THE JAPANESE MENTAL LEXICON

THE JAPANESE MENTAL LEXICON

PSYCHOLINGUISTIC STUDIES
OF KANA AND KANJI PROCESSING

JOSEPH F. KESS

TADAO MIYAMOTO

University of Victoria

JOHN BENJAMINS PUBLISHING COMPANY
PHILADELPHIA/AMSTERDAM

TM   The paper used in this publication meets the minimum requirements of American National Standard for Information Sciences — Permanence of Paper for Printed Library Materials, ANSI Z39.48-1984.

Library of Congress Cataloging-in-Publication Data

Kess, Joseph F.
    The Japanese mental lexicon : psycholinguistic studies of kana and kanji processing / Joseph F. Kess, Tadao Miyamoto.
        p.   cm.
    Includes bibliographical references and index.
    1. Japanese language--Psychological aspects. 2. Japanese language--Orthography and
        spelling. 3. Psycholinguistics. I. Title. II. Miyamoto, Tadao, 1948-
PL513 .K46   1999
495.6'01'9 21--dc21   99-044919
ISBN 90 272 2189 8 (Eur.) / 1 55619 761 6 (US) (Pb; alk. paper)

John Benjamins Publishing Co. • P.O.Box 75577 • 1070 AN Amsterdam • The Netherlands
John Benjamins North America • P.O.Box 27519 • Philadelphia PA 19118-0519 • USA

TABLE OF CONTENTS

PREFACE

This text is intended to serve as an introduction to the psycholinguistic dimensions of written word access to the mental lexicon in Japanese. Ten chapters focus on the nature of such psycholinguistic inquiry, its history, lexical access studies in kanji, kana, romaji, and mixed text processing, laterality preferences in kanji/kana processing and their implications for scientific discussions of language and cognition, evidence from eye-movement studies, the acquisition of orthographic skills by Japanese children, and a review of the implications and conclusions that arise from the contributions of such research.

The text is directed at filling the need for an overview of such research not only because of its potential impact on linguistics and psychology, but also on aphasiology, mathematical and statistical linguistics, educational practices and governmental intervention in respect to language policies, and to a lesser degree, linguistic and cultural history. Ours is an unabashedly interdisciplinary view of psycholinguistics, contending that inquiry into such research questions is not the exclusive prerogative of a single field or academic discipline. As the following text will demonstrate, the consolidation of our knowledge about language processing in respect to Japanese orthographic access to the mental lexicon is not the accomplishment of any single scientific paradigm. Rather, an information processing view of such mental events relies on the convergence of a disparate number of research strands which, when taken together, form a cohesive whole. We have, therefore, attempted to present an integrated history of the development of research ideas, and their relative successes, in the psycholinguistic study of ortho-graphic pathways to the mental lexicon. This small area within cognitive science also reflects our interdisciplinary commitments to understanding the structure of human LANGUAGE, together with the structures of specific languages, in their relationship to human cognition.

When we first surveyed the rich field of Japanese psycholinguistics, we quickly realized that the most fertile area for research has been the area of kanji and kana processing. This was true even before the focus on the mental lexicon became fash-ionable in Western psychology and psycholinguistics, for Japanese scholars have always been keenly interested in possible differences between Japanese orthographic systems and other systems found in the world's languages. As a result, we focussed our attention on this area, organizing our book into 10 chapters, which, except for the Introduction, represent the diversity of Japanese psycholinguistic research into the nature of written word processing in Japanese. The first chapter provides a brief introduction to the history of Japanese psychology, and the development of the interdisciplinary field of Japanese psycholinguistics within this scholarly tradition. Chapter 2 charts the early emergence and subsequent development of the Japanese orthographic systems in historical terms. It also presents a brief history of more recent developments in governmental policy directed at controlling the number and type of kanji in both the media and the schools, as well as a glance at scholarly attempts to characterize the orthographic symbols which actually do appear in written Japanese. The next four sections are organized around experimental or descriptive treatments of kanji, kana, romaji and mixed-text processing. These chapters survey the theoretical issues in lexical access, word recognition, and the way in which the Japanese mental lexicon reflects processing strategies which are tied to the quadripartite Japanese orthographic system.

Chapter 7 presents a cursory survey of research on the acquisition of Japanese reading and writing skills by young children. Although the field of reading comprehension as a whole is too wide an expanse to cover usefully or profitably here, we feel it is useful to see how the acquisition of these skills in Japanese differs from acquisition of such skills in other orthographic systems. Chapter 8 reviews the recent developments in current research on eye movements in reading different text types in Japanese, and how this reflects universal vs. language-specific issues in orthographic systems and reading. Chapter 9 examines the reported results for studies of lateralization and hemispheric specialization in respect to the special demands made by the Japanese orthography and its dual nature.

Lastly, Chapter 10 offers our summative conclusions about the implications of such research for those universal vs. language-specific issues which arise from processing models of language perception, language production, and language acquisition. Many of the research directions that have informed the last four decades of psycholinguistic research have shared similar intellectual sources with Japanese psycholinguistics. But there are also many instances in which Japanese research is unique in the research questions it has chosen to follow, and the answers to these questions are often enlightening in ways that we have not considered. We offer commentary on these research avenues, and the way that the interplay between universalistic and language-specific issues in Japanese inform theoretical debates about the universalistic nature of language processing in psycholinguistic terms.

Finally, we should acknowledge those colleagues that have been so helpful in supporting the completion of this book. First of all, we must note E. F. Konrad Koerner, whose collegial genius for organization has been recently recognized by the Royal

Society of Canada. It is his editorial tenure at John Benjamins Publishers that has allowed this book, and many another scholarly text, to see the light of day in published format. At the same time, we wish to acknowledge the contribution of our editor at John Benjamins Publishers, Kees Vaes, who encouraged this book and ensured its realization in its final printed form.

We have also been particularly fortunate to have Japanese colleagues who have made this project as much their quest as ours. Their expertise as outstanding scholars in the field, as psychologists and linguists, and their kindness in introducing us to their own work, as well as to that of their colleagues, has been the infrastructure which allowed this work to proceed. The distinguished scholar of whom this is especially true is Dr. Kan Kashu, recently retired as Dean of Humanities and Professor of Psychology at Kwansei Gakuin University in Kobe, Japan. It has been his enthusiastic leadership in our research group that has served as the inspiration for our own commitment to this project. We are also grateful to Dr. Shoichi Yokoyama, of the National Language Research Institute in Tokyo, for his kindness and collegiality in helping us to access the right contacts in the realization of our research goals, particularly in the early stages of our work. We also wish to acknowledge those scholars who took the time to read and comment on various stages of the manuscript, giving freely of their wisdom. Our gratitude goes to Professors Shoichi Yokoyama and Eric Long of the National Language Research Institute, Che Kan Leong of the Hong Kong Institute of Education, Takeshi Hatta and Hirofumi Saito of Nagoya University, Hiroyuki Kaiho and Nobuo Ohta of Tsukuba University, Kan Kashu and Jun Ukita of Kwansei Gakuin University, Michio Inoue of Kobe Yamate University, Katsuo Tamaoka of Hiroshima University, Hironari Nozaki of Nagoya City University, Tomoyoshi Inoue of Doshisha University, Thomas M. Hess of the University of Victoria, and Gary D. Prideaux of the University of Alberta. With their advice and support, the final product is unquestionably a much better portrait of Japanese psycholinguistic research in this area.

Finally, and most importantly, we wish to acknowledge the research support we received from a continuous grant between 1994-1999, on *Comprehensive Research on the Role of the Japanese Language in the International Community* (*Kokusai Shakai ni okeru Nihongo ni tsuite no Sogoteki Kenkyu*; #06NP1201, 07NP1001, 08NP0701, 09NP0701) provided by the Ministry of Education, Science and Culture Grant-in-Aid for Creative Basic Research. There is little question that this massive research undertaking owes its very existence to the organizational genius of Professor Osamu Mizutani, now retired as Director General of the National Language Research Institute in Tokyo. His congenial, but insightful touch has been evident in every aspect of the overall research plan and its realization. We have been truly fortunate to have him as our project director, and our collective research efforts have profited in myriad ways from his wise stewardship.

In closing this preface, we want to also acknowledge those special ones who figured in our thoughts during the time of our writing. Joseph F. Kess: I dedicate this book to my son Tony, the last in an unbroken line of 'knezhashki mahacheks', and we hope, the first in a continuing line of many more yet to come. Our times together in Japan gave us the opportunity for a 'walkabout' neither of us will ever forget! Tadao Miyamoto: I dedicate this book to my wife Susan, who allows me to pursue my academic interests.

Chapter 1

INTRODUCTION

INTRODUCTORY COMMENTS

The purpose of this book is to chart the contemporary focus of one of the most vibrant areas of research in the field of psycholinguistics in Japan. Japanese research in psycholinguistics in the area of lexical access and word recognition, and the way in which the four orthographic types (katakana, hiragana, romaji, and kanji characters) in the modern Japanese writing system affect processing, has been one of the longest and richest traditions in modern Japanese psycholinguistics. The larger aim of our research into Japanese psycholinguistics has been to produce a comprehensive overview of Japanese attempts to focus on how natural language is produced, comprehended, stored, and recalled. But we quickly came to the realization that Japanese scholarship into the nature of the mental lexicon represents one of the most important Japanese contributions to the field of cognitive science. Japanese scholarship has often followed an independent line of development in certain areas of scientific endeavor, and the study of language is a prime instance in which the motivating intellectual force for research has been derived from specifically Japanese perspectives. For example, Japanese research into psycholinguistic questions of lexical access and word recognition is a good illustration of this, and it is exactly this rich tradition in the discipline of Japanese psychology that we hope to bring to the fore.

THE HISTORICAL DEVELOPMENT OF JAPANESE PSYCHOLOGY

Contemporary scholarship in Japanese psycholinguistics reflects recent developments in cognitive science, and the traditional interests of cognitive psychology, linguistics, artificial intelligence, neuroscience, and philosophy, and to a lesser extent, those in social psycholinguistics, mathematical linguistics, and cognitive anthropology. But contemporary developments in psycholinguistics also reflect the century-old history of psychology in Japan, and it is worth reviewing the historical evolution of that disciplinary history.[1]

Some trace the beginnings of psychology in Japan back to the first use of the word *Shinrigaku* (心理学) 'Psychology'[2] in Amane Nishi's 1878 translation (*Heban-shi Shinrigaku* 'Haven's Psychology') of Joseph Haven's (1869) Scottish school treatise on *Mental Philosophy* (see Hoshino, 1979; Hoshino, & Umemoto, 1987).[3] Some see Yujiro Motora's 1889 return from Johns Hopkins University, where he received a doctorate under G. Stanley Hall's tutelage in Wundtian psychology, as a turning point. Motora was immediately appointed Lecturer in Psychophysics at the Imperial University in Tokyo, and under his leadership, the first laboratory of psychology was established there in 1900 (Azuma & Imada, 1994). But it was not until Matataro Matsumoto, Yujiro Motora's student, that one sees the formal establishment of laboratories for experimental psychology in 1903, both at the Tokyo Higher Normal School (where he was a professor) and the Imperial University in Tokyo (where he was a lecturer)[4] and then at Kyoto Imperial University in 1908 where he became Professor and Chair of that newly established department. Another laboratory focus was consolidated in 1913 at Tokyo Imperial University, when Matsumoto moved there as Motora's successor (Tanaka, 1966; Hoshino, 1979; Hoshino & Umemoto, 1987). In 1918, this experimental laboratory of psychology grew into the first university Department of Psychology, and Matsumoto became its first Chair. Matsumoto remained at the Imperial University in Tokyo until his own retirement in 1926.

His study tour of the United States and Europe certainly exposed him to mainstream developments in the social sciences, especially what was becoming the most scientific of those social sciences, the scientific psychology promulgated by the founder of the first

---

[1] An earlier, much reduced version of this historical overview appears as "The Origins of Modern Japanese Psycholinguistics within the Japanese Psychological Tradition" in Embleton, Joseph, and Niederehe (in press).

[2] Nishi employed *Shinrigaku* to avoid overlap with existing schools of thought which had already co-opted the term *Shingaku* (心学) for a kind of popular psychology which was essentially a type of conventional morality. The root *Shin*(心)- is still used in other psychological applications, as for example, the recently coined *Shin-teki Jisho* (心的辞書) 'Mental Lexicon' for semantic structures in the mind.

[3] Tanaka (1966) places Nishi's translation later, in 1880, and Haven's text earlier, in 1857.

[4] Hoshino and Umemoto (1987) credit Motora with establishing this first experimental laboratory at the University of Tokyo in 1903, while Tanaka (1966) gives credit to Matsumoto for its creation in 1903. Azuma and Imada (1994) credit Motora's leadership with its first appearance in 1900. All, however, agree that it was at the Imperial University in Tokyo that the first institutionalized laboratory was set up.

experimental laboratory, Leipzig's Wilhelm Wundt (see Kess, 1983). The first academic journal in the field, *Shinri Kenkyu* 'Journal of Psychology' had been published in Tokyo in 1912, but the first official organ attached to a professional society, *Shinrigaku Kenkyu* 'Japanese Journal of Psychology',[5] appears with the establishment of the Japanese Psychological Association in 1926. Not surprisingly, Matsumoto was both the first president of the Japanese Psychological Association (JPA) and is often credited with founding its journal (Hoshino & Umemoto, 1987).[6]

Ever since, the development of psychology in Japan has reflected the same trends and directions that psychology has taken throughout the world.[7] At first, Japanese psychology, like psychology elsewhere, followed Wundtian structuralism as the main theoretical framework until the 1920s. Wundt's death in 1920 and the post-World War I collapse of German intellectual hegemony in the sciences caused a theoretical vacuum, soon to be replaced by developments in Gestalt psychology. After the decline of Wundtian psychology in Europe (see Kess, 1983), psychology in Japan was largely influenced by the European movement in Gestalt psychology. By the second world conflict, psychology courses were being taught at Imperial Universities in Tokyo, Kyoto, Kyushu, Hokkaido, Seoul and Taiwan, as well as in the private universities Keio and Waseda in Tokyo, Doshisha in Kyoto, and Kwansei Gakuin in Kobe (Hoshino, 1979).

Not surprisingly, World War II precipitated a decline in independent psychological research in Japan. The period after World War II saw the introduction of theoretical goals and methodological strategies derived from American psychology, and these became the predominant influence in applied, social, clinical, and experimental psychology (Tanaka, 1966). Gestalt psychology continued as a force until the 1950s, but quickly gave ground to Skinnerian behaviorism and Hullean Neo-Behaviorism in the 1960s.

The ongoing development of the discipline of psychology in Japan as one moves into the 1970s reflects a breadth of interest which sees multiple directions taken in research pursuits. The methodology in psychological research since then has been particularly

---

[5] Another Japanese Psychological Association journal, *Japanese Psychological Research,* appeared in 1954, and continues on ever since, in a largely English language format.

[6] Tanaka (1966) places the year of the association's establishment at 1927, but the appearance of the journal at 1926. Both Hoshino (1979) and Tanaka (1966) place the first professional meeting of the JPA at 1927 at the University of Tokyo; Azuma and Imada (1994) place the year of the association's establishment at 1925, and place the first professional meeting of the JPA at 1925.

[7] It has been a extremely active participant in following those trends, typically sending a sizable contingent of conference participants to every national and international conference in the discipline, and in 1972, hosted the Twentieth International Congress of Psychology in Tokyo.

influenced by the goals of cognitive psychology, as has been much of Anglo-American psychology.[8] Behaviorism in its many forms remained the mainstream paradigm until the 1970s surge of interest in cognitive psychology, and its natural interdisciplinary ally in the newly minted Cognitive Science which developed in the 1980s. The steady progression of research articles in the professional literature give evidence of this steady and inexorable shift from one major school of thought to the next major school of thought, generally reflecting the direction of world trends (Miyamoto & Kess, 1997).

Japanese psychology has always been attracted to the applied side of psychological research, and this has been particularly true of post-war research interests, as the interaction between psychology and society was shifted to socio-cultural activities (for example, see Tanaka's 1966 and Tanaka & England's 1972 inventories of scholarly activity, as well as Japanese Applied Psychology Association, 1954). Between 1874 and 1932, over 700 of the 1300 professional studies in psychology were in applied fields (Hoshino & Umemoto, 1987). The percentage of psychological research with applied connotations has probably risen higher since the post-war years, and especially in the last decade. Group dynamics and group processes, social engineering, ergonomic efficiency, and mass culture are typical areas where such research has had an impact.

Another important event which affects psychology in that post-war period relates to reform in the educational system. As a result, such post-war developments in education saw expansion by national and private universities into a number of areas, among them the field of psychology. Inevitably, these institutions began to compete with the Imperial universities for both students and research programs. Recent overviews chart eleven particularly vibrant fields of interest, among them memory, perception, cognition and understanding, developmental, animal, social, educational, and clinical psychology, as well as comparative cross-cultural research (see Misumi & Peterson, 1990). Many of these research areas have dedicated professional followings, as well as a professional journal.[9]/[10] The count stood at a total of 14 professional associations in psychology in

---

[8] But the designation of *cognitive* in this sense does not have quite the same meaning as in the earlier *cognitive psychology* focus attributed to the Gestalt cognitive psychology of the 1930s. Both are, however, similar in their theoretical and methodological rejection of behaviorism (see Neisser, 1967), and their attention to general learning principles in the broader sense of general biological and cognitive foundations of human behavior.

[9] The number of professional psychology journals has grown, but they still only represent a fraction of the total number of professional publications. For example, in 1969, there were over 1,000 scholarly and semi-scholarly journals which carried social science articles in Japan (see Kuroda, 1969). The intervening twenty-five years may easily have seen the number double.

[10] For example, among them may be listed the Japanese Educational Psychology Association (founded in 1952), the Japanese Social Psychology Association (founded in 1960), the Japanese Criminal Psychology

1987, and has probably risen to a score by now (Hoshino & Umemoto, 1987; Azuma & Imada, 1994). The most recent of these, the Japanese Cognitive Science Society [*Ninchi Kagakukai*], founded in 1983, has a membership derived from a variety of disciplines, reflecting world trends in multi-disciplinary approaches to charting the structure of the human mind and the nature of mental representations for information and decision-making.

Psycholinguistic studies, of course, are germane to all of these areas, by virtue of the role language behavior plays in the realization of these diverse areas of human behavior. In particular, current research into cognition, understanding, and memory are most compatible with psycholinguistic interests within Japanese psychology, and often pursue the theme of cognitive differences related to information processing, especially of the linguistic type. Such studies also reflect the Japanese view that human cognitive activities are embedded within socio-cultural activities, as well as the Japanese penchant for elucidating cognitive practices that are unique to Japanese culture.

THE HISTORICAL DEVELOPMENT OF JAPANESE PSYCHOLINGUISTICS

The history of Japanese psycholinguistics, like that of Western psycholinguistics, is a relatively recent one but can be linked to psychological interests in language behavior over this century. Our own interest in the research field of psycholinguistics in Japan was piqued by the apparent richness of scholarly activity in Japan, and resulted in a recently published inventory of Japanese scholarship in this area (see Kess & Miyamoto, 1994).[11]

In tracing the history of Japanese *psycholinguistics*,[12] one could, of course, take a strictly historical approach in listing dates and events, noting, for example, the following

---

Association (founded in 1963), the Japanese Clinical Psychology Association (founded in 1964), and the Japanese Psychonomic Society (founded in 1981).

[11] This annotated bibliographic inventory contains about a thousand of the several thousand entries in our collection, and is organized into 17 sections which can be said to be representative of the major interests in psycholinguistic research in Japan, thus giving some insight into what has motivated recent Japanese work in this area.

[12] There are actually two interrelated usages in Japanese, *Gengoshinrigaku* and *Shinrigengogaku*, which could be discriminated when translating into English. The first might be better translated as 'the psychology of language', since most of these scholars are psychologists and not as focussed on linguistic knowledge as defined by the field of linguistics (T. Inoue, p.c.). We have chosen to translate them both as 'psycholinguistics' in order to provide a sense of the disciplinary breadth that this field encompasses.

as the first texts with the term *psycholinguistics* in their titles: K. Jimbo, *Gengo-shinrigaku* [*Psycholinguistics*], (1934), and Kanji Hatano, *Gengoshinrigaku* [*Psycho-linguistics*] (1936).[13] But given the tenor of the times and the *Kokugo Kyoiku* 'National Language Education' series both appear in, the modern use of the term best awaits a later candidate. One could cite, for example, the following as the first textbook with the term *psycholinguistics* in its title: I. Sakamoto, K. Okamoto, S. Muraishi, and Y. Sato, *Gengoshinrigaku* [*Psycholinguistics*], (1956). Or the following as the first psychological text dealing with the issues of psycholinguistics in its modern sense: I. Sakamoto, *Kotoba no Shinri* [*The Psychology of Language*], (1952).

Other texts appear, some with 'psycholinguistics' in their titles (Iritani, 1964, 1975, 1983; Sakano & Amano, 1976, 1993; Haga, 1988; Hieshima, 1994) and some without (Hatano, 1958; Kikushima, 1964; Iritani, 1965, 1971; Sanseido, 1977; Haga, Y. 1979; Endo, 1983; Iwata, 1987; Ukita & Kashu, 1996). But most give evidence of a modern and thus contemporaneous view of the field of psycholinguistics and the psychology of language. Some even make it into the lucrative popular market of pocket books, but without quite the same technical prowess (see Miyagi, 1953, 1954). Like Western psycholinguistics, the field has been confined largely to the discipline of psychology, although more recently attempts have been made to incorporate current linguistic theory into the core of research directions (see, for example, Otsu, 1989).

Other texts appear with psycholinguistic motifs, but these are usually tied to a specific sub-discipline. The richest of these areas has been education (Sakamoto, 1955; Okubo, 1968; Okada, 1969; Fukuzawa, 1996) and developmental psychological concerns with the growth and fostering of first language abilities in children (Yatabe, 1956, 1983; Muraishi & Hayashi, 1958; Iwabuchi, 1968; Murata, 1968, 1972, 1977, 1981, 1983; Okamoto, 1982; Fukuzawa, 1987; Ito, 1990; Muto, 1991; Kobayashi & Sasaki, 1997). There have, of course, been more specialized interests, such as clinical preoccupations (too numerous to mention since Omori, 1955), metaphor (Haga & Koyasu, 1990), and bilingualism (Haga, J. 1979). The most recent of these specialized interests has been the alliance of cognitive psychology with the aims of cognitive science, as Japanese psycholinguistics keeps pace with research interests elsewhere (Ota & Tajika, 1991; Mori, 1992; Tajika, Kawaguchi, Ikegami & Yama, 1992; Abe, 1994; Nakau, 1994; Yoshimura, 1995; Moro, 1997).

---

[13] For example, Hatano's companion volume in Iwanami Shoten's series entitled *Iwanami Kooza Kokugo Kyooiku* 'Iwanami Lectures in National Language Education' and *Kokugo Kyooiku no Gakuteki Kikoo* 'Scholastic Organization of National Language Education' was Zenri Tabata's *Shakaigaku yori Mitaru Gengo* 'Language as Viewed from Sociology' (1936), and gives an idea of the thrust of such scholarship.

But our purpose here is not to chart the history of Japanese psycholinguistics itself, and as a result, we do not pursue the distant past too vigorously.[14] We instead choose to focus on a tightly related network of issues that psycholinguistics is currently pre-occupied with, and suggest that this approach may be more illustrative of the robustness of modern Japanese psycholinguistics. We pursue both senses of the term *Japanese psycholinguistics*, the discipline of psycholinguistics as pursued within Japan itself and the international research in modern psycholinguistics which targets the Japanese language as the focal point of empirical procedures or deductive analysis in psychology, linguistics, psycholinguistics, and cognitive science. We are especially careful to focus on Japanese psycholinguistics in Japanese, as suggested by the eminent neuropsychologist Takeshi Hatta in his criticism (1986b) of those who choose to ignore this robust literature. We searched the Japanese literature for scholarly insights, peering into published reports and memoirs of research institutes and universities, as well as journal articles, books, and collections. This treasure trove of data and insightful commentary is complemented with an equally thorough survey of the Western literature, for Japanese psycholinguistics has also been influenced by European or Anglo-American theoretical concerns.

The resultant outcome is that some focal areas in Japanese research have been complemented or even enriched by these influences. Among these may certainly be counted the point-counterpoint status of the long-standing Japanese interest in kana/kanji processing,[15] and Western parallels in elucidating the cognitive mechanisms involved in lexical access, word recognition, and the structure of the mental lexicon. Similarly, neurolinguistic advances in hemispheric correlates for the comprehension and production of the syllabic kana versus the logographic Chinese-derived kanji characters are enhanced by the current medical technology found in PET scan, CT scan, and Magnetic Resonance Imaging techniques which pinpoint tissue damage for aphasic diagnoses. Lastly, modern aspirations to harness even more clever generations of computational devices which can read, parse, and even translate between languages, intersect with the boom in psycholinguistic work on morphological aspects of language processing.

---

[14] For example, we are aware that the psychology of Leipzig's Wilhelm Wundt set the intellectual paradigm for work in the psychology/language interface at the end of the Nineteenth Century. We could have written on the likelihood that the general post-World War I decline of Wundtian psychology in favor of American behaviorism was slowed in Japan as a result of the influential purchase of Wundt's entire library by Sendai's Tohoku University after Wundt's death in 1920.

[15] This long-standing Japanese interest in the psychology of *kana/kanji* processing is tied to the even longer tradition of meditation on the nature of the Japanese language and the unique characteristics of its writing system for philological reasons. There are countless scholarly inquiries directed at the latter topic in the sub-fields devoted to *Nihongogaku* 'the Japanese language' and *Kokugogaku* 'the National language' (see, for example, Sato, 1992).

THE SCOPE OF THIS BOOK

This book thus surveys a constellation of inter-related issues in Japanese psycholinguistics that impact models of lexical access and word recognition right across languages as different as Chinese, Japanese, and English. We first attempt to summarize how relevant areas have been approached and synthesized in respect to the Japanese data, and then to show how these psycholinguistic findings enrich and possibly modify our view of what is universal and what is language-specific about natural language processing in regard to lexical access procedures in word recognition across orthographic types.

Orthographic systems are normally classified as one of three types. Although there are variations in the way they are named, they are generally grouped in respect to which aspect of language they primarily represent. Thus, there are alphabetic systems like English, Greek, and Russian which employ symbols for individual phonemes, syllabic systems like Cherokee, Miao, and Japanese which employ symbols for syllables, and logographic systems like Chinese and Japanese which employ symbols for morphemes or words (see Gelb, 1963, for a traditional explanation). The relationship between phonology and orthography differs across these languages, with some languages boasting a close relationship between the two and others not. We know that because different orthographies are based on different aspects of language (namely, phonemes, syllables, and morphemes, or the intersection of these features at the morphophonemic level), these orthographies can present such linguistic information in different ways. But we are not always sure of the cognitive processes which might handle these orthographic representations and how the human processor takes information out of these various orthographic shapes. For example, Chinese has been held out to exhibit an opaque relationship between phonology and orthographic type, and English a closer relationship, but these assumptions do not always find themselves reflected in the facts. For example, Chinese has phonetic radicals, and English has oblique spellings for familiar words which are read at processing glance, instead of through phonological decoding. Moreover, English itself is not such a simple phonemically-based writing system; rather, graphemic units are often tied to an intermediate morphophonemic level before they are related to sound (see Venezky, 1967). And although Chinese is morphemically-based, Chinese allows, and sometimes requires, phonological information to be accessed during its word recognition procedures. The fact is that the phonemically-based orthography of English is more morphophonemic than we give it credit for, and in turn, Chinese has many phonetic elements which can be used in reading *hanzi* (see Leong, 1986, for an excellent outline of just such processing hints).

Hanzi are the logographic written symbols used in the Chinese orthography, commonly known as Chinese characters. *Kanji* are those logographic written symbols imported into Japanese orthography from Chinese in several separate and distinct historical periods. In Chinese, their use constitutes the only writing system, but in Japanese, the use of Chinese characters is complemented by other orthographic script types. And because Japanese borrowed in separate and distinct historical periods, different pronunciations came over for those kanji, thus complicating reading in the modern writing system. As a result, Japanese is a mixed system, employing two syllabaries which match the relatively simple syllabic structure of the language, and a large inventory of logographic kanji which can have varying pronunciations derived from either borrowed Chinese readings or native Japanese readings. The issues in lexical access for Japanese words are complicated by the fact that Japanese does not have a single script type.

Actually, with the increasing use of the Latin alphabet-based *romaji*, it now has four script types. Japanese may have the unique distinction of employing all three extant means for transferring sound to written symbol, namely, the alphabetic, the syllabary, and logographic writing systems. The Japanese system of orthographic scripts thus provides an informative counterpoint to current research on written word recognition because of its use of several different systems at the same time. The fact that it uses a logographic script type and a syllabary script type allows us to compare the processing strategies which each script type might involve. Then again, because there are two kana syllabaries which occupy somewhat different usage domains, we are able to assess relative processing differences and issues of frequency and script familiarity.

Another set of useful insights arises from the fact that Japanese may appear to use the same system as other logographic languages, but its actual deployment is different in respect to how that script type is realized in representational and processual terms. For example, Chinese characters are used in China, Korea, and Japan, and although all three languages use the same script, their respective uses of logographic script are far from identical.[16] Logographic kanji usage in Japan is, however, the most complicated, because kanji often have more than one reading. Despite the fact that Japan has one of the highest literacy rates in the world, there are often times when even an educated person does not know the appropriate reading for a kanji that one has seen before; more commonly, one might not know the reading or perhaps the meaning of an unfamiliar kanji. And increasingly these days, one might not recall the exact stroke configuration for an infrequent kanji when pressed to write that kanji by hand, due to the extensive use of word processors.

---

[16] Chinese characters were also borrowed into Vietnamese to write borrowed Chinese words and the occasional Vietnamese word, serving as the impetus for a native script based on similar principles which survived until replaced by Roman letters several centuries ago (see Martin, 1972).

There are many more characters commonly in use in written Chinese, while the Korean kanji which remain in use number about 2,000. Even with this smaller number, their common use in Korean has been severely curtailed and each is associated with only a single reading (Taylor, 1988).[17] Although there are 1,945 officially sanctioned characters in non-specialist writings in the Japanese press and government documents, this number swells as general texts add characters to represent personal and place names. The number of potential characters is another matter, and different figures reflect the different degrees of coverage in dictionary inventories. For example, the 12-volume *Daikanwa Jiten* lists 49,964 characters, sufficient to read even the classic Japanese texts of the past. More compact treatments list less, as for example, the *Daijiten Dictionary* with 14,924 and the *Shinjigen Dictionary* with 9,921 kanji (see Gottlieb, 1995).

Unlike Chinese or Korean, Japanese kanji characters can have two possible types of reading for a given kanji; *on* Chinese readings, derived from several periods of historical borrowing from China, can compete with *kun* Japanese readings of the same kanji. Multiple pronunciations, or readings, for individual kanji are common, with one or more *on*-readings and one *kun*-reading of the character often the case. Although it is common for individual kanji to have more than one possible reading, it can happen even on the kanji compound level. For example, the same temple, 清澄寺 on the Boosoo Peninsula flanking Tokyo Bay has highway signs pointing to *Seichoo-ji* (清澄寺) at one point and *Kiyosumi-dera* at another point. The first employs the *on*-reading and the second the *kun*-reading for the same place.

And there is no predictability for which kanji will have Chinese or Japanese readings, or how many readings there will be. Some kanji have an *on*-reading, but no *kun*-reading; for example, the kanji which combine to create the compound word 気候 *ki-koo* 'climate, weather' only have *on*-readings. When kanji appear as singles, in isolation, they usually take a *kun*-reading, if they have one. For example, 頭 'head' is read as *atama* in isolation, but as *too* when in compounds with other kanji. When kanji occur in compounds, there is a tendency to expect the pronunciation to have an *on*-reading, but this is by no means a given.

Another crucial consideration derives from how the characters are linked in morphological deployment of word-building preferences. One count of 40,000 common

---

[17] Korean scholars and officials read and wrote in Chinese characters from the Fourth Century on, with the 28-letter Hangul alphabet a secondary writing system until the middle of the Twentieth Century. King Sejong had obviously intended Hangul to fulfill that function for the common, uneducated masses, as his preface to the Fifteenth Century *Hun-Min-Jung-Um* (訓民正音) 'Proper Sounds for the Instruction of the People', so clearly indicates: "Because Korean and Chinese are different languages, the use of Chinese characters (for expressing Korean) is not convenient for communication...[of] many things that the 'foolish masses' wish to express...." Like Japanese, it was not until this century that the shift to a nativized script was expedited, and for Korean, the shift from kanji was even later (see Shim, 1987).

Chinese words showed 65% of those words to be two-character compound words (Liu, Chuang & Wang, 1975, cited in Hatta & Kawakami, 1996). In contrast, compound words in the inventory of Japanese common words might only be as high as 40%, with single kanji common words running over 45% (Hatta & Kawakami, 1996). Thus, there is simply no *a priori* guarantee that the processing mechanisms adduced to deal with instantiations of logographic characters are the same for Chinese hanzi and Japanese kanji. Even though Chinese hanzi have come to be employed in Japanese, the structuring of the mental dictionary for Japanese kanji will inevitably be unique in many ways. The same is obviously true for Korean, which has also employed Chinese characters over the centuries. According to Ki (1986), the vocabulary inventory of Modern Korean may be classified into two distinct groups, with the salient factor being whether the Korean word finds its origins in a phonological rendition of an original Chinese character or characters. Sino-Korean words, or Korean *Han-ja-ə* (漢字語) 'Chinese character words', are the Korean equivalent of Japanese *on*-readings and have had an enormous impact on how the Korean mental lexicon is structured.

One of the most vibrant areas of research for Japanese psycholinguistics, therefore, has been tied to the architecture of its orthographic system, and the way that this system accesses the Japanese mental lexicon. There has been a recent explosion of interest in this area, as a 'cognitive science' of the mind attempts to elucidate the processing mechanisms by which humans process linguistic information through the printed medium in Japanese (see, for example, Tamaoka, 1994; Ukita, Sugishima, Minagawa, Inoue & Kashu, 1996; Yokoyama, 1997; Leong & Tamaoka, 1998). But Japanese research has long been keenly interested in the structure of the mental lexicon not only because of possible differences in syllabic kana vs. logographic kanji processing, but also because of possible differences in processing Japanese vs. non-Japanese orthograph-ic layouts. This is a long-standing interest, and one which reflects the Japanese view of the written dimension as the important medium in language studies. Western linguists have been largely guided by Saussure's (1916) suggestion that spoken language is the first and foremost province of true language study, and that written language is but a pale and uninformative imitation of 'real' language, while Western psychologists have tradition-ally used the written word as the experimental stimuli in their inquiries. Ebbinghaus' (1885) pre-World War I foray into memory for nonsense syllables is direct-ly mirrored in the post-World War II pursuit of paired associate learning, evidence for which may be gathered by a glance at any issue of the *Journal of Verbal Learning and Verbal Behavior* through the 1950s and 1960s. In time, the linguist's preoccupation with the spoken word slowly but surely made its way into Western psycholinguistics, but this was not so with Japanese psycholinguistics. Here the preoccupation with the rich orthography prompted more than enough psycholinguistic inquiry (see Inoue, 1995), and grounded Japanese research more in the written aspects of language than was the case in its Western counterparts.

In Japanese psycholinguistic studies of the orthography, the questions at first ran along easily discerned boundaries. Are there processing differences between kana and kanji script types? Are words written in kana named faster than the same words written in kanji? Are there hemispheric differences in laterality preferences that are associated with kana processing vs. kanji processing? The early literature even entertained the notion that the two types of writing system, kana syllabary vs. kanji logographs, would not only employ different mechanisms but also different sides of the brain. Such early studies quickly discovered that the nature of the cognitive task is what predicts laterality preferences, not the stimulus type itself. Kess and Miyamoto's (1996) survey of the Japanese experimental literature on kanji processing shows a clear interaction between the experimental stimuli involved vs. the specific tasks posed. The stimulus type is not what drives the particular cognitive demands arising from the various types of experimental tasks asked of subjects when dealing with kanji. Although the stimulus type *per se* does make its own specific processing demands, the cognitive task type is a crucial consideration in evaluating laterality preferences when subjects deal with logographic kanji.

Current research has evolved to match modern psycholinguistic concerns with the role of 'top-down' processing mechanisms vs. 'bottom-up' processing mechanisms. The experimental range of such research is worthy of note, and the results fascinating for both a theory of kana/kanji processing and for psycholinguistics in general. Our understanding of the cognitive architecture which underlies access and storage of linguistic information in the mental lexicon is certainly enriched by Japanese research into the possible interaction between graphemic, phonemic, and semantic information in kana vs. kanji processing. Our goal is to survey and evaluate these findings, in the light of current speculation about the cognitive processes that underlie lexical access for visual word recognition and reading for languages in general. We expect that such work will inevitably shed light on the architecture of the mental lexicon in human languages, by spanning the necessary bridge between phonological and semantic realms in graphemic symbols which represent Japanese words, phrases, and sentences written in kana and/or kanji.

Chapter 2

A HISTORY OF THE JAPANESE ORTHOGRAPHY

INTRODUCTORY COMMENTS

The history of the Japanese scripts is a developing history, tracing its origins from millennium-old adaptations of Chinese characters and still subject to manipulation in the legislated literacy of recent times (see, for example, Kabashima, 1977, and Koizumi, 1991). The tangible result we currently see are the two kana syllabaries,[1] which match the relatively simple syllabic structure of the language, and a large inventory of logographic kanji which can have varying pronunciations. It is no stretch of the imagination to declare Japanese one of the most intricate, most elegant, and yet most difficult writing systems in the modern world.

A variety of reasons come together to make this the case. For one, the intricate flow of stroke patterns that gives rise to the art form we know as calligraphy also gives rise to countless variations on their presentation. The result is an **enormous inventory** of configurations that must be mastered, stored, and recalled in order to access the written form of most Japanese content words. It is true that simplified kanji lists numbering below 2,000 have been the product of various orthography reforms, but mastering 2,000 items is a far different task than mastering an alphabetic inventory of 26 symbols in English or a syllabic inventory of 85 symbols in Cherokee. As if this task were not enough, many, if not most, kanji have more than one way of being read. And even if this hurdle is cleared, and kanji are mastered in their representational function for normal vocabulary words, many proper names and place names continue to pose problems because of their exceptional or obscure status. Then too, kanji are only part of the total picture, because since the turn of the century Japanese orthography is a system which freely mixes three sets of script types in an orthography that also expects mass literacy.

---

[1] We have opted for a slightly modified version of the Hepburn Romanization system in our transliteration of Japanese words. A more complete description of this system is to be found in Chapter 5, the chapter on romaji.

This orthographic system relies on the use of kanji in conjunction with the two syllabaries, hiragana and katakana.

Historically, the inventory of **Japanese vocabulary** contains three types of lexical items. There are native Japanese words, either historically or contemporarily derived from native elements (やどや *yadoya* 'hotel'); there are Chinese words, either borrowed historically in one of several periods of importation (旅館 *ryokan* 'hotel') or words which combine those Chinese roots to make up new Sino-Japanese words (哲学 *tetsugaku* 'philosophy'); and lastly, there are borrowings from other languages, loanwords which have found their way into Japanese from languages as diverse as English (ホテル *hoteru* 'hotel'), Portuguese (天婦羅 tempura <TEMPERO 'tempura-dish'), Dutch (チョッキ *chokki* <JAK 'vest'), Geman (カルテ *karute* <KARTE 'medical file'), and French (パンタロン *pantaron* <PANTALON 'lady's trousers'). Along similar lines, Japanese does not employ a single script type, but instead represents those vocabulary items variously with its three orthographic types. There is no strict one-to-one correspondence between type of vocabulary item and script type, although one generally sees Chinese borrowings in kanji characters, native Japanese content words in kanji or hiragana, native Japanese function words in hiragana, and the borrowings from other languages in katakana. It is no wonder that there has been considerable discussion about reform ever since the Meiji Restoration of 1868 underwrote aspirations for modernization (Twine, 1983), and that various principles of orthographic reform have waxed and waned during most of this century. Ever since the Meiji Restoration, the general thrust, or at least, the general intention, of government-sponsored inquiries into language reform has been to foster simplification and standardization of the orthography.

KANJI SCRIPT

Kanji History

The first features of the Chinese writing system, an orthography which itself dates from the second half of the second millennium B.C. (see Boltz, 1994), were borrowed into Japanese as the Fourth Century turned into the Fifth Century, just as they were also borrowing other useful structures. Chinese elements were borrowed in several historical periods, but the legacy of the 'Han characters' (*han-zi* in Chinese) associated with the Han Dynasty period seems to predominate. *Kan-on* (漢音), or 'Kan readings', were borrowings which were often associated with aspects of Confucian scholarship, giving rise to the term *kan-ji* for Japanese characters. It is this group of Chinese hanzi now become Japanese 漢字 *kanji* that was and still remains the most productive set of readings when one encounters Chinese characters in Japanese. It is also the most productive set in creating new words in the contemporary Japanese lexicon. Other *on*-readings derived from imports coming in during the Wu,[2] Soong, and Tang dynasties, and are called *go-on* (呉音), *soo-on* (宋音), and *too-on* (唐音) respectively. As a result, Japanese characters often have **multiple readings** for many characters that have only a single reading in Korean or even in Chinese (see Taylor & Taylor, 1995, for a comparison of Chinese, Korean, and Japanese writing systems).[3]

But Chinese was vastly different from Japanese in structure, and the **morphological aspects** which fostered this script type in Chinese were simply missing in Japanese. Although many of the Chinese hanzi stood for individual morphemes, many of the original Chinese characters stood for bound morphemes which were parts of larger compound words (換金 *kan*(change)-*kin*(money) 'cashing'; 作曲 *sak*(make)-*kyoku*(song) 'song-writing').[4] At first this was no problem, for Chinese was the written language of texts in Japan, with Japanese the spoken, but unwritten vernacular. In general, the whole situation is very reminiscent of the way in which Latin served as the only written language of Europe, until the spoken vernaculars in the Middle Ages each claimed an orthography and ensuing legitimacy for themselves. In time, Japanese did acquire written status as well, but that writing system relied and still relies heavily on the Chinese logographic system.

The other historical result is that the core vocabulary of Japanese comes to include the essential components of an entirely new set of **word formation** procedures based on the imported Chinese readings of characters. These procedures come to be limited not just to an inventory of learned, technical words (科学 *kagaku* 'science'; 社会 *shakai* 'society'), but also to common vocabulary words (食事 *shokuji* 'meal') which compete with native Japanese words (めし *meshi* 'meal'). This situation is in its turn reminiscent of the Latin and Greek borrowings which came into English and gave rise to an entirely new method of word coinage. The net result, of course, has been a historically-based dichotomy in the lexicon which contrasts classical words with native Anglo-Saxon words. The lines have been blurred over the centuries, and in both English and Japanese the original etymologies of many words are only a distant memory.

The Japanese also went on to make up their **own characters**, simply by analogy with the traditional ones. Some of these have only *kun*-readings (for example, 辻 *tsuji* 'crossroads' and 峠 *toge* 'mountain pass'), while others have only an *on*-reading (癌 *gan*

---

[2] The *go-on* of the Wu Dynasty period came in with Buddhist terminology, but spread into other domains as well (see Martin, 1972).

[3] And to some extent, the Japanese readings thus often represent more accurately the historical pronunciations of the Chinese characters than do the Modern Chinese readings.

[4] Even the Chinese word order of verb-object is retained in these compounds.

'cancer'). Still other unique Japanese creations have both *kun-* and *on-*readings, as for example 働(く) *hataraku* 'to work, labor' and 働 *doo* 'to work, labor' (see Martin, 1972). And some of these Japanese creations reflect unique Japanese assignments, in the *ateji* (当字) or *jukujikun* (熟字訓) manners of construction. *Ateji* give a phonetic rendition of *on-*readings to create a reading for a native Japanese word, as for example, 風 *fu* and 呂 *ro* being put together to form a kanji for 風呂 *furo* 'bath'. *Jukujikun* are simply irregular *kun-*readings for characters put together on the basis of some vague semantic context. For example, 梅雨 *tsuyu* 'early summer rain' comes from the characters for 'plum', a blossom of late spring and 'rain', 土産 *miyage* 'souvenir' from the characters for 'local soil' and 'produce', and 田舎 *inaka* 'countryside' from the characters for 'rice field' and 'reside'.

Other structural differences between Japanese and Chinese presented problems which required other kinds of adaptation. One such problem was the fact that the Chinese tones do not have counterparts in Japanese, and the distinguishing tone placement on Chinese morphemes was lost into what often becomes Japanese **homophony**. Another problem was how to apply the new orthography to pre-existing lexical items in Japanese which needed representation in the newly imported orthography. For example, how would one deal with proper names and place names which pre-dated the Chinese imports? An already established Chinese method for representing proper names by using the phonetic values of existing hanzi found a Japanese application in the representation of Japanese proper names by the Seventh Century.

Simplification and adaptation to a broader population of users was another underlying problem which slowly found its own solutions. By the middle of the Eighth Century, abbreviated forms for the phonetic kanji mentioned above began to be displayed as the representation of the full kanji; often a single, simpler part of a larger kanji was isolated out to act as the orthographic symbol. Another evolutionary line of development saw orthographic symbols written in a more cursive format; this strategy simplified certain kanji while at the same time focussing on the fluidity allowed by a cursive representation of that kanji shape. In time, these isolating and cursive forerunners of the modern kana syllabaries began to appear as distinctive forms associated with increasingly exclusive formats: the isolating *katakana*-like symbols were more common as glosses in Chinese Buddhist texts, and the *hiragana*-like symbols were more common in private letters, poetry, and secular texts in general (see Seeley, 1984a). There were also gender preferences, with marginal katakana notes in Buddhist texts typically men's writing and the bulk of classical writing by women (for example, the *Genji Monogatari* (源氏物語) 'Tale of Genji') appearing in hiragana (Unger, 1987).

Kanji Policies

In the Twentieth Century, a writing system which reflects both the standard and the colloquial orthographic styles emerges and becomes increasingly familiar across a broader spectrum of the general population. The scene for this was already set, with the wave of political, economic, and educational reforms that were propelled toward the Japanese nation after the Meiji Restoration. This tsunami simply inundated the conservative structures so carefully nurtured by the Edo shogunates from 1603 to 1867, and Japanese life was changed forever. One of the Meiji goals was the acquisition and importation of knowledge, and the old orthographic system seemed to pose severe limitations on new ideas about mass education, and certainly the mass prosyletization of the new regime's even newer ideas. The push and pull of reformist vs. conservative social philosophies has swayed language policies since the turn of the century, but, generally speaking, **orthographic reform** has had its cumulative effect over time. For example, one telling effect of this thrust can be found in the fact that the number of commonly used kanji with official approval has dipped, hovering somewhere around the 2,000 mark. The Interim Committee on the National Language first recommended restricting the number of kanji to 2,108 characters in 1923, but official support for major orthographic revisions was only realized in the post-Word War II sweep which effectively reduced the number of kanji in sanctioned formats as early as 1946 (Seeley, 1984b). At that time, the kanji inventory within the Japanese writing system was whittled down to a set of *Tooyoo Kanji* (当用漢字) characters, and later modifed to a slightly expanded set of *Jooyoo Kanji* (常用漢字) characters to be used in the educational system. Both sanctioned lists were official attempts to restrict the number of kanji that could be learned effectively. The *Jooyoo Kanji* were not as restrictive as the *Tooyoo Kanji* list, and reflected contemporary use of kanji in government and the mass media; but they did exclude academic, professional, and artistic specializations. After 200 committee sessions and public hearings involving representations from professional, academic, and mass media circles, a first subset of 2,300 kanji was chosen out of 4,200 candidates. From these, a final 1,945 kanji characters were settled on (see Yasunaga, 1981).

Although there has been a slow, but inexorable drift toward simplification of the writing system since the turn of the century, this has not always meant a lineal progression toward reform and simplification. For example, earlier reform attempts in this century were often blunted by **conservative trends** or by major events which set the tenor of the times. For example, the Manchurian Incident in the Thirties and the Pacific War in the Forties were effective obstacles toward any liberalization of language policies and orthographic reform. The prospect of abandoning traditional language policies to pursue the direction of simplification struck the miltarists of the period as not only imperiling the spirit of the Japanese language (*kotodama* 言霊), but by extrapolation the very spirit of *kokutai* (国体) and the sense of Japanese nationhood (see Collier-Sanuki, 1996). Then too, there were simple, but practical reasons to be found in the very events of the time, and these too affected orthographic reforms in their parallels to national directions. One practical example of this can be found in the fact that increased activity in Manchuria translated into an increase in the number and type of Chinese characters which began appearing in the journalistic outlets which reported the events of the day.

The end of the Pacific War, however, finally opened the door for those who favored sweeping reforms in the political and educational arenas, and the enthusiasm for these reforms provided a platform upon which orthographic changes could also be realized. The long-repressed enthusiasm of the reformers was well-matched to the sentiments emanating from the General Headquarters of the American Occupation Forces, which also hoped that educational reforms would facilitate democratization of post-war Japan. In 1946, the learning of the *Tooyoo Kanji* characters was legislated by the Ministry of Education. Upon entering the *Shogakkoo* 'Elementary School' children were to master 966 of the 1,850 *Tooyoo Kanji* list by Grade Six, and then master the rest of the 1,850 by the time they passed out of *Chuugakkoo* 'Junior High School' at Grade Nine (see Seeley, 1984b).

But even this *Tooyoo Kanji* list, aptly named as the 'List of Kanji for Current (or Temporary) Use', is eventually modified by the give and take between various interest groups and the pressing educational and journalistic demands of the post-war era. The results of such compromises are embodied in the official promulgation of a set of 1,945 *Jooyoo Kanji* in 1981, now clearly named the 'List of Kanji for Daily Use (常用)' (see Seeley, 1984b, for the nuances in the keen debate which accompanied adoption of this change). Although **Jooyoo Kanji** and **Tooyoo Kanji** do not differ dramatically in number, the new list strove to more accurately reflect actual kanji usage in modern society, as for example, kanji use in laws, ordinances, official texts, newspapers, magazines, and the media. This *Jooyoo Kanji* list in fact builds on the earlier *Tooyoo Kanji* list, and even makes a few extra additions. For example, it adds 166 kanji which are used only to write proper names, and it also adds 110 miscellaneous common words which use kanji with irregular readings. Like its predecessor, the list of *Jooyoo Kanji* is also presented in graded waves: first-graders were expected to learn 76 kanji, second-graders 145, third-graders 195, fourth-graders 195, fifth-graders 195, and sixth-graders 190, for a total of 996 (Shimamura, 1990). Once again, there is an expectation of mastery of the complete set of 1,945 by the time that Grade 9 of Junior High School is completed. The reality of literate Japan, however, is that most Japanese know many more kanji than the simplified list, and indeed, in order to wade through the daily newspaper, 3,000 or more kanji are probably required.

Both the *Tooyoo Kanji* and the *Jooyoo Kanji* lists, it should be noted, are not simply the product of sudden and sweeping post-war reforms, but are based on earlier **pre-war suggestions** which were unable to be realized sooner. Many of these ideas had been around for a half-century or more, and simply provided the foundation upon which post-war kanji reforms were built. The first serious attempt at kanji reform can be traced to a suggestion by the *Mombusho* 'Ministry of Education' in 1900 to limit primary school mastery of the logographic system to about 1,200 kanji. But these suggestions were repealed in 1908, as considerable opposition to kanji quotas and kana changes arose. The ramifications of other socio-political questions have swirled around the orthographic debates, and have variously strengthened or weakened the thrust of the reform move-ment. The drive to improve literacy levels and accessibility to newspaper journalism was tied to the principles of democracy generally taking place in Japan and added credibility to the movement, but after the Manchuria Incident in 1931, nationalism mixes well with the conservatism which undermines the movement. Reforms which had been proposed much earlier were thus only realized when the post-war swing in both official and public mood proffers support for orthographic change. But their implementation would not have been realized as efficiently without the groundwork which had already been carried out beforehand.

This drama has not reached its denouement yet. This is one of the border frontiers in the continuing skirmish between **conservatives and reformers**, and language policy is constantly evolving, always reflecting the changes and moods in the social and political Zeitgeist. For example, the political conservatism of the ruling Liberal Democratic Party re-emerged to prompt a re-evaluation of language reforms. Its appointed committee reported back in 1968 that earlier reforms had unfortunately resulted in a conspicuous lowering of reading skills. The committee moved to retain older forms of kanji, return to historical spellings, and relax kanji limits, all proposals which certainly reflected a re-surgence of conservative perspectives on language policy. At the very least, these pro-posals serve as a re-affirmation of kanji as central to the Japanese orthographic system. However, the nostalgia for pre-war kanji forms[5] and historical spellings never did catch on, and these suggestions were never acted upon (see Gottlieb, 1995). But the practical realities of journalistic practices have led various organizations in the publishing industry to modify their in-house kanji standards and to increase the inventories they saw a need for. The downward drift toward kanji reduction has thus been checkmated by the official

---

[5] Despite the nostalgia for the 'golden age' of kanji erudition by the common person, Shimamura's (1997) comparison of the actual figures in surveys of kanji abilities between 1916 and 1985 shows the opposite to be true. Modern Japanese children on the average seem to evidence better kanji knowledge scores than pre-war children as a whole. And her example of the mediocre performance by young 1936 draftees recalls how this reality caused the military authorities to adapt technical manuals for its inductees during the period of the Pacific War (see Gottlieb, 1995).

increase in the *Jooyoo Kanji* inventory from 1,850 to 1,945, as well as by newspaper publishing tendencies to add and standardize kanji for their own uses.

Kanji Frequencies

The reality of kanji usage inevitably reflects three practical facts, namely, their absolute numbers, their frequency of usage, and their ease of access through human or artificial memory. The number of extant kanji characters is enormous, and 'comprehensive' kanji dictionaries contain anywhere between 12,000 and 50,000 entries (Kindaichi, 1991; Morohashi, 1989). But dictionary entries do not tell the whole story, for frequencies are crucial to understanding not only usage but the way in which the mental dictionary is accessed. As a result, psycholinguistic and cognitive science inquiries in the West have used, and continue to find, new applications for such frequencies. Though they are early attempts, and now perhaps dated, we have **word frequency lists** for American English such as the *Thorndike-Lorge Count* (Thorndike & Lorge, 1944), the *Brown Corpus* (Kucera & Francis, 1967), and the *American Heritage Word Frequency Book* (Carroll, Davies & Richman, 1972). But there have been few comparable word frequency lists for Japanese. Although the 1946 *Tooyoo Kanji* and the 1981 *Jooyoo Kanji* lists legislated by the Ministry of Education reflect frequency considerations, they are not strictly word frequency counts. They will not tell you, for example, how often a given token appears in the mass media texts of popular magazines and newspapers.

Until recently, a good source has been the word frequency list published by the National Language Research Institute (国立国語研究所) in 1962 (and re-issued in floppy disk format in 1997). This list was based on a corpus derived from 90 journals and magazines in five genres published in 1956. It was later complemented by the National Language Research Institute's kanji frequency list in 1976, a frequency list which was based on a newspaper corpus of the *Asahi, Yomiuri,* and *Mainichi Shimbun* newspapers in 1966. There was also statistical analysis of kanji in daily usage by Nomura (1984), which showed just over 3,000 of the possible 50,000 kanji are typically used in contemporary magazines and newspapers. He found less than 200 kanji accounted for 50% of daily usage, while 1,000 kanji accounted for 90% of daily usage. An inventory of 2,000 kanji accounted for 99%, suggesting that the actual number of discrete but **frequently-used kanji** is considerably less than one expects.

Now these earlier attempts have been replaced by a more current and more comprehensive analysis of Japanese newspaper corpora which does much to tease out the factors which impact word recognition strategies in Modern Japanese.[6] For example, of the thousands of potential kanji characters in the 110,000 articles spanning one year of morning and evening editions of the *Asahi Shimbun*, 4,476 different characters appear at least once.[7] Of these, the first 1,000 most frequently-used characters account for about 95% of the total number of kanji characters in newspapers (Nozaki & Yokoyama, 1996; Nozaki, Yokoyama, Isomoto & Yoneda, 1996; Yokoyama & Nozaki, 1996b; Yokoyama, Sasahara, Nozaki & Long, 1998).[8] The story seems to be much the same for magazines and periodicals. Here Nozaki, Yokoyama, and Chikamatsu (1997; see also Nozaki, Yokoyama, Chikamatsu & Isomoto, 1997) found that the top 500 kanji accounted for around 75% of kanji usage, the top 1,000 for 90%, the top 2,180 for 99%. The remaining items, taking us up to a total number which includes the top 3,200 kanji, accounted for the last 1%.

Diachronic Factors in Kanji Frequencies

Statistical data point to a decline in the overall use of kanji over the long term. For example, novels written in 1900 employed text which was 39.3% kanji, while those written in 1950 employed only 27.5% (Nomura, 1984). The same decline can be illustrated by charting the frequency of **kanji usage** in major Japanese newspapers published during the Meiji (1868-1911), Taisho (1912-1925), and Showa (1926-1989) eras (see Kajiwara, 1982). The use of kanji in the 'big newspapers' (大新聞 *ooshinbun*) which were aimed at bureaucrats and intellectuals was at first extremely high, with kanji running as high as 65%. Government notices cited in such papers exhibited a kanji ratio which even went as high as 95%. High frequencies for kanji were observed even with the earlier versions of the 'small newspapers' (小新聞 *koshinbun*) which were aimed at the common people; here the occurrence ratio was reported at around 55%. Throughout the last century, however, kanji have somewhat decreased in Japanese newspapers,

---

[6] Such newspaper inventories can also be used for other kinds of analysis, as Inoue and Tsujino (1992) demonstrate with an overview of the National Language Research Institute collection of newspaper articles assembled between 1953 and 1988.

[7] Interestingly, a recent analysis of a 1,800,000-character corpus of Chinese modern usage reveals that 4, 574 hanzi comprise 100% of that inventory (*Xiadai Hanyu Pinlu Cidian* 'Modern Chinese Frequency Dictionary', cited in Tan & Perfetti, 1997).

[8] But frequency must be counter-balanced with familiarity. For that reason, the new *NTT Psycholinguistic Database*, scheduled for publication in 1999, contains familiarity scores for 6,700 kanji, as well as subjective and objective complexity scores (S. Amano, personal communication at the International Conference on the Mental Lexicon, September, 1998).

spurred on to some degree by governmental decrees[9] reducing the number of officially approved kanji, but probably more by the self-serving motive of making newspapers available to a larger readership. This is also seen in the complementary drift toward use of more colloquial language in the newspapers; according to Kajiwara (1982), the tendency towards colloqualization and limitations on kanji usage was the most marked in the decade between Taisho 6 (1917) and Showa 2 (1927).

Even with the downward drift over time, the ratio of kanji to kana in modern Japanese newspaper text can run as high as 42% at times (see Kaiho & Nomura, 1983), and the centrality of kanji in the orthography cannot be overlooked. The type of outlet has an effect on the **kanji ratio**, with the highest percentage (38.2%) appearing in political and economic weeklies. Weekly magazines and newspapers favored exclusively by male readers and female readers have the lowest kanji ratios, 23.6% and 25.2%, respectively. The low figures here reflect the specialized, often imported vocabularies that accompany coverage of such activities, for example, sports coverage of ongoing baseball, rugby, and soccer matches for the male readership. For these specialized weekly publications directed at a sports-minded male readership, Nomura (1980) found that katakana weighed in at a hefty 15.4%, while the kanji ratio for publications aimed at general readership showed a 29.7% figure.

But the most interesting fact about contemporary usage is that the relative kanji frequencies in more contemporary newspaper copora appear to have not changed dramatically over the past thirty years. Chikamatsu, Yokoyama, Nozaki, Long, Sasahara, and Fukuda (1998, n.d.) compared the first 3,000 frequency ranks between the 1966 and 1993 kanji frequency rankings, and found a very high correlation between the two usage periods. As the following scattergram with axes values corresponding to degree of frequency illustrates, the overall pattern of kanji usage has not significantly changed between 1966 and 1993.

---

[9] According to Kajiwara (1982), the 1923 restriction of kanji use to 1,963 characters through the government decree of *Jooyoo Kanjihyoo*, and the further restriction of kanji in 1946 to 1,850 characters through the issue of the *Tooyoo Kanjihyoo*, contributed to a decrease in occurrence rate of kanji by as much as 5% and 6.9%, respectively, to 1980.

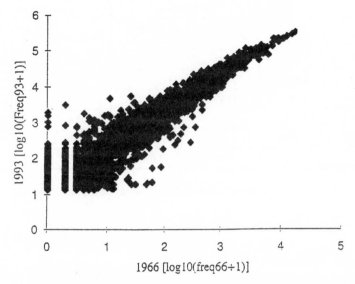

Figure 2.1 Kanji usage scattergram of correlation between 1966 and 1993.
(Reprinted with permission from Chikamatsu, Yokoyama,
Nozaki, Long, Sasahara, and Fukuda, n.d.)

According to Yokoyama and Nozaki (1996b), the correlation between kanji usage during these two chronological points was r=.95 (n=4543), even when including all the lower frequency kanji. For example, 445 kanji ranked in the top 500 kanji in the 1966 analysis of frequencies were still ranked in the top 500 in 1993. And the remaining 55 kanji were still in the top 1,000 in the 1993 corpus. A recent study by Tamaoka, Yanase, and Kirsner (n.d.) postulates an even higher correlation ratio of r=.97 (n=1945) for *Jooyoo Kanji* between the 1976 and 1998 analyses. Where there are shifts in kanji frequency, it is typically in the low-end kanji, the ones which are not in the top percentiles. Very simply, high frequency kanji tend to stay in their relative positions, but low-frequency kanji are more likely to shift in respect to their usage over time (see also Nozaki, Yokoyama & Chikamatsu, 1997).

Inevitably, some kanji have changed their **relative position** in the frequency wars; some have increased in frequency, while others have lost their place of prominence in the print media. For example, the following pair of tables illustrate these increases and decreases in counts taken in 1966 and 1993 (from Yokoyama & Nozaki, 1996b).

Kanji	Kuten-code[10]	1966 Survey		1993 Survey	
		Ranking	Frequency (%)	Ranking	Frequency (%)
狙	3332	1983	0.010	854	0.205
崩	4288	1722	0.024	771	0.245
訟	3057	1687	0.027	967	0.161
阜	4176	1663	0.029	968	0.160
削	2679	1460	0.052	855	0.204
葬	3382	1448	0.053	892	0.189

Table 2.1 A sample of kanji whose frequency in use has increased.

Kanji	Kuten-code	1966 Survey		1993 Survey	
		Ranking	Frequency (%)	Ranking	Frequency (%)
鍵	3091	734	0.291	1907	0.013
才	2645	625	0.356	1565	0.033
蚕	3862	948	0.169	1871	0.014
胃	1663	893	0.190	1739	0.021
綿	4442	850	0.216	1582	0.033
糸	2769	687	0.314	1340	0.063

Table 2.2 A sample of kanji whose frequency in use has decreased.

More recently, even more **comprehensive evaluations** of these kanji frequencies have been forthcoming, as computer technology allows us to treat multiple dimensions

---

[10] According to Lunde (1993), the *kuten* code is a machine-independent way of indexing characters in JIS X 0208-1990 and JIS X 0212-1990 sets, and the corporate character sets derived from them. The term *kuten* (区点) itself literally means 'ward-point', but should be interpreted to mean 'row [and] cell'. With the *kuten* code, all the two-byte characters in a code are identified by their position in a code table. The table is divided into 94 rows (only rows 1 to 84 have characters assigned in JIS X 0208-1990), each of which has 94 characters. So the first number in the *kuten* code identifies the row, and the second number identifies the position of the character within that row. Most punctuation characters are in ROW 1, the Latin alphabet is in ROW 3, hiragana in ROW 4, katakana in ROW 5, and kanji begin in ROW 16. The *kuten* code is the most universal way of referring to particular characters, but the actual binary code used in any particular computer implementation must be calculated from the *kuten* code.

of such corpora for linguistic and psycholinguistic research. Chikamatsu et al. (1998; see also Yokoyama, Sasahara, Nozaki & Long, 1998) present a detailed analysis of that one-year CD-ROM collection of *Asahi Shimbun* morning and evening runs from 1993 (*Asahi Shimbun* [Newspaper], 1994). Their published results make available the JIS code, the ranking, raw frequency, frequency ratio by percentage, and cumulative frequency ratio for each of the 4,476 kanji characters that appear in the 24 million kanji total. A sample table from Chikamatsu et al. (1998) may serve to illustrate.[11]

Kanji	83JIS	Ranking	Raw Frequency	Frequency Ratio (0/00)
日	3892	1	336465	14.37379
一	1676	2	285089	12.17900
十	2929	3	254534	10.87369
二	3883	4	223075	9.529766
人	3145	5	218967	9.354272
大	3471	6	218693	9.342566
年	3915	7	216931	9.267294
会	1881	8	214989	9.184332
国	2581	9	199502	8.522727

Table 2.3 Ten highest ranking kanji in frequency.

This newspaper publishes a daily run of ten million copies, and that daily paper is probably perused by twice that number of readers before being recycled. Thus, one can be assured that such frequency lists are representative of a large segment of the reading population, and play a role in contemporary word recognition strategies for more than just a few.

But we should also note that newspapers comprise a special literary genre, especially in respect to **kanji density**. Kaiho and Nomura (1983) found the ratio of kanji to kana to hover around the 42% mark in newspapers, while Hatta, Kawakami, and Hatasa (1997) cite the ratio of kanji to kana in the nationwide daily *Asahi Shimbun* as 46.1% to 41.4%. The 54,606,769 printed units in the 1993 corpus of the *Asahi Shimbun* that were recently analyzed by Chikamatsu et al. (n.d.) yielded the following ratios: 42.86% were kanji, 37.92% were hiragana, and 6.60% were katakana. The popular medium of magazine

---

[11] This character frequency list is available from the National Language Research Institute in Tokyo through the Internet on the World-Wide Web at **http://www.kokken.go.jp/asahi-news-db**. And it has just been published as Yokoyama, Sasahara, Nozaki, and Long (1998).

journalism offers a 30% ratio in Kaiho and Nomura's analysis, more in keeping with its more narrative or conversational style of prose. The other consideration is that word frequency and character frequency counts invariably reflect the genre from whence they are derived. Newspapers invariably focus on the dramatic and negative in social and political matters, and employ more technical terms in political, economic, governmental, and scientific arenas than might normally be found in lighter publication outlets.

Kanji in the Computer Age

The modern availability of word processors, electronic dictionaries, and personal computers, and their impact on current kanji awareness, cannot be overlooked (see Kabashima, 1984). In 1978, the available word processors on the commercial market were roughly equivalent to a middle manager's annual income (see Ikeda, 1988). But twenty years later it seems as if everyone has at least one, if not two, such devices. This ready access has made kanji easily available through facile input strategies, such as typing in romaji or kana to access kanji images on the screen. Even homonyms are no longer a problem, for the entire list of homonyms is instantaneously retrieved, and choices are easily made. Unfamiliar kanji can also be retrieved through accessing the radical or the number of strokes, and the immediacy of electronic retrieval has transformed a tedious task into a simple manipulation.

Engineering applications now show interest in further simplifying **kanji retrieval**, by making use of whatever distinctive or redundant features might be applicable to establishing kanji codes (see Araki, 1985, Saito, 1988, and others as examples of the continuing quest to achieve maximum access and yet minimum redundancy). The retrieval problem is obvious when one compares older and newer versions of common kanji configurations, such as 龍 and 竜 for *ryuu* 'dragon', 櫻 and 桜 for *sakura* 'cherry', and 曾 and 曽 for *soo* 'formerly'. Older texts, as well as the modern texts showing such personal preferences, may show the older variants of these kanji. Optical readers have to be able to see both configurations as the same, just as the educated human eye does. Even the educated reader is not up to the task of handling all variations, and recourse to the JIS inventory does not always provide a listing for a surprising number of those variants which are commonly called *itaiji* (異体字) **'deformed characters'** (see Nakahara, 1991).

There are other problems too, such as those presented by the existence of *yuurei kanji* (幽霊漢字) **'phantom kanji'** which appear in modern newspapers and yet are not listed formally in the dictionary because they may be *ad hoc* variants of the historically correct shapes of lesser used kanji or created amalgamations of existing shapes (see Sasahara, Yokoyama, Nozaki & Yoneda, 1998; Yokoyama, Sasahara, Nozaki & Long,

1998; Yokoyama, Sasahara, Nozaki & Yoneda, 1997). For example, Sasahara et al. examined kanji listed in the JIS X 0208 standard used in personal computers, but which are not listed in major kanji dictionaries. Of 129 such kanji searched for, examples of 34 characters were found in the newspaper corpora. They also found *yuurei kanji* with doubtful authenticity which are defined in the JIS set and which are substituted for standard dictionary listings. Both findings certainly underscore the value of electronic corpora for ascertaining the true usage dimensions of such low frequency kanji. Once again, the human eye may recognize such variant shapes, despite their illegality, and engineering applications seek to emulate the successful resolution that we human readers take for granted.

One of the most efficient proposals to account for all the variations has been the implementation of a **4-byte code** to replace the 2-byte code currently used in much electronic retrieval. The National Language Research Institute is currently pursuing a research project which uses a four-byte system, supporting the establishment of a standard digitized code for the entire inventory of kanji used in China, Korea, and Japan (Saito, 1994). Saito (1998) suggests that its adoption allows more flexibility, and gives better coverage for such varied uses as historical names of people and places in Japan, not to mention the same possibility for presentation of the same kanji facts regarding personages and events in China, Korea, Taiwan, and so forth. This is predicated on the overarching principle of making kanji coding compatible for all kanji-using orthographies, a driving principle behind much work. The fact is that Japanese kanji often do not match the Chinese simplifications which have taken place for their hanzi characters. The Japanese did adopt some simplified shapes for kanji after the Second World War, both for kanji as whole units and for radical elements within kanji characters. However, when the People's Republic of China simplified its hanzi inventory, the results were often different from the Japanese simplifications. The net result is that Chinese and Japanese characters have less in common in the latter half of the Twentieth Century than they did in the latter half of the Nineteenth Century. The most telling evidence of this is the difficulty that Chinese students of Japanese as a Second Language have with mastering kanji from a *hanzi* background, although there are pedagogical aids which do capitalize on the similarities between the readings for Chinese hanzi and the *on*-readings for Japanese kanji (see, for example, Kayamoto, 1995). And there is even more differentiation among kanji-using cultures, because Singapore and Hong Kong often followed China, while Taiwan maintained older versions of the hanzi (see Martin, 1972; Takata, 1991). If these logographs are ever to have any common values for access, an enlarged set of coding principles will be needed to cope with such variation. One possible solution for dealing with this problem of character variations was recently put forward by the Mojikyo Research Society (文字鏡研究会), a non-profit organization which has been developing software/fontware encompassing approximately 90,000 kanji fonts (see Mojikyo Research Society, 1999). This inventory of fonts is claimed to include all the possible characters which have ever been used in China, Hong Kong, Taiwan, Singapore, Korea, and Japan.[12]

The **standardization** of character codes in Japanese itself is far from settled for other reasons as well. At present, the computerization of Japanese kanji characters involves three possible coding systems: the Japanese Industrial Standard (JIS), the Shift-JIS (SJIS) and the Extended Unix Code (EUC). Choice depends upon the system one is using; for example, personal computers often use the SJIS code, but the Internet, and the original UNIX stations which went with early uses of the Net, use EUC as their standard coding system. Thus, working across systems or cross-tasking often requires a conversion filter if one treks across the three types of codes in any way (see Chikamatsu et al., 1998).

For the average person, however, the attractions of the electronic age have resulted in a basic push-pull conflict between the number of kanji actually used vs. the number of kanji possibly used. On the one hand, the drive to reduce and simplify kanji in this century has seen its effects in the proclamations regarding officially sanctioned kanji in the education system. But the reality is that ease of access has in fact increased the number of kanji made available to users, and greater computing power has been matched by more and more kanji being added to processing systems. Nomura (1991) observes that the commercial availability of computers and word processors has led to an **expansion of the kanji** in use, with each new stage meeting new challenges, at the same time that it poses new challenges with the increased computing power it has just made available. But there are also those who see the traditional writing system on a collision course with the exponential leaps in scope and number of computer applications. Unger (1987) claims that unless a fundamentally different type of computational device can be built, the sheer inefficiency of using traditional Japanese orthography in computer environments will bring the whole system to a halt. The question is not whether computers can handle Japanese script at all, it is rather whether that script can be handled as cheaply and efficiently as alphabetic writing is. And some, like Unger (1984, 1987), maintain that the answer is 'no', unless some innovations in orthography for purposes of data processing are enacted.

Scholars from the *kokugogaku* (国語学) 'National Language' school of thought think otherwise, and sing the praises of the narrowly selected *Jooyoo Kanji* as a foundational set, claiming that the modern word processor requires only a limited range of 3,000 or so kanji to fulfill most writing requirements (Tanaka, 1991). While this may be true, the general drift allowed by increased computing power is toward expanded numbers. For example, in 1978 the **JIS list** standardized the kanji capacity in electronic

---

[12] Information on the Society, as well as how to obtain free software/fontware on *mojikyo*, is available on the Web: **http://www.mojikyo.gr.jp.**

devices at 2,965, with a secondary list of 3,388 available for more specialized uses. By 1990 a tertiary JIS list of 5,801 had brought the total to 12,154 (Gottlieb, 1995; Koizumi, 1991; Satake, 1991), although many in the secondary and tertiary lists are rare or seldom used characters that even kanji scholars might not know (Koizumi, 1991). Such developments obviously invite a wider range of kanji usage by the average user, and the advantages offered by word processing packages and electronic retrieval support this invitation. Many argue that these same benefits are not without their costs, since they weaken the active retrieval of kanji configurations from the human mental dictionary, and frustrate their conscious use in text production because the kinetic component involved in actual writing has been lost.

Commercial publishers of magazines, books, and newspapers often maintain larger inventories for the specialized demands made on them by proper names, place names, and specialized or technical vocabulary, and the JIS lists at least offer a uniform standard reference point. After all, there are occasions when one needs an old character for ancient texts, drama or song titles, or even company names, and specialized systems act as repositories for these needs.[13]

Many suggestions have been made about limiting the expansion of kanji beyond the current list of **personal names**,[14] using the commonly used kanji forms for family registry and record-keeping procedures (see Nomura, 1991), and even controlling the number of *on-* and *kun*-readings (see Kabashima, 1991). But what is common in one place may not be common elsewhere, and it is a matter of perspective. Using his own extraordinary *koseki* (戸籍) name as an example, 樺嶋 *Kaba-shima*, Kabashima (1991) notes that in Kyushu, Fukuoka, and Saga prefectures, variants of the name are far from extraordinary, and that in Fukuoka one can buy a ready-made variant of the name's *hanko* seal for cheap just about anywhere. He also recounts how his attempt to use the simplified character 島 for the actual 嶋 *-shima* part of his name only resulted in manuscript rejection, and the injunction to use his legal *koseki* family register name. Obviously, feelings run strong on the matter of maintaining or rejecting any kanji which serves as a family name.[15]

---

[13] The Mojikyo Research Society (1999) offers free services for their society members to create any character fonts which are not in their inventory of 90,000 fonts.

[14] By Showa 56 (1981), the number of approved personal names had swollen to 2,111, and by Heisei 2 (1991) the number was up to 2,229. Moreover, Ishiwatari (1991) notes that if the kanji 潤 *man*, with its 43 written variations, is any bellwether of trends in personal name assignments, this poses potential identification complications for the keepers of family registry data.

[15] Satake (1991) offers a similar scenario for the various *Watanabes* who share the same reading, but for whom the actual kanji differ.

Though tremendous advances have been made in simplifying access and reproduction, new improvements are always sought in commercial applications for kanji character readers and word processors. Some of them reflect everyday applications of kanji processing demands, as for example, how to have hand-written kanji read by an optical reader linked to the computer, how to have the computer convert a sequence of type-written letters into output which has kanji and kana at appropriate places in the sentence, and perhaps most importantly, how to build user-friendly capabilities which reflect knowledge from natural language processing into the word processor (see Kurosu, 1984, for an early statement of the potential of such devices). It may turn out that the question of how many kanji exist will cease to matter as a practical question, as increasing numbers of users simply plug into the easy accessibility afforded by mechanical devices. There may even come a time in Japan when there will be two character sets in actual practice; one will be for reading comprehension, a **read-only set**, while the other set will be a **write-only set**, the set that literate Japanese will have to be able to produce in handwriting tasks (see Takata, 1991). The former set could even include relatively rare characters, as well as an inventory of frequent, but complex characters with multi-stroke configurations; the latter set might be high in their frequency or simple in their configuration, or both. Perhaps the reality is that the Japanese are already there.

KANA SCRIPTS

There are two syllabary types in Japanese, the katakana syllabary and the hiragana syllabary, in which the kana unit represents a sound unit which roughly corresponds to a syllable. In fact, it is the mora that the Japanese syllabary system employs kana symbols for, although for all practical purposes the overlap with syllables is very close. Both kana scripts contain 46 basic symbols and an additional 25 symbols with diacritic marks. Hiragana and katakana share the same syllabic reference point, so that the same syllable can be transcribed by either system. For example, the syllable /sa/ is transcribed as さ in hiragana and as サ in katakana.

The **katakana syllabary** is more angular in the shape of its symbols, and is commonly declared as the appropriate transliteration medium for loan words coming into Japanese from other languages. However, it sees a good deal of use in modern printed Japanese as a kind of visual italics, useful for highlighting exclamations in everything from literature to *manga* comics. It also sees extensive use in citing neologisms, and has been seized upon as a perceptual focal point in advertisements in order to call attention to brand names or brand qualities. **Hiragana**, on the other hand, is more cursive in the formation of its symbols, and its shapes are more easily discriminated one from the other. Although it is used for writing some content words, it is more commonly used in writing the non-content words and the grammatical morphemes not usually presented by the kanji characters. In short, hiragana is used for some content words, as well as for all the morphological endings, function words, and the rest of the grammatical scaffolding of Japanese sentences. Kanji may roughly constitute a third of the total number of symbols in the average sentence (see Saito, 1981a), but what is not kanji is usually hiragana.

Just as was the case with kanji legislation, there have been some **kana reforms** in the evolution of the Japanese orthography during this century. The Ministry of Education attempted to facilitate kana acquisition as early as 1900 by limiting the number of kana symbols to be considered as standard. It also promoted a more straightforward relationship between kana symbols and their pronunciation, attempting to replace the historically-based principles of kana assignment to one based on pronunciation (see Seeley, 1984b). Considerable debate, if not downright opposition, ensued, and the Ministry backed down in 1908 by rescinding its earlier regulations about kana symbols and their assignment. Forty years later, post-war reformers once again attempted to re-align the kana system with their modern pronunications, rejecting some of the older conventions based on historical principles. The 1946 promulgation of *Gendai Kanazukai* 'Modern Kana Usage' by the Cabinet ironed out kana usage practices, and also placed kana in closer conjunction with kanji roots in words by standardizing *okurigana* placement of kana after kanji roots when showing inflectional endings. But even so, there is still considerable variation in actual practice, and various authors will differ in how they incorporate the final syllable(s) of the root shown by the kanji character, as exempled below.

柔(ら)か	/yawa(ra)ka/	'soft'
後(ろ)	/ushi(ro)/	'back'
動(き)	/ugo(ki)/	'movement'
調(べ)る	/shira(be)ru/	'to examine'

Kana has never replaced kanji, and there are a variety of reasons why this never came about. A common argument is that Japanese has too many **homophones**, words with the same pronunciation whose differing meanings are efficiently shown by their having different kanji characters. For example, if one looks at overlapping *on*-readings in just the first standardized grouping of JIS kanji, there are 102 kanji read as *koo*, 95 kanji read as *shoo*, 76 kanji read as *shi*, and 61 kanji read as *too*. There are also many instances of overlapping *kun*-readings, with 45 kanji read as *ka*, 44 kanji read as *o*, and 41 kanji read as *to* (see Kaiho, 1987). In discussing design problems associated with Japanese keyboard input, Yamada (1983) cites a vocabulary count of one popular Japanese dictionary as showing as many as 36.4% of the entries to be homophones. Some words may be distinguished due to the placement of pitch accent in their spoken rendition (for example, /ha'na/ 'flower' and /hana/ 'nose'), but this advantage disappears in their written rendition and they are exactly identical in their printed kana shapes (はな 'flower, nose'). In contrast to hiragana transcriptions, katakana is often considered to portray loanwords or native neologisms unambiguously, simply because they are far fewer in number and already unique by virtue of their origins. But it too offers homonyms, as for example, ダイヤ *daiya* meaning both 'diamond' and 'time schedule', バンド *bando* both 'brass-bound' and 'belt', and バック *bakku* both 'back' and 'bag'.

The distaff side of this classic argument about potential ambiguity in the orthography is that spoken Japanese seems to flow effectively without visual support of the kind claimed as necessary through kanji. Correct interpretations are, for the most part, immediately and accurately assigned simply on the basis of discourse and contextual cues. But counter-arguments about whether orthographic reform is possible, or even desirable, may be missing the real ember that motivates much of the heat in this debate. That is the degree to which the uniqueness of the kana and kanji writing system permeates many aspects of **Japanese life**. There is little question that the writing system acts as more than a convenient notation system for the spoken language; it has taken on a life of its own, engendering its own art forms (like *shodoo* (書道) 'calligraphy') and popular belief sets. For example, traditional expectations about intelligence and level of education lead the average Japanese to judge written compositions that display few kanji as being the product of one who is lacking in one or both of these attributes. In this respect, one would have to agree with the countless Japanese authors (for example, see Suzuki, 1969, 1975, 1977) who consider spoken language and written language in Japanese so closely intertwined that one cannot fully understand the Modern Standard Japanese setting without taking into account the writing system that the Japanese language employs.

All of the above factors are in some way reflected in the dimensions of the mental lexicon in Japanese, and are certainly played out in the range of individual differences displayed by language users as they access their respective mental dictionaries. The nature of the multi-faceted Japanese orthography must be viewed as a formative agent which exerts some influence, if not power, over the spoken language itself, and by extension, over the processing strategies employed in lexical access and word recognition procedures. Needless to say, a knowledge of the historical events which precipitated the current versions of standardized kanji and kana practices is central to understanding the attempts to improve orthography acquisition in reading and writing skills. They also provide a useful background when reviewing reports of language impairment and language loss, but most importantly, they provide a necessary backdrop to lexical access and word recognition procedures for the average Japanese reader.

Chapter 3

KANJI PROCESSING

INTRODUCTORY COMMENTS

As is well-known, Japanese employs kanji characters borrowed from the morphemically-based logographic system developed for Chinese orthography. Beginning in the seventh century, kanji were actively imported and transduced into Japanese orthography from Chinese hanzi in several distinct historical periods. In Chinese, their use constituted the only writing system, but in Japanese, the use of Chinese characters came to be complemented by two other sets of orthographic symbols, the hiragana and the katakana syllabaries, both of which are themselves ultimately derived from kanji simplifications. Massive borrowing not only transformed the vocabulary but also established new patterns for the creation of lexical items; the obvious result of this is the fact that content words in Japanese are often lexical items which are typically presented by Chinese-derived kanji characters.

In cultural terms, kanji have achieved a special place in Japanese education, aesthetics, and even in popular notions about the psychology of language. It is not surprising, therefore, that this orthographic system has attracted enormous interest in a wide range of psycholinguistic studies.[1]

---

[1] To give some idea of the unique role, if not the place of prominence, that is accorded to kanji, we might note that some psycholinguists have even examined the knowledge that the blind might have about kanji. Even the blind receive some training in kanji, and several studies (Kaiho & Sasaki, 1984; Sasaki, 1984a) have charted the possible correspondence between spoken words and written kanji, asking sighted subjects and subjects who were blind before any school experience which words might be expected to have corresponding kanji characters. Subjects produced as many kanji as possible, based either on the sound or on the radical (*bushu*) for the kanji. The blind subjects did exhibit some sensitivity to the correspondence between words and kanji, though obviously to a lesser degree than the sighted. In fairness, it should be noted that this is probably due to their naive, but nevertheless accurate, grammatical assessment of words into part of speech classes which have a statistical probability of receiving kanji assignments. Not suprisingly, although the blind do have some kanji knowledge, their knowledge of actual form is extremely poor; however, once form is acquired, it has a long residence in memory for the blind. The point to be

Current psycholinguistics is quite preoccupied with the structure of the mental lexicon, and the processes underlying lexical access and word recognition. And so also is the Japanese psychological literature, although largely through the medium of kanji processing. The mental representation for lexical items presented through kanji invites a number of processing questions which must be answered before we have a clear picture of word recognition. We need to know which informational features are invoked in lexical access procedures for written kanji words, and then we can ask how these features contribute to the final stage of successful word recognition. In some ways, the issue of kanji orthography offers an ideal test for cognitive models of lexical access and word recognition. This is because the kanji inventory does not offer an internally obvious algorithm of ordering words, other than the traditional, but nevertheless *ad hoc* strategies of lexicon look-up by radicals or by number and direction of strokes. In this sense, kanji offer an ideal example of an inventory ordered by spreading activation between units within the system because kanji are potentially linked by a larger number of nodes than alphabetically arranged words. The mere fact that kanji display a large array of graphic configurations which partially or totally overlap increases the number of potential contact points for activation to take place. And this is what a number of psycholinguistic studies have attempted to ascertain.

Another key processing question for kanji recognition involves the role of phonological vs. semantic factors, and their possible application in a parallel mode vs. a sequential mode. Similar to the debate in Chinese lexical access (see Chen, 1996), can meanings of words written in kanji be understood even when their phonetic codes are not retrieved from the written transcriptions? Unlike Chinese, however, the problem of phonological activation in Japanese is complicated by the problem alluded to above, namely, that there is usually more than one reading for a given kanji. A second key question is whether the ostensibly semantic quality of the component radicals in individual kanji characters actually have much to do with lexical access approaches to the mental lexicon. Radicals are larger than individual strokes, and are rather those stroke clusters which can be considered the identifiable structural pieces which make up the kanji. The question is, then, whether the 'semantic' qualities of certain radicals are in any way employed during the semantic interpretation of kanji words? The third key question has to do with the fact that many common and technical Japanese words are typically compounds, and not words represented by single kanji. The issue to be accounted for here is whether compound kanji are recognized and processed as integrated units, or whether their successful recognition is contingent upon the recognition and processing of their individual kanji components.

---

made, of course, is that kanji are felt to be uniquely Japanese, and researchers apparently expect even the blind will have some psycholinguistic knowledge of both their form and function.

We will attempt to survey some of the experimental answers to these basic questions below, carefully examining both Japanese and Western research reports, in an attempt to elucidate what we have learned about the role of kanji features in the mental lexicon for Japanese vocabulary items.

THE STRUCTURE OF KANJI WORDS

Kanji Architecture

The compositional principles that generate Chinese characters were borrowed, and kept, in their original design features. That is, the spatial construction of Chinese characters proceeds from *left-to-right*, *top-to-bottom*, and *outside-to-inside*. This is true for simple kanji, as well as for complex kanji: for example, contrast the following simple kanji with complex kanji constructions which are created by following the same directional principles of stroke architecture.

Direction	Simple Kanji	Complex Kanji
Left-to-right	川 *kawa* 'river '	明 *akari* 'light'
Top-to-bottom	三 *san* 'three'	家 *ie* 'house'
Outside-to-inside	王 *oo* 'king'	国 *kuni* 'country'

Chinese characters are traditionally classified into four major groupings, according to the basis of their formation (see Saito, Inoue & Nomura, 1979, but see also Ito, 1979). A very, very small percentage of kanji are actually ideographic or diagrammatic, a somewhat larger proportion are compound semantic, and by far the largest proportion are phonetic-semantic in their formation, with this latter group hovering around the 80% mark (Sato, 1973, cited in Saito, Inoue & Nomura, 1979).

Ideographic kanji (象形文字 *shookei moji*) present a stylized version of some object or concept, as for example, the peaks and valleys suggested by 山 *yama* 'mountain'. Diagrammatic kanji (指事文字 *shiji moji*) portray a logical, geometric, or conceptual relationship by some arrangement as for example, the up-down spatial relationships shown by 上 *ue* 'up' and 下 *shita* 'down'. Compound-semantic kanji (会意文字 *kaii moji*) typically put two simple characters together to form an ostensibly transparent character which is supposed to represent the additive value of the original units. For example, compare 明 *akari* 'light, bright' with its components, 日 *hi* 'sun' and 月 *tsuki* 'moon'.

But these three types are only a minority of the totality of Japanese kanji, representing no more than 20% of the total. By far the largest number of kanji are phonetic-semantic kanji (形声文字 *keisei moji*), containing a semantic 'radical' which gives a rough approximation of where the kanji fits categorically and a 'phonetic' which may suggest the Chinese reading for the kanji by its similarity to a basic kanji embedded in this larger phonetic-semantic compound. The semantic radical is often found on the left-hand side of the phonetic-semantic kanji, and the phonetic on the right-hand side, and are known as the *hen* and *tsukuri*, respectively .

Pronunciations	Phonetic Radicals	Semantic (water) Radical
/kai/	悔 'to regret'	海 'sea'
/sei/	晴 'clear weather'	清 'clear water'
/sen/	銭 'money'	浅 'shallow'
/shin/	侵 'to invade'	浸 'to soak'

But these are only two of the seven categories that phonetic-semantic compounds divide themselves into. A total inventory of potential compositional elements would include all of the following constructional elements.

Radicals		Examples	
Hen	(left-hand)	波 'wave',	河 'river'
Tsukuri	(right-hand)	清 'clear water',	晴 'clear weather'
Kanmuri	(top)	草 'grass',	花 'flower'
Ashi	(bottom)	熊 'bear',	馬 'horse'
Kamae	(enclosure)	国 'country',	囲 'to enclose'
Tare	(top-left)	庭 'garden',	店 'shop'
Nyoo	(left-bottom)	返 'to return',	逃 'to escape'

The presentation of a Chinese character is meant to fit within an idealized box-like configuration which dedicates the same relative space to the individual characters in running text. As the following chart (adapted from Kaiho & Nomura, 1983, and Tamaoka, 1991) illustrates, this principle of equidimensionality means that each character occupies the same imaginary box-like space which has an identical size. Thus, the same element which served as a character in isolation might now shrink in size as it forms part of a larger, more complex character.

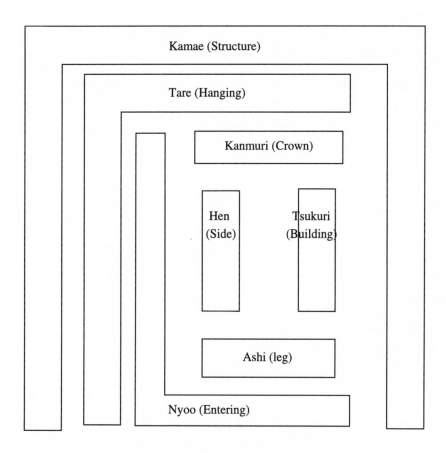

Figure 3.1 Equidimensionality of kanji characters.

In running text, moreover, the box-like spaces containing these single, complex, and compound characters run on without special markings like capitalization or special spacing for word boundaries, as shown below.

> この辞典は、国語辞典であるとともに、学術専門語並びに百科
> 万般にわたる事項用語を含む大総合辞典として編集された.

> 'This dictionary was compiled as a language dictionary, as well as a
> large-scale encyclopedia, containing not only academic technical
> terms but also terms dealing with every aspect of daily events.'

On-readings vs. Kun-readings

But where the architectural design of Japanese kanji is essentially the same as their Chinese hanzi origins, their implementation is not. Reading written Japanese is not as simple as memorizing a limited number of single characters which represent single words with single readings. A number of orthography-specific requirements interact to make kanji processing a many-faceted, and often unpredictable, cognitive task in Japanese. Homophones are not only possible, but are in fact very common. Kanji characters with different meanings often have the same pronunciation; for example, the syllable /ki/ could, to cite just several, be any of the following kanji: 木 'tree', 気 'feeling', 機 'chance', 輝 'to glow', or 期 'period'.

More importantly, Japanese kanji characters often have varying pronunciations (or 'readings'), a fact which arises from the history of their implementation. There are two possible types of reading for a given kanji: a kanji can have a native Japanese reading, known as its *kun*(訓)-reading, or it can have an imported Chinese, or *on*(音)-reading. Furthermore, the Chinese *on*-readings can also vary; a given kanji can have *on*-readings which correspond to any one or several of the periods of historical borrowing from China they arrived in. As a result, a given character can have one or more readings in each of the *on* or *kun* traditions. For example, the kanji 頭 for 'head, chief, top, beginning', can be read *too, do, zu, ju*, in the Chinese way, or as *saki, atama, kashira, koobe, kaburi, tsumuri* in the Japanese way, depending upon the context (see Coulmas, 1989).

There has been some suggestion that the *kun*-readings have a primacy over *on*-readings in search procedures (Kaiho & Nomura, 1983; Nomura, 1978, 1979). For example, Nomura, (1979) placed *furigana* readings[2] in the margin next to the actual kanji

---

[2] Such *furigana* glosses are reading aids, whereby the reading of a kanji is written in hiragana next to the kanji. In left-to-right texts like this one, the kana gloss is placed after the kanji in question, as for example, 恐竜 (きょうりゅう in hiragana) 'dinosaur'. In traditional vertical texts, as well as modern newspapers, magazines, and comic book *manga*, it is placed to the right of the column in which the kanji appears. The system remains in active use, coaching young children in textbooks, as well as adults reading technical

to contrast the effect of *furigana* which were *on* Chinese readings with *kun* Japanese readings of the kanji. Both reading and recall of kanji were affected by the presence of furigana, but the presence of the *kun* Japanese reading of the kanji in furigana significantly enhanced its processing, suggesting to Nomura that readers attribute some primacy to the Japanese *kun* style. However, this finding must invariably be conditioned by the frequency of the kanji and the frequency and regularity of its *kun*-readings vs. its *on*-readings (see also Yamada, 1992a, for an explication of selective frequency of kanji readings for common kanji).

Such claims of *kun* superiority, however, have not been based on robust experimental evidence and may be largely speculative as to the role of 'native' vs. 'foreign' words (in this case, Chinese borrowings which have been part of the language for over a millenium). Unless tutored in the differences in the origins of *on-* vs. *kun*-readings, most Japanese would not attend to many such differences and simply take the bound *on*-morphemes as Japanese bound morphemes (which they are). Even if one is literate and knows that such differences exist, many Japanese think of some kanji readings, such as 肉 *niku* 'meat' and 駅 *eki* 'station', as *kun*-readings ... which they are not. But there is another important issue which this debate touches upon, and that is the issue of **multiple readings** and the potential competition between them. Kayamoto, Yamada, and Takashima (1998) have addressed exactly this issue in a pair of experiments designed to tease out the effect of single- vs. multiple-readings on naming latencies for single kanji words. A first experiment compared single- and multiple-reading single kanji in two frequency ranges, high vs. mid, and found a substantial naming delay of 76 msec. for kanji that had multiple readings. But the naming delay was not at the expense of one of the two readings; the mean naming latency was not significantly different between the dominant and the subordinate readings. All kanji in this experiment had both an *on-* and a *kun*-reading; so this was true for high frequency kanji, such as 数 *kazu/suu*, as well as for mid-frequency kanji, such as 訳 *yaku/wake* 'translation/reason'. How often could this state of affairs happen? Kayamoto et al. had no difficulty in finding 633 single kanji words which had one *kun-* and one *on*-reading.

But this does not necessarily mean that all multiple-reading kanji will act this way, for it is still possible that there are some multiple-reading kanji which have dominant readings strong enough to overwhelm the competing, and thus secondary, readings. And so a second experiment tested multiple-reading kanji which had a dominant *kun*-reading to see if these could be named as fast as the single-reading kanji. For multiple-reading kanji of this type, such as 島 *shima/too*, this is just what happened. These kanji typically elicited the dominant *kun*-reading, and not the subordinate *on*-reading. In this respect,

---

descriptions in reference books and encyclopedias, as well as everyday literature containing unfamiliar kanji with technical designations, place names, or proper names.

one must admit that Nomura (1979) has touched on the right point with his suggestion about the superiority of *kun*-readings, but only for some kanji and not necessarily because the *kun*-readings are 'native' readings. It would also appear, at least according to Kayamoto et al.'s conclusions, that Nomura's (1978) *on-kun* frequency ratio is a fairly reliable predictor of the strength of the dominant reading for such words.

Simple Kanji vs. Complex Kanji

In terms of **graphic configuration**, kanji characters can be simple or they can be complex. That is, a simple character is one that can stand alone, and like the original Chinese they are derived from, there are many of these simple basic characters. A certain number of these may also be used as a 'radical' which forms part of a larger, more complex single character; it may appear in its original, but reduced shape, or it may appear in a somewhat altered shape. Like the original Chinese, there are historically 214 of these radicals, and this aspect of kanji design reflects the pseudo-semantic basis for categories that kanji historically fall into. For example, 木 can stand alone as *ki*, the word for 'tree', or it can enter into the formation of larger, more complex characters, such as 松, 椿, 梅, 杉 *matsu, tsubaki, ume, sugi* 'pine, camelia, plum, Cryptomeria cedar'. The radical also appears in kanji for words related to trees, their components, and their woody by-products, as for example, 枝, 根, 板 *eda, ne, ita*, 'branch, root, board', and so forth.[3] But this 'system' of **semantic categorization** has its limitations in reading Modern Japanese, and this is easily seen in the complex characters 橋, 枕, 机, 村 for *hashi, makura, tsukue, mura* 'bridge, pillow, desk, village', as well as many others of their ilk. In an age when pillows and bridges were made of wood, such assignments of the radicals must have made immediate sense. But time passes, circumstances change, and the same loss of conscious meaning, with ensuing semantic opacity, that one sees in the etymological origins of compounds in English is a feature of kanji components.

But these radicals are not always stand-alone radicals. For example, the 'water' radical is physically different from the character for 'water' 水 *mizu*, though it may be historically an abbreviated form of the full character. It is the left-hand component in characters as well-bounded as the complex characters 涙 *namida* 'tear', 湯 *yu* 'hot water', 酒 *sake* 'sake', 池 *ike* 'pond', 河 *kawa* 'river', 海 umi 'sea', 波 nami 'wave' and 港 minato 'port'. But you will never see the abbreviated component on the left side of these characters stand alone.

---

[3] The use of these radicals may even be extended in this way. For example, the kanji for *hiiragi* 'holly', a relatively new introduction, is written with the 'tree' radical to the left of the character for 'winter' to produce a complex kanji creation, 柊.

In some cases, the meaning of a given radical in a complex character makes no sense at all, as in the case of the radical 口 for 'mouth' forming the radical for the kanji 石 for 'stone'. And in many cases, it is not always transparent which is the radical in a complex character, and determining the radical and its semantic contribution is an exercise which often works better in specialized historical exegesis than in daily practice. Then, too, there are homophonic instances when different kanji may have the same radical, such as 力 (force), with the remainder of the kanji providing the semantic nuance.

/Tsutomeru/ 'To engage'
勉める 'to study'
努める 'to endeavour'
勤める 'to work (in an office)'
務める 'to serve (in government)'

At other times, the same homophonic reading conveys the same general semantic intention, but a completely different kanji which shares no graphic overlap whatsoever is employed. In such cases, the notion of the 'semantic' radical denoting the conceptual range within the lexicon simply founders. Contrast, for example, the following three kanji:

/Tsukuru/ 'To make'
作る 'to make/manufacture'
造る 'to form/mold/ferment/build'
創る 'to establish (an institution)'

Then again, many complex characters are a combination of two or more radicals which cannot stand alone as simple characters. And some complex characters are kanji which are composed of one or more radicals which are juxtaposed with a combination of several strokes which never appear other than inside a complex character. Consider the following pieces which remain after we have separated the radicals out: 凌 *ryo* 'to overcome' without the radical (冫) on the left; 殿 *den* 'mansion' without the radical (殳) on the right; 富 *tomi* 'wealth' without the radical (宀) at the top; and 弊 *hei* 'vice' without the radical (廾) on the bottom.[4]

---

[4] At least in contemporary Japanese, these left-over components do not function as independent characters (T. Inoue, p.c.).

Kanji Attributes

Turning from design features to processing considerations, we might note that there is a correlation between morphological simplicity and frequency of use. Although there is no equivalent of Zipf's Law[5] in Japanese, the simpler a kanji is, the more likely that this fact will be reflected in its frequency ratings. But orthographic simplicity vs. **orthographic complexity** does not necessarily result in processing difficulty. In fact, orthographic complexity may facilitate processing by underwriting the uniqueness of a kanji configuration. One can conceivably even make the same case for English, given that unique configurations and a large number of letters in a word makes words like *morphophonemics* and *Vladivostok* unique and thus easily identifiable. The large number of strokes in such kanji can be compared to a largish number of letters in a word, and in this respect, logographic and alphabetic systems might actually converge. In fact, if the average number of strokes is, as Wang (1971) suggests, 4 or 5 in modern, simplified Chinese characters, this figure is about the same as the number of letters in the average English word.

High frequency kanji are also typically easier to read, because of the likelihood of familiarity. But when frequency is held constant, more complex kanji are easier to read than less complex kanji, simply because their orthographic complexity in terms of strokes facilitates their reading. Kawai (1966) tested adults and college students on 160 more complex and 160 less complex kanji, and found that the more complex kanji were more easily read than the less complex ones. And in fact, when frequency of usage and complexity were both high, they were easier yet to read. They are also easier to learn for retention, as Kawai (1966) further demonstrated with 12 random, meaningless patterns whose complexity was graded according to the number of lines involved. Once a specific meaning was assigned to each of the figures, undergraduates who were charged with learning the association between the figures and given meanings found the complex figures easier to retain than less complex ones.

For kanji of 13 strokes or less, difficulty in kanji processing increases proportionally to the **number of strokes**; however, after this point, increase in the number of strokes actually facilitates kanji processing (see Kaiho, 1979), probably because the kanji is taken as a chunk with its own perceptual identity as the whole unit. Although the order of writing strokes for kanji occurs in fixed order, from left to right and top to bottom,

---

[5] Zipf's Law accounts for George Kingsley Zipf's finding that the length of a word in English is inversely related to its frequency. In simplest terms, the more frequent the word, the more likely it is that it will be a short word.

kanji processing does not involve deconstruction of the kanji production process.[6] This is especially noticeable in the results for high-end kanji where the large number of strokes in such unique kanji offers a visual signature which often elicits shorter recognition times.

Subjective judgments of visual complexity in kanji are very sensitive to orthographic attributes like the number of strokes and symmetry in the horizontal, parallel, and diagonal planes. Kanji with fewer strokes are considered less complex, but so also are symmetrical kanji (see Kashu, Inoue & Ishihara, 1980; Kashu, Ishihara, Inoue, Saito & Maeda, 1979). Attempts to determine the interactive effect of stimulus exposure time and stimulus complexity on kanji identification reveals that complex kanji and symmetrical kanji are easier to identify than less complex and asymmetrical kanji under minimal exposure conditions (see Saito, 1986).

When the basic 881 kanji were evaluated on **ten potential components** through the Semantic Differential technique, subjects showed high reliability for the eight of the ten componential features measured. The scales for complexity, compactness, elongation, openness, straightness, roundness, stability, and symmetry were deemed as appropriate for measurement of the configurational perception of these basic kanji, and probably for others as well (Kaiho & Inukai, 1982). A subsequent factor analysis classified the kanji into 4 tighter groupings based on the correlations between these Gestalt characteristics. Some idea of these perceptual groupings may be gleaned from the following kanji groupings situated in the four quadrants determined by a factor analysis of the original eight scales (adapted from Kaiho, 1987; Kaiho & Inukai, 1982).

---

[6] There is some question as to whether kanji themselves are decomposed and analyzed during processing. The only attempt to examine this problem, however, does not use Japanese subjects. Koga and Groner (1989) attempted to track eye movements for European subjects before and after they learned kanji of varying degrees of complexity. Kanji with identifiable radicals were presented under two learning conditions: through stroke-order where the kanji was presented stroke by stroke and through holistic presentation where the kanji was presented as a single image. Koga and Groner report that eye fixation patterns in the pre-learning phase were neither very regular nor very organized, whereas in the post-learning phase, subjects' eye-movement patterns changed dramatically. Fixations were concentrated on the more informative pieces, namely, the radicals. Of the two radical positions, the left-hand and right-hand positions, eye fixation patterns seemed to concentrate more on the right-hand patterns, and these are in fact the more informative of the two radical components.

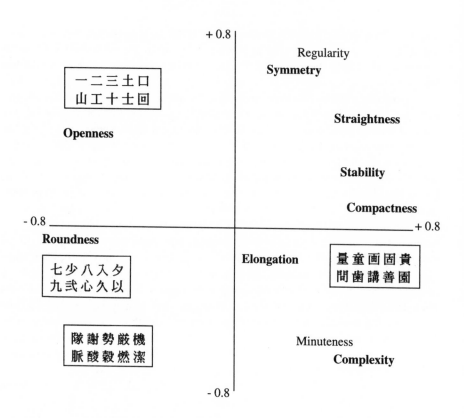

Figure 3.2 Evaluation of visual complexity of kanji on ten potential components.

Kitao, Hatta, Ishida, Babazono, and Kondo (1977) surveyed 1,000 undergraduates for the attributes of **concreteness**, **hieroglyphicity** (iconicity), and **familiarity** for the same 881 kanji. Based on 'yes-no' answers for concreteness and a seven-point scalar evaluation for the other two attributes, the results indicated a positive correlation between concreteness and hieroglyphicity, but a negative correlation between either of these attributes and familiarity. A supplementary examination revealed concreteness to be the essential attribute in recognition of the kanji. Such subjective explorations provide a fuller picture of the perceptual factors which could play a role in lexical access, and should be noted in any serious model of how the various informational features attached to kanji entries influence one another in a spreading activation fashion.

PHONOLOGICAL INFORMATION IN KANJI WORDS

Some suggest that there is a 'universal phonological principle' inherent in accessing the mental lexicon, no matter what the language (Perfetti & Zhang, 1995; Perfetti, Zhang & Berent, 1992). Very simply, this means that whichever writing system is used, be it alphabetic, syllabic, or logographic, lexical access ultimately invokes the phonological characteristics of the word stored away. It is only a question of where and when this phonological information is accessed during the quest for recognition.

Chinese orthography, the source from whence Japanese kanji are derived, is morphemically-based. Yet Chinese allows, and sometimes may even require, phonological information to be accessed during its word recognition procedures. The majority of Chinese logographs are phonographs (Wang, 1981), and it is this type of logograph which has typically drawn experimental attention in questions of automatic **phonological activation** in studies of Chinese lexical access and word recognition. Phonographs exhibit two possible constituent parts: traditionally, there is a radical or *signific*, usually on the left side of the character, which refers to meaning; on the right side of the character, there is often a *phonetic* which refers to pronunciation (see Chen & Yuen, 1991). In Chinese psycholinguistic research, it has been the set of phonographs which have pronunciations which are identical to their phonetic radicals that has served as the focal point of experimentation into phonological activation during lexical access and word recognition procedures.

It was this system which, in principle at least, was borrowed into Japanese. Although the characters imported from China into Japanese often retained these phonetic radicals, such phonetic radicals are nowhere as reliable or useful in reading Japanese kanji as they are in Chinese. Various figures have been given for these phonetic radicals; Ito (1979) reckoned that 61% of the 1,933 kanji she inventoried could be categorized as **phonetic kanji**, while Saito (1981a) cites earlier literature as claiming 80% of kanji combine a semantic radical and a phonetic radical. But a recent inventory of the first standard JIS corpus by Saito, Kawakami, and Masuda (1995b) claims that only a third of the complex kanji in that set of 2,965 kanji characters have the same pronunciation as their right-hand phonetic radicals. (Interestingly, they also found that 4% of that set have the same pronunciation as their left-hand radical; for example, compare 巧 *koo* 'skilled' and 効 *koo* 'effect'.)

The central issue in Chinese hanzi processing has revolved around this dichotomy between phonological and semantic properties of characters, and attempts have been made to examine whether the phonological properties of a given hanzi character must be invoked before its meaning can be accessed. The basic difference in frequency and transparency of phonetic components makes the discussion of phonological activation inherently different for character recognition in Japanese discussions of lexical access.

The issue of phonological activation is, of course, worthy of interest whether or not there are so-called phonetic radicals within the logographic symbols for either language. It is just that their presence in Chinese has been more closely tied to such inquiry in Chinese psycholinguistics, in Japanese considerably less so. One important reason that this has not been as crucial an issue in Japanese psycholinguistic research into lexical access as it has been in Chinese research is undoubtedly because Chinese only has the one system of orthography, namely, logographic representation. Japanese has complementary, if not alternative, orthographic systems based on the kana representation of syllable shapes, and therefore the issue has simply never assumed the major proportions in Japanese work that it has in Chinese. Nevertheless, the same psycholinguistic question arises in respect to Japanese kanji processing, namely, whether phonological and semantic processing interact in parallel or sequential modes when the mental dictionary is consulted. There has been some fruitful work on this issue, and it is useful to report the findings on phonological activation in Japanese for those kanji which do have reliable phonetic radicals.

One influential view, the **speech recoding view**, claims that character processing in lexical access automatically proceeds from the written form of the word through the speech coding for the word. The idea is that activation of the phonological properties of a word is an automatic and integral component in the path of accessing the word's identity in the mental lexicon. And there have been various forms of support for this hypothesis. Hirose (1992b), for example, presented subjects with kanji stimuli, differing in their combinations of left- and right-hand radicals, and had them judge as quickly as possible whether sequentially-presented kanji (活/括 katsu; 信/侵 shin; 程/停 tei) had the same pronunciation or not. Right-hand radicals played a significant role in phonological processing of kanji, in that kanji pairs which shared the same right-hand radicals exhibited the fastest reaction times, reminiscent of priming effects. A second experiment employed pairs of kanji which had the same radicals on the left- and right-hand side of the kanji characters (採/彩 sai), respectively. The left-hand radicals had no facilitating effect on the phonemic processing of kanji, suggesting that the information carried by the right-hand radicals does play some role in the phonological processing of kanji for Japanese readers, but only for those kanji which have such reliable phonetic radicals.

Saito, Inoue, and Nomura (1979) review two experiments which suggest that kanji processing does involve some phonological processing, and that phonetic and semantic processing is carried out simultaneously. Subjects were presented with three sets of kanji: homonym pairs which were graphically different (草 soo, 倉 soo), pairs which were graphically similar but had different pronunciations (草 soo, 単 tan), and pairs which were both graphically and phonologically different (草 soo, 君 kun). When subjects saw the first member of the pair, they were asked to produce the on-reading for the kanji, to ensure that the homonym relationships, if any, were in fact in place. They then saw the second kanji and were asked to make judgments about the relationship of the second kanji to the first. A first experiment tested for identity, with results revealing that reaction times improved not only for graphically similar kanji, but also for homonym kanji. The results are even more interesting when one recalls that phonological processing was not being tested as the basis of decision-making by the subjects in this experiment. When the second experiment did ask subjects to make phonological judgments as to whether two kanji had the same pronunciation, reaction times mirrored the pattern revealed in the first experiments, namely, that reaction times improved when both homonymic and graphemically similar kanji were presented. These experimental results do not locate the point of phonological processing, but they do point to an interaction between graphemic, semantic, and phonological processing (see also Inoue, 1980; Inoue, Saito & Nomura, 1979).

The primacy and number of readings for kanji is also a consideration for fluent Japanese readers. Saito and Tsuzuki (1989) investigated retrieval for homophonic bi-syllabic kanji compounds in order to establish norms of retrieval variability for kanji readings. Subjects were presented with words transcribed in hiragana and then asked to write as many kanji words as they could for that pronunciation within 60 seconds. Correct kanji words tended to be recalled within the first 30 seconds, with a large number of widely differing incorrect kanji words emerging in the last 30 seconds. In the cases of incomplete retrieval, kanji for the first syllable were retrieved three times more often than kanji for the second syllable, reminding one very much of the classic *tip-of-the tongue* experiments (Brown & McNeill, 1966; Kohn, Wingfield, Menn, Goodglass, Gleason & Hyde, 1987) in which the basic phonological frame of the word was recalled, with greatest success on the initial segments or syllable.[7]

However, the use of phonological information may not be as much at issue as is the temporal time frame for interaction between phonological and semantic information in processing kanji. When Wang (1988) asked subjects to find a target kanji word from each of three lists of homographs, homophones, and homonyms, processing of homographs was the quickest. Processing the other two lists took exactly the same time. That is, orthographic targets were processed faster than the phonological or semantic targets, which seemed to evidence the same response times. A second experiment repeated the same test, using kanji compounds which consisted of four kanji instead of two, and

---

[7] But the *tip-of-the-tongue* phenomenon in Japanese, because of the nature of the mixed script system, reflects different strategies for storage of lexical items written in kana and kanji. In two experimental probes, Murakami (1980) presented subjects with ten relatively rare katakana loanwords, and then with ten kanji compounds. Subjects had to recall the words, recording those segments which they could recall. Retrieval of katakana loanwords was phonologically guided by the syllabic units found in the words, but retrieval processes for kanji compounds suggested that the individual kanji were the units that were being accessed.

showed exactly the same results. These results were taken to suggest that phonological and semantic information about kanji are available in a parallel mode rather than a sequential mode, but the more appropriate inference may be that pattern matching is not only quick, but does not invoke phonological and semantic processing for kanji.

The interference effect of **homophonic overlap** between words is a fairly reliable finding, and that effect from homophonic words has been used alone, or in conjunction with various semantic categorization tasks, to test the time course of phonological activation. An early study by Erickson, Mattingly, and Turvey (1977) tested whether silent reading of kanji requires short-term phonetic storage. Four sets of kanji words were prepared as stimuli, with kanji stimuli sets presented in phonetically similar, semantically similar, orthographically similar, or neutral conditions. When subjects were required to write the kanji word which appeared on the screen one second after a probe word, recall of the phonetically similar kanji words was worst among the four stimuli sets, suggesting that even silent reading of kanji requires phonetic short-term storage, and that phonological overlap between kanji items produces interference.

When a semantic categorization task is added to the variable of phonological overlap, the results for Japanese bear considerable similarity to the results that are reported for English. Let us review the results for English first. Early on, differences in reaction times were reported for lexical decisions for non-words which were homophones with real words (*brane*) vs. non-words which were not (*melp*) (Rubenstein, Lewis & Rubenstein, 1971). Van Orden (1987) and Van Orden, Johnston, and Hale (1988) added a semantic task, giving English-speaking subjects a category name like *flower*, and then having them decide whether a later target word was a member of that category. But they manipulated target words to include targets like *rows*, which is a homophone with the word *rose*, obviously a real member of the category of *flower*. Both experiments found that subjects made more categorization errors with, and spent more time on, the homophone foils than they did on the spelling controls. What this means is that when the category was *flower* and the target word was *rows*, the existence of homophone foils like *rose* gave more problems than target words (like *robs*) which were spelling controls. This should not be the case if orthographic representations are used exclusively in word identification; one should expect no differences in the error rates for homophones vs. control words.

In fact, such homophonic overlap gave rise to problems even when the target words were non-words. Van Orden, Johnston, and Hale (1988) introduced as targets non-words that were homophones. For example, *brane*, was presented for possible inclusion in the category entitled *a part of the human body*. The reasoning is that since non-words such as *brane* are obviously not entries in the mental lexicon, there must be a mandatory phonological activation of such words if categorization errors occur. And indeed, this is just what happens with *brane*, because it is a homophone with *brain*; it does not happen with non-word spelling controls like *blane*. What we infer from such results is that there is automatic activation of phonological information in lexical access for English words.

Are there similar results in Japanese kanji processing? Three experiments reported by Wydell, Patterson, and Humphreys (1993) also found a significant homophone effect for Japanese two-kanji compounds. Homophonic target words elicited longer reaction times and more errors than their controls when subjects were posed the task of making semantic category judgments for such kanji words. But Wydell, Patterson, and Humphreys also found a significant effect which arose from orthographic similarity. That is, incorrect target words that were visually similar to correct examplars, and that fit the semantic category, were also responsible for longer reaction times and higher error rates, although not to the same extent as the results obtained from phonological overlap in homophones. The effects were strongest when both factors intersected, that is, when homophonic targets were also visually similar in orthographic shape to correct exemplars of the semantic category specified. We may infer from their results that, in Japanese, lexical access for kanji invokes both orthographic and phonological representations for the appropriate information, but germane to the discussion here, phonological information is part of that process.

When Sakuma, Sasanuma, Tatsumi, and Masaki (1998) pursued the same issue of whether phonology plays a role in visual word recognition in Japanese, they came up with results which placed an even greater emphasis on orthography as the primary source of activation of meaning for kanji words. The first two of their three experiments with familiar kanji words provided results which pointed to both phonology and orthography as contributing to the activation of kanji words. And in this respect, they suggest that their results are generally compatible with the earlier findings reported by Van Orden (1987) and Wydell et al. (1993). But a third experiment, which employed masking conditions, continued to show a strong effect of orthography, while the effect of homophony was shown to be relatively reduced, although it remained significant on errors for orthographically similar foils. The findings by Saito, Kawakami, and Masuda (1998), described earlier in this chapter, also support the notion of an **interactive relationship** between orthographic shape and phonological information. Recall that their four experiments focussed on sub-word components in the radical positions, and the way in which they might be activated in kanji recognition. What is relevant at this juncture is that homophony between probe and source kanji elicited false alarms when they were graphically similar; subjects made many more errors on the probe kanji when it was a homophone with previously seen source kanji. But they did not elicit false alarms when probe and source were graphically dissimilar, suggesting that accessing both phonological and graphic information during kanji recognition is a profitable strategy because the two are statistically tied in Japanese.

Taken as a whole, these results all point to orthography as the primary source of activation, even though they accede to the fact that the phonology of kanji words is automatically activated and may even partly contribute to semantic activation. Such findings, of course, weaken the exclusivity of the phonological mediation position, but are consistent with a parallel access view of informational features in lexical access, one in which both phonology and orthography come into play.

Interestingly, when this experimental paradigm was applied to **Chinese word recognition**, the situation seems to be quite different. Chen, Flores d'Arcais, and Cheung (1995) applied semantic categorization tasks to their investigation of hanzi processing, and report results which differ from the English and Japanese findings. In one experiment, Chinese subjects silently read a category name and then looked at a fixation point. A target character was then presented, and the subjects had to judge whether the target was a member of the category that had just been presented by pressing a response key labelled 'yes' or 'no'. Subjects were relatively accurate at making judgments about semantic categorization, and produced the same proportion of false positive categorization errors, showing the same decision latencies on homophone foils as on the non-homophone controls. The confounding factor of phonological information did not seem to affect the semantic task in this instance, and the authors concluded that phonological information associated with a character does not become active in processing the character for semantic decisions.

A second experiment added orthographic similarity as an extra condition to check whether there were possible interference effects arising from orthographic overlap. Such interference would reveal whether the orthographic code is active during the process of coming to a semantic decision. This time subjects made more errors and produced longer response times on graphemically similar foils than they did on the corresponding controls. Such clear effects from visual similarity in the Chinese characters on the semantic categorization task stand in sharp contrast to the absence of phonological effects, suggesting that phonological information is not automatically activated during semantic processing for Chinese characters. Chen, Flores d'Arcais, and Cheung did not rule out the possibility of optional phonological activation, but observe that their results do not support the notion of automatic phonological activation.

Even so, variations on the experimental task defined above seem to produce conflicting results, as suggested by Chua's results (1995) for this same general semantic task in three experiments. Chua had subjects decide if a target logograph fit a previously presented definition. Contrary to Chen, Flores d'Arcais, and Cheung (1995), his results show phonological recoding as obligatory, and not optional. In addition, this recoding was not easily inhibited, and took place before semantic access was completed, thus making it a candidate for pre-lexical automatic activation. As with the van Orden studies in English, Chua's subjects were sensitive to the presence of homophones, showing higher error rates and longer reaction times in making decisions.[8]

An interesting twist in kanji retrieval is provided by Hatta, Kawakami, and Tamaoka's (1998) examination of kanji errors in the two-morpheme (two-kanji) compound words which appeared in spontaneous handwritten compositions by Japanese students. When a kanji word is recruited from the kanji lexicon, and it is incorrect, the search is nevertheless an ordered search which reveals storage parameters. In this case, analysis of such writing errors revealed that phonologically-related kanji errors outnumbered both orthographically-related and semantically-related errors.

Interference from Concurrent Vocalization

If we add concurrent vocalization to the interference dynamic, some interesting, though not necessarily conclusive, findings bear upon the issue of phonological activation. Concurrent vocal interference involves subjects repeating irrelevant material aloud while reading or making judgments. It is thought to disrupt the auditory/articulatory channels because it interferes with the phonological code but leaves the visual code unaffected.

Concurrent articulation has been found to affect reaction times in one semantic processing task for kana words, thus confirming the interference effect of concurrent articulation in decoding orthographic symbols which require phonological processing. And it also had a significant delaying effect when subjects were posed with the same semantic processing task with kanji words overlaid with the concurrent articulation condition (Mizuno, 1997). But the results are not equivocal, and can sometimes simply be contradictory. For example, concurrent articulation affected reaction times in a semantic processing task for kana words in Kimura (1984), but kanji words did not evidence impaired performance. When subjects were asked to judge whether pairs of words written in kana or kanji were related in meaning, concurrent articulation impaired the reading of the kana, but did not affect decisions about the kanji words as subjects

---

[8] In another type of task, Wang and Kikuchi (1989) found processing of the semantic component precedes the processing of the phonological component for kanji words when they are presented under conditions of extremely brief duration and under masking conditions. Two-kanji compound words were paired with both synonymous and homophonous words; each of the masked words was presented on an oscilloscope for durations of 15, 25, 35, or 45 msec., followed by the corresponding synonymous and homophonous words. Subjects had to select either the synonymous word or the homophonous word depending on the instructions given. All exposure durations were found to be insufficient for complete accuracy in recognition for the masked words, but the accuracy in choosing the semantically similar words was invariably higher than for the phonologically similar words. Of course, another interpretation is also possible, namely, that the kanji shape cues the meaning range in a way that the kanji shape cannot under masked conditions.

worked their way down the list of written words. Kimura and Bryant (1983) also report that concurrent vocalization had no effect on reading and writing kanji, although visual interference, via the presentation of similar kanji shapes, did have an effect. Once again, however, concurrent vocalization did have an effect on reading and writing kana words.

It may be that interpretation of concurrent articulation results should be tempered by consideration of the type of processing task it is intended to confound. For example, Kinoshita and Saito (1992) found that concurrent articulation interfered more with judgments about kanji words than of kana-transcribed words when the task involved rhyme decisions or homophone decisions. However, concurrent articulation of irrelevant material did not disrupt the lexical decisions for words presented in either kanji and kana when the task was simply to determine whether or not the target string was a word.

If we move down the age scale, the results are more indicative of levels of advancement in reading skills and the role of individual differences in reading comprehension. Leong and Tamaoka (1995) report a lexical decision task with single kanji characters which were given to Japanese fourth-, fifth-, and sixth-graders who had been classified as skilled and unskilled readers. On the basis of overall configurations or the phonetic components, they were asked to decide on the lexicality of kanji and pseudo-kanji during concurrent articulation. Not surprisingly, the younger readers or less skilled readers were less accurate and less automatic in comparison with their older or more skilled counterparts. But the results suggest that kanji recognition may be accompanied by phonological processing, at least some of the time, especially with rare or difficult kanji characters. Difficult characters which have phonetic components may be decoded with some kind of phonological processing taking place, since they seemed to be more susceptible to interference from concurrent articulation. Leong and Tamaoka are careful to point out that they do not consider phonological processing to be an all-or-nothing proposition, but best thought of as probabilistic in nature (cf. Perfetti, Zhang & Berent, 1992). That is, the likelihood of invoking the phonological information attached to a specific kanji depends on the features inherent in that kanji, its frequency and familiarity, and the age and level of knowledge of the individual reader, be they child or adult. It might even be a by-product of the access procedure, so that if the phonological information is known, it automatically becomes available, though not necessarily used, as part of the storage package which uniquely identifies a given kanji word.

Tamaoka, Leong, and Hatta (1992) similarly report on the effect of vocal interference on children's processing of kanji and kana. One hundred and eight elementary school students from grades 4-6, classified as skilled and less skilled readers, were asked to judge sentences as being semantically correct or incorrect. Embedded in each sentence was a commonly-used word, usually written in kanji but here presented in kanji or in hiragana (野球/やきゅうはスポーツです 'Baseball is a sport'). Two treatment conditions involved either no interference or vocal interference, which was created by having subjects count repeatedly in Japanese from one to ten while performing the task. The results indicate that even though words in kanji were processed faster than words in hiragana, vocal interference had a similar effect on the processing of both scripts. Once again, interference impaired less skilled readers more than skilled readers and younger children more than older children. A second study used a similar methodology and had the same students judge the semantic correctness of sentences containing a commonly-used word, usually written in katakana (オルガン/おるがんは楽器です 'An organ is a musical instrument'), but here presented in katakana or in hiragana. Again, the authors found that vocal interference inhibited less skilled readers more than skilled readers and younger children more than older children. The authors conclude that both the grade level (that is, age) and reading ability of children affect lexical access.

Relevant Chinese Studies

We should also briefly review the range of relevant Chinese studies which shed light on the possibility of automatic phonological activation for kanji in Japanese. Early work (Hung & Tzeng, 1981; Tzeng, Hung & Wang, 1977; Tzeng & Wang, 1983) suggested **phonological activation** for Chinese, as well as the possibility that meaning for Chinese hanzi cannot be accessed without first accessing the phonological identity of that hanzi. An early experiment by Tzeng, Hung, and Wang (1977) on short-term retention visually presented target lists of four Chinese characters which differed in syllable structure from each other. This was followed by an oral interference task which contained items that were either phonemically similar or dissimilar to the target list of characters. Imme-diately after visual presentation of the target list, subjects had to say aloud the interference words which they had just heard. They were next asked to write down the target characters which they had first seen, and in the order that they had appeared. If speech recoding takes place, one would expect that phonological similarity between the target and the interference characters would disrupt the memory for the items that subjects had to recall. The results demonstrated that phonological similarity did have a significant effect; in particular, it was vowel similarity in the pronunciation of the characters that elicited interference on recall abilities, and given the phonological principles of canonical shapes for Chinese syllables, this makes the findings even more significant.

The second experiment tested grammaticality judgments for sentences, manipulating normal vs. anomalous sentences that contained phonologically similar words vs. phonologically dissimilar words. As in the first experiment, phonological similarity again interfered with subjects' performance, affecting not only their short-term memory for unrelated characters, but even the reading of the normal meaningful sentences. Both experiments were taken as early evidence suggesting that phonological factors have a very real cognitive presence in processing.

Similarly, Tzeng, and Hung (1980) found subjects to be more accurate in detecting logographs that contained a target radical with a phonetic value in the pronunciation of the hanzi in which it appeared. To put the example into English terms, this would be like reporting where the letter *e* appears. Is it easier to notice in words like *red* or in words like *date*? In the word *red*, the letter *e* is directly linked to the pronunciation of *red* and is therefore more readily noticed than the *e* in the word *date*. Because the 'silent *e*' in *date* is not linked to its pronunciation, it might not be reported as having been seen as often.

Seidenberg, Waters, Barnes, and Tanenhaus (1984) have suggested that it may be frequency that conditions whether English words are recognized on a visual basis or through phonological mediation, and Seidenberg (1985) reports that this is true for Chinese as well as English. If a large pool of lexical items in every writing system is recognized on a visual basis, then differences between orthographies will really reside in how lower **frequency** items are represented phonologically and thus the degree to which phonology plays a role in reading. The extent to which written words encode phonology is irrelevant to the recognition of high frequency words, but in both lan-guages, phonological recoding appears to be tied more closely to the processing of lower frequency words. It is of course a fact that lexical items are skewed in their dis-tribution, with some lexical items more common than others, and a small number of words account for a large percentage of the words that actually appear in written or spoken text. This is certainly obvious for function words, such as '*the, of, with, because*', which are by their nature extremely frequent and also typically exceptions to any phonological recoding rules in English. But for some content words the key to the degree of phonological recoding may have to do with their frequency. If this analysis is correct, given that frequency plays an important role in much of kanji processing, then differences in processing strategies may depend not so much on differences between orthographic type, but on the relative frequency of the lexical item. This analysis may allow us to see more similarity between logographic and alphabetic languages, and the way in which they deploy the cognitive abilities resident in the human information processing system.

Nevertheless, Seidenberg did find some critical differences between the two writing systems for Chinese and English. All of the Chinese hanzi took longer to read aloud than even the lowest frequency exceptions in English. And the main effect of frequency was much greater in Chinese, so that some very real differences remain between the two orthographic types. For example, naming latencies for lower frequency words in English averaged under 600 msec., while higher frequency hanzi in Chinese averaged over 700 msec. This difference must be due to the transparency of phonological representation in English, as opposed to its presentation in Chinese. This also matches with our ex-perientally-based intuitions that learning to write and recall hanzi configurations is a more labor-intensive exercise than is the acquisition of orthographic and spelling abilities in English, which is in turn harder than Tagalog and other more closely aligned scripts with so-called shallow orthographies.

Several more recent studies offer support for **automatic phonological activation** in Chinese. Lam, Perfetti, and Bell (1991) took as their working hypothesis the automatic availability of the phonetic code of the first language or first dialect to proficient readers of that dialect or language. They compared subjects who were bidialectal in Cantonese and Mandarin with subjects who were unidialectal in Mandarin, expecting that, because some hanzi have different pronunciations in Cantonese and Mandarin, there will be interference in Mandarin for native Cantonese readers. They suggest that it is the phonetic representation in the first language that will be indelibly stored in memory, and that this will be the one automatically retrieved from memory in reading individual characters. Thus, the inference is that when making judgments about whether pairs of hanzi are pronounced the 'same or different' in Mandarin, the Cantonese phonetic representations will be automatically invoked, causing the interference. When subjects were given pairs of characters and had to determine whether they had the same pronunciation in a given dialect, Mandarin or Cantonese, this task revealed that reading judgments were more automatic, that is, both faster and more accurate in the first dialect. The authors suggest that phonetic values in the first dialect were automatically recalled and that automatic acoustic activation necessarily takes place.

Perfetti and Zhang (1995) also report results which bear on the notion of phonological activation in two experiments which manipulated **synonym judgments**. In keeping with their *at-lexical* view of the identification event in word recognition, they tested both factors of phonological interference and semantic interference. Giving precedence to neither, they probed whether Chinese readers suppress phonological activation when a semantic judgment is required, and then probed whether semantic activation can be suppressed when phonological judgments are required. In the first experiment, subjects were asked to judge whether a given pair of hanzi was synonymous or homophonic. When the characters were homophones, negative judgments resulted in longer reaction times than when the characters were not. The second experiment used a similar experimental design with synonym judgments to check the time course of such interference, and found that phonological interference took place within 90 msec. of stimulus onset. Semantic interference, on the other hand, was initiated much later, at the 140 msec. boundary. Thus, in a task in which phonological activation has no obvious value, the name (or pronunciation) of the character is activated within 90 msec. of processing. This, of course, does not rule out semantic activation, but does show that visual processing of a hanzi for a semantic judgment task will nevertheless bring up its phonological characteristics. And it will do so automatically, even if it has no particular strategic value.

The **opposing view** to the notion of automatic phonological activation claims that hanzi recognition accesses semantic properties directly in Chinese (see Chen, 1996). This view is more closely tied to traditional views of Chinese and Japanese logographic representations, and is aligned with other corollaries about processing Chinese characters, namely, that lexical access is more direct or quicker for hanzi than for alphabetic words, that hanzi are more distinctive in shape than alphabetic words, and that hanzi can facilitate recall through graphic features like semantic radicals to access semantic categories (see Hasuike, Tzeng & Hung, 1986). These premises cannot be taken as proven, however, as a series of ten experiments by Liu, Zhu, and Wu (1992) have shown in their examination of the visual superiority effect in Chinese subjects' performance with hanzi in the immediate free recall and serial paradigms. Rather, their results suggest a **multivariate set of factors** for such reported findings; they demonstrate that Chinese subjects exhibit visual superiority effects for a complex of reasons, not simply because Chinese lexical access is simple, rapid, and direct (see Leong, Cheng & Mulcahy, 1987, for another multi-variate analysis, as well as Tan, Hoosain & Peng, 1995).

One of the key factors that accounts for visual superiority in some studies rests on the confounding of integrity vs. separability of component parts in the individual character. Leck, Weekes, and Chen (1995) contrasted integrated characters, which contain strokes that are not separable, with those single characters which contain at least two identifiable and separable component parts. They found that visual information was more central to the recognition of the integrated characters, while the characters with separable constituents relied more on a combination of informational factors; that is, visual, phonological, and semantic information all made a contribution to the recognition process. The separability factor is underscored by recent work on contrasting the stroke and the stroke pattern as the functional orthographic unit in Chinese word recognition. Chen, Allport, and Marshall (1996) present compelling evidence that visual analysis of Chinese characters by skilled readers is based upon the utilization of recurrent, well-defined, and well-integrated stroke patterns (see also Hue & Erickson, 1988). This is a larger set than the traditional list of 189 *Bu Shou* 'radicals' listed in typical Chinese dictionaries, although it likely contains the majority of these *Bu Shou* radicals. In a same-different matching task, the number of individual strokes had no influence on speed or accuracy of performance, but stroke patterns definitely did. Although most of the stroke patterns are not explicitly taught as functional elements independent of word context, and are often not even nameable, they are intuited as being crucial elements in written word production and recognition.

Retention of hanzi configurations in short-term memory in visual or verbal formats have also been shown to depend upon their frequency and familiarity (Hue & Erickson, 1988). When radicals or characters were frequent enough to have their pronunciations well-known by literate Chinese subjects, they were maintained in verbal form in short-term memory. However, when they were of low frequency, and pronunciations not well-known, they tended to be stored in their visual form. Memory span is typically shorter for the latter, since chunking of familiars is not as easy. Moreover, memory for unfamiliar hanzi is more influenced by orthographic complexity, and memory for unfamiliar radicals is influenced by inter-character frequency. In addition, short-term memory for unfamiliar hanzi is more subject to interference by intervening visual tasks, while intervening verbal tasks interfere more with the frequent, well-known hanzi.

Summary Conclusions

In sum, phonological information about Japanese kanji and Chinese hanzi appears to be part and parcel of the identity of a lexical item, and activation of that phonological information may even be a necessary component of word recognition. It may be that phonological and semantic processing levels are automatically and simultaneously activated, but whatever the time course, both seem to appear on the access path to final word recognition. But if phonological activation does take place, current research has not definitively answered the question of when that phonological information is made available. Does it take place at the pre-lexical stage before word recognition has been achieved? Or at the post-lexical stage once word recognition has been achieved? Or is it at the *at-lexical* event as an integral part of the word recognition event, as Perfetti and Zhang (1995) suggest. Current wattage does not fully illuminate this issue, and one wonders if future research will provide a definitive answer about the time course for phonological information.

SEMANTIC INFORMATION IN KANJI WORDS

The traditional belief has been that kanji need not invoke phonemic recoding in accessing semantic features, because logographs represent words instead of sounds and because 'semantic radicals' cue meanings. There is little question that Japanese readers can use the cues provided by the component parts of kanji in order to ascertain the meaning of a new kanji when those cues are reliable. Certainly, such components can help readers of Japanese to infer the meaning of unfamiliar technical words in a way that meanings of words transcribed in kana cannot. For example, one experiment matched 30 unfamiliar, technical terms with their definitions; the transparency of the kanji compounds was obvious, much like Latin- or Greek-derived technical terms operate for English readers (Hatano, Kuhara & Akiyama, 1981). When other subjects were given the 30 definitions and corresponding kana words, and asked to change these into kanji, the correct matchings were also statistically significant. And when subjects provided the correct kanji encodings, they typically inferred the correct meanings as well. It appears likely that experienced readers of Japanese have an inventory of kanji building blocks that relate to compound words, especially learned ones, and that by referring to this inventory, as well as knowledge about compounding schemata, world knowledge, and contextual information, Japanese readers are able to figure out the meanings of many unknown kanji words.

This is not, however, the same as the traditional belief that the semantic radicals provide a built-in conceptual categorization system which guides the semantic search through the mental lexicon. In some processing tasks, such radicals inside the whole kanji are treated as relevant units, rather than as an unorganized clutter of strokes. There is little doubt that analysis by 'chunking' of the component parts of a kanji character does take place, but there is also strong evidence for correlation of memory span with well-known chunks which are not traditional radicals or even characters (Hue & Erickson, 1988). Sometimes semantic radicals are important chunks to be taken into account in many types of analysis, and sometimes kanji are taken in at a processing glance, so that they are treated as a whole unit, rather than analyzed into their component parts. Hatta and Kawakami (1996) report an informal query into subjective awareness of kanji components, in which not one student in two university classes admitted to dividing kanji into radicals and stem as they scanned textbooks for information. The only time they admitted to doing this was upon encountering an unfamiliar kanji or when they focussed on a specific kanji for a while; then, and only then, would the various component parts come into conscious view.

Function of Semantic Radicals

What then is the role of the 'semantic' radicals in kanji processing which is automatic and not self-conscious? Their function poses a set of interesting questions for a theory of word recognition, not only for Japanese, but for universal strategies of written word recognition. For Japanese readers specifically, do readers of kanji process at some un-conscious level the semantic information which the radicals embedded within complex kanji are purported to carry? More interestingly, do they process such information when the radical embedded within the larger complex kanji has only a tenuous, opaque re-lationship to the meaning of the total complex kanji. The answer to this question is important for a universal theory of word recognition, for it is the Japanese version of the debate regarding analytic decomposition of morphologically complex words in alpha-betic languages like English. The closest analogy to the issue of prefix-stripping in

English words such as *relish* vs. *retrain* may be the Japanese complex kanji.[9] Does analytic decomposition of complex kanji take place in Japanese, and if decomposition takes place, is such analysis optional or obligatory for the reader?

Such questions about kanji have most often been probed with semantic priming tasks (see Ohta, 1991, for a review of the literature on direct priming), because for kanji as whole logographic units representing words, the results are often supportive of a spreading activation model of lexical access (see Kawaguchi, 1985, 1987; Naka, 1984). For example, Naka (1984) has paralleled Western findings with ambiguous lexical items, namely, that both meanings of an ambiguous homograph are activated (up to 0.6 sec.) before one of the meanings is selected as the one linked to a context word (after 1.2 sec.). Priming experiments which examine lexical access procedures for complex kanji thus offer some interesting perspectives on the full-listing vs. **decompositional/affix-stripping** positions on how word recognition is supposed to take place (see Kess, 1992). But like the evidence for decomposition in languages like English, the evidence for this is mixed as regards Japanese kanji.

This may be because the semantic radicals often offer only vague, and sometimes unreliable, information about semantic groupings in the mental lexicon. Certainly this is the impression one gets from Flores d'Arcais and Saito's (1990) failure to find clear priming effects for semantic components of complex kanji characters when the relationship between the complex character and the single component was opaque in its relationship. For example, imagine we prime with 石, the kanji for the word 'stone'. It contains an opaque component, the radical 口 for 'mouth' in its configuration. Further suppose that we then present 目 'eye' as the target kanji; 目 'eye' is known to be semantically related to 口 'mouth' because subjects have previously shown that 'eye' and 'mouth' prime one another in semantic priming trials. But will the prime 'stone' facilitate recognition of the target 'eye'? Just because the reader is not consciously aware of this relationship does not mean that some activation of potentially relevant elements might not go on below the level of awareness, or so the hypothesis goes.

Subjects were presented with a prime like 石 'stone', followed by a target kanji, and were asked to name the target word as quickly as possible. If the target word contained active components of the prime word, and the meaning of the target word was associated with the meaning of such a component, then theoretically subjects should name the target word more quickly than if the prime word did not have an active component in the character representing the target word. In the end, however, Flores d'Arcais and Saito's

---

[9] For instance, based on the measurement of eye movements, Lima (1987) reports that such pseudo-prefixed words as *re-lish* receive longer fixations than such prefixed words as *re-vive*, because the reader spends extra time to unsuccessfully look up non-morphological fragments such as *-lish* in the mental lexicon.

results for this task failed to show a significant difference in response times when prime and target words were so 'related'.

Because Flores d'Arcais and Saito thought that this simple naming task might be too shallow to reveal the true effect of semantic priming, they then tried for effects when subjects judged whether word pairs were semantically related, but now they were asked to do so under speeded judgment conditions.[10] Their reasoning was that if two words are related along the semantic dimension, as 'eye' and 'mouth' are, subjects will quickly reply 'yes'. If they are unrelated in meaning, as is the case for 'rope' and 'emperor', they will quickly reply 'no'. But if the two words are unrelated and if one of the two characters contains a component that has a meaning similar to the meaning of the other character, it should take longer to judge the words as unrelated. This would happen, once again, because the presence of the semantically related components in the pair 石 'stone' and 目 'eye' interferes with the production of a negative response. The interfering component in this case is the opaquely related radical for 'mouth' 口 which appears in the kanji for 石 'stone', and primes the semantically related kanji for 目 'eye'. The conjecture is that the meaning of the hidden radical is accessed in processing, at least sufficiently to produce interference in making a semantic judgment which requires the subject to say "No, this pair of kanji is NOT related". And this is what did happen. Negative responses took longer to verify; the implication is that semantic information about components of complex characters is accessed during processing for such a semantic judgment task. This, however, may be the case when processing attention is called to such semantic components, but leaves open the question of automaticity and reliability of such information.

These data are not entirely persuasive[11] that it is more difficult to decide that two kanji are unrelated when the prime contains a radical which by itself represents a word that is related in meaning to the target. And so the paradigm was further expanded in a later report in which Flores d'Arcais and Saito (1993) again used a speeded semantic categorization task. Readers were required to decide if two kanji represented words which were related in meaning, and once again, the two kanji were unrelated in meaning, except for the embedded element which was opaquely related in meaning to the other

---

[10] There is, of course, an upper-limit to how 'speeded' the judgment conditions can be. For example, when primes and targets were presented for 5 msec., with pre- and post-masking of 50 msec., Wang and Kikuchi (1991) found no priming effects for repetition priming, semantic priming, and phonological priming conditions for single kanji primes and targets.

[11] One problem with this second experiment was the limited number of Japanese subjects (10), and the fact that the authors themselves characterize the subjects as *rather atypical*.

kanji.[12] These results again showed interference in making negative semantic judgments for pairs of characters which were only 'related' through the opaque semantic values of the embedded radical component. The evidence also seemed to point at part-whole relationships in kanji pairs: 石 'stone' and 口 'mouth'; 虹 'rainbow' and 虫 'insect'; and 粗 'rough' and 米 'rice'. The first of each of these pairs contain the simple kanji within their configuration; that is, the radicals for 'mouth', 'insect', and 'rice' appear inside the complex characters for 'stone', 'rainbow', and 'rough'. However, this latter finding might also be interpreted as giving evidence for the orthographic interference which arises from graphically similar parts, especially in the left-hand side of the characters where calligraphy usually begins. This possibility is enhanced by the fact that a third condition in the same experiment did show interference for exactly that fact in graphically similar characters. That is, graphically similar kanji all produced interference effects in making negative semantic judgments. Consider the perceptual overlap between graphically similar kanji such as the following: 革 'leather' and 草 'grass'; 全 'all' and 企 'project'; and 仲 'friend' and 伸 'to extend'. As noted earlier, physical similarity in terms of graphic configuration seems to produce effects, and may even be what accounts for interference in the part-whole condition of 石/口 'stone/mouth'. It does not, however, provide an obvious answer for the interference produced in hidden radicals, such as the 石 /目 'stone/eye' pair.

There is, of course, another way of looking at the component parts of such complex kanji. Chen, Allport, and Marshall (1996) agree that a character like 石 'stone' contains a smaller unit 口, which means 'mouth' in isolation. But they do not consider 口 'mouth' to be the radical for 石 'stone', because their findings point to stroke patterns as the key factor in word recognition. They note that 石 'stone' is already the smallest stroke pattern of some relevance in processing, and rightly warn against positing systematic 'phonetic' or 'semantic' kanji components on the basis of traditional notions about etymological origins of kanji constructions or *ad hoc* intuitive criteria.

Interaction of Phonological and Semantic Information

Then, too, there is the question of positioning for the embedded radicals, and how the information they carry might contribute differently to processing. Flores d'Arcais, Saito, and Kawakami (1995) contrasted the contributions of the semantic radical (the *hen* component on the left-hand side of complex characters) with the phonetic radical (the *tsukuri*, on the right-hand side). Two experiments manipulated characters that did or did

---

[12] Once again, examples included the following: 石 'stone', containing the radical 口 'mouth', matched with the target 目 'eye'; the kanji 始 'to begin', containing the radical 女 'female', matched to 男 'male'.

not encode both phonological and semantic information separately in their left and right radicals.[13] The method was to present the semantic and phonetic radicals with an onset asynchrony, so that either the phonetic or the semantic radical was presented 60 or 180 msec. before exposure of the whole character. Assuming that both components are activated in the lexical search, this would give a momentary advantage to either the phonological information or the semantic information, depending on which radical was presented ahead of the entire character. The results suggest that both phonological and semantic information are activated, since subjects in these two experiments made use of the information as soon as it was supplied. Phonological information seems to become available more effectively in the naming task; earlier exposure of the phonetic radical at 180 msec. before the exposure of the whole character facilitated the naming response, and so did the 60 msec. point of exposure, but in a somewhat weaker fashion. Exposure of the semantic radical had only a weak facilitation effect at the 60 msec. point and none at the 180 msec. point.

But not all components play such a role in semantic activation. And their placement may also have crucial or trivial consequences as factors in lexical access.[14] Saito, Kawakami, Masuda, and Flores d'Arcais (1995, 1997) report that more than half of the 2,965 standard kanji listed in the first-level JIS grouping are complex kanji of the type constructed with components on both the left and right sides. This works out to 1,668 complex kanji with left or right radical components, or a total of 56.3% (see also Saito, Masuda & Kawakami, in press). Of these, 760 groupings cluster around right-hand *tsukuri* radicals, while only 247 groupings cluster around the left-hand *hen* radicals. The processing consequence of this asymmetry in the population of complex kanji is that if the right-hand radical is correctly identified, the field of choice narrows to an average of 2.2, that is, 1,668 divided by 760. The field of choice is wider for the left-hand radical cluster, for even if it is correctly identified, the average here still works out to 6.8, or 1668 divided by 247. Obviously, the two offer different degrees of information, with the right-hand *tsukuri* offering a better set of clues in respect to reducing the potential range of possible kanji groupings. This, of course, presumes that kanji identification relies on bottom-up processing of all the component cues; if this is the case, the right-hand radical sometimes provides phonetic cues, sometimes semantic cues, sometimes both, but it

---

[13] Examples are as follows: (a) 粉 *fun* 'powder' [+semantic (Left Radical)/+phonemic (Right Radical)]; (b) 粒 *ryu* 'grain' [+semantic (LR)/-phonemic (RR)]; (c) 粧 *sho* 'make-up' [-semantic (LR)/+phonemic (RR)]; and (d) 粋 *sui* pure [-semantic (LR) /-phonemic (RR)].

[14] Recall that embedded components in complex characters are more variable than left- vs. right-hand placement. Phonetics can be found to the left, above, below, or inside the stem, as well on the right-hand side, and we have already noted that the *hen* and *tsukuri* are complemented by the *kanmuri* 'crown', *ashi* 'leg', *kamae* 'structure', *tare* 'hanging', and *nyoo* 'entering' components in other kanji configurations.

always provides configurational clues crucial to making the final decision as to identity. As such, Saito et al.'s figures certainly underscore the contribution of other elements besides the traditionally cited left-hand *hen* radical.

Collocational Possibilities

Furthermore, just because an element is considered a radical for historical reasons does not mean it is commonly used. Martin (1972) observes that although there are roughly 200 radicals, more than half of all kanji include one of the 20 most frequent radicals. And Saito, Kawakami, and Masuda (1995a) rightly point out that the average subject in a psycholinguistics experiment, let alone the average reader, relies more on configurational considerations than on historically-derived etymological considerations. In fact, they extracted 857 basic radicals from the JIS first set, by focussing on their configurational similarity, resulting in a figure somewhat different than the 214 historical categories. Of these, the majority (610 or 71%) appear on the right-hand side of the complex characters; only 97 (or 11%) appear in the left-hand position. And some radicals appear on either the left- or the right-hand side; this moveable group was actually larger than the set of left-hand radicals, 150 in number (or 18% of the total 857), and Saito et al. called this set the 'floating radicals'. The following chart (adapted from Saito, Masuda, Kawakami & Flores d'Arcais, 1997) illustrates how these **left**, **right**, and **floating radicals** fit together to create a complex kanji.

Left-Anchored Radical	
糸 'string'	線 *sen* 'string' 綿 *men* 'cotton' 紋 *mon* 'crest' 經 *kyo* 'scripture'

	Right-Anchored Radical
順 *jun* 'turn' 項 *koo* 'section' 類 *rui* 'kind' 頭 *too* 'head'	頁 'piece'

Floating Radical		
紡 *boo* 'to weave' 訪 *hoo* 'to visit'	方 'direction'	族 *zoku* 'group' 旅 *ryo* 'travel'

But even these absolute numbers are not the final story, for the three radical types have different collocational possibilities with other components in creating complex kanji of this left-right kind. The right-anchored *tsukuri* radicals combine with an average of 2.0 left-hand components, the left-anchored *hen* radicals with an average of 8.6 right-hand components, and the floating radicals with an average 5.5 components on the right side and 2.9 on the left side. When Saito, Masuda, Kawakami, and Flores d'Arcais (1997) tested subjects to see whether they could estimate the number of kanji characters that could be formed with a particular radical, they found that subjects could correctly evaluate the number of possible characters as a function of the number of possible collocations with that radical. For example, for left-hand radicals, they offered subjects such pairwise choices as the following, in order to ascertain the dimensions of their knowledge about companion collocations (adapted from Saito, Masuda, Kawakami & Flores d'Arcais, 1997).

扌 makes 133 kanji characters
打 *utsu*   'to hit' 授 *sazuku* 'to grant' 投 *nageru* 'throw' 折 *oru*   'to snap' etc.

工 makes 4 kanji characters
項 *koo* ' section' 功 *koo* ' skill' 巧 *koo* ' skillful' 攻 *koo* ' to attack'

They did find that subjects could indeed evaluate the number of possible characters, and that this was a function of the number of possible collocations with that radical. But they also found that the subjects were better in estimating that number for left-hand radicals than with right-hand radicals, although this may result from the kinetic storage considerations we mentioned earlier, namely, that writing is realized in left-to-right, top-to-bottom sequences and the multiple acts of practice create a motoric image for storage in the mental lexicon. Thus, we have a contrast between two aspects of subjects' knowledge, recognition vs. recall. In recognition, the right-hand radical *tsukuri* is more informative, because they collocate with a smaller number of companions on the left side to make a complete kanji. This makes sense when one considers that fewer candidates facilitate recognition because there are fewer to sort through. On the other hand, in recall, the left-hand radical *hen* is more useful in evaluating its number of companions in a specific kanji family. Whether this is because the left-hand radicals recall a larger number of kanji with a more centralized semantic pivot, or because of kinetic associations in writing practice, is uncertain. But the fact is that the two component types each play a role in the knowledge subjects have about complex kanji, and which they ultilize in tasks as varied as recall and recognition.

These considerations have other processing repercussions, as Flores d'Arcais, Saito, Kawakami, and Masuda (1994) illustrate with **radical migration** in a delayed matching test. They used a delayed matching task in which subjects were first shown two kanji, each of which was made up of two component pieces, a left-hand and right-hand radical component, as in 略 (*ryaku* 'abbreviation') and 伴 (*han* 'to accompany'). These source kanji were then followed by a probe kanji, which might have one of its components the same as the source pair, as in the kanji probe 畔 (*han* 'path around a rice field'). The subject now had to decide whether the probe just presented was the same as one of the kanji characters provided briefly in the earlier source set. Graphic similarity had an effect, especially when they were in the same position in the kanji probe, that is, in left- vs. right-hand position.

They also found a **homophony effect**, and so did Saito, Kawakami, and Masuda (1998) for a conclusive demonstration of an interactive relationship between ortho-graphic shape and phonological information. Four experiments focussed on these same sub-word components in the radical positions, and the way in which they might be activated in kanji recognition. They again used a delayed matching task. The subject now had to decide whether the probe, such as 畔, just presented was the same as one of the kanji characters provided briefly in the earlier source set, such as 略 and 伴. What is relevant here is that *on*-reading homophony between probe and source kanji elicited false alarms when they were graphically similar, even though this was strictly a visual pattern-matching task. But they did not elicit false alarms when probe and source were graphically dissimilar. Phonological processing was not the object of the exercise, but homophony did contribute to determining identity. Saito et al. thus conclude that phonological information for both the whole kanji and its sub-word radical components are activated during access procedures, and that this intersects with the graphic configuration of the kanji because the two are statistically tied in Japanese. At the very least, there is a reliable contribution to word recognition that is made by the right-hand radical that cannot be overlooked statistically, and seems to be best explained by spreading activation among components related by similarities in both graphic and phonetic shape.

Hatta and Kawakami (1996) have also examined the relative contributions of the component parts of kanji, but their two experiments presented subjects with non-prototypical kanji. As a corollary to the question of whether component parts like radicals are activated in kanji recognition, they tested for variations among those component parts by manipulating **transparency of meaning** as shown by the compositional radicals, position, and **degree of separability** in non-prototypical kanji. Because non-prototypical kanji violate perceptual grouping mechanisms, they offer insights into the contribution of component positioning to kanji recognition. The method was simple, and followed the inverse logic of procedures reported for the experiments above; that is, subjects in front of a computer screen had to decide whether the stimulus presented to them was the result of decomposition of a real kanji. Stimuli were grouped into four types, as illustrated below.

Transparent/Horizontal   Opaque/Horizontal

Transparent/Vertical   Opaque/Vertical

Group 1 kanji, such as 話 *hanashi* 'talk', consisted of transparent components (言/舌 'word/tongue') which were displayed horizontally in relation to one another. Group 2 kanji, such as 背 *se* 'back', did the same for transparent components (北/月 'north/moon') which were oriented vertically to one another. And group 3 kanji, such as 神 *kami* 'god', and group 4 kanji, such as 売 *uru* 'sell', did this for opaque components, breaking up the kanji into its components and presenting the pieces in vertical orientation to one another.

They found that the degree of transparency of the individual component's meaning produced different levels of activation, with the effect stronger in transparent components than in opaque components. Secondly, they also found significant effects for the orientation of kanji configurations, confirming that some positions for components are more important in the recognition process than others. The interaction of these two factors reveals that transparent components in the upper and lower positions of a character play a crucial role in lexical access, while opaque components on the left and right sides are not as crucial.

In essence, Liu (1983) found similar results for Chinese characters. When Liu removed components from the various quadrants of the character and compared reading times and error rates for characters with missing elements, the components in the left-hand and the uppermost-top areas had the greatest effect on processing success. Although Hatta and Kawakami issue disclaimers that theirs is a "preliminary" study, their results are a welcome and insightful approach to the problem. What such studies remind us of is that there are degrees of contributory value to different components, as well as the orientation of these components, and that this must be taken into account in a full explanation of kanji word recognition. There is no question that features such as parallelisms and symmetries are attended to by the perceptual system in general, and there are plenty of these in the top and bottom quadrants of kanji configurations. Consider, for example, the parallelism of the repeated constituents in the 'bamboo' radical at the top of the kanji 算 'to count', the grass radical at the top of the kanji 花 'flower', or the 'four dots' at the base of the kanji for 馬 *uma* 'horse' and 鳥 *tori* 'bird'. If the visual parallelism of doubled lower case letters like <l> can have an effect in English words like *spill, gill, hollow, follow* (see Oden & Rueckl, 1986), we should expect such parallelisms to offer perceptual cues to the more complicated kanji configurations.

Summary Conclusions

Taken as a whole, these findings regarding semantic radicals suggest the following compromise as to their real role. The role of the 'semantic' radicals is not semantic in recognition of many complex characters, for the recognition units which contribute to access procedures are simply not isomorphic with the semantic radicals as traditionally conceived. Upper and lower configurations, as well as repeated or parallel elements, are also critical. The evidence cited for priming effect between characters with same semantic radicals is mixed and may in fact result from graphic interference in some cases. Where the semantic radicals may be of particular significance is in those cases where kanji is unfamiliar or unknown, and one searches for any and all clues that may give some indication of its range and identity.

COMPOUND KANJI

Introduction

The focus on individual kanji, simple or complex, does not necessarily illuminate the cognitive procedures employed in dealing with the many common Japanese words which are compounds of two or more kanji. It is not just the technical vocabulary in Japanese that is presented by Sino-Japanese compound words. Many common words in Modern Japanese are represented by neither a simple nor a complex character, but by a compound *jukugo* (熟語) which is a polysyllabic composite of two to four kanji usually carrying an *on*-reading.[15] Although the word-level and character level units are the same in many cases (for example, 顔, 本, 犬 *kao, hon, inu* 'face, book, dog'), an equal, if not larger, number of cases of common vocabulary words in literate Japan are compounds. Consider, for example, common words such as 会社, 誕生, 証券, 緊張 *kaisha, tanjoo, shooken, kinchoo* 'firm, birth, securities, stress'. Such compounds are typically combinations of two characters, any of which may be a simple or a complex character. And all variations are possible: simple-simple (山刀 *yamagatana* 'mountain-knife'), simple-complex (山脈 *sanmyaku* 'mountain ranges'), complex-complex (銅脈 *doomyaku* 'counterfeit'), and complex-simple (銅山 *doozan* 'copper mountain'). Longer compound words are created by compounding a character or another compound word, as 誕生日, 緊張感, 証券会社 *tanjoo-bi, kinchoo-kan, shooken-gaisha* 'birthday, stressful feeling, security firm'.

Compound kanji comprise more than 50% of most dictionaries, and can often be homonymic in their *on*-readings. Gile (1986) has experimentally demonstrated that spoken word compounds are difficult to identify in isolation for native speakers, and further suggests that spoken word recognition in Japanese is slower, more contextually dependent, and more energy-consuming than spoken word recognition in European languages. Some research into written word recognition for compound kanji suggests

---

[15] Some compound kanji do not have such readings and are simply irregular, requiring mastery as singular orthographic events. For example, 土産 *miyage* 'souvenir' does not show correspondences between the component kanji in the compound and their expected readings. Such *'jukuji-kun* (熟字訓) compound characters' have a *kun*-reading and some vague semantic attachment which motivates their reading, as in *miyage* 'souvenir' which is derived from 'soil' (土) and 'produce' (産), creating the flavor of 'local product brought back as a souvenir'.

that **recognition units** in kanji processing are formed on the word level rather than on the level of the individual kanji character. That is, many two-kanji compound words are stored and accessed as whole word units. In this respect, compound kanji seem to parallel lexical access for opaque derivational compounds in English. Compounds such as *ribcage, briefcase, shoehorn* are semantically unpredictable from their constituent parts, and such compounds appear to have their own **lexical address** in the mental dictionary.

Early work in English found that familiar compounds with a primary-tertiary stress pattern, such as *stock market* were not primed by their respective components (*stock* and *market*) in either spoken (Gipson, 1984) or written (Osgood & Hoosain, 1974) presentations. Such compounds did, however, prime themselves as whole units, with *stock market* priming *stock market*. Kanji compounds often present a similar deployment of component kanji. Single kanji and compound kanji may contain identical components, but often they are not employed in the same way.[16] Single kanji words and compound kanji words may often be stored with different addresses in the mental lexicon. Just because they share the same graphic shape does not automatically mean that they share the same lexical address.

Whole-Word Access

Like the evidence for compounds in languages like English, the evidence for lexical access procedures is mixed as regards Japanese kanji compounds. But it does seem certain that the phonological rendering of a kanji is highly dependent on the **intra-word context,** and is finalized at the word level instead of at the character level. A series of six experiments by Wydell, Butterworth, and Patterson (1995) confirm that Japanese is different from both English and Chinese in this respect. In English and Chinese, considerations at the sub-word level are important in determining the pronunciation of a word. For example, in English the consistency found across look-alike words with

---

[16] This is reflected in the occasional piece of data from Japanese aphasiology. For example, one patient with left parietal lesions was able to read the single kanji 手 *te* 'hand' and 紙 *kami* 'paper', but could not decipher their coupling in 手紙 *tegami* 'letter' (Matsuda, Shotenmoku, Nakamura, Nakatani & Suzuki, 1996, cited in Hatta, Kawakami & Tamaoka, 1998). Conversely, another patient had less difficulty naming kanji compound words than single kanji words; for example, he was able to read 乗馬隊 *joo-ba-tai* 'cavalry', but could not read the individual kanji components 乗, 馬, 隊, when presented separately (Sakamoto, 1940, cited in Sasanuma, 1980). Yet another patient with multiple sclerosis was able to read the compound 自然 *shizen* 'nature', but could not read one of its single kanji, mistaking the upper right-hand component of the single kanji 然 *-zen* for the entire kanji and rendering it as 犬 *inu* 'dog' (Higuchi, Saito, Tominaga, Shimada, Yamaguchi, Motomura, Kashiwagi & Yamadori, 1996, cited in Hatta, Kawakami & Tamaoka, 1998).

similar orthographic shape will influence the speed and accuracy of decisions about how to pronounce a word. For example, imagine that we encounter for the first time the orthographic shape *gown*. Is the pronunciation to be /gon/, in line with the pronunciations of *blown, mown, sown*? Or is it to be /gawn/, in line with the pronunciations of *town, clown, frown*? In Japanese it is the word level which is important because such cohorts can not be applied in the same way. Recall that Japanese can have two types of reading for its kanji, the *on*- or the *kun*-readings. These readings vary for individual kanji on the level of intra-word context, and are not ultimately determined by the individual pieces of the character in respect to phonetic or semantic radicals. This means that Japanese readers must choose the correct reading for a kanji which has alternative pronunciations through context at the word level, and not through the individual kanji itself. Thus, the correct reading is conditioned by the other kanji in the compound. For example, 父親 *chichi-oya* 'father' and 両親 *ryo-shin* 'parents' both contain the same kanji, 親, for words which belong to the same general semantic category. But the kanji 親 has a *kun*-reading in the first compound and an *on*-reading in the second. The upshot of this is seen in the lack of consistency in naming effects in the results for two-kanji compounds and single kanji words reported by Wydell, Butterworth, and Patterson. In essence, although there are many clues as to a likely pronunciation, Japanese readers come to learn that, in the final analysis, the only reliable level is the whole word level.

This is further confirmed by Morton, Sasanuma, Patterson, and Sakuma's (1992) experimental inquiry into how single and compound kanji are related within the organization of the Japanese lexicon (see also Morton & Sasanuma, 1984). They too addressed the question of whether compound kanji are recognized as integrated units or whether their recognition is contingent upon the recognition of their individual kanji components, but they did this from a different perspective. Two priming experiments revealed that both single and compound kanji words are facilitated only by pre-training with the identical word, not by kanji units contained in the compound. That is, **no priming facilitation** was observed between compound kanji pairs which shared a character, nor was facilitation observed between single kanji and compound kanji words in which the single kanji appeared. There was facilitation neither from a single kanji to the compound, nor from the compound to the single kanji contained in the stimulus compound. Thus, there was no priming from the component character 道 *michi* 'road' to 坂道 *sakamichi* 'slope', nor was there any significant priming from the component character 花粉 *kahun* 'pollen' to 花 *hana* 'flower'. For their subjects, recognition units for kanji compounds were most often formed on the word level rather than on the level of the individual kanji character, implying that such compounds are stored and recognized as integrated units, not according to their component kanji members.

Sakuma, Itoh, and Sasanuma (1989) also compared kanji characters and word units as the recognition units in lexical access for compounds. A first experiment had two-kanji target words preceded by primes which consisted of a single identical kanji, two-kanji words which shared one identical kanji, or an identical two-kanji word. A priming effect was again observed only when the primes were the identical single kanji word or the identical two-kanji compound word. That is, a single kanji word will prime itself, and a two-kanji compound word will prime itself, but a single kanji word will not prime a two-kanji compound word in which it is a member, nor will a kanji member of a two-kanji compound word prime that same kanji when it appears as a single kanji word. A second experiment examined whether priming effects appeared with single-kanji words. Once again, priming effects were observed only when the primes preceding the targets were the identical kanji characters. Simple kanji characters which corresponded to the radicals of the target words also failed to elicit any priming effect. Sakuma, Ito, and Sasanuma also concluded that lexical access for Japanese words written in kanji utilizes word units as the basic element in searching the mental lexicon, and not the kanji character units or analyzable parts thereof.[17]

There is some indirect evidence which touches on this same issue. Since the appropriate reading of kanji characters in a kanji compound is ultimately decided by the **whole-word context**, whole-word translation from orthography to phonology is the most dependable processing procedure. Whole-word access seems to outweigh sub-lexical considerations which would access probabilistic values for readings of the constituent kanji. This being the case, Sasanuma (1992) notes that because the whole word is the most dependable and over-learned level of translation, this makes it the most resistant to neurological impairment through damage or disease. Two patients whose abilities deteriorated through progressive Alzheimer-type dementia continued to display near-normal pronunciation of kanji words after three years. This ability stands in contrast to the fact that all other cognitive skills became non-functional in this longitudinal study. Each word written in kanji has a unique whole-word pronunciation, Sasanuma observes, and this processing route keeps its integrity in certain forms of impairment until the last because of its stability through overlearning.

In fairness, it should be noted that patients with *gogi aphasia* (語義失語), who suffer profound word meaning loss, also suffer from a selective impairment in reading aloud

---

[17] This may be related to the fluidity with which compounds appear and disappear in Japanese. This is exemplified in Saito and Kawakami's (1992) examination of how pseudo-compound kanji words might relate to the mental lexicon. Subjects were given 248 kanji compounds (/kagaku/: 科学 'science', 化学 'chemistry', 歌学 'musicology')) and 368 pseudo-compounds (/kagaku/: 可学, 火学, 歌楽), and asked whether they knew the compounds and whether the compounds could be found in the dictionary. Two-thirds of the subjects judged that approximately 20% of the pseudo-compounds could be found in the dictionary, suggesting that readers differentiate pseudo-compounds from kanji compounds not so much on actual lexical addresses as on their lexical likelihood. However, to be able to then access the actual lexical address one must know the compound as an existing compound word, with its own unique configuration of phonological and semantic attributes.

kanji words (see Sasanuma, 1992). This impairment is manifested in oral reading errors for kanji which are essentially *on-kun* confusions in assigning the correct reading to the component character of a kanji compound. The more typical *on-* or *kun*-reading is given to the constituents, suggesting that the sub-lexical procedures are employed for such words and that the 'irregular' readings are thus regularized. This is especially noticeable in response to the *jukuji-kun*, those 'compound characters' which have a unique *kun*-reading. Thus, 相手, 田舎, 煙草, 真面目, 人形, 時雨, 土産, 海老 *aite, inaka, tabako, majime, ningyoo, shigure, miyage, ebi* 'opponent, countryside, cigarette, serious, doll, rain shower, souvenir, prawn' may be instead read with their more common assignments on the sub-lexical level. Thus, these *jukuji-kun* compounds might instead turn out as *soo-shu, den-sha, kemuri-kusa, shin-menboku, jin-kei, toki-ame, do-san, kai-roo*.

Essentially, therefore, we have evidence for two processing strategies, one which addresses the whole word as word and another which takes into account the sub-word values of the constituent kanji in kanji compounds. Either one of these strategies can remain or be impaired, depending upon the neurological circumstances. The question, of course, is what happens in normal readers, and the best explanation might be that kanji compounds are stored and accessed as whole words, except when they are unknown or unfamiliar. In such instances, kanji compounds are analyzed by breaking them into their component parts, searching for the most likely fit in terms of both pronunciation and meaning.

In a different vein, Shimomura and Yokosawa (1995) tested for functional differences between character-level and word-level units by posing a **proofreading** task to subjects who had to detect 'mis-spelled' characters. Many kanji characters are visually close to one another, and it is relatively easy to change one component of a kanji to create an incorrect character which is close to the correct target. The results of this exercise revealed that subjects used information about word shape more than the details of the individual characters in their proofreading. That is, they were better at detecting mis-spellings when the whole word or phrase was presented at a time than when an individual character was presented. The inference is that individual kanji are attended to more accurately in larger units where they have actual meanings than when they appear in isolation. Obviously, reading is a holistic process which does not decipher the message kanji-by-kanji, but rather employs top-down processing units like words and phrases to achieve this goal. Very simply, subjects appear to pursue recognition of the word before they attend to recognition of its constituent parts, even if they are whole kanji within the compound.

Sub-Lexical Access

Tamaoka and Hatsuzuka (1998) pursue this matter in their exploration of the relative roles of morphological semantics vs. word semantics in two-kanji compounds. That is, does the reader access the individual semantic values for the two individual kanji which constitute the compound, or does one first access the semantic values of the compound as an integrated whole word. Just how much processing of the individual kanji in the compound does take place? If whole-word representations are typically accessed for familiar words, are the individual units in unfamiliar compounds accessed? Tamaoka and Hatsuzuka had their subjects perform both lexical decision and naming tasks with real compounds and pseudo-compounds created by combining two real kanji. The compounds were of three types: compounds containing two kanji which were semantic opposites (長 'long' + 短 'short' = 長短 *choo-tan* 'length'); compounds containing two kanji which were semantically similar (柔 'soft' + 軟 'flexible' = 柔軟 *juu-nan* 'pliable'); and control compounds containing two kanji which are closely bound but do normally appear together (荒 'wild' + 野 'field' = 荒野 *koo-ya* 'wilderness'). Interference in lexical decision times was present for both semantic opposites and similars, but particularly strong for the semantic opposites, suggesting that **semantic activation** does take place at the level of the individual kanji because delays are best explained as conflict between morphological semantics (the individual kanji) and word semantics (the compound as a whole). The same general picture emerged for the naming task, again without such interference for the control word compounds. Here, an alternative explanation might be that accessing individual kanji components of compounds is a back-up strategy for compounds which are unfamiliar or unintelligible.[18]

It may also be that frequency of the two component kanji in a two-kanji compound word has an effect on the path of lexical access. Hoshino (1991) had subjects read kanji compounds from left to right and classify them as words or non-words to test whether non-words with high-frequency characters would take longer to categorize than non-words with low-frequency characters. The non-word strings were created by reversing the characters of an existing word, but the results revealed that subjects were able to

---

[18] A useful analogy is found in the complications offered by place names which often have locally derived readings which are often unpredictable. The readings are confirmed at the word level, but achieving successful recognition of the phonological identity is often possible only through specific knowledge. Recall our earlier example of the same temple (精澄寺) on the Boosoo Peninsula being identified by highway signs as the *on*-reading *Seichoo-ji* at one point and the *kun*-reading *Kiyosumi-dera* at another point. The driver searching for this temple in fact produced the *kun*-reading as *Kiyozumi-dera*, with the expected morphophonemic change of voiceless /s/ to voiced /z/ in the second kanji. Such examples abound in place name assignments, and another example might be the kanji in 鴨川, for the *Kamogawa* River running through Kyoto, contrasting with the same kanji 鴨川, for the *Kamokawa* township found on the Boosoo Peninsula.

classify words more quickly than non-words, and that the frequency rating of the characters did not influence classification times for non-words. Access procedures are striving to achieve the word-level address, so that subjects may ignore the frequency factor for individual kanji when such information does not provide the crucial cues to whole-word recognition.

Tamaoka and Hatsuzuka (1995) also tested for an effect from **kanji frequency** by using both naming and lexical decision tasks. A first experiment using the naming task created 80 two-kanji compounds by controlling frequency (high vs. low) and position (left-hand vs. right-hand character in the compound). The results revealed that high frequency kanji in the left position in the compound facilitated accuracy and speed in the whole-word naming responses. Of course, since naming initiates phonological activation, the frequency of the left-hand character will inevitably affect naming. A second experiment using the lexical decision task augmented the above stimuli with the same number of pseudo-homophonic compounds, whereby one of the compounding elements in a given kanji was replaced with a homophonic kanji. Subjects were then asked to judge as quickly and accurately as possible whether the stimulus compound was a legitimate kanji compound or not. In this case, high kanji frequency in the right position facilitated accuracy and speed in the lexical decision task. Of course, because the lexical decision task cannot be ultimately realized without processing the right-hand kanji in order to decide if the stimulus is a word or not, the frequency of the right-hand kanji inevitably shows an effect.

But Shimomura (1998) reports that when primes were in the **first position** in targets, faster responses were elicited than when the primes were in the second position. Her experiment manipulated the nature of the primes, however, so that they were either kanji characters which could be used as a word by itself (for example, 本 *hon* 'book' and 花 *hana* 'flower') or which could not stand alone (for example, 基 *ki* and 化 *ka*). This distinction between primes which were word-type kanji, such as 本 for 本箱 *honbako* 'bookcase' and 花 for 花束 *hanataba* 'bouquet', and nonword-type kanji both prompted faster lexical decision times for her subjects, although the faster responses were found for the nonword-type kanji like 基 *ki* and 化 *ka* that only exist as constituents in kanji compounds such as 基本 *kihon* 'basics' and 化石 *kaseki* 'fossil'. Recalling the Tamaoka and Hatsuzuka (1995) findings of a frequency effect, she did find a familiarity effect for the word-type kanji primes, but an inverse effect. Thus, a low-familarity target would yield a large priming effect, as in 山 (*yama* 'mountain') > 山荘 (*sansoo* 'mountain retreat'); but high-familiarity targets yielded no priming effect at all, as in 人 (*hito* 'person') > 人間 (*ningen* 'human being'). Shimomura's findings may also shed some light on Makioka's (1994) findings for the effect of position within compound words. In detecting target words like 実用 *jitsuyoo* 'utility' with probes like 実証 *jisshoo* 'proof' and 応用 *ooyoo* 'application', subjects showed high false alarm rates when the critical single kanji in the priming compound matched the same position as the same single kanji in the target compound, just as Shimomura reports for both positions. Although Makioka concluded that these results demonstrate that information about within-compound positions in kanji compounds is used in word recognition, it may just be that this information is more attuned to the pattern matching aspects of the task he posed his subjects, and the fact that primes which are sub-word level nonword-type kanji constituents can cue their *doppelgangers* in two-kanji compound words in either position. It would appear that their non-lexicality is what allows them a certain freedom in cueing the same kanji in a larger compound target.

A lexical decision task in Hirose's (1992a) three priming experiments also demonstrates some support for **the role of the first kanji** in the storage and retrieval of kanji compounds in memory. A first experiment probed for the features used to retrieve compound words from memory, and found that the initial, or left-hand, character of the pair primes kanji compounds. A second experiment tested the effect of kanji primes which differed in pronunciation, but which were identical to the initial kanji in the compound to be activated; there was no significant effect attributable to difference in pronunciation, suggesting that it is the graphic shape or the meaning associated with a character that is doing the priming in the retrieval process. Hirose suggests that the first kanji narrows down the number of choices as to the right-hand kanji in real compounds in the cohort. Although he concludes that compounds which share an initial kanji are clustered together in the mental lexicon according to the meaning of the first kanji in the compound word, it may also be the graphic configuration of the kanji which provides the cues. His third experiment manipulated kanji primes in respect to their frequency of occurrence as elements in kanji compounds; low frequency kanji primes showed a greater priming effect than high frequency kanji, suggesting that low frequency has an effect on whether that first kanji will play a role in activating the compound. The implication is that the total number of two-kanji compound words in which a single kanji plays a construction role has an effect. That is, compound words which contain a kanji which often enters into such compound constructions will take longer to process than those which contain a kanji which does not often enter into such constructions.

Tamaoka and Takahashi (1999) had subjects write two-kanji compounds after they were dictated, and their findings also demonstrate some support for the role of the first kanji in the storage and retrieval of kanji compounds from memory. Their goal was to contrast the relative weighting of word frequency and orthographic complexity, as measured by number of strokes. Not surprisingly, stroke complexity affected low frequency compounds, but not high frequency compounds. But the interesting finding here is that word frequency facilitated initiation times, as well as writing times, for the left-hand character. But the word frequency effect was not apparent in the writing times for the right-hand character.

Yamada and Kayamoto (1998) have also examined the effect of associative values on the recognition of two-kanji compound words. Imagine that we are considering the first kanji in a two-kanji compound before us. That kanji has associative values with other compound words in which this kanji appears, as either the kanji in the left-hand position or the right-hand position. This is its 'valency'. We can assume that **high-valency kanji** may have higher probability, as well as higher potential for forming new words, and that such words are generally richer in meaning because they activate more related meanings in the mental lexicon than words with low-valency kanji. And it is also easier to venture a guess as to their semantic identity. For example, Yamada and Kayamoto set the valency of kanji 禁 *kin* in a word like 禁止 *kinshi* 'prohibition' at 12, because it appears in first position in 10 words (like 禁煙 *kinen* 'no smoking') and in second position in 2 words (like 解禁 *kaikin* 'removal of the ban'). In contrast, the valency of the kanji 賠 in the word 賠償 *baishoo* 'compensation' is only 1, because it appears in only 1 word, the very word 賠償 *baishoo* itself. And this is what their subjects reflected in lexical decision times for words and non-words in the high and low valency conditions. Lexical decisions were faster for real high-valency words than for low-valency words. But decisions were slower for non-words in the high-valency condition than in the low-valency condition, probably because a high frequency kanji appearing in the first position makes a non-word look more word-like. The lexical decision thus takes longer. This also implies that unfamiliar or low-frequency two kanji compounds are read sequentially, rather than holistically. Although valency appears to be an informational feature of some processing import, these results really underscore the role of the first kanji in a compound as keying the access code for both real words and non-word recognition. It is the frequency of this first kanji, as well as of the whole kanji compound itself, that remains the best predictor of ease of word recognition (see also Hirose, 1992a) and the likelihood of any given word being judged as a real lexical entry (see Saito & Kawakami, 1992).

Tamaoka and Hatsuzuka (n.d.) also investigate the role of word-construction frequency, by contrasting this value with the fact of kanji printed frequency in Japanese printed texts. When they counterposed these two factors, **word-construction frequency** and **printed frequency**, they found that kanji printed frequency had a stronger effect in naming and lexical decision tasks for two-morpheme compound words. Obviously, the relative weighting of the following three factors form the interactive matrix which leverages success in searching the mental lexicon: (a) individual kanji frequency, (b) frequency with which an individual kanji enters into construction to form compounds, and (c) the frequency of the resultant compounds.

Frequency also interacts with the type of morpheme represented by a kanji in a kanji compound. Not all kanji represent content words, and not all kanji are free morphemes. Some kanji fall into the category of bound morphemes, and can only be used in that context; for example, 宇 *u*, only appears in the compound meaning 'universe', 宇宙 *u-chuu*. Similarly, the kanji for the bound morpheme 娯 *go* only appears in the compound meaning 'entertainment', 娯楽 *go-raku*. Their meanings are so vague and restricted that Japanese speakers would be hard-pressed to provide a definition. But some kanji like 緊 *kin* are freer in that they can be used to form several compounds, such as 緊急 *kinkyuu* 'emergency', 緊張 *kinchoo* 'tension', and 緊密 *kinmitsu* 'tight'. Yamada (1994a) contrasted their relative status in an experiment in which 30 subjects were given an audiovisual tachistoscopic task in which they had to name as quickly as possible the bound morpheme kanji under one of the following three conditions: (i) the single bound morpheme kanji (宇 *u*) when not part of a compound word; (ii) the two-kanji compound, when containing the single bound morpheme kanji, as the initial element in the compound ('universe', 宇宙 *u-chuu*); (iii) possible kanji compound words which could be generated from the bound morpheme given (in the case of 宇 *u*, a limited set of one possible compound, but a larger set for other bound morphemes, such as 緊急 *kinkyuu* 'emergency', 緊張 *kinchoo* 'tension', and 緊密 *kinmitsu* 'tight' for 緊 *kin*). Subjects took longer to name the kanji compound words from which only the initial bound morpheme kanji was given than to name the single bound morpheme kanji. Yamada's results favor pre-lexical access over post-lexical access explanations because such single bound-morpheme kanji seem to be named by directly accessing the phonological level instead of directly accessing the lexical level. This suggests **competition** between the two access routes, phonological vs. lexical, with subjects using the most opportunistic route. In this case, when presented with a single bound morpheme like 宇 *u*, some time is needed to access the relevant lexical entry, and so subjects tended to rely on the faster phonological route in the naming task. But a second important point, insofar as our discussion is concerned, has to do with the variable status that kanji have. Not all kanji should be considered to have the same function or access path in the architecture of kanji storage in the Japanese mental lexicon.

Summary Conclusions

Given the mixed findings, we seem to be left with two different possibilities as to which are the relevant recognition units for kanji compounds. First, there is strong evidence that the kanji compounds are themselves the recognition units. But there are also some claims that the individual kanji are the relevant recognition units, and frequency is a crucial factor in these assertions. There can be little question that kanji frequency is a critical factor in word recognition because frequency is the key to how often such judgments are made. High frequency kanji in the first position in kanji compounds facilitate access for naming, because this is where access procedures are first initiated, and successful naming will depend upon the accuracy of matching phonological information to the kanji embedded in the compound. But the number of possible readings must first be gone through before the correct reading comes up for an accurate naming response. The frequency with which this association appears is inevitably an extension of frequency considerations. High frequency kanji in the second position in kanji compounds faciliates access for lexical decision tasks because this is the end point at which the final information for real kanji is crystallized. One decides on whether a given compound is in fact a real kanji compound, and that decision can only be taken once the final pieces of the processing puzzle are in place. Once again, the frequency with which this association appears inevitably is an extension of frequency considerations. The frequency factor is not a contradictory element after all because the high frequency of an individual kanji is also a reflection of the frequency of its appearance in kanji compounds. The final arbiter of successful naming responses is in fact the contextual level for kanji compounds, for this is where final decisions have to be made for the correct reading of a particular kanji, and thus the correct pronunciation of the compound. But accuracy in deciding whether a kanji compound is in fact a real word will reflect knowledge about how often this configuration appears and whether a lexical address for this configuration is commonly accessed.

KINETIC INFORMATION IN KANJI WORDS

There is also a kinetic aspect to kanji acquisition by Japanese children, resulting in a kinetic memory which can be unlocked by the priming of the initial steps of a motor program (see Nihei, 1991). The motor representation of the kanji can be retrieved directly, without retrieving the accompanying phonetic or semantic representations, though these informational features may be activated automatically (Watanabe 1991). This is confirmed by research on **'slips of the pen'**, the graphemic equivalent of verbal 'slips of the tongue'. It is possible to induce 'slips of the pen' by activating the motor memory of a similar character, revealing that repeated use of a motor activity can cause other motor memories to become active. For example, slips of the pen during rapidly repeated writing can be induced by writing a similar character prior to the target character, also under speeded or repeated conditions (Nihei, 1986a, 1986b, 1988). Usually there is some common identity between the intended characters and the mistakes: some begin with similar strokes, or proceed through common turning points in cursive writing, or end in similar ways. The motor programs for writing the intended and mistaken characters obviously share common segments in sequences of movement, and such results suggest that Japanese kana/kanji storage incorporates not only the expected phonetic, semantic, and configurational features, but also their motoric sequences in terms of kinetic movement.

There is also evidence that certain aphasics are able to comprehend kanji which were previously unreadable when they are allowed to trace the kanji, suggesting the facilitating aspects of this **kinetic memory** when it is initiated (Nihei, 1991). In general, it seems that the graphic representations in kanji storage that are used for motor output incorporate kinetic information and form part of the mental representation for a given kanji. These facts are certainly in keeping with a spreading activation view of the mental lexicon, but one in which such kinetic components are among the stored elements.

But this kinetic facilitation is not only true for kanji/hanzi characters. Naka and Naoi (1995) report four experiments on whether repeated writing (that is, rehearsal by writing) is an effective strategy for memory. In general, the findings point to repeated writing as facilitating recall for such varied stimuli as meaningless graphic designs for both Japanese and American subjects and Arabic letters for Japanese subjects. It facilitates memory for unfamiliar graphic designs, but not for familiar linguistic symbols, and appears to be culture-independent. The facilitation effect is observed in free-recall, but not in recognition, because repeated writing encodes specificity in visual-motor information. That this kinetic factor should be stronger for Japanese and other logographic languages simply reflects the enormous amount of time spent learning by physically practicing kanji production by hand, and the continuing belief that **repeated copying** is the tried and true way of learning how to write (but see Onose, 1987, 1988). At least this continues to be true in an age where children are still taught kanji by continuous writing regimens; whether it will continue to be so in an age of keyboard-generated computer lookup is another question for many kanji.

Another area where the kinetic values attached to kanji comes into play is perhaps best observed in the traditional practice known as *kuusho* (空書), the **finger-writing strategy** for recalling the form of a kanji. When Japanese writers are unsure of a kanji, they may begin tracing the outline of the kanji on the palm of their hand to initiate the motor sequence which unlocks the remainder of the kanji configuration. Or when the identity of a homophonic kanji is unclear in conversation, one of the co-locutors may trace the kanji in the air or on a flat surface to indicate which specific kanji was meant. This activity recalls the motoric strategy inculcated by teachers and students alike when internalizing characters as a series of strokes which must be exactly memorized in respect to number and order. *Kuusho* finger-writing obviously serves as a probe which accesses motoric- or action-based representation, as well as serving as an external mnemonic to facilitate a conscious mental process (see Endo, 1988, and Sasaki, 1987a).

There is no report of finger-writing in non-kanji cultures, though it appears as early as 10 for Japanese children. It does appear in other **kanji cultures**, and Sasaki (1987a) found that both Taiwanese and Japanese subjects used this strategy to solve kanji anagram tests. In an examination (Sasaki, 1984b) of 500 school children between the ages of 7 and 12, the following developmental sequence emerges for *kuusho* use. When children were required to provide correct kanji after exposure to integral parts of the kanji, the number of children using this strategy directly correlates with age: 11.8% of the 7-year-olds, 5.6% of the 8-year-olds, 22.2% of the 9-year-olds, 56.7% of the 10-year-olds, 57.3% of the 11-year-olds, and 66.7% of the 12 year-olds employed a finger-writing strategy to aid recall. The figures suggest that children have largely acquired this behaviour by the age of 11, and employ this finger-writing strategy wherever needed, in space and on the surface of objects. When the children were prohibited from finger-writing in solving kanji integration tasks in a second experiment, the results showed a decrement in correct performance as a result of the prohibition. When 105 female college students were required to perform kanji integration tasks, Sasaki and Watanabe (1983) found that all but two subjects exhibited finger-writing in space (44%) or on surfaces like a hand, desk, or thigh (66%). When a second experiment presented kanji integration tasks both orally and visually, and subjects were prohibited from finger-writing, they exhibited poor performance in kanji integration tasks in both modes.

Sasaki and Watanabe (1984) extended this paradigm to other orthographic cultures, comparing Japanese subjects with Chinese subjects and subjects from non-kanji cultures who had some knowledge of both Japanese and kanji. Both the Japanese and Chinese subjects used finger-writing in solving a kanji integration task, but such behaviour was absent among the subjects from non-kanji cultures. When finger-writing was prohibited, the percentage of correct answers for the Chinese students was much worse than for their Japanese counterparts. Chinese writers typically know three times the kanji that Japanese know, and the results suggest that Chinese rely even more upon finger-writing as a puzzle-solving and memory strategy. A second experiment employed various English spelling tests, and both Chinese and Japanese subjects used finger-writing to solve the English spelling tasks. The non-kanji subjects did not, confirming that the finger-writing strategy is a culturally-based external tool in cueing the motoric and action-based aspects of mental representations.

FONT-TYPE INFORMATION
IN PROCESSING KANJI WORDS

One issue that has not been addressed in any of the kanji recognition models is the range of **font type variation** in printed Japanese. A glance at any newspaper or magazine page reveals an enormous variety of font types, as can be seen in the following *Asahi Shimbun* advertisement for new books for sale. Each book title runs in vertical mode and differs in font type.

Figure 3.3 A sample of font type variation.
(Reprinted from *Asahi Shimbun*, Tokyo morning edition, March 26, 1999)

While the aesthetic and/or attention-getting nature of these font choices need not be discussed in any detail here, their effect on lexical access is certainly worthy of mention. They certainly do have an effect on information transmission, as the work by Hagita and his collegues on degradation in the presence of **visual noise** confirms.

It is often difficult to distinguish character parts from noise for kanji which have been degraded by noise in transmissions such as faxed messages. The geometrical features of kanji patterns can easily be marred by stains and blurs, as well as by the graphic designs that re-orient newspaper headlines and advertising headings. Most conventional methods used in mechanical character recognition try to extract geometrical features of kanji, such as stroke direction and connectivity, in order to compare them to reference patterns stored in a dictionary database. Thus, any such distortion or noise must be removed before recognition can take place (Sawaki & Hagita, 1996), and some success has been achieved in improving the success rates for graphic images embedded in noise (see Sawaki, Hagita & Ishii, 1997), particularly by projection methods which extract text-line regions by contrasting the complementary relationship between characters and background (Sawaki & Hagita, 1998). If anything, such research reminds the psycholinguist that word recognition in the real world is complicated by more than the neat presentations that tachistoscopes and computer terminals allow. Reading words and text in real time and space offers an additional dimension of distortion that lexical access procedures must deal with in achieving word recognition, especially in Japanese where a wide range of font manipulations is possible.

In terms of the connotative features, Japanese readers have definite opinions as to which font-types are more traditional, more legible, more aesthetic, and so on. For example, Langman and Saito (1984) compared kanji written in the five standard styles of calligraphy: 'block' (楷書 *kaisho*), 'scribe' (隷書 *reisho*), 'semi-cursive' (行書 *gyoosho*), 'cursive' (草書 *soosho*), and 'seal' (篆書 *tensho*).

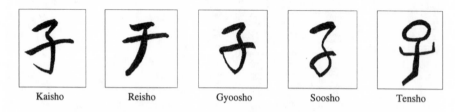

| Kaisho | Reisho | Gyoosho | Soosho | Tensho |

Figure 3.4 A sample of kanji in five standard calligraphic styles.

They presented them to a group of native Japanese speakers and a group of English speakers who knew no Japanese. When they examined their judgments of **prototypicality** in regard to the writing styles, the patterns of prototypicality ratings were strikingly different for the two groups. The Japanese subjects rated the 'block' *kaisho* and 'semi-cursive' *gyoosho* styles as prototypical kanji, likely because these are the most commonly used styles in reading and writing, respectively. The English-speaking subjects, with no knowledge of such conventional uses, rated the *tensho* and *soosho* styles as prototypical because of their iconicity.

This confounding of prototypicality for kanji with their appearance in commonly used styles in reading and writing appears to be confirmed by Saito and Langman's (1984) examination of how native Japanese speakers would rate the prototypicality of unfamiliar, obsolete kanji in Japanese. These Saito and Langman labelled as 'Chinese kanji', and presented them to subjects in each of the five styles. When an iconic meaning was given for the kanji, the Japanese rated these 'Chinese kanji' just as the Americans did in the previous study, rating the *tensho* style as most prototypical. However, when non-iconic meanings were provided, the most familiar styles were once again rated as more prototypical than the rarer styles. The inference is that when sufficient graphemic-semantic overlap makes the character iconic, subjects from different cultures rate the prototypicality of styles in a similar way; however, when such overlap does not exist, the Japanese will rate the most familiar style as the most prototypical.

Chapter 4

KANA PROCESSING

INTRODUCTORY COMMENTS

Japanese text is never limited to just kanji, but is intermixed with kana syllabary symbols in what is known as *kanji/kana majiribun* 'kanji/kana mixed sentences'. This is true of both the traditional *tategaki* (縦書) 'vertical' top-to-bottom style or the Western-derived *yokogaki* (横書) 'horizontal' left-to-right style. There are two of these kana syllabary types in Japanese, the **katakana** syllabary and the **hiragana** syllabary. Hiragana and katakana are syllabic scripts in which each symbol represents a sound unit which corresponds to a mora, for which the canonical shape is most often a Consonant-Vowel (CV) combination. There are also five vowels, for which there are five kana symbols, as well as a morphophonemic nasal which also has a separate kana symbol (ん). The grapheme-to-mora correspondence ratio is extremely high for kana in both syllabary systems, and the idealized one-to-one principle in orthographic correlations is close to being realized in Japanese orthography.[1]

The **mora** is a suprasegmental feature which is best defined as a unit of length, and its use in Japanese phonetics is often explained by claiming that morae are pronounced with equal time durations. In musical terms, the mora is a rhythmic element which is measured by dividing the whole sequence into parts which carry equal time values. In linguistic terms, then, each segmental structure that consists of a vowel, a consonant plus a vowel, a consonant plus a glide plus a vowel, and so forth, lasts one such unit of length in Japanese (see Akamatsu, 1997). If we pose Japanese as a "syllable-timed language" in the old sense of the term (see Kess, 1992), morae traditionally constitute the basis of its subjective timing and its rhythm in poetic genres like *haiku* (俳句) and *waka* (和歌), with each mora given equal time duration. More recently, Otake, Hatano, Cutler, and

---

[1] Some exceptions are to be found. The hiragana symbols は and へ are read as /ha/ and /he/ normally, but when they function as case-marking particles after nominals, they take on an archaic reading of /wa/ and /e/.

Mehler (1993) have demonstrated its centrality even in objective measures of syllable perception and syllable manipulation. Kubozono (1989) has also demonstrated the psychological reality of the mora and mora boundaries through the patterns underlying speech errors in Japanese. In particular, the analysis of blend errors suggests that mora boundaries, and not syllable boundaries, are the most common switch points in Japanese speech errors and are essential for significant generalizations about phonotactics in Japanese.

SYLLABARY INVENTORIES

Both kana scripts contain 46 basic symbols, with an additional 25 symbols which employ diacritic marks taking the total to 71 kana symbols (Kindaichi, Hayashi & Shibata, 1988). The diacritics appear in the upper right-hand quadrant of the kana symbol: a pair of quotation-like marks signal the change from a voiceless consonant to a voiced consonant, as in the shift from た *ta* to だ *da*. The basic kana are generally arranged in sets of five, with the various consonants appearing before the five vowels /a i u e o/ in CV combinations. In one set, /ha/ alternates morphophonemically with /ba/ and /pa/, and this trio of kana shows up as the basic, unmarked は *ha*, the marked ば *ba* with the two marks in the upper-right quadrant, and the marked ぱ *pa* with a small circle in the upper-right quadrant. Another 33 syllables created by the cluster of consonant plus semi-vowel /y/ plus vowel results in a grand total of 104 kana configurations for syllabary deployment to represent the various morae. The table of hiragana and katakana symbols can be seen in the following tables, where the hiragana symbol appears first and is followed by its katakana counterpart in parentheses.[2]

---

[2] Some idea of the actual frequencies of hiragana and katakana symbols can be derived from a recent analysis of a Japanese newspaper corpus spanning a full year of morning and evening editions of the *Asahi Shimbun* (see Nozaki & Yokoyama, 1996; Yokoyama & Nozaki, 1996b).

Table 4.1 Total inventory of kana syllabaries.

あ (ア)	a	い (イ)	i	う (ウ)	u	え (エ)	e	お (オ)	o
か (カ)	ka	き (キ)	ki	く (ク)	ku	け (ケ)	ke	こ (コ)	ko
さ (サ)	sa	し (シ)	shi	す (ス)	su	せ (セ)	se	そ (ソ)	so
た (タ)	ta	ち (チ)	chi	つ (ツ)	tsu	て (テ)	te	と (ト)	to
な (ナ)	na	に (ニ)	ni	ぬ (ヌ)	nu	ね (ネ)	ne	の (ノ)	no
は (ハ)	ha	ひ (ヒ)	hi	ふ (フ)	fu	へ (ヘ)	he	ほ (ホ)	ho
ま (マ)	ma	み (ミ)	mi	む (ム)	mu	め (メ)	me	も (モ)	mo
や (ヤ)	ya	い (イ)	i	ゆ (ユ)	yu	え (エ)	e	よ (ヨ)	yo
ら (ラ)	ra	り (リ)	ri	る (ル)	ru	れ (レ)	re	ろ (ロ)	ro
わ (ワ)	wa	ゐ (ヰ)	i	う (ウ)	u	ゑ (ヱ)	e	を (ヲ)	o
ん (ン)	n								
が (ガ)	ga	ぎ (ギ)	gi	ぐ (グ)	gu	げ (ゲ)	ge	ご (ゴ)	go
ざ (ザ)	za	じ (ジ)	ji	ず (ズ)	zu	ぜ (ゼ)	ze	ぞ (ゾ)	zo
だ (ダ)	da	ぢ (ヂ)	ji	づ (ヅ)	zu	で (デ)	de	ど (ド)	do
ば (バ)	ba	び (ビ)	bi	ぶ (ブ)	bu	べ (ベ)	be	ぼ (ボ)	bo
ぱ (パ)	pa	ぴ (ピ)	pi	ぷ (プ)	pu	ぺ (ペ)	pe	ぽ (ポ)	po
きゃ (キャ)	kya			きゅ (キュ)	kyu			きょ (キャ)	kyo
しゃ (シャ)	sha			しゅ (シュ)	shu			しょ (ショ)	sho
ちゃ (チャ)	cha			ちゅ (チュ)	chu			ちょ (チョ)	cho
にゃ (ニャ)	nya			にゅ (ニュ)	nyu			にょ (ニョ)	nyo
ひゃ (ヒャ)	hya			ひゅ (ヒュ)	hyu			ひょ (ヒョ)	hyo
みゃ (ミャ)	mya			みゅ (ミュ)	myu			みょ (ミョ)	myo
りゃ (リャ)	rya			りゅ (リュ)	ryu			りょ (リョ)	ryo
ぎゃ (ギャ)	gya			ぎゅ (ギュ)	gyu			ぎょ (ギョ)	gyo
じゃ (ジャ)	ja			じゅ (ジュ)	ju			じょ (ジョ)	jo
びゃ (ビャ)	bya			びゅ (ビュ)	byu			びょ (ビョ)	byo
ぴゃ (ピャ)	pya			ぴゅ (ピュ)	pyu			ぴょ (ピョ)	pyo

The **internal structure of the syllabary** is in principle based on phonetic criteria which mesh closely with morphophonemic criteria. For example, the principle by which diacritics are added to show *dakuon* (濁音) 'voiced sounds' not only links voiceless/voiced consonant pairs like /t-d; k-g; s-z/ together, but also reflects their pairing in morphophonemic alternations in inflection and derivation.[3] Columns reflect consonantal groupings, as in k/g, t/d, h/b/p; rows reflect which of the five vowels the particular consonant occurs with, as in /ka ki ku ke ko; ga gi gu ge go/. The mental map of the syllabary that users carry about in their heads contains these dimensions of spatiality and distance, as can be seen from Itsukushima's (1981) inquiry into that organization of ordering judgments in respect to the Japanese syllabary. But these results also reveal that organization of the columns in the Japanese syllabary by consonants facilitates discrimination, while organization of the rows by the five vowels does not. Two experiments had subjects judge the proper order of two syllables in respect to their position in either a column or a row of the Japanese syllabary. Two factors which shortened the time required to make such judgments reflected whether there was a large separation between two syllables, and whether syllable pairs appeared in their proper order.

Hiragana and katakana share the same syllabic reference point, so that the same syllable can be transcribed by either system. For example, the syllable /sa/ is transcribed as さ in hiragana and as サ in katakana. In appearance, the katakana syllabary is more angular in the shape of its symbols, and is commonly taken as the appropriate transliteration medium for loan words into Japanese from other languages. However, it also sees a good deal of use in modern printed Japanese for native vocabulary items as a kind of visual italics, useful for highlighting exclamations in literature and comic strips, citing neologisms, and catching the eye in advertisements which call attention to brand names or brand qualities. Hiragana, on the other hand, is more cursive in the shape of its symbols, with these shapes more easily discriminated one from the other. Although it can be and is used for writing some content words, it is more commonly used in writing the non-content words and grammatical morphemes not usually presented by kanji characters. In short, it is used for morphological endings, function words, and the rest of the grammatical scaffolding of Japanese sentences.

Kana has never replaced kanji completely for a variety of reasons. A common argument is that Japanese has too many **homophones**, words with the same pronun-

---

[3] Japanese morphemes with an initial voiceless obstruent in isolation sometimes occur with an initial voiced obstruent as the second element of compounds or stem-affix formations (*te* 'hand' + *kami* 'paper' > *tegami* 'letter'). This consonant alternation, known as *rendaku* (連濁), is not an automatic process, but usually obeys the constraint that the initial consonant of a morpheme never undergoes the process if that morpheme already contains a voiced obstruent (*hitori* 'one man' + *tabi* 'travel' > *hitoritabi*/*hitoridabi* 'travel without company'). Although this phonological constraint is highly regular, experimental results show it to be psychologically real for only a small number of speakers (see Vance, 1980).

ciation whose differing meanings are efficiently shown by their having different kanji characters. For example, in discussing design problems associated with Japanese keyboard input, Yamada (1983) cites a vocabulary count of one popular Japanese dictionary as showing 36.4% of its entries to be kanji homophones. Although some kanji words may be distinguished due to the placement of pitch accent in the spoken words, they appear exactly identical in print in hiragana and katakana presentations. Katakana is typically taken to be more unique in its portrayal of foreign loanwords and native neologisms, but it also offers homonyms that are written and pronounced identically but which have different meanings.

The flip side of this classic argument about potential ambiguity is that spoken Japanese seems to flow effectively without excessive visual support of the kind claimed as necessary through kanji. Correct interpretations are, for the most part, immediately and accurately assigned simply on the basis of discourse and contextual cues. Some scholars (see Suzuki, 1977) even insist that homonyms "thrive and prosper in daily speech" because of the disambiguating function of kanji. The claim is that homonyms in other languages are discouraged because of the competition between overlapping forms, whereas in Japanese phonetically identical forms in speech can be easily distinguished because of the distinctive kanji in print. The implication is that Japanese language users are somewhat dependent upon the graphic image of the word that is stored in their minds, and knowing the kanji shape for the word is then an important factor in their comprehending what was just said. Just how true this is, and to what extent, is of course one of those areas of popular culture that psycholinguistic studies of lexical access to a mental lexicon which stores kanji vs. kana formats is all about. The real issue here may be more cultural than it is psycholinguistic, however. As Unger (1984) points out, there are many aspects of the problem that are really cultural, and not linguistic, reflecting the widespread belief that kanji are simply indispensable for writing Japanese. Obviously, the Japanese language is not the same as Japanese writing, but there are cross-modal influences and interaction. Even in the computer age, much of the debate about what constitutes an efficient set of protocols for data entry and word processing in Japanese juxtapose some of these **cultural beliefs** in contrast with efficiency measures as an impatient information age looks for optimal solutions.

PROCESSING DIFFERENCES BETWEEN KANA TYPES?

Although Japanese research has been concerned with the possible processing differences between the two orthographic types of syllabary vs. kanji, some work has also attended to possible processing differences between its two syllabary types, hiragana vs. katakana. Some have taken this to mean that the two syllabaries are **domain-**

specific, with the main function of katakana tied to its representational function for foreign loan words. Hatta, Katoh, and Kirsner (1984), for example, contrasted lexical decision rates for English-speaking learners of Japanese with native Japanese speakers, in order to tease out the nature of lexical representation for loan words in Japanese. They suggest that native Japanese readers possess two separate, but partially overlapping lexicons: a foreign word lexicon to which katakana corresponds and a Japanese word lexicon to which hiragana script corresponds.[4] In contrast, they claim that native English learners possess only one lexicon, a Japanese word lexicon, to which both hiragana and katakana correspond. Exactly the opposite conclusion, however, is to be found in Komendzinska's (1995) naming experiment. That is, her results suggested that Japanese readers have one internal lexicon for both kana scripts, while the foreign learners of Japanese turned out to be the ones with two separate lexicons for katakana and hiragana words. Obviously, the ease with which the two lexicons concept can be replicated is not assured. Nevertheless, Komendzinska's 15 foreign graduate students, with an average learning time of 3 years, did name katakana loan words faster when they were written in their conventional katakana format. Japanese words normally written in hiragana were also read faster when they appeared in their normal hiragana format. If anything, this demonstrates that the familiarity effect can be assumed for language users at all stages of fluency; that is, familiarity has an effect in the speed of naming and even learners can access a lexical entry by making use of a stored whole word pronunciation.

Katakana vs. Hiragana Vocabularies?

Tamaoka, Hatsuzuka, Kess, and Bogdan (1998) seem to offer some support for this notion of overlapping vocabulary sets, given Japanese subjects' performance on words and pseudo-words written in hiragana and katakana. Common two-kanji compound words (for example, 教育 *kyooiku* 'education') written in hiragana (きょういく) elicited faster lexical decision judgments than the same presented in katakana (キョウイク), suggesting that perhaps such kanji words have a *doppelganger*, 'shadow' lexical representation in hiragana as well. When one considers that such kanji compounds are often first seen by children in early grades in their hiragana forms, and that even later they may be written with *furigana* (振仮名) glosses on the side to aid reading, the likelihood of this double entry concept is strengthened. It also strengthens the explanation from the point of view of script familiarity. And once this concept of double entries is accepted, it paves the way for Tamaoka et al.'s explanation for the same findings for pseudo-words in

---

[4] Okada (1985) queries the rationale behind some of the processing assumptions of their model, and even challenges whether their conclusions are consistent with their analyses of the data.

hiragana only minimally changed from existing kanji compound words (みょういく *myooiku*, a pseudo-word derived from きょういく *kyooiku* (教育) 'education'). A second experiment, however, found the opposite to be true for actual foreign loanwords of low frequency, as well as for pseudo-words similarly adapted from such loanwords. That is, in such cases lexical decisions were faster for katakana script presentations. Thus, for both the actual low-frequency loan words normally appearing in katakana (for example, エクスプレス *ekusupuresu* 'express'), as well as for pseudo-words in katakana constructed on their frame, the katakana versions were processed faster. While these findings do seem to suggest the possibility of a roughly defined 'script boundary' separating the two large, but overlapping vocabulary sets of 'native' vs. 'foreign' words, they may also be reflecting confounding factors which arise from the canonical phonological patterns associated with foreign loanwords vs. native words assimilated by native Japanese readers. They may also be reflecting the simple expectation of Japanese readers that if the form is appearing in katakana, it must be a new word and thus categorically more familiar in the katakana script than in the hiragana script. Very simply, one has more experience seeing such new and often unique phonological sequences in katakana, and this confers a familiarity factor to anything that is written in katakana because it defines the nature of the reading experience.

As far as **foreign learners** of Japanese are concerned, katakana words are strictly Japanese. Beginners, and even advanced learners, often complain of the fact that katakana words are typically more difficult to decipher (see Hatta, Katoh & Kirsner, 1984). The graphic distinctiveness of hiragana is typically easier for foreign learners to use in discriminating Japanese words, whereas the graphic overlap of the angular katakana is often a source of processing difficulty. The real issue here reflects the perceptual difficulty that non-native learners of Japanese have with katakana, a problem that is confirmed by recent experimental testing. Beginners' recognition of katakana words takes longer than recognition of hiragana words on Japanese lexical judgment tests (Chikamatsu, 1996). Hatta and Hirose (1984) also report two experiments testing whether foreign learners of Japanese differ from Japanese in processing kana words. A first experiment presented 200 Japanese words and English loanwords to 26 Japanese native speakers, while the second experiment presented them to 14 Australian students of Japanese with an average of 4.2 years of study behind them. Both Japanese words and English loanwords were processed faster by Japanese subjects when these words were presented in their conventional kana types (that is, hiragana for Japanese words and katakana for loanwords), but the effect was most pronounced for the foreign loan words in katakana presentations. In contrast, hiragana facilitated processing for the Australian subjects, while katakana failed to do so.

These findings can be related to pedagogical practice, since there is a common misconception among Japanese teachers of foreign students that katakana words will be mastered without difficulty since they are originally loan words from English and therefore 'familiar' (Prem, 1991; Tomita, 1991). If anything, there is support for the opposite conclusion; learners are not facilitated by katakana, and initially are unable to take advantage of the visual familiarity offered by katakana for loan words as read by Japanese native readers (Tamaoka, 1994). The pedagogical implications are that the principles of how katakana words are created to transliterate loanwords should be taught more carefully to foreign learners of Japanese, and both morphological principles and word frequency considerations are central to that task.

The very fact that kana is used to transcribe real words gives it an informational value, much as grammaticality contributes to the recognition and recall of sentence-like strings. Thus, Miura (1978) found a **word superiority effect** for hiragana when testing for the effect of syllabification by tachistoscope. Orthographic regularity in respect to symbolization is an important feature of the kana syllabary, but the fact that the kana appears in a real word is a key factor which leads to this word superiority effect. Very simply, just as alphabetic letters are more accurately identified when presented in a real word (BLINK) than when presented alone or in a legal non-word (FLINK) because of the 'lexical status effect' (see Taft, 1991), so also is kana identification superior in real words to identification of kana in *on*-morphemes or when presented alone.

Some authors suggest that the nature of the resulting phonological representations may even be different for scripts based on **alphabets vs. syllabaries**. Shimomura and Yokosawa (1995) suggest that kana (and perhaps even kanji) function midway between words and alphabetic letters, representing higher level processing units than alphabetic letters. That different script types evoke different learning protocols in children at early stages of segmentational analysis is possible, but ultimately both kana syllabaries are based on the syllabic structure of Japanese, and are thus converted into phonology. Besner (1990) claims that the phonology derived from reading syllabic Japanese kana script is more closely tied to articulatory activity than is the phonology derived from reading the alphabetic English orthography, and that the nature of these two orthographies gives rise to different forms of phonological representation. But Tamaoka and Taft (1994) found that the smallest unit of phonological processing in Japanese is the phonemic segment, not the mora which is orthographically represented by kana. They modified katakana words for a lexical decision task in which words like *ka-me-ra* 'camera' could appear in three altered shapes: the vowel of the initial mora was altered, giving *ko-me-ra*; both vowel and consonant of the initial mora were altered, giving *so-me-ra*; or two initial morae were altered, giving *so-ki-ra*. Subjects were presented with 30 stimuli sets on a videoscreen and asked to decide whether the stimulus was a word or not. Longer response times were required for *ko-me-ra*, suggesting that subjects were engaged longer in seeking a lexical address for the first type. Although the mora is the smallest unit of orthographic representation, Japanese subjects were obviously sensitive to phonemic segments in processing these kana 'words', suggesting that phonemic segments are relevant to phonological processing of kana representations.

Orthographic Attributes of Katakana vs. Hiragana

The three scripts have different historical routes, and they also carry different informational values in their shapes. Reading monosyllabic kana is faster than reading monosyllabic kanji (Umemura, 1981). But the number of syllables in polysyllabic kana words does affect their reading times, whereas the number of syllables in single kanji words does not affect their reading times (Tada, 1975). Kanji, hiragana, and katakana recognition are also differentially affected by noise levels. When these three script types are filtered through several levels of visual noise (15%, 20%, and 25%), kanji is better recognized than kana at all noise levels by both humans and Optical Character Readers. There is no significant decrease in recognition rate for kanji as the noise level increases, but there is a linear decrease for kana, with katakana typically worse than hiragana in the presence of noise. Yokoyama and Yoneda (1995) attribute this robustness of kanji recognition to iconicity and the distinctive number of strokes involved (see also Yokoyama, 1995).

Orthographic **design attributes** also contribute to making the kana symbols hard or easy to read. A lack of distinctiveness, compounded by the similarity between certain kana shapes, can interfere with legibility for both hiragana and katakana. Models of kana recognition by both humans and mechanical devices rely on perceptual features such as symmetry, regularity, and complexity in making perceptual judgments, although to different degrees (Kaiho & Toda, 1981). For example, when 200 students were asked to cross out specified symbols from sets of katakana and hiragana as quickly and as accurately as possible, simplicity and less curviness contributed to hiragana legibility,[5] while simplicity and the presence of a horizontal or parallel line (vs. the absence of a diagonal line) contributed to katakana legibility (Matsubara & Kobayashi, 1966). An excellent inventory of the various design features which are incorporated in kana symbols is to be found in Tamaoka and Hatsuzuka's (1997) detailed characterization of each item in the hiragana and katakana syllabaries, and is therefore reproduced below.

---

[5] Hayashi (1991) takes this to be a reason for introducing katakana to children before hiragana, claiming that the straight-line katakana offer learning advantages over the curvy hiragana shapes.

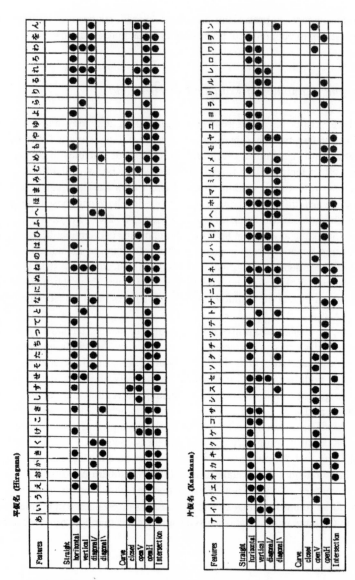

Table 4.2 Design attributes of kana syllabaries.
(Reprinted with permission from Tamaoka and Hatsuzuka, 1997)

Both syllabary types, however, offer examples in which graphic overlap contributes to a lack of discriminability in the kana symbol. This is true for katakana where one encounters pairs such as シ/ツ *shi/tsu* and ソ/ン *so/n*, and it is also true for hiragana pairs such as め/ぬ *me/nu* and ね/れ *ne/re*. Of the two syllabary types, katakana appears to pose a greater possibility of **perceptual overlap** than hiragana. Kaiho's (1968) multiple regression analysis charts the factors which affect katakana legibility, and shows that frequency of katakana symbols have no positive effect on katakana legibility under noise conditions.[6] But salient orthographic features such as horizontality, longitudinal directionality, and redundancy do have a positive effect on legibility. This is corroborated by work on the effect of different letter sizes on subjects charged with haptic recognition by touch. Accuracy increased as size increased (3.0 x 3.0, 5.5 x 5.5, and 8.0 x 8.0 mm.) for the alphabetic letters and katakana presented to subjects, but katakana recognition was typically worse than alphabetic (Tasaki, 1992; cf. Yokoyama & Yoneda, 1995).

Although we devote an entire chapter (Chapter 8) to **eye-movement** studies, it is worth noting here that some eye-movement studies show differences for katakana and kanji in terms of fixation periods and saccade distances, as well as differences between katakana and hiragana. Osaka (1989) compared hiragana-only texts, katakana-only texts, and kanji-based texts, to find that the katakana texts required the longest fixation periods and the shortest saccade distances covered by the eye movements. Kanji-based texts, on the other hand, required the shortest fixation periods and the longest saccade distances, with kanji acting like stepping stones to aid the reading process. Of course, the interpretation of these findings must take into account the issue of script familiarity on a textual scale. Kanji-based mixed texts are the norm, and hiragana-only texts are not common, although they are a primary vehicle in elementary school training. Katakana-only scripts are far less common in contemporary Japanese, but when they do occur, they apparently invoke more processing attention.

DIRECT ACCESS FOR KANA

Early views projected processing differences between kanji-reading and kana-reading, and questioned whether kana would take more or less time to read than kanji. The experimental results showed that kana took less time to read aloud than kanji did, but that, in a silent reading condition, kanji took less time to access their semantic referents, at least as measured by a sentence judgment task (Saito, 1981b). Kana reading

---

[6] Mathematical models of letter identification generally assume that letter identification involves the two processes of evoking a candidate set of letters and a decision process which reflects the probability of possible responses (Inui, 1983).

speed was said to slow down in proportion to moraic length as the number of kana increased, while the number of kanji did not affect reading speed for kanji in the same way (Saito, 1981b, 1982). Three experiments by Tada (1975) contrasted the effect of syllable length in kana and kanji word recognition, demonstrating that the number of syllables in kana words affected recognition times, but not for polysyllabic words which consisted of a single kanji. Recognition times were affected, however, by the number of syllables in kanji compound words which consisted of two kanji and were typically longer.

The early notion was that kana require phonemic intervention in order to access their semantic referents, but that kanji would directly access their semantic referents (see Saito, 1981a, 1981b). The meaning, or semantic representation, of a given kanji, therefore, was thought to be assessed directly from the visual form of its graphemic representation. But later kanji research suggested that some tasks might evoke the phonemic representation of the lexical unit involved, suggesting that both kanji and kana involve graphemic, phonemic, and semantic processes. The main difference in reading kanji and kana was at first postulated as involving differing processing routines, varying in the specific path of lexical access. Kana was said to invoke graphemic, phonemic, and then semantic processing, while kanji would invoke graphemic, semantic, and then phonemic processing (Saito, 1982; Saito, Inoue & Nomura, 1979). This early view about lexical access for Japanese words also seems to reflect the traditional belief that words written in kana necessarily rely on their **phonological values**, while words written in kanji would be accessed from the mental lexicon directly from their visual image. But it soon became obvious that visually familiar sequences of kana, particularly common katakana words, are often treated as chunks in reading, in a way that visually unfamiliar sequences are not. This implies that kanji are not the only forms that can be accessed directly from their orthographic image, and opened up new avenues of word recognition research.

Many experimental reports came to demonstrate that high frequency kana words allow **direct access** to their meaning, while low frequency kana words slow down access procedures, presumably because the latter require phonemic processing. The effects of script configuration on word recognition were particularly noticeable for words written in **katakana**, possibly because of their special visual status as 'one of a kind'.[7] For example, Besner and Hildebrandt (1987) found that visually and orthographically familiar words written in katakana were named faster than both non-words and visually

---

[7] Although this is generally truer for katakana words than for hiragana words, some katakana words are written in more than one way, depending on their pronunciation. For example, consider the differences between バイオリン *baiorin* and ヴァイオリン *vaiorin* for 'violin', クラスメイト *kurasu meito* and クラスメート *kurasu meeto* for 'classmate', and アイデアー *aideaa* and アイデイアー *aidiaa* for 'idea'.

unfamiliar words. Katakana words were presented in three conditions: visually familiar words usually written in katakana, visually unfamiliar words usually written in kanji but here presented in katakana, and non-words. When Japanese subjects read these stimulus words aloud as rapidly as possible, naming latencies revealed that orthographically familiar words were named faster than both unfamiliar words and non-words. This also shows up as an advantage in oral reading over those kana words that must resort to sound-spelling correspondence rules, and one infers that lexical access for some familiar words printed in katakana can be achieved without recourse to the preliminary steps involved in phonological recoding.

If some frequent katakana words allow direct access to their stored representations directly from their whole-word orthographic shape, even pronunciation features might be accessed through this "addressed" phonology route instead of the "assembled" phonology route requiring phonological analysis and recoding. Feldman and Turvey (1980) tested the availability of phonological information by comparing latency differences in naming kanji and kana words. Response latencies in naming color words that were written in kana were consistently faster than the words written in their familiar kanji counterparts. They hypothesized that naming words written in kana exploits both an orthographic strategy (based on letter-sound correspondences) and a word-specific strategy (based on visual shape), whereas naming words written in kanji only allows the latter because kanji have no phonological properties. They also postulate that kana shapes support greater facility in naming because the phonologically-based nature of kana supports greater facility in verbally naming the form.[8]

This finding was even more impressive, given the fact that color words are normally written in kanji and not kana. However, when one looks closely at the actual stimuli, the choices for the six color names presented to the two Japanese subjects almost predicts the conclusions. The six color names (黒, 緑, 茶色, 灰色, 朱色, 栗色 *kuro, midori, chairo, haiiro, shuiro, kuriiro* 'black, green, brown, gray, vermilion, chestnut') obviously vary in word frequency, as well as in the **frequency of script type**. An equally plausible explanation might be that such color names are presented in kana as commonly as in kanji, and that this is what accounts for the rapid naming response. But both inter-

---

[8] This superiority effect for kana over kanji has been reported elsewhere. Nomura (1981a) investigated potential differences in processing kanji and kana in three experiments which measured reading speeds for kanji, kana, and kanji which were accompanied by *furigana*. The results of all three experiments suggest that kanji is processed by a conceptually-driven (top-down) processing mechanism, whereas kana is processed by a data-driven (bottom-up) processing mechanism. In reviewing the results of five previously published experiments with kana and kanji script, Nomura (1981b) illustrates how they must be processed differently in respect to graphemic, phonemic, and semantic properties, and how both data-driven and conceptually-driven processing must then interact to achieve lexical access and recognition. But the fact remains that kana transcriptions of some common kanji words are named faster than their normal kanji counterparts in isolation, although the reading latency for kana embedded in sentences is slower.

pretations still mean that either path, access through phonological assembly or the familiar visual configuration, are possible in varying degrees for some kana forms in a way that emulates that for kanji forms.

Yamada (1992a) challenges Feldman and Turvey's finding that colors conventionally written in kanji are named slower than are unconventional kana transcriptions of the kanji color words, and offers an explanation as to why such kana words might be named faster than kanji words. Feldman and Turvey attributed this superiority of kana over kanji to the closer relationship of kana to phonology, consonant with the dual-route hypothesis which has kanji processing going directly to meaning and then to sound, while kana processing goes directly to sound and then to meaning. Yamada shows how selection difficulty will have an effect on whether unconventional kana words are always named faster than the corresponding conventional kanji words. His detailed results with numerals illustrates how kanji numerals are named faster than are corresponding kana numerals, and that the selection difficulty inherent in most kanji is what explains the apparently conflicting results between this study and previous findings. The resolution of these conflicting findings rests in the selection difficulty inherent in retrieving certain types of kanji readings from long-term memory because most kanji represent both free and bound morphemes, with bound morphemes appearing more frequently in familiar forms than as free morphemes. For example, numerals such as 三 *san* 'three' and 五 *go* 'five' are examples of such familiar kanji words. Such numerals are considered free morphemes, though they are commonly used as bound morphemes, as in 三人 *san-nin* 'three people'. Thus, a typical subject named such kanji numerals faster than the kana numeral, while common kanji nouns continued to be named slower than their kana counterparts. The response time data were also reflected in the introspective judgments made by the subjects, who confirmed that numerals were easier to name in kanji than kana, but that common nouns were easier to name in kana than kanji. While word type seems to be a factor, the real key may be that the more readings for a kanji, the more ambiguous the potential reading, and the slower the response time. Even common kanji nouns typically have more readings and thus more ambiguity than numerals do.

There is other evidence that low frequency katakana words require phonemic processing, while high frequency katakana words allow direct access to their meaning. Tanaka and Konishi (1990) presented high frequency katakana words (ホテル *hoteru* 'hotel'), high frequency kanji words (電気 *denki* 'electricity'), low frequency katakana words usually written in kanji (ジシン *jishin* 'earthquake'), and low frequency hiragana words usually written in katakana (てれび *terebi* 'TV') to adult subjects, who had to discern non-words from words, as well as sort the words into semantic categories. There was a clear **frequency effect** separating high and low frequency katakana words, with high frequency words processed faster than their low frequency counterparts.[9] There was also a word-length effect for low frequency words, so that the longer the word, the slower the processing time. Reaction times increased in proportion to word length for unfamiliar script words, but this increase was not found with the familiar script words.

Some indirect evidence for the **role of orthographic shape** comes from experiments testing for priming effects derived from the physical characteristics of katakana words. Harada (1987) physically inverted katakana words which were paired with their non-inverted counterparts in order to test the priming effects of the former on the latter. Regardless of task condition as perceptual or semantic, there was a clear priming effect from the inverted katakana words, suggesting that the holistic shape of the katakana word can also be a relevant factor in processing (see also Fujita, 1992).

But priming effects arise only when subjects can identify the items for processing. Kamiya, Tajika, and Takahashi (1994) failed to find priming effects when words which were subliminally presented could not be successfully read. When Tajika, Kamiya, and Takahashi (1993) contrasted the effects of subliminal perception on explicit memory tests (free recall and recognition) vs. implicit memory tests (for example, word fragment completion and perceptual identification), they again found that reading words can elicit a priming effect on implicit retention tasks as long as they are identified. They also note that good performance on memory tests arises when there is a match between mode of processing (for example, reading rather than generating words) and the type of retention test (for example, a word fragment test rather than a recall test), once again recalling for us the importance of the familiarity factor.

The number of loan words in Japanese has increased by exponential leaps and bounds in recent decades, and an official policy of adoption of foreign loan words through katakana spellings was promulgated in 1991 (Gottlieb, 1995). The trend toward internationalization and the constant interaction with Western culture in Japan has seen an enormous increase in the **loan word inventory** of the Japanese lexicon. A 1991 survey conducted by the Japan National Broadcasting Corporation (NHK) reports 90% of adults responding that loan words were used more than ever before (Ishino, 1992). Such subjective reports are corroborated by Nomura's (1984) comparison of 'new word' dictionaries published in 1960 and in 1980. Fully 58% of all new words added in the 1980 edition were loan words (in katakana); only 27.7% were kanji words of Chinese derivation, and 12.7% were words of Japanese origin (in hiragana). However, a comparison of three commonly-used Japanese dictionaries by the Agency for Cultural Affairs (1987) shows the average frequency of loan words in the regular dictionaries as 6.3%, as opposed to a 12% occurrence rate for newspapers and 9.8% for magazines. And

---

[9] They also report a visual field difference; the low frequency words showed the involvement of the right visual field, whereas the high frequency katakana words did not.

many of the loanwords listed in those three dictionaries are no longer in common use. Obviously, loan words written in katakana are increasingly frequent and cannot be considered a marginal or exotic element in the lexicon of Modern Standard Japanese.

A recent **katakana word frequency list** based on a newspaper corpus (Nozaki & Yokoyama, 1996; Yokoyama & Nozaki, 1996a, 1996b) charts the frequency curves for the katakana words that appear in modern Japanese journalism. A small number of high frequency words are used repeatedly, while a large number of katakana words are barely used. Yokoyama and Nozaki (1996a, 1996b) found that the cumulative frequency of the most frequent 375 words accounted for 50% of total katakana word use. Furthermore, the most frequent 1,000 and 3,000 words accounted for 65% and 80% of the total usage, respectively; the remaining 50,000 words covered only 20% of total katakana usage. Frequency considerations being as central as they are in word recognition, such details are a prerequisite to choosing stimulus materials for future experiments, as well as offering the necessary backdrop to interpreting the results of past experiments.

Much of the work on direct access has focussed on the typicality of katakana shapes, despite the fact that hiragana frequencies are far higher than katakana frequencies (see Hotta, 1984). The effects of **script type frequency** on word recognition are abundantly clear for words written in katakana, but the same must in principle be true for many words that are typically written in hiragana. This must be true for hiragana words of the grammatical type and is probably true for some of the content type. A distinction between content words and function words should be made, for it is unlikely that phonological recoding is needed in accessing all lexical items. Japanese, like English and other alphabetically-based orthographies, probably elicits whole-word access for the configurational shape of most, if not all, function words, but word recognition studies have typically focussed on lexical access for content words. All of the function words are normally presented in hiragana, and one suspects that direct access is the rule here as well.

There is some evidence for the role of **lexicality** in word recognition for hiragana words. Yamada (1992a) constructed hiragana non-words as a control measure in an experiment contrasting kanji vs. kana readings of common words, and found that orthographically unfamiliar hiragana words (やま *yama* 'mountain', うえ *ue* 'up') were named faster than orthographically unfamiliar hiragana non-words (やた *yata*, うと *uto*). This is a hiragana mirror image of Besner and Hildebrandt's (1987) findings of the same lexicality effect for katakana words vs. katakana non-words. Taken together, these findings for hiragana and katakana, respectively, confirm that lexicality plays a role in access, since words typically take less time to name than non-words in both kana scripts.

THE ISSUE OF SCRIPT FAMILIARITY FOR KANA

Hiragana and katakana formats do not constitute completely separate and distinct lexical representations, but they also do not constitute completely identical entries. The findings confirm the potential role of both scripts as orthographic renditions of words, and serve to rule out the notion of script exclusivity. At some level, the two scripts are seen as alternate paths to the same lexical address. But a common finding in the lexical access literature is that word familiarity, in addition to word frequency, is closely related to the ease of word perception. In fact, it may just be that word familiarity is a better facilitator of word recognition than word frequency, though the two do interact. In a language like Japanese where more than one script can be the orthographic 'carrier' of the word, the fact of which script commonly appears with a word cannot be ignored. In fact, a central issue embedded in the foregoing discussion has to do with the fact of script familiarity for the two kana types.

Script Variation

Although the hiragana and katakana syllabaries represent the same inventory of moraic shapes in Japanese, they overlap in actual usage in some interesting ways. The **choice of script** is not always consistent and may vary, depending on a writer's intention or even in-house publishing practices. For example, the word for 'eel' is pronounced /unagi/, but could be written as うなぎ in hiragana in one context, but as the katakana ウナギ in another context. There is also variation between the kana scripts and kanji: the word for 'egg' is pronounced /tamago/, but could be written as たまご in hiragana in one context, but as the kanji 卵 in another context; the same is true for the kanji 斡旋 *assen* and the hiragana あっせん *assen* 'mediation'. Some words allow variation between the kanji and the katakana representations: 癌 and ガン *gan* 'cancer'. And some allow variations between all three orthographic types: 風呂, ふろ, and フロ *furo* 'bath' (see Inoue, 1995, or Ukita, Sugishima, Minagawa, Inoue & Kashu, 1996, for an exact account of the types of variations and their relative frequencies).

These variations cannot be said to be extraordinary in their appearance; Inoue, Sugishima, Ukita, Minagawa, and Kashu (1994) report that variation is common even among high frequency words for which kanji is the typical representation. Basing themselves on an National Language Research Institute (1962) analysis of magazines, they found that 16.8% of the highest frequency 750 words showed variation in their representational manifestations. When Kashu (1995) examined the **subjective frequency** of script type for these 750 common words with Japanese college students, the results revealed that more than half of the words were identified as words which could be seen in more than one script. A newspaper analysis undertaken by the National Language Research Institute (1983; re-classified by Inoue, 1995) showed that in newspaper headlines alone, 14% of the words (4,916 out of 34,477 words) showed variations in their orthographic formats. This fluidity in orthographic practice not only leads to the expectation of script variation in printed Japanese text, but also implicitly encourages such fluidity in written production as well (see Kashu, 1994).

At the same time that it offers fluidity for some items, it also reinforces script type for other items. Ukita, Sugishima, Minagawa, Inoue, and Kashu (1996) found a positive correlation between high frequency content words in print and script type expectations that such words were most appropriate in kanji representations. Very simply, a high exposure rate for a common word is usually matched by a high subjective frequency that the word will appear in kanji format. But unusual words, with low familiarity and low exposure rates, usually showed variation in written forms. And this observation was also true across generations, with the consequence that low frequency words in printed outlets showed large generational differences in script variation. It should also be noted that, in addition to the topical treatments that newspapers focus on, there are also educational differences in kanji exposure which come into play here and which also underwrite such generational differences.

There are also modality considerations to familiarity ratings for Japanese words, such that script frequency expectations will also contribute to **modality dependency**. Amano, Kondo, and Kakehi (1995) had 11 subjects select the orthography (that is, hiragana, katakana, and kanji) they thought to be most familiar for 62,001 aurally presented words, and then had the subjects perform the same task with visually presented words. In addition to orthography appropriateness scores, they also measured familiarity ratings for Japanese words. Familiarity ratings for words (that is, 'know' vs. 'don't know') were more modality dependent than they were for similar examinations in English, with a correlation coefficient of .808 for Japanese vs. .930 for English between auditory and visual ratings. Essentially, this means that a substantial proportion of the Japanese mental lexicon is modality dependent. This modality dependency was especially true of low familiarity words, and seemed to be much larger for kanji words than for kana words. Thus, the difference in modality ratings between low-frequency and medium- to high-frequency items is related to orthography, in that kanji words may have multiple pronunciations and usually represent meaning whereas hiragana or katakana words have a single pronunciation and may not represent meaning as such.[10]

---

[10] A new *NTT Psycholinguistic Database* containing 80,000 words, with familiarity ratings by 32 subjects in three modalities (auditory, visual, and audio-visual) is scheduled for publication in 1999 (S. Amano, personal communication at the International Conference on the Mental Lexicon, September, 1998).

Script Type Frequency

There are processing implications attached to bi-scriptalism, and although we can say that the two symbolic systems are functionally equivalent, we cannot say that they are functionally equal. External factors such as script familiarity can exert an influence on lexical decision tasks. A common finding has been that fluent native readers of Japanese words can read familiar stimuli faster than unfamiliar stimuli. This means that words which are normally written in katakana are recognized faster in katakana than when they are written in hiragana. Conversely, this means that words that are normally written in hiragana are recognized faster in hiragana than when they are written in katakana. Reaction times will increase in proportion to word length for unfamiliar script words, that is, in inverse proportion to the frequency with which a given word is normally seen in either katakana or hiragana script. Conversely, this increase is not found with familiar script words. This is certainly a finding which is in keeping with experimental reports of word recognition results which show that the more familiar and frequent words are, the more quickly and the more accurately they are recognized. For example, Hirose (1984) examined the **effect of script type frequency** on lexical access by having subjects classify words into semantic types. Script type frequency was manipulated to form three groups: words written in kana though their regular script type is kanji (low-frequency kana words: ヤキユウ *yakyuu* 'baseball'); words written in kana just as they are usually represented (high-frequency kana words: ラグビー *ragubii* 'rugby'); and words written in kanji (kanji-words: 野球 *yakyuu* 'baseball'). The low-frequency kana words took longer to process than both the high-frequency kana words and the kanji words, but there was no difference between high-frequency kana words and kanji words in processing time.

Hatta and Hirose (1984) found response time differences between Japanese subjects and Australian subjects reading native Japanese words and foreign loan words which were directly related to experience with script type. The Japanese subjects employed both visual-orthographic strategies based on script type familiarity and phonological recoding strategies based on symbol-to-sound analysis; but the Australian subjects, because of their lack of experience with the script type correlations, were only able to use the phonological recoding strategy. Hirose (1985) also found evidence for both the script familiarity effect and the cross-script priming effect in a two-trial lexical decision task. Subjects were first asked to decide if words appearing on a screen were legitimate words or not. The katakana stimuli were of two types: Japanese words, whose normal orthographic representation is in hiragana, and loanwords, whose normal representation is in katakana. Not surprisingly, in the first trial the Japanese words written in katakana were processed slower and less accurately than the loanwords. A second trial differed from the first in that half of the stimuli were repeated from the first trial, and this time the Japanese words which were written in katakana were processed faster and more accurately than in the first trial, showing a clear **facilitation effect**. Reaction times for the foreign loan words written in katakana stayed at a steady state, and showed no such increase in facilitation. Hirose implies that exposure to the Japanese words in katakana in the previous trial served to establish some degree of familiarity for those words in kata-kana formats, and that this is what facilitates the increase in their reaction times.

Kawakami (1993) also examined the influence of script familiarity on lexical access procedures by contrasting familiar/unfamiliar words, three to five kana in length. The words were written in both their regular kana script and the kana script they are not usually written in. Subjects who judged whether these stimuli words were real words showed reaction times which increased in proportion to word length for unfamiliar script words, but not for familiar script words. A second experiment then had subjects make lexical decisions, but reading from right-to-left instead of in the usual left-to-right order. This unusual reading condition increased reaction times for both familiar/unfamiliar script words in direct proportion to word length. We may infer that visually familiar sequences of kana are treated as chunks in reading, in a way that visually unfamiliar sequences are not. But when this **visual chunking** is disrupted, as in reversals of the type used as stimuli in this experiment, the cueing benefits of the visually familiar shape are diminished.

Similarly, Sasanuma, Sakuma, and Tatsumi (1988) concluded that orthographically familiar kana words have a more **direct access** to the lexicon on the basis of the orthographic code, while orthographically unfamiliar words require recourse to pho-nological recoding. Their conclusion is based on reaction time differences in lexical access procedures for different types of kana strings. Orthographically familiar 'kana words' (words which are normally written in kana: いとこ *itoko* 'cousin') were con-trasted with non-words and 'words in kana' (words which are not normally written in kana, as for example, kanji transcribed into kana or katakana loan words transcribed into hiragana (れたす *retasu* 'lettuce')). Response times for orthographically familiar words were significantly faster than for non-words, as well as for orthographically unfamiliar words when those words were noun loan words, adverbs, and grammatical morphemes like *shikashi, donata, asoko* 'but, who, there'. When the orthographically unfamiliar words were native nouns, however, there was no significant difference between ortho-graphically familiar and unfamiliar words. Sasanuma et al. perspicaciously point out that this latter finding reflects the more than occasional fluctuation in orthographic renditions of the same content word, a topic we will address next. The use of katakana as a kind of orthographic italics is consistent with this latter finding for the so-called orthographically "unfamiliar" native words in the sample.

Addressed or Assembled Phonological Route?

Yamada, Imai, and Ikebe (1990) also contrasted the efficiency of the **addressed phonology route** with the **assembled phonology route** by testing for the effect of variables such as lexicality (words vs. non-words), kana type (hiragana vs. katakana), string length (long vs. short), and vocal interference (silence vs. concurrent vocalization). Their results confirm the influence of the first three variables, but most importantly for our discussion here, they show that the more conventional strings are, the more quickly they are recognized. And they also found that for familiar katakana words the pronunciation can be reached both by phonological recoding and directly addressing the visually-based orthographic lexicon. However, for unfamiliar words, only the assembled route which required phonological recoding was possible. Non-words were processed through the assembled phonological route, since there can be no conventional template for such words. Such findings confirm that lexicality (word status) and conventionality of kana strings contribute significantly to whether a word is taken in holistically by its visual shape or on a phonologically analytic basis. The frequency of a kana configuration, in terms of frequent word shapes, is obviously an important factor in word recognition. We must conclude that the type of orthography *per se* does not exclusively control processing time; familiarity with the frequency of the orthographical shape is a highly influential factor in lexical access.

But there were also **individual differences** in Yamada et al.'s study which must be taken into account, since individuals favor specific strategies. For example, their subjects divided into two groups, orthographic lexicon users and phonological assemblers, in respect to their use of sight vocabularies. Response times for the first group were the same for both long (アシスタント *ashisutanto* 'assistant') and short (アルミ *arumi* 'aluminum') katakana words, but they were slower for long hiragana strings (くりすます *kurisumasu* 'Christmas') than for short ones (らいす *raisu* 'rice'). The reason may be, of course, that longer hiragana words are not as common, thus negating the visual shape factor in word recognition. Shorter hiragana words are common, and this factor can have an influence. The second group showed slower response latencies for long words than for short words in either kana script type. Nevertheless, even this latter group of predominantly phonological assemblers also recognized some sight words according to their visual shape. These results point to individual strategies favoring the possible involvement of either direct access via the orthographic shape or access via the phonological assembly route, as well as the differential weighting of factors such as frequency, familiarity, and conventionality determining which one of the two routes will be taken.

This availability of both the assembled phonology and addressed phonology routes for fluent native users of the language may be what accounts for Komendzinska's (1995) findings. Her results suggested that Japanese readers have **one internal lexicon** for both kana scripts, while the foreign learners of Japanese turned out to be the ones with two separate lexicons for katakana and hiragana words. Her explanation for this unexpected finding (cf. Hatta, Katoh & Kirsner, 1984) is that there is not much difference between the speeds at which assembled phonology and addressed phonology routes arrive at the correct pronunciation when the automaticity and speed of reading these two shallow kana scripts is so undeveloped.

Script Type Effects

But familiarity cannot be just defined in binary terms, as familiarly seen in just one script or the other. Ukita, Sugishima, Minagawa, Inoue, and Kashu (1996) charted the subjective frequencies of the three script types to ascertain just what kinds of familiarity we are talking about. For 750 common words in 36 semantic categories, they established **ten classificatory types** to describe the degree of **interactive frequency** between the three script types. Those frequency types were as follows:

1. words written frequently in kanji but rarely in hiragana or katakana
2. words written frequently in hiragana but rarely in kanji or katakana
3. words written frequently in katakana but rarely in kanji or hiragana
4. words written frequently in kanji
5. words written frequently in hiragana
6. words written frequently in katakana
7. words written frequently in kanji and hiragana
8. words written frequently in kanji and katakana
9. words written frequently in hiragana and katakana
10. words written frequently in each script type

They also found that Japanese speakers are quite prepared to make subjective judgments of appropriateness as regards typicality of script type for everyday words. Japanese readers have a keen sense of the subjective frequency of script types for written forms in Japanese, and will easily make an evaluation of the script type that is, in their opinion, frequently seen for a given word. For example, when Ukita, Minagawa, Sugishima, and Kashu (1991) had subjects judge the subjective frequencies of the three script types for 119 extremely common words (for example, *megane* 'glasses' and *hako* 'box'), their evaluations were confirmed by subjects in a second experiment who also judged the appropriateness of the scrip type for each of the words again. Such experiments demonstrate consistency in subjects' judgments, as almost half of these words were deemed to be best as kanji (see also Ukita, Sugishima, Minagawa & Kashu, 1993, and Inoue, Ukita, Minagawa, Sugishima & Kashu, 1995).[11]

Ukita et al. (1996) also found **generational differences** between college students and middle-aged subjects. If anything, younger students are more likely to evaluate hiragana as the high frequency script type for many words, except for the high frequency kanji words. It seems that younger age groups exhibit a greater subjective variety of script types than older age groups, with the boundary between kanji and hiragana not as sharply defined in absolute terms.

The subjective evaluation of script type has also been measured by the Semantic Differential (SD) technique. Common words (for example, *isu* 'chair' and *tokei* 'watch') were presented in kanji, hiragana, and katakana to undergraduate subjects, who evaluated them on a seven-point SD scale. **Script effects** were obvious, with the angular scripts inherent in kanji and katakana factoring out separately from the more cursive hiragana. This finding may be due to the historical derivation of katakana directly from kanji, with hiragana coming through a slightly different path of origin (see Sugishima & Kashu, 1992).

Repetition priming experiments consistently show that words written in katakana or hiragana substantially facilitate the second presentation of a word when it appears in the same orthography. But this repetition priming effect is also found when the second presentation of the word is in the other kana syllabary. Although lexical representations in Japanese are not script-specific and tied to only one kana script, they are not perfectly equivalent either, for there is a difference in the strength of the repetition priming effect across syllabary types. For example, Hatta and Ogawa (1983) found the priming effect to be half as strong as same-script priming when they primed across script types for their non-word kana strings.

The degree to which the same lexical address is accessed by the two kana syllabaries has also been probed by repetition priming with kana in word-fragment completion. Komatsu and Naito's (1992) three experimental tests manipulated katakana and hiragana

---

[11] An interesting twist on the notion of script type preferences is reported by Yokoyama and Sasahara (1998a, 1998b). They matched revised and traditional forms of kanji from the JIS character set to see which form was preferred and the subjective reasons why this might be so. Consider, for example, the simplified version of *hinoki* 'cypress' as 桧 or its traditional, more complex version as 檜. A 1997 survey of women college students revealed a surprising preference for many older versions as more aesthetic, more distinctive, and more elegant when seen in print. While there was a general tendency to prefer the revised form to the traditional form, there was a distinct preference for traditional forms when neither revised nor traditional form was in the *Jooyoo Kanji* list, when the traditional form was frequent, and when there was a noticeable difference in their shapes. For example, the traditional form of 籠 *kago* 'basket' was preferred 81% to 19% over the revised form 篭. One does wonder, however, whether the same preferences would emerge if the subjects were also pressed to reproduce the same kanji in handwriting, as in the days before word processing packages made it all so much simpler.

to determine the effects of a script change between study and test on later word-fragment completion with stimuli that consisted of foreign loan nouns normally written in katakana. The results revealed reliable cross-script priming between katakana and hiragana. Subjects who studied a list of foreign loan words in either katakana or hiragana were easily able to then perform a word-fragment completion test in which the word fragments were presented in either katakana or hiragana. Not surprisingly, matched script completions were enhanced by previous study, but so also were completions when the scripts differed between the study and completion test conditions. It was found that the katakana fragments ((ボ)クシン(グ) *bokushingu* 'boxing') were completed more easily than hiragana fragments ((ぼ)く しん(ぐ) *bokushingu* 'boxing'), but given that the test materials were derived from foreign loan words, the issue of script familiarity probably accounts for this advantage. It is obviously not the case that the target loan words were imaged in katakana only, since there was significant cross-script priming from one kana script to the other.

Komatsu and Naito also found substantial cross-modal priming when the presentation modality was changed from auditory to visual. In this experiment, subjects heard a list of foreign loan words and then performed a word fragment completion test in either katakana or hiragana. Despite the fact that the target words were loan words normally written in katakana, subjects had no difficulty performing word completion in hiragana or katakana. The size of the cross-modal priming was almost the same for the hiragana condition as it was for the katakana condition, ruling out **script exclusivity** again. A variation on this theme then tested subjects for native Japanese words which would be written normally in hiragana, and found no significant difference between katakana and hiragana completions of native Japanese words.[12]

When Hatta, Hatae, and Kirsner (1984) tested for interference effects in letter recognition by presenting hiragana test letters to foveal vision and irrelevant orthographic stimuli (English letters, pictures, hiragana, and katakana) to parafoveal vision, they found no support for the hypothesis that the systems are mutually antagonistic. But they find support for the familiarity effect, such that the magnitude of interference arising from the presence of the irrelevant parafoveal stimuli reflected the strength of the system from which the secondary stimuli came. What this means is that the greatest interference effect arose when foveal and parafoveal stimuli were both hiragana; and there was also a weaker, but significant **interference effect** when the foveal and parafoveal stimuli were hiragana and katakana, respectively.

---

[12] Brown, Sharma, and Kirsner (1984) report similar cross-over for bilinguals recalling words written in the closely related languages Hindi and Urdu. Despite the fact that Hindi is written from left-to-right in the Sanskrit-derived Devanagari script, and Urdu right-to-left in an Arabic-derived script, their bilingual subjects showed nearly complete transfer effects in performance and comparatively poor memory for which script the phonologically identical words had been presented in.

But ruling out script exclusivity does not rule out script familiarity. If anything, same-script presentation does seem to enhance certain tasks. Words written in their common written form are generally easier to grasp than when words are presented in an unusual written form. For example, in solving anagrams, hiragana targets are best solved when the anagrams are presented in hiragana strings; the same is true for katakana targets derived from katakana anagrams (see Ukita et al., 1996). Naito and Komatsu (1988) manipulated four possible combinations of kana and kanji script types, and found that priming effects were greater when the script type was held constant. Script type does seem to function as a **memory attribute**, as Kamiya (1985) found when he unexpectedly gave an orthographic recognition test to subjects to check their recall for whether words presented sometime earlier had been given in kanji or kana. Scores were far higher than chance, and when another group of subjects were tested for recall of the words them-selves, results were best when the presentation phase and the recall phase were in the same script type. There is also considerable evidence of domain specificity from aphasic studies, in that kanji words are best read aloud when they are presented in kanji formats; the same is true for hiragana words when presented in hiragana formats (see Ukita et al., 1996). In general, these findings generally point to the fact that script familiarity exerts considerable influence on many tasks, and that storage of the word as word seems to include script type as one of the key informational features when processing the word as a unit in such tasks.

There are also **stylistic consequences** to script variation, and in this arena, the three symbol systems are not functionally equivalent. They convey different nuances and invoke different connotations, each script type painting a unique tapestry of emotive imagery or synesthesia. At the very least, their availability allows the author to play with the endless variation that having more than one script allows. For example, the same children's song titled entirely in kanji 赤蜻蛉 'dragonfly' will present the word differently at various points : it is the hiragana あかとんぼ akatombo in the first verse and a mixed kanji-hiragana 赤とんぼ akatombo in the final line (Kindaichi, 1988, cited in Inoue, 1995).

Kanji seems to offer a more scientific tone, whereas the use of hiragana offers a softer, more emotional feeling (see Inoue, 1995). This arises in part from the fact that certain categories are more commonly thought of as seen in kanji; for example, envi-ronmental words are thought to be more appropriate for kanji representation, while animal names are thought to be more appropriate in katakana (see Ukita et al., 1996). Other categories are considered more appropriate in hiragana; for example, seasonal words in haiku (and in fact, the whole network of emotive words) were measured by the Semantic Differential as presenting a 'good, soft' image when presented in hiragana formats. Very simply, connotative meanings, imagery, and synesthesia can all be correlated to the subjective frequency of the written forms (see Ukita et al., 1996). It is obvious that the study of variation in script types is as much a literary study as it is a scientific study. The study of script variation should be analyzed not only from the passive point of view the reader takes, but also from the active perspective the writer employs when producing a piece of written Japanese. The writer may consciously choose to place a specific word in a particular script type for the 'feeling' it invokes.

Memory and Recall

There has been considerable interest in the interrelationship between language and memory in Japanese psycholinguistics (see, for example, Ito, 1995; Ukita & Kashu, 1996; Yokoyama, 1995), and within this context the effect of script frequency on the recall of kana and kanji words has also specifically been examined. For example, Sugishima, Ukita, Minagawa, and Kashu (1993) manipulated script representations to create stimuli words for both reading aloud and incidental recall tasks for undergraduate subjects. The stimuli words were words which were regularly written in kana (kana-type: あご *ago* 'chin'), words which were regularly written in kanji (kanji-type: 青 *ao* 'blue'), and words which were regularly written either way (kana/kanji type: あさがお/朝顔 *asagao* 'morning glory'). In the reading aloud task, the kanji- and kana/kanji-type words which were represented in kanji was as fast as the same types of words represented in kana, confirming that the kana (that is, phonological) mode of representation does not necessarily enhance reading speed. And in the recall task, recall for kana-type words which were represented in kana were as good as those represented in kanji, indicating that the kanji (i.e., the so-called semantic) mode of representation does not necessarily enhance recall speed. Obviously, **script familiarity** plays a significant role in not only lexical access, but also in repeated lexical access under recall conditions, underscoring the fact that the mental lexicon is not controlled by a simple dichotomy between kana and kanji.

In fact, orthographic information about script type is recorded during input, as Kamiya (1985) reports for incidental learning. Subjects who had to perform a semantic or structural orienting task recalled whether the target words they had manipulated were kanji or hiragana at a level significantly better than chance when long-term memory was probed. And when such orthographic information was manipulated in another experiment, recognition performance and reaction times were also facilitated by the detection of orthographic familiarity.

Psycholinguistic experiments which examine the difference in memory and recall between kanji and kana words have also found some differences for low-imagery and high-imagery words, with kanji items more likely to be tagged for this informational feature (see Yokoyama, 1991b). For example, when subjects are unexpectedly asked to recall kana and kanji words, already ranked in terms of high vs. low imagery, **imagery** has a greater impact on the recall of kanji words (Yokoyama, 1995), particularly for the recall of low-imagery items (Yokoyama & Imai, 1989; Yokoyama, Imai & Furukawa, 1991). Free recall was tested in the incidental memory paradigm, and the number of correct items which emerge in the unexpected memory test is greater for the kanji low imagery items than for the kana items. But when a semantic orienting task is added, there are no differences in the rate of recall between kana and kanji words in respect to high vs. low imagery (Yokoyama & Imai, 1989). Yokoyama, Imai, and Furukawa (1991) also used the incidental memory paradigm, and had college students read aloud high- and low-imagery kana and kanji words, two to four morae in length. The college students were then tested in an immediate recall test, and the results of this immediate recall test showed a difference in recall peformance, with low-imagery kanji recalled much better than the low-imagery kana items. High-imagery words in kana and kanji did not show much of a difference along script type lines. Within script categories, the low-imagery kanji were recalled better than the high-imagery kanji items, and there was better recall for high imagery kana words than for the low imagery kana words. They then gave the same stimuli to another group, with a delayed recall interval of 30 seconds. Although both experiments required subjects to read each stimulus word aloud in order to direct their attention to the sounds of the words, the second group had to free-recall the stimuli after performing simple mathematical problems for 30 seconds. The delayed recall test now found better recall for high-imagery kanji items than for their kana counterparts. In general, there do seem to be different coding processes for kanji and kana words, insofar as recall procedures are organized, with kanji being more commonly marked by such features as imagery.[13]

The effect of imagery and orthographic familiarity on the recall of loanwords has also been examined. Yokoyama (1991a) had undergraduates read aloud loanwords, which had been classified into high vs. low imagery words. Stimuli words were written both in katakana (the typical orthographic form for loanwords) and hiragana (the atypical way of representing such loanwords). In one experiment, using the incidental learning paradigm, the subjects read aloud stimulus words, and then were unexpectedly asked to recall as many words as possible in a 60-second period. Here the high imagery words were better recalled than low imagery words, but there was no significant orthographic effect. A second experiment had another group of undergraduates perform the same task, but had them engage in a mathematical task for 30 seconds before recalling the words.

---

[13] Park and Arbuckle (1977) found interesting results for Korean subjects when words were presented in kanji or hangul. Words in kanji were remembered better than words presented in hangul on both recognition and free recall tests. And concrete words were generally recalled better than abstract words. One confounding factor in the Korean results, however, may have been the increasingly unique status that kanji characters have for younger generations not drilled in them as explicitly as they once were in Korea.

The result was that high vs. low imagery had no effect on recall, but there was now a significant orthographic effect. The orthographically unfamiliar hiragana words were now recalled better than orthographically familiar katakana words, perhaps because of the original cognitive effort required to read the orthographically unfamiliar words; this effort and the special treatment they were given seemed to act as a memory aid in their subsequent recall.

CONCLUSIONS

In general, then, hiragana and katakana syllabaries share a great deal as script types. But they also differ in the way in which they are tied to the words which they represent, and not in the simple way they have been traditionally viewed as carriers of native vs. borrowed words. They show differential frequencies with individual words, and this issue of script familiarity has its own consequences in processing and even production terms. In the larger view, of course, the simple view that kanji are processed directly as 'sight words' and kana are processed through phonological recoding is simply not the case either. If anything, both logographic and syllabary scripts give evidence of both types of informational features being accessed, depending upon the task, the frequency and familiarity of the individual word, and the linguistic context. One has a greater appreciation of the cognitive complexities of orthography which the human mind is capable of handling in achieving literacy in this language.

Chapter 5

ROMAJI PROCESSING

ROMAJI

Japanese has a **fourth script** which is not formally recognized as part of the traditional orthographic system. But it is omnipresent, and used in a number of interesting ways to complement the appearance of kana and kanji in printed text. This script is called *romaji* (ローマ字), because the Japanese use 22 of the 26 letters of the Roman, or Latin, alphabet. In addition, Arabic numerals have also appeared to take the place of kanji numerals in most horizontal *yokogaki* writing; but vertical writing, or *tategaki*, remains largely committed to kanji numerals.

Not a great deal has been done with this alphabetic script in a psycholinguistic sense. Discussions of literacy and word recognition in Japanese research are usually limited to the three scripts we have just reviewed. But the romaji script has made such inroads into popular Japanese printed media that it must at least be noted as a separate system within the totality of the Japanese orthographic inventory.

There was some post-war discussion about **romanization** of the current orthography, with romaji support groups encouraged by the general thrust of the American Occupation Forces and the US Education Mission. But any such possibility was destroyed by the governmental decision to maintain the practice of kanji-kana mixing in the orthographic presentation of printed text. And the appearance of Japanese word processors in the 1980 cemented this decision in position by making access to kanji easier than it had been. At the same time, this development established romaji in a crucial support role in many electronic devices (see Gottlieb, 1995). Romaji has become the vehicle by which computer keyboards often access the other three Japanese scripts in word processing and dictionary software packages. Kana entry is a competing system, with keys representing the kana inventory instead of the alphabetic inventory. The **romaji keyboard** typically copies the traditional QWERTY sequence, although one would expect the kana keyboard to take advantage of the frequency counts for spoken syllables, and therefore, for kana symbols in the language (see Ishii, 1991). One also finds systems that have both romaji and hiragana merged on the same keys, and either way, familiarity with romaji is facilitated, as a more efficient system replaces the traditional 'hunt-and-peck' method of sorting through the 3,000 base characters in Japanese typewriting and typesetting. Romaji has become the key to unlock the ergonomic puzzle to entering input simply and conveniently, and the task of kanji retrieval has been efficiently re-organized (see Yamada, 1983). For example, for homonyms a list of the relevant kanji flashes on the screen once the romaji equivalent has been entered. The list is usually ordered according to frequency statistics, discourse genre, and/or likelihood, and users then make a choice from among the array. The net result of these orthographic search procedures is that this generation of electronically savvy students is at home with romaji in a way that previous generations were not.

Romaji Usage

But owning a word processor is not the entire explanation, however, since Imai (1987) reports a survey with 9,000 kindergartners that revealed roughly 10% of them could read most of the English alphabet. The ubiquity of romaji in the modern world must account for this surprising finding. For example, romaji is common in road signage, railway station designations, and exterior placards for companies, stores, and eating places of all kinds. It flourishes in **media advertising**, perhaps because its distinctive character in a field of kana and kanji make it 'stick out', thereby giving prominence to that which it denotes. It is noteworthy in the increased number of periodicals, magazines, and newspapers that employ romaji either exclusively for their names or in conjunction with kanji and/or kana that announce that title once more. It also has become increasingly common to represent lexical items that denote a commonly understood semantic range; for example, consider *OB* 'old boys', as in 'old boys' network' and *OL* 'office ladies or office girls'. Many company names are abbreviated romaji acronyms of the original Japanese, as in KDD = *Kokusai Denshin Denwa* 'International Telegraph and Telephone', and compete with romaji acronyms derived from English company names, as in NTT = *Nippon Telephone and Telegraph.*

Romaji has also become indispensable for designating certain commercial layouts, sizes, or conventions. Consider the standard format for real estate ads exemplified by *3DK*, meaning '3 rooms, plus Dining room and Kitchen', or the L, M, S sizing for *T-shatsu* 'T-shirts' or *V-nekku suetaa* 'V-neck sweaters'.

According to Saint-Jacques (1987), the **increase in romaji** is exponential, and the cumulative effect of such usage is that it is no longer regarded as an alien form of writing, exotic and incomprehensible to the average Japanese. Words from English, French, German, and other languages that only a few years ago were written in katakana are now often imported and written in the original Roman alphabet in genres like advertising, as seen in the following advertisement for Tokyu Hands.

Figure 5.1 A sample use of the Roman alphabet in advertising.
(Reprinted from *Asahi Shimbun*, Tokyo morning edition, March 26, 1999)

Even some Japanese words and proper names have begun to appear in romaji, occasionally in the middle of a normal Japanese sentence. Aside from the advertising panache attached to foreign imports, the reason is simple. A romaji word will stand out from the rest of the script presentation, simply because it is so different, and thus it invites processing attention. As a result, it has even seen recent use in word play and naming in areas that want to make a statement or at least stand out as different, innovative, or just plain cute. Consider, for example, the name of the pop music group who are Japan's most popular contribution to the alternative music paradigm, written as シヤ乱Q *sharankyuu* 'Sharan-Q'. The *Q* here plays on the homophonic effect in the two orthographies as /kyuu/, and allows one to create a name which is not entirely Japanese, but yet is essentially Japanese.

L1 Script Transfer Effect

Romaji is not a pedagogical subject in the same way that the kana syllabaries are, although the romaji chart is introduced as early as Grade 4 textbooks. Some educators see its introduction as a **disadvantage** in English language studies, arguing that romaji hinders rather than facilitates the acquisition of English vocabulary because the gap between English source words (*table, computer*) and Japanese borrowed renditions (*teeburu, kompyuutaa*) is simply too large to be anything but confusing. There is, however, experimental evidence to show that knowledge of romaji is linked to the ability to read English words (see Yamada, Matsuura & Yanase, 1988). And the use of romaji in learning Japanese is certainly a benefit for foreign learners of the language whose native language employs an alphabetic script. Tamaoka and Menzel (1994) found that **students of Japanese** whose native languages employed a Latin alphabet transposed these skills effectively when presented with word-naming, lexical judgment, and text reading tasks. These subjects expedited such tasks twice as fast with romaji-presented words than with kana-presented words. In contrast to these English-, French-, and German-speaking subjects, Chinese and Japanese subjects showed the reverse, with kana-presented words and text processed more efficiently. More recently, Tamaoka (n.d.) further reports that text-reading is faster for English-speaking students when the texts are presented in romaji instead of the kana/kanji mixed texts. Comprehension was the same for English students, regardless of script type, and this was also true for those students of Chinese background (who obviously have adduced their *pinyin* skills). There were three times fewer errors in word pronunciation, and they were evaluated by Japanese judges as sounding more Japanese on a seven-point SD scale. In sum, there was no negative interference from the romaji presentation, and in fact, a **facilitating effect** was the case for both comprehension (text reading) and production (pronunciation). Obviously, there is a practice element here which cannot be overlooked for those wishing to more efficiently master Japanese script. Unfortunately, the use of romaji in teaching Japanese to foreign learners has often been criticized in Japanese pedagogical circles, despite the fact that there are definite benefits to be derived from taking advantage of script practices that have been internalized.

We also know that there are such L1 script effects which facilitate kanji recognition. Mori (1998) has shown that there is **transfer** of learners' L1 orthographic processing strategies to L2 kanji processing in Japanese. For example, for English-language L1 students, providing phonologically accessible characters, such as characters whose inner radical was a pronounceable katakana character, made such pseudo-characters easier to recall from memory than those which did not have this feature. If such supportive features arise in the area of kanji recognition in Japanese, one expects that analogous features can be adduced in other areas of learning that involve the Japanese mental lexicon and its orthographic representations.

Transliteration Systems

But the alphabetic habits ingrained by traditional script practices also raises the question of which **transliteration system** forms the basis of the romaji choices being made, for there is not universal agreement on which romaji system is to be employed. One of the most common systems in use is the Hepburn System, a system of transcription proposed as early as 1885 by the Romaji Association, and adopted by James Curtis Hepburn in the third edition of his Japanese-English Dictionary (Unger, 1987). Given the fact that it is perfectly tailored to English orthographical practices, it is often favored by English speakers. And this fact may have led to the generalized basis of many romaji applications by the Japanese themselves in the post-war press, advertising, signage, and so forth.

There are two other transliteration systems, differing slightly between one another, the *Nipponshiki* (日本式) 'Japanese style' actually pre-dating the *Kunreishiki* (訓令式) 'Cabinet style'. The latter is the more common, given that it was formalized as the Japanese standard by Cabinet Order in 1937 and again in 1954. Although this system has many advantages, not the least of which is its more precise representation of underlying phonemic and morphophonemic relationships, we have chosen to employ a modified Hepburn System because of its familiarity to English speakers. For those more familiar with the other two systems, the Hepburn Romaji system of transcription differs from the *Kunreishiki* and *Nihonshiki* romanization systems in the following crucial ways.

Hepburn	Kunreishiki	Nihonshiki
shi	si	si
sha	sya	sya
shu	syu	syu
sho	syo	syo
ji	zi	zi
ja	zya	zya
ju	zyu	zyu
jo	zyo	zyo
chi	ti	ti
cha	tya	tya
chu	tyu	tyu
cho	tyo	tyo
ji	zi	di
ja	zya	dya
ju	zyu	dyu
jo	zyo	dyo
tsu	tu	tu
zu	zu	du
fu	hu	hu
o	o	wo

Table 5.1 Transcription differences among Hepburn,
Kunreishiki, and *Nihonshiki* romanization systems.

Ever mindful of one of the themes in Japanese psycholinguistic research on the
mental lexicon, namely, the role of script types in word recognition, we have chosen to
employ an adapted Hepburn System because this basic consideration allows parallels to
the language (English) employed in this book.

Chapter 6

KANJI-KANA MIXED TEXTS

KANJI-KANA MAJIRI-BUN

The basic fact of everyday printed Japanese is that phonetic and non-phonetic script are intermingled in ordinary text to be read. Like Chinese, Japanese was traditionally written top-down in vertical columns which traveled right to left across the page. Although this style of *tategaki* is still common is newspapers, books, and magazines, it is also increasingly common to find Japanese script running left to right, in horizontal lines which progress down the page. A common example of this left-to-right *yokogaki* style is to be found in scientific articles, as for example, the source psychology journals of the type cited in this book. In both styles, Japanese is typically written in the *kanji-kana majiribun* 'kanji-kana mixed sentence' style, and all three scripts can appear in the same sentence in ordinary written Japanese. The more typical case, however, is that kanji and hiragana usually are the two script types that present the bulk of most Japanese prose. Examples of both orthographic scenarios appear below, a sentence containing all three script types and a sentence containing the more usual pairing of kanji and hiragana.

漢字仮名プロセシングの問題は、サイコロジーのいちフィールドとして多くのリサーチャーの関心をあつめている.
漢字仮名処理の問題は、心理学の一分野として多くの研究者の関心をあつめている.
'As a branch of psychology, kanji and kana processing attracts the interest of many researchers.'

Because Japanese is written in mixed script style,[1] this means that psycholinguistic research on Japanese lexical access interacts not only with fundamental principles of orthographic processing at the word level, but also with **higher-level 'top-down' processes** which have an impact on phrasal and sentence level decisions. A very good example of this is found in Shimomura and Yokosawa's (1995) failure to find any differences in the detection of certain **'mis-spelled' kanji** which had some small component of the total kanji configuration wrong. When 'mis-spelled' kanji, such as those shown below, appeared in isolation as individual kanji forms, their detection was relatively quick.

Mis-spelled Kanji	Correctly Spelled Kanji		
徴熱	微熱	*binetsu*	'slight fever'
残署	残暑	*zansho*	'lingering summer heat'
桃戦	挑戦	*choosen*	'attempt'
会議窒	会議室	*kaigishitsu*	'meeting room'
後維者	後継者	*kookeisha*	'successor'

But when these 'mis-spelled' kanji were constituents in compounds and presented as whole words or presented together with postpositions as a phrase (for example, 桃戦が *toosen-ga*(-nominative)), their recognition and detection was not as likely as when they appeared as individual kanji forms. These results suggest that the phrase level and sentence level decisions are important, and that lexical access and word recognition procedures may be influenced by processing goals at these higher levels (see also Watanabe, 1993).

Thus, one must be careful to discriminate between those models of word recognition and the mental lexicon which pose explanations through autonomous (modular) vs. interactive models. Such explanations differ crucially in their treatment of contextual effects on lexical access; the **autonomous model** denies contextual effects, whereas the **interactive model** depends upon them. We know from previous work on lexical ambiguity that resolution is tied to later processing stages, and that at a very early stage of processing, for homophonic words at least, multiple readings unaffected by context are considered. This initial stage is then replaced by the selective reading which fits the contextual restrictions (see Kess, 1992; Kess & Hoppe, 1981; Kess & Nishimitsu, 1990).

---

[1] In fact, some word compounds can be combinations of mixed script juxtaposition within the same word. Many compound words are formed by combining katakana and kanji words, as in テスト-会場 *tesuto-kaijoo* 'test place'. Other compound words are formed by combining kanji and katakana fragments, as in 朝-シャン *asa-shan* 'morning shampoo', 板-チョコ *ita-choko* 'chocolate bar', and 滿-タン *man-tan* 'full tank'.

Ultimately, natural language processing will have to be explained by a model which accepts that processing strategies for information in lexical access can be variously autonomous or interactive, but for now we concentrate instead on assessing what we do know of mixed texts in Japanese (see Yi, 1987).

Kana-only vs. Kanji-mixed Texts

Because printed Japanese typically intersperses kanji and kana in printed sentences, **reading times** are faster for the kana/kanji-mixed sentences as normally integrated syllabary-logograph texts, than they are for the kana-alone type (Kitao, 1960; Sakamoto & Makita, 1973). Mixed texts are also processed faster than the hiragana-only texts, as Kitao (1960) demonstrated when he had subjects fill blanks with appropriate words in a cloze test. Mixed texts facilitated more accurate responses than hiragana-only texts, were easier to read than hiragana-only texts, and seemed to facilitate the extraction of meaning from the text as well. Nomura (1981a) found that the reading latency for kana script targets embedded in sentences is slower than that of kanji. But subjects can accommodate to hiragana-only texts, given the practice effect derived from several repetitions; Kitao (1960) further reports that differences in reading times grew smaller as the number of trials grew larger. The number of compound kanji in mixed texts can also exert an influence, despite the fact that specific content words, like technical or scientific terms, tend to be learned as kanji at their first appearance in school. Although these words are commonly written in kanji at all stages in the education system, texts such as nursery tales are still read faster than scientific essays.

There are also differences between kana-only and mixed texts in how the concurrent **vocal interference effect** plays out in reading comprehension. Recall that concurrent vocal interference involves subjects repeating irrelevant material aloud while reading or making judgments (see Chapter 3). It is thought to disrupt the auditory/articulatory channels because it interferes with the phonological code but leaves the visual code unaffected. Hayashi and Hayashi (1991) therefore measured reading comprehension for kana and mixed kana/kanji sentences in the presence of concurrent vocal interference. Script types for sentences were either mixed kana-kanji or kana alone in eight stories whose contents were either scientific essays or nursery tales. Mean reading times were computed for each condition and taken as an estimate of the relative difficulty of reading a given sentence under the various conditions. Reading times were significantly faster in the kana-kanji mixed text than in the kana-alone text, but surprisingly, concurrent vocal activity did not affect reading times in either of the script conditions. Intra-sentential comprehension was found to be worse for the scientific essays than the nursery tales, and inter-sentential comprehension of the scientific essays was especially affected by the concurrent vocalization task when written in the kana-only script type. One explanation, of course, is that general or basic content words, such as those in the nursery tales, may have been experienced in both the kana and kanji scripts, while specific content words tend to be learned as kanji at their first appearance, and it is more natural for these words to continue to be written in kanji.

Another explanation, however, must reflect the fact that kana-only texts do not have the same familiarity as mixed kana/kanji texts. Entire texts written in katakana are very rare indeed, and Japanese readers do not usually see hiragana-only texts that much after they leave the elementary grades. Even so, when hiragana-only texts are encountered, they pose kana-specific processing problems because of the lack of **word boundaries** between lexical items. For example, consider the following identical texts. In the first two sentences, the hiragana and katakana words show no discernible boundaries when there is no kanji, except those syntactic boundaries hinted at by the presence of case-marking particles. In the third sentence, the presence of the kanji words offers useful breaks in the kana stream.

おなじことばをあらわすかんじでもそのもじのかたちによってかんじがかわる.
オナジコトバヲアラワスカンジデモソノモジノカタチニヨッテカンジガカワル.
同じ言葉を表わす漢字でもその文字の形によって感じが変わる.
'Even with the same kanji characters, depending on their calligraphy types, their impressionistic 'feeling' differs.'

Because Japanese is typically written as the kana/kanji mixed sentence style, computational processing requires conversion of sentence-length input utterances into appropriate kana/kanji-mixed output in the final text product. This requires natural language parsing algorithms far more sophisticated than the currently available parsing techniques which employ dictionary look-up strategies to come up with a probable output. The available algorithms for automatic conversion of *betagaki-nyuuryoku* (べた書入力) 'pure phonemic input' are superior to manual conversion, but are still plagued by problems of inaccuracy and restricted input length. The challenge is to create an optimally automatic conversion which is reliably accurate to at least the sentence level in utterances, one which is capable of detecting inaccuracies and distortions in the natural language input, and yet flexible enough to insert the typical kana-to-kanji ratio in the written output. In sum, the creation of an **effective conversion system** is one of the pressing engineering problems for Japanese orthography in the immediate future. And this is a task which is particularly dependent upon psycholinguistic research in lexical access and word recognition, and the way in which relevant informational features are deployed in kana/kanji selection strategies when retrieving items from the mental lexicon. If ever there was a case for the research relevance of psycholinguistic studies of the mental lexicon in the computer age, this must be just such a case.

NON-LINGUISTIC SYMBOLS

A number of studies have tried to compare processing strategies for linguistic symbols as opposed to non-linguistic symbols, and typically report that linguistic symbols differ from the non-linguistic symbols in the way they are processed. For example, we know that words can be named more quickly than **pictures** in both Japanese and English, but that pictures can be categorized more quickly than words (see Flaherty, 1993b, 1994; Potter & Faulconer, 1975). In Japanese, this is true for words written in either kana or kanji. The suggestion that kanji occupies an intermediate position between pictures and phonetically-based scripts is simply not supported. Based on the results from Japanese subjects who read and categorized words and photographs, Flaherty (1993b) has demonstrated that kanji words are not read in a more "pictorial" fashion than kana or even English words. Moreover, linguistic displays, be they kanji or kana words, also differ in being less sensitive to sequential and configurational ordering. Figural representations are sensitive to **ordering** considerations in a way that verbal representations are not (Eko & Nakamizo, 1989). For example, when subjects have to verify if a comparison array contains the same elements as the original stimulus array they viewed, spatial considerations in respect to the way the array is configured has a significant effect on response times for figural stimuli, but not so for verbal stimuli. Verbal representations are much more constrained by sequential ordering, and this is equally true for both kanji and kana.

But such inquiries may be pre-destined to find inherent differences in both processing and recall. When Tatsumi, Itoh, Sasanuma, and Fujisaki (1985) tested subjects for their ability to retain word lists given as speech, kana, kanji, and line drawings, the experimental results led the authors to construct a model of short-term memory which has word information processors at various auditory and visual levels of linguistic information. They even posited six separate short-term memories for phonemic, graphemic, pictorial, graphemic word shape, phonological word shape, and semantic information. The different **memories** are postulated to employ different encoding systems to retain the stimulus information, and exhibit capacity and decay characteristics which are different from the corresponding characteristics for the other memories. As an example, the semantic memory is able to maintain a large amount of information, with a decay time which is much longer than that of the other memories.

Numerals have often been used in such experiments with non-linguistic symbols, with some interesting results. The English orthographic system generally treats numerals and letters as belonging to different classes of stimuli, with numerals such as [1, 2, 3, 4, 5, 6, 7, 8, 9, 0] commonly thought of as being logographic symbols, along with the miscellaneous set containing [$%&#-@*+?]. In Japanese, of course, the Arabic numerals are an import which see service along with the traditional Chinese kanji numerals for 1 to 10, namely, 一, 二, 三, 四, 五, 六, 七, 八, 九, 十 '1, 2, 3, 4, 5, 6, 7, 8, 9, 10'. Kana, kanji, and Arabic numerals invoke different processing strategies depending upon the type of test posed to subjects. For example, when testing for visual vs. auditory memory for random digits in series, Hamada (1986) found that visual presentation induced better performance than auditory presentation in both forward and backward recall. This suggests superiority of visual memory to auditory memory for numerals, and is reminiscent of the memory enhancement found in visual presentation for kanji recall. Similarly, Fujihara (1989) investigated kana and numeral stimuli under noise conditions, and found different patterns for noise effects. Undergraduate subjects categorically classified target stimuli flanked by noise, and their reaction times for classifying the targets showed that noise influenced the stimuli processing stage more than the response processing stage for kana; noise only influenced the response processing stage for numerals.

But such findings may also be correlated with **individual differences** and task type. Hishitani (1980) examined how coding strategy differs according to the properties of both the individual and the stimuli by contrasting high school students who had been divided into two skill levels on the abacus. Subjects memorized a list of five auditorily-presented digits and alphabetic symbols, while also solving a mental calculation problem presented auditorily. The results indicated that the mental calculation task did not interfere with the memorization of digits in the skilled group, but memorization of the alphabetic symbols was impeded in both skilled and unskilled groups. Assuming that mental calculation involves linguistic coding, Hishitani concludes that skilled abacus users use visual imagery to code digits, while unskilled abacus users code them linguistically. Alphabetic symbols are coded linguistically irrespective of the subjects' abacus skill.

Some effects with numerals are tied to whether numerical values are presented as Arabic numerals (4, 7) or as words ('four', 'seven'). In English, subjects are influenced by irrelevant variations in physical size when making comparison judgments between Arabic numerals. That is, when the numerically larger number is also physically larger, subjects make such judgments faster than when both numbers are the same physical size. In contrast, subjects are slower when the numerically larger number is physically smaller. Thus, if a numerically larger numeral like 7 is presented in a physically smaller print size from the numerically smaller **4**, this variation in physical size confounds rapid performance of the task. However, when numerical value and physical size are congruent, or when the two numerals are the same size, no such delays arise for Arabic numerals. In contrast, such Stroop-like effects do not occur when subjects are making judgments about number words, and not numerals, in English (see Besner & Coltheart, 1979). Takahashi and Green (1983) compared such **numeral judgments** for numbers 1 through 9 with Japanese subjects. Stimuli were written in kanji and kana, and similar to the English results, Stroop-like effects emerged for the kanji numerals, with a different pattern for the kana numerals. It is hard to know what to make of the reaction time differences for comparative judgments of numerical distance in the two scripts, but either the two scripts are retrieving different mental representations or they interact with other cognitive procedures when performing such a mental task. There are parallels in the aphasia literature for European languages, where a patient's ability to read Arabic numerals may be much less affected than the ability to read alphabetically printed words. In Japanese too, we also have a long history of reported instances of separate impairment for kanji vs. kana processing, and there is some question as to whether numerals can be contrasted so clearly from alphabetic symbols on the one hand and from kanji symbols on the other hand.

But some have raised questions as to whether numerals simply pose a separate problem, with processing strategies closely aligned to some writing systems and not to others. For example, Green, Meara, and Court (1989) found that, popular notions to the contrary, both letters and numerals yielded the same search strategies for English-speaking subjects, while non-alphanumeric shapes yielded different search strategies. When the same task was given to Chinese-speaking subjects, they discovered that Chinese readers did not use the same search strategies for Arabic numerals that they did for Chinese numerals. They conclude from these results that Chinese numerals and Arabic numerals do not form the same logographic set for Chinese readers, and that Arabic numerals do not form a special set of logographs within the English alphabetic system. This interpretation suggests that different writing systems encourage their readers to develop characteristic search procedures for identifying symbols like numerals, but another interpretation is that numerals invoke a script familiarity effect during processing. Takahashi and Tamaoka (1992) presented undergraduates with 42 number pairs in different scripts: Arabic and Arabic; Arabic and kanji; Arabic and hiragana; and Arabic and alphabetic. As the pairs appeared on a computer screen, they were to judge as quickly as possible which of the two numbers was greater in value. Script types did not affect accuracy, but familiarity did affect numeral processing: familiar scripts (kanji and Arabic) were processed faster than unfamiliar scripts (hiragana and alphabetic representations).

Younger subjects have also been tested for such differences. Tamaoka, Leong, and Hatta (1991) presented two numerals of unequal values to fourth-, fifth-, and sixth-graders who had been grouped according to skill level. Arabic numerals were matched against other Arabic numerals, as well as numerals written in kanji, hiragana, or kata-kana. Not surprisingly, the older and more skilled the children, the better their performance. In general, children did best when presented with Arabic/Arabic pairs, like **6** and **8**. They did next best with Arabic/kanji pairs like **6** and 八 *hachi* '8'. Kana matches were processed less efficiently, with Arabic/katakana pairs worse than Arabic/hiragana pairs. Several insights emerge from these findings. First, Arabic numerals pose no processing difficulty in Japanese, with this efficient treatment reflecting their common use in daily life. So too for kanji numerals, which are most often used in the top-down writing style of *tategaki*. Secondly, the unconventional appearance of numerals affects the efficiency with which they are treated, and reflects the script familiarity problem discussed earlier in the book. Thirdly, like words and kanji characters, the numerals do not form a seamless set, but invariably reflect usage frequencies and script familiarity factors.

STROOP TEST RESULTS

The Stroop test is an experimental technique which first dates from the 1930s, and tests an individual's ability to separate word and color stimuli (see Stroop, 1935). Color naming provides some insight into how the two perceptual planes intersect, because results typically reveal that **interference** arises when subjects have to name the color represented by a color word, when that word is actually presented in a color of ink that is different from the color the word is naming. There are typically several conditions: for example, some color words are printed in black ink, some symbols are printed in colored inks, and some words are printed in colors which do not match the actual color named by the word. Subjects are typically found to more quickly name colors when the stimuli presented are color patches or symbols in the specific color than when colors are presented as words written in orthographic symbols which are colored differently than the color to be named. The point of the experimental probe is to create a conflict between the ink color and the printed word itself. Very simply, there is no conflict when the subject has to read the word and ignore the color; the printed word easily takes precedence and subjects read the word without difficulty. But it is very difficult to verbalize the name for an ink color, say, for example, **red**, when the word that is actually presented in print before you is *blue*. The tendency, of course, is to blurt out 'blue', even though the ink color you were supposed to name was red. The Stroop test, replicated often and with very reliable results, has been cited as a good example of **automaticity**, because the word's phonological properties are automatically accessed, even when we do not need it for the task the Stroop task poses to us, namely, to name the color of the ink.

There have been some interesting findings in respect to logographs in **Chinese**, with early (Biederman & Tsao, 1979) and persistent (Chen & Tsoi, 1990) findings that Chinese hanzi characters are much more potent than alphabetic script as an orthography in producing Stroop interference. Given the reports that Chinese and English subjects exhibit different patterns of results in naming tasks when Stroop interference is interposed, the inference that many have made here is that different processing mechanisms might be activated when dealing with Stroop stimuli in logographic as opposed to alphabetic languages. For example, Biederman and Tsao (1979) offer an explanation based on **competition** for processing resources in the right hemisphere. That is, since both the perception of color and the perception of pattern configuration are functions that at the time of their writing were assigned to the right hemisphere, they conjectured that the Stroop test invites these two functions to come into conflict.

Whatever the reason for greater Stroop test interference in logographic languages, apparently it is more difficult for Chinese subjects viewing Chinese hanzi to verbalize the name for the ink color **red** when the hanzi itself is naming a different color. Even logographic readers cannot seem to get away from reading the printed word unconsciously, even though they are not supposed to; as in English, it is as if they have to suppress the drive to process the printed word instead of simply naming the color as we were instructed to do. The reason why we have difficulty verbalizing the name for the ink color **red** when the word that is presented is *blue* is because this tendency interacts with the notion of automatic phonological activation, or so would say proponents of this hypothesis. But opponents instead take these results to claim that Chinese hanzi permit more direct access to meaning than do English words in alphabetic orthography, since we can not confirm the locus of this processing difference beyond saying that certain processing strategies may be affected by the type of writing system.

The **Japanese results** with kanji in the Stroop condition are even more interesting. In general, response times for incongruent Stroop stimuli are also longer than response times for congruent stimuli where ink color and color name are the same, but the morphemically-based aspects of the Japanese writing system, namely, the Japanese kanji, produce much greater interference in Stroop tasks than does the Japanese kana syllabary. Studies of the Stroop effect in Japanese have reported greater interference for kanji than for kana (Fang, Tzeng & Alva, 1981; Hatta, 1981a; Hayashi, 1988; Morikawa, 1981). For example, Hatta (1981a) reports mean magnitudes of 92 and 68 msec. for kanji and kana presentations, respectively. Hatta also notes a highly significant interaction of visual fields with the stimulus materials, so that there is greater interference when the right hemisphere is involved in single kanji recognition of Stroop phenomena. Kana did not show such differences between left and right visual fields in terms of size of Stroop effect. Like Biederman and Tsao (1979) before him, Hatta also suggests that a right hemisphere advantage for processing both color information and individual kanji might lead to competition between perceptual processing resources in the right hemisphere, accounting for the larger Stroop effect with kanji.

Kanji **frequency** in Japanese has a significant Stroop effect, but the number of strokes does not. When Morikawa (1986) matched kanji stimuli for high vs. low frequency and high vs. low stroke counts, and presented them in four colors (red, blue, yellow, and green), the number of strokes had no significant Stroop effect, but kanji frequency did in dampening the extent of the color-naming consequences in the Stroop test. Color matching tasks can also show Stroop effects, though to a lesser extent than the oral naming task, and semantic relatedness will affect the amount of interference from the Stroop effect on tasks involving both auditory-visual stimuli and visual-visual stimuli (Hayashi, 1988; Ishio, 1990). Although it has been suggested that the difference between color-naming and word-reading times could be used as a measure of cognitive processing, there is no evidence of correlation between speed of retrieval from semantic memory and speed in the Stroop test (Tajika, Taniguchi, Kamiya & Neumann, 1991).

One factor that should be addressed is the degree of familiarity. For example, adding a practice condition will increase correct answer rates (Hakoda & Sasaki, 1990), and once subjects know what is happening, they begin to adjust their perceptions. Paradis, Hagiwara, and Hildebrandt (1985) also note that color terms used in studies are those usually written in kanji, thus making their kana counterparts less familiar. For example, if the kanji, 青, 黄, 緑, 赤 *ao, ki, midori, aka* 'blue, yellow, green, red' are presented as the kana shapes あお, き, みどり, あか, they claim that this makes it impossible to determine whether differences in Stroop effects for **kanji vs. kana** are therefore due to the script type *per se*, or to the factor of unfamiliar kana shape (cf. Hatta, 1981a). But Fang et al. (1981) seem to have anticipated this problem in their citation of word-naming experiments with words simply printed in black; here the color terms written in kana were named much faster than color terms written in kanji. This is congruent with the Feldman and Turvey (1980) results, which also saw faster naming times for kana formats for color terms, despite their possibly being written more frequently in kanji format. Although familiarity with the procedure, and with the actual orthographic shapes themselves, obviously exerts an influence, it does not appear to be the controlling factor.

Toma and Toshima (1989) postulate a **hierarchical process** through which the perceptual systems of word recognition, color recognition, and verbal responses are functionally organized in Japanese. Whereas first-, second-, and third-graders, as well as university students, all showed significant Stroop interference in both hiragana and kanji versions, there was a clear qualitative difference before and after the third grade. It is at this point that more errors appear in the kanji words than in the kana words, presumably because the cognitive architecture which organizes the processing subsystems involved in word recognition, color recognition, and verbalization has matured into a fully integrated system. It would appear that the word recognition system does not have as strong a tendency to be verbalized in the first grade, and fewer Stroop errors occur. The second grade sees developmental progress in the integrative system, with Stroop errors increasing throughout this and the third grade, until one sees real dissociation between the recognition systems for hiragana and kanji. Although this provides a developmental frame of reference for the emergence of Stroop interference, it does not answer the question of why kanji and kana produce different levels of interference. Toma and Toshima suggest that it may be due to the functional proportions of kanji to kana in the increasing amount of written material provided to children during their school careers, but the answer here must certainly lie elsewhere.

The Stroop phenomenon has also been used to study inter- and intra-language relations for **bilinguals**. Such inquiry has been variously tied to whether the two languages are fused or separate in respect to the organization of mental representations, as well as to the question of whether one language must be dominant in respect to semantic access. When bilinguals are tested by naming ink colors on printed words across their two languages, they may show interference of the Stroop type. But the magnitude of this Stroop effect is always greater in the intra-(same-)language condition than in the inter-(across-)language condition (see Fang et al., 1981). There can be **inter-language interference**, but when it does occur, two factors should be taken into account. First of all, bilinguals show patterns which usually correlate with their degree of knowledge in the second language, and which reflect whether the bilingual's second language is native or not. There is no uniformly predictable metric here. For example, when one set of Chinese-English bilinguals was presented with the Stroop task, and given English words to name in English, they showed patterns in English which were more similar to English subjects than to Chinese subjects (Chen and Tsoi, 1990). But when Japanese-Korean bilinguals, who were born in Japan and had learned Japanese as their first language and Korean at school, were tested, the dominant language (Japanese) displayed stronger interference. Interference between Japanese and Korean was not high, suggesting psycholinguistic independence for the two languages. But the age at which the education in the second language (Korean) was started had stronger effects on linguistic interference for these 10-to-20-year-olds than the length of the education (Kim, 1990).

Another consideration to be noted is the possibility that the specific characteristics of the two languages a bilingual has under control might exert some specific effect on how the languages overlap. To be specific, will the degree of their **overlap** have an effect on the degree of Stroop interference, as for example, similarities in word shape between the two languages? If a Spanish-French bilingual were to be tested for possible inter-language interference between *verde/vert* 'green' and *negro/noir* 'black', the effect might be found for the first, but not the second. If a Japanese-English bilingual were to be tested for possible inter-language interference between 緑 *midori* 'green' and *green*, the effect might not be found at all. But it might be found between the katakana shape グリーン *guriin* 'green' and *green*.

In essence, monolinguals usually show the slowest naming times in their own language, while for bilinguals naming is slowed in relation to the strength of the language system in the second language (see also Ikeda, Matsumi & Mori, 1994). Stroop interference will also be lessened in proportion to the degree that subordinate second-language color names are dissimilar to the word in the native language (see Fang et al., 1981). All this being said, however, one has to conclude that while the Stroop test is an interesting exercise, its much-touted promise of being able to provide essential clues as to the script processing mechanisms in logographic languages is yet to be fulfilled. On the face of it, it does seem to offer some support for the classic view that kanji address meaning directly, since the search for the semantic designation of the color seems to conflict with the search for the identity of the printed word. Because kanji elicit greater interference than kana, this was the interpretation often given. However, it does not answer the vexing question of why this should interfere with the verbalization of the response, for the essence of the Stroop test is to provide a vocal response, and the vocal response is what is slowed for kanji. Taken in this light, one could make as much of a case for the possibility of automatic phonological activation for kanji, and claim that this is what slows the verbal response for kanji. But this explanation then begs the question of why kana elicit less interference. In sum, one has to say that the Stroop test is an intriguing, attention-getting classroom demonstration, but it is not a set of findings to base a theory on. The one fact which does incontrovertibly emerge from Stroop findings is that the word recognition system is powerfully linked to the verbalization system, certainly in a way that the color recognition system is not.

CONCLUSIONS

Japanese typically mixes kanji and hiragana in printed text, and this is the fastest text format to both read and comprehend. Kana-only texts are more difficult to read and slower to comprehend, although performance on such texts can improve with repeated exposure. This may be because of script familiarity for kana-kanji mixed formats in longer passages, but it may also be because the kanji in normal mixed-text sentences provide for convenient fixation points in the onward progression of the sentence. This is a question that is further elucidated in the forthcoming chapter on eye-movements by data which appear to support this likelihood.

Chapter 7

ACQUISITION OF ORTHOGRAPHY SKILLS

ORTHOGRAPHY SKILLS AND READING

That there are various writing systems in the world's languages does not change the fact that reading and writing are secondary processes. Phonetic short-term storage is necessary to the primary linguistic activity of speech processing in its basic state, and writing systems exploit this processing fact to varying degrees according to the demands of various processing tasks (see Erickson, Mattingly & Turvey, 1977). The basic purpose of orthographic representation is that it represents language, and language is essentially a system which represents words in phonological terms. This is true no matter which system we consider, and must be true even of classically logographic systems like Chinese and recently logographic systems like Japanese. DeFrancis (1989) calls this "the diverse oneness of writing systems", and notes that each child learning to read and write in a language must come to master the specific vagaries of this relationship in the language at hand. In this chapter, we will briefly survey what it is that the child must learn in acquiring orthographic skills in a symbol system that employs Chinese characters, two syllabaries, alphabetic romaji, and both Chinese and Arabic numerals. Since this is not a text in the educational foundations of reading abilities, we will confine ourselves to those aspects of **orthographic acquisition** which relate to the interaction of script types with script processing.

Learning how to read and write in Japanese officially begins at the age of six, and thereafter takes up a good deal of the time spent in education at the elementary, junior and senior secondary school levels. It is safe to say that learning how to read and write is a life-long process, at least insofar as acquisition and maintenance of kanji inventories are concerned. This is true since kanji are constantly being acquired and lost during one's reading life; it is certainly the case if one moves into technical and specialized fields which always provide an array of new kanji. Acquiring new knowledge is more than learning new vocabulary words appropriate to the field of knowledge, it also implies acquiring the kanji by which that new knowledge is codified. Even without such requirements of specialized knowledge, one of the hallmarks of erudition in Japan has traditionally been the ability to display one's knowledge of arcane or rare kanji, and better yet, the ability to write them from memory on demand.

There is a considerable body of research which examines reading and writing skills, but this is typically found in the pedagogical literature. If one limits the scope to work which qualifies as psycholinguistic inquiry, or to work which impacts on universal vs. language-specific issues in the acquisition of orthography skills and reading, there is considerably less. We will consider some of those psycholinguistic issues in the following pages.

Controversy rages over the value of phonological recoding as opposed to **sight reading**. In earlier discussions of lexical access, we saw similar positions counterposed in two access routes which relied on either assembled phonology (that is, phonological recoding by grapheme to phoneme correspondences) or addressed phonology (that is, sight reading by orthographic shapes). When applied to the reading process, phonological recoding involves the way in which the child (or adult) is taught to match the regularities of the orthographic system in order to transform spellings into pronunciations with meanings which the reader can recognize. The meaning of the word which has been thus accessed is recognized from the pronunciation of the word, not from any of the holistic print cues embodied in its shape. The other reading route is the one along which sight reading travels, and here words are recognized holistically and rapidly. This is possible because readers are postulated to use the memorized shapes of words to access them rather than by decoding their orthography-to-phonology relationships. This is a system which is more difficult to learn, easier to forget, and near impossible to decipher when lost to antiquity. One only has to consider the fate of Egyptian and Mayan hieroglyphics, or even classical Japanese and Chinese texts, to be reminded of how difficult it is to reinstate semantic assignments once they are lost.

This debate also extends into the exact contribution of orthographic knowledge as a **metalinguistic ability**. Metalinguistic awareness refers to the knowledge that users of a language have about their knowledge of the language. Such metalinguistic abilities reflect the fact that language rules are not only used by the child, but that the child can reflect on and infer from those rules of language. In the case of orthography, it refers to how the child becomes able to recognize relevant units of the spoken language, such as phonetic and phonemic segments, the onsets and rimes within a syllable, the syllabic unit itself, and then to be aware of how these features relate to the features of the orthographic system. Metalinguistic awareness appears to be a crucial factor in reading, but it must ultimately be linked to individual differences in the way that metalinguistic skills typically are (see Leong & Joshi, 1997).

KANA ACQUISITION

Much has been written about the speed and early age at which the highly regular kana are encountered and mastered by young Japanese children. Some reports even credit toddlers with acquiring some orthographic knowledge under direct conditions of direct tuition (see Steinberg, Yoshida & Yagi, 1985). Although **pre-schoolers** are generally untutored, they typically come to the institutional learning experience knowing some kana, perhaps even some common kanji. A recent survey (Shimamura & Mikami, 1994) of pre-schoolers in Tokyo and Aichi Prefecture for their reading and writing abilities for hiragana illustrates that three-year-olds can read 26.2% of the 71 hiragana configurations tested for; four-year-olds could read 70%, and five-year-olds 92.8%. In contrast, three-year-olds can write only 6.3% of the 71 hiragana, four-year-olds 20.9%, and five-year-olds 62.8%.[1] When compared with surveys carried out by the National Language Research Institute in 1954 and 1967, children's abilities in reading and writing hiragana appear to have improved considerably over the intervening four decades. For example, a survey by the National Language Research Institute in 1954 reported that Tokyo children entering elementary school read an average 30 out of 46 hiragana, as well as knowing an average of 5.8 katakana, 5.4 kanji, and 7.9 Arabic numbers. And even children in rural areas were not that much further behind, being able to read an average of 23.8 hiragana, 3.6 katakana, 4.4 kanji, and 6.5 Arabic numerals (see Sakamoto & Makita, 1973).

Early longitudinal comparisons of children's abilities in respect to hiragana and kanji recognition show that recognition skills for both improve with age. Tanaka, Iwasaki, and Miki (1974) tested 600 children aged 5 to 14, by having them cancel matching letters in lists of kanji and kana. Hiragana recognition was easier for children between the ages of 5 and 7, while kanji was easier for older subjects. In general, female students showed better performance than males across all age groups. Imai's (1987) recent synthesis of several **large surveys** with thousands of kindergartners reports that most kindergartners can read most hiragana symbols; those who cannot read even one kana number less than 2%. Their knowledge of katakana is, however, quite limited; 50% do not know more than 10 katakana. This stands in stark contrast with the 10% who could read 20 or more kanji. In general, kana recognition for those kana presented in familiar words is better than for those presented in unfamiliar words.

Even some of the finer points of kana principles appear to have been intuited, as Endo-Misawa (1990) has demonstrated. Pre-schoolers with a mean age of 6;0 were tested for their abilities with regular kana and the miniature-sized *yo-on* (拗音) kana

---

[1] Interestingly, the children in Aichi were better than those in Tokyo in both reading and writing abilities. Kindergarten children were superior to those at nursery schools, and girls were superior to boys.

(syllables with a /y/ as the second consonantal onset, as in きゃ, きゅ, きよ kya, kyu, kyo and しゃ, しゅ, しよ sya (=sha), syu (=shu), syo (=sho)). When parents were queried to see whether any systematic instruction had been given to the children, the results revealed that most children were able to read and spell most yo-on before entering elementary school and without receiving any systematic instruction. This may not be too surprising, if the acquisition of kana is related to the frequency of use of the particular orthographic symbol and its corresponding syllable, as Hotta (1984) claims. He recorded conversation from college students, three-year-olds, and five-year-olds, and analyzed them for the frequency of each syllable; the same was done for textual data derived from the text of picture books. The combined data from conversational and textual frequency were compared with data on children's reading and writing skills taken by the National Language Research Institute in 1972, with the results showing that **frequency of use**, both in conversation and in written text, is a significant factor in the acquisition of the orthographic kana symbols. If this is true, mastery of the /Cy-/ yo-on syllables simply reflects their relative frequency in both spoken and written language, and the advantage that frequency of occurrence gives.

But kana mastery is not all there is to reading kana. Kana may be regular and are thus mastered early, but **reading mastery** does not automatically follow. Even four- and five-year-old children who master all 46 hiragana make mistakes about the basic nature of the reading task, as exemplified by their tendency to read the vertical *tategaki* columns from left to right, instead of the correct direction from right to left across the page (Akita, Muto, Fujioka & Yasumi, 1995). And there are reports that children who read in terms of larger units, such as syllable groupings, comprehend more than those who read a kana syllable at a time (Akita et al., 1995). Lastly, kana mastery certainly does not confer knowledge about the conventional rules of how stories and books are organized textually or how the discourse type in print is organized in simple physical terms. And knowing how the situational script, scene, frame, or scenario is organized, and what expectations arise from that, is also crucial to mastery of what reading comprehension is really aiming at (Ishizawa & Furugori, 1990). As a result, various strategies have been promoted to enhance the acquisition of kana reading skills by presenting kana in familiar words (Imai, 1987), introducing pictures (Imai, 1983),[2] syllable decomposition (Imai & Sakai,

---

[2] In fact, what Imai (1983) found was that learning katakana representations for low familiarity words was not enhanced by the presentation of pictures, and that learning katakana representations for high familiarity words elicited better performance without pictures. Two other groups of slightly older subjects (mean ages of 5;9 and 7;2) learning to read hangul script representations were, in contrast, facilitated by the presentation of pictures and sentences. Nevertheless, Imai's net conclusion on these findings is that pictorial aids do facilitate learning to read words with low familiarity. Interestingly, Sugimura (1974) found the same non-results for pictures when presented along with kanji or katakana words. If anything, the pictures

1991), and so forth. Some studies suggest that form-quality, speed, and span for kana-copying are associated with reading and writing abilities, and that these measures could be employed as a predictor of reading and writing achievement in Japanese pre-school children and possibly beyond (Yamada, Sasaki & Motooka, 1988). Copying span and copying speed has even been suggested as a rough measure of reading comprehension in general, since copying abilities show a moderate correlation with reading, dictation, and spelling ability in general (Mori & Yamada, 1988). However, individual differences in reading and writing abilities lower the magnitude of the correlation, and just as in English, reading remains an elusive skill for some and a skill which quickly reveals the reality of individual differences.

Segmentation Skills and Script Type

There has been some discussion of what alphabetic vs. syllabic systems enhance or suppress because of the levels of language which they focus upon. For example, what is the nature of the segmentation process, and the role that it plays in mapping orthographic symbols onto phonetic segments? Various streams of research in the literature generally agree that **phonemic awareness** is necessary for early reading (Leong, 1991), and some even suggest that there is a causal connection (see, for example, Bradley & Bryant, 1983). Some go even further than this, claiming that, at the early stages at least, knowing an alphabetic system or being trained in one is the key to being able to manipulate speech sounds (see Read, Zhang, Nie & Ding, 1986). But the final resolution of the claim that phonemic awareness develops only in learning to read and write in an alphabetic language is yet to be empirically and conclusively validated (see Leong, 1991). Nevertheless, the theoretical basis of this question rests at the core of the debate about what constitutes the basis for successful acquisition of reading skills, as well as for what might be underlying causes for poor reading skills or even reading disabilities. One influential view insists that **phonemic segmentation skills** are crucial to reading in alphabetic systems, and this hypothesis has some interesting consequences for how and when these skills are acquired in other script types. The notion is that segmentation skills are inferred by children as they learn to use sound-to-spelling rules in learning to read, and further, that learning to think of spoken words as a sequence of discrete phonemic segments is essential to becoming able to read and write those spoken words. This position is supported by the reliable correlation between segmentation skills and reading

---

seemed to present a competing stimulus which distracted the learners' attention away from the kana and kanji targets, resulting in lower correct answer rates.

abilities for young children in the first few grades (see Liberman, Shankweiler, Liberman, Fowler & Fischer, 1977).

In principle, **alphabetic literacy** relies on a segmental conception of language, and thus in practice implicitly fosters segmentation skills. There is considerable evidence for the training protocols derived from learning to read in an alphabetic system; that is, alphabetic spelling carries over into enhanced abilities in phonemic segmentation skills. For example, in comparing literate and illiterate adults in rural Portugal, Morais, Cary, Alegria, and Bertelson (1979) found that their literate subjects could add and delete word-initial consonants, while their illiterate counterparts could not. The same has been found to be true for pre-literate English-speaking children, namely, that they too are unable to perform simple substitutions with single consonantal segments (see Fox & Routh, 1975; Liberman, Shankweiler, Fischer & Carter, 1974). It is only when they go to school that there is a dramatic jump in their segmenting abilities, obviously tied to the formal experience of learning how to read and write in the alphabet system. When Read et al. (1986) tested Chinese adults who were only literate in hanzi characters, they were found to be unable to add or delete individual consonants in Chinese words. However, a control group of Chinese adults who were literate in alphabetic spelling because of post-1958 schooling in *pinyin* phonemic writing performed this task readily and accurately. In fact, even adults who had once learned this alphabetic writing, but who no longer were able to use it, were able to perform the task. The difficulty does not lie with the task, because adding or deleting a syllable-initial consonant is a task well-suited to Chinese syllable structure; moreover, it is also implicit in language manipulations like rhymes, minimal pairs, phonetic radicals, and speech errors of the metathesized Spoonerism type. Apparently, learning to read and write alphabetically implies learning to segment spoken syllables into phonemic units, and provides an automatic set of explicit training protocols. In contrast, learning to read and write in a logographic system does not automatically entail such segmentation practices, regardless of the reading fluency achieved in that system.

The evidence for how **Japanese children** segment out the initial consonant is even more interesting, because orthography acquisition starts with the syllabary first. Mann (1986) reports on four experiments which compared awareness of morae/syllables and phonemes among Japanese and American children at different ages. The results clearly show that the Japanese children's approach to phonological counting and deletion tests is influenced by their having learned to read a syllabary instead of an alphabet. Knowledge of the kana syllabary tended to confound their performance on tasks that assessed ability to manipulate phonological units. In contrast, American first-graders could more accurately count the number of phonemes in words and remove initial phonemes from nonsense words, suggesting that learning to read an alphabet must have facilitated their awareness of phonemes at this age. By the fourth grade, the Japanese children were able to manipulate both syllables and phonemes, whether or not they had been instructed in use of an alphabet. With increasing age and educational experience, Japanese children obviously become capable of manipulating phonemes, whether or not they are literate in an alphabet.

These results notwithstanding, it should be said that children in general find syllable manipulation an easier task than phoneme manipulation, and that learning to read a syllabary or alphabet is not the sole determinant of phonological awareness. Pre-schoolers in Japan are often adept at kana manipulation, and after they have entered the Elementary School at age 6, their mastery of hiragana is soon completed. According to Amano (1970), Japanese children are relatively adept at syllable segmentation at an early age, and very adept at 'syllable segmentation' as soon as they have mastered the majority of the hiragana. But it is harder for them to find a specific syllable in a polysyllabic word, and so there has been some discussion of what kind of awareness of moraic units is a necessary prerequisite for reading the kana syllabary (see Dairoku, 1995). The mastery of this skill also seems tied to having the orthographic tools for carrying out the task, and along with mastery of the hiragana inventory comes the ability to point out exactly the syllable in question, as for example, pointing out the /-ra-/ in /hi-ra-ga-na/.

Katakana makes a relatively early appearance in the formal school setting, being formally introduced in the latter half of the first grade and completed by the end of the second grade. Obviously, learning one system has a learning effect far beyond the system itself, and the regularity and similarity principles underlying the hiragana system condition the related skills which arise from that experience. The net result is that **katakana skills** are acquired relatively early in the school setting, once introduced. But katakana skills seem to always lag behind hiragana skills. Tanaka (1977) reports that recognition success rates are always better for hiragana over katakana. In the age range between six and eight, the ordering is hiragana best, followed by katakana and kanji, in that order; between nine and ten, the ordering is hiragana, kanji, and then katakana, and above the age of eleven, the ordering is kanji, hiragana, and katakana. Eventually the reading skills even out, so that fluency is achieved in reading abilities and orthography-specific skills mature into skills which may also apply to other systems.

Measuring Skilled Readers

The issue of phonological knowledge has been applied to the measurement of skilled vs. less skilled readers in Japanese, with some results reminiscent of the findings for phonological activation accompanying lexical access. For example, Mann (1984) investigated the relationship between temporary **memory** for linguistic vs. non-linguistic material and Japanese children's reading ability. She first manipulated spoken nonsense words in order to determine whether efficiency in phonetic decoding and storage is a contributing factor in distinguishing between good and poor readers, and in a second experiment, compared memory for two kinds of visual linguistic material with that for two types of visual non-linguistic material. Second-graders whose reading ability had already been assessed by their teachers as good, average, or poor, were auditorily presented with 80 test items in random order; 48 nonsense words appeared as non-recurring stimuli, while 8 occurrences of each of four nonsense words served as the recurring stimuli. The children were then asked to decide whether each item was new or previously given. The second experiment used four types of visual stimuli (that is, hiragana, kanji, abstract designs, and photographs of faces) for the same type of recurring recognition tests as the first experiment. Both experiments show that good readers surpass poor readers in memory for the spoken nonsense words, suggesting that effective use of phonetic representation is significant in reading efficiency, even for a language which uses non-alphabetic script types. In addition, the good readers excelled in memory for both kana and kanji compared to the poor readers. In fact, the poor readers' memory performance was markedly worse on the kana material as compared to the kanji material. The good readers also performed better in the memory tasks for abstract designs, but no significant difference was found in their memory for faces. Lastly, memory for kana was correlated to memory for spoken words, but not to memory for either of the non-linguistic materials. Memory for kanji, in contrast, was correlated both to memory for spoken words and to that for abstract designs, suggesting the involvement of a graphomotor coding strategy in both kanji and abstract design memory.

Flaherty (1993a) tested similar dimensions in eight-, ten-, and twelve-year-old Japanese children via the tasks of reading kanji aloud, object-naming of the same objects in photographs, and semantic categorization tasks for lexical items. Reaction times were faster when they read the kanji aloud than when they named the objects in photographs. Naming and semantic categorization were the same for the eight- and ten-year-olds, while the twelve-year-olds were faster in placing the objects into semantic groupings. Flaherty also concludes that the **phonetic code** is a critical informational feature in reading, possibly even accessed prior to the semantic code for these children when reading kanji.

In a critical application of Perfetti's (1985) *verbal efficiency theory* to Japanese children, Kuhara, Kojima, Hatano, Saito, and Haebara (1996) tested whether **vocalization latencies** are a universal measure of skilled vs. less skilled readers. By implication, they also address the question of whether the phonological information is activated during lexical access (see Perfetti, Zhang & Berent, 1992). Three experiments did in fact provide results that are compatible with findings for American elementary school children, who typically show single-word vocalization latencies which are shorter for skilled readers. Vocalization latencies for both kanji and hiragana presentations were shorter for skilled readers in dealing with both real words and pseudo-words. Some differences were noted, however, between the Japanese and the American children. Vocalization latencies were greater for real words than for pseudo-words for the Japanese fifth graders in both kanji and hiragana presentations. This was true for the Japanese children whether pseudo-words were presented as a block in the same sub-session or in separate sub-sessions from the real words. One consequence of this finding is that further consideration should be given to the practice of using the speed of pronouncing pseudo-words as a metric for differentiating skilled from less skilled readers, for it may only be applicable to alphabetic systems like English. In fact, it may have to do with the regularity of the sound-to-letter correspondences, and English may even differ from Spanish or Finnish in this respect. At any rate, as Kuhara-Kojima et al. point out, by the fifth grade Japanese school children have already reached the upper limits of their abilities in orthographic decoding for hiragana. Thus, these fifth graders exhibited vocalization latencies and error rates which matched those of Japanese college students. This comparison can definitely not be made for American fifth-graders, and speed of vocalization for pseudo-words may be confounded more by regularity of orthographic type than by the orthographic type itself. The fact that pseudo-words did not show such differences for pseudo-word kanji was because the two kanji in a compound will carry an individual reading for each component, whether it represents a morphemic part of a real word or not. Thus, the *han* and *yoo* in the pseudo-word 半用 *han-yoo* invite readings whether or not they are part of a real word. And in this case, the derived *on*-reading compound of our pseudo-word *han-yoo* could indeed be uttered as a possible word meaning 'half-use'.

   Concurrent articulation has also been used as a confounding factor in reading probes, in order to separate skill levels. Recall that concurrent vocalization is a technique which was used to test the presence or strength of phonological activation because it is assumed to block phonological analysis. Tamaoka, Leong, and Hatta (1992) found that reading comprehension deteriorated under concurrent articulation conditions. One hundred and eight elementary school students from grades 4 through 6, classified as skilled and less skilled readers, were asked to judge sentences as being semantically correct or incorrect. Embedded in each sentence was a commonly-used word, usually written in kanji, presented in kanji, or the same word presented in hiragana. Two treatment conditions involved either no interference or vocal interference, which was created by having subjects count repeatedly in Japanese from one to ten while performing the task. The results indicate that even though words in kanji were processed faster than words in hiragana, vocal interference had a similar effect on the processing of both scripts. But interference did impair less skilled readers more than skilled readers and younger children more than older children. A second study used a similar methodology and had the same students judge the semantic correctness of sentences containing a commonly-used word, usually written in katakana, presented in katakana, or the same word presented in hiragana. Again, the authors found that vocal interference inhibited less skilled readers more than skilled readers and younger children more than older children. Obviously, age has a stabilizing effect, but so also does skill level when taken as a measure of an individual's level of reading competence.

KANJI ACQUISITION

Kanji Attributes

Kanji are not taught in the school system until children are six or seven years of age. Despite the facility with which the regular kana syllabaries are acquired, at the earliest stages the holistic shapes afforded by simple kanji make them the easier units to acquire in terms of unit recognition. This is true even for multiple stroke kanji, such as the sixteen-stroke kanji 橋 *hashi* 'bridge' and 薬 *kusuri* 'medicine' (see Steinberg & Yamada, 1978-1979). But the key to such early learning is **meaningfulness**, not shape. When kanji are presented together with their meanings, simple single kanji are more easily learned than kana by even three- and four-year-olds (see Steinberg, Isozaki & Amano, 1981; Steinberg & Yamada, 1978-1979). For example, Steinberg, Yamada, Nakano, Hirakawa & Kanemoto (1977) report that kanji words such as 雪 *yuki* 'snow' and 新(-しい) *atara(-shii)* 'new' are easier to learn than the individual hiragana れ and い (*re* and *i*), or the individual katakana レ and イ (*re* and *i*).

It appears to be the quality of meaningfulness that explains this early mastery of a small set of symbols, and this is confirmed by their pairing meaningful words with kana symbols instead of trying to have children learn meaningless symbols. Steinberg et al.'s results reveal that it is easier to learn the kana symbols つくる for *tsukuru* 'to make' or the kanji symbol 作 for *tsukuru* 'to make' when they are paired with the real spoken word than it is to match the individual kana つ *tsu* with the syllable /tsu/. Similarly, Steinberg and Yamada (1978-1979) report that three- and four-year-old subjects learned kanji more easily, despite their being vastly more complex graphically. For example, 37% of the 84 kanji tested were learned within 3 trials, and 15% were learned on the first trial; some of the counter-matched 84 kana symbols were not learned at all.

Haryu (1989) has also demonstrated the **centrality of meaningfulness** with four-year-old kindergartners, by presenting them with targets which could be kanji with a word reading, hiragana with a syllable reading, kanji with a syllable reading, or hiragana with a word reading. The results show that the meaningfulness of the reading signif-icantly facilitates the learning of the characters, with figural complexity having a much less significant effect. Oka, Mori, and Kakigi (1979) have demonstrated the effect of meaningfulness on learning to read hiragana on very young children. A first experiment revealed that, after a week's delay, three- and four-year-olds retained kanji verbs (50%) and adjectives (52%) far better than hiragana (10%), confirming the effect of meaningfulness on kanji retention. But a second and third experiment taught the children to read hiragana by using word association (for example, the さ *sa* of *sakura* 'cherry'). The results now showed that when hiragana were taught through such word associations, their retention rate rose to the level of kanji retention. This finding is founded in the fact that the children treated such hiragana as complete words (that is, さ *sa* means *sakura* 'cherry') rather than as kana symbols for syllables.

But **figural complexity** does play a role in decoding and memorizing, and complements meaningfulness in facilitating children's learning to read kanji and kana. Ozawa & Nomura (1981) compared pre-schoolers' discriminatory and decoding processes in the reading of hieroglyphs, kanji, and kana. Experimental results with kindergartners aged between 4;8 and 5;8 found that, while meaningfulness and repeated reading of scripts facilitated the process of decoding the scripts in general, simpler kanji were learned more quickly than the complex ones. Obviously, both discriminating and decoding processes affect the reading process, and even at the earliest stages, figural complexity is a perceptual factor.

What emerges from such studies is that it is not the perceptual complexity of the item to be learned that determines the difficulty of the learning, but rather the **language level** at which the learning is aimed, meaning vs. phonetic analysis. Obviously, the complexity of 雪 *yuki* 'snow' vs. つ *tsu* will play a role, but at this early stage, the level of metalinguistic ability needed to take advantage of perceptual clues is such that meaningfulness is the cue which is readily seized upon. Given these findings, it is easy to see why some advocate teaching kanji reading to young children on the principle that reading kanji is easier than reading kana (see Yamada, 1984). But it is not so much that kanji are easier to learn at this stage than kana, but rather that meaningful symbols are easier to learn than non-meaningful symbols, certainly those non-meaningful symbols that require refined phonetic skills.

Kanji reading and writing poses a memory burden, despite popular beliefs about the centrality of kanji in an orthography which is credited with an extremely high literacy rate. Surprisingly, there is no official Ministry of Education definition for what constitutes literacy as such. Nevertheless, Sakamoto and Makita's (1973) contribution to a collection of comparative reading studies from around the world put Japan's **literacy rate** at over 99%, with the major exceptions to this figure to be found among the mentally retarded. This is the result of a compulsory nine-year education system which requires six years in elementary school and then three years in junior high school. This compulsory aspect of the system then sees 95% of its students going on to senior high school, and half of those going on to post-secondary education. This is of course a product of the last century or so, and owes much to the provision of government funds for a national compulsory education system as of 1900. Between *Meiji Gannen*, 'the first year of Meiji' in 1868, and 1920, this measure caused an increase in the enrolment rate, and thus the literacy rate among children, to jump from 30% to 99% (see Sakamoto & Makita, 1973).

Kanji Curriculum

In every grade, at every level, the Japanese language is a mandated subject in the curriculum. In this compulsory system, there are **set rates** for how many kanji should be mastered at each grade level. Before 1971, the *Tooyoo Kanji* were first presented in the Elementary School, with first-graders expected to learn 46 kanji, second-graders 105, third-graders 187, fourth-graders 205, fifth-graders 194, and sixth-graders 144, for a total of 881. The entire set of 1,850 *Tooyoo Kanji* were to have been mastered by the end of Grade 9 of Junior High School, meaning that the remaining 969 kanji had to be learned during that period (Sakamoto & Makita, 1973). After 1971, the *Jooyoo Kanji* list increased the number of kanji to be learned to 1,945, so that the number to be learned in the Elementary School increased to a total of 996. These characters and a total of 2,005 possible readings associated with them are distributed according to grade, as shown below.

Grade	Number of Assigned Kanji Characters	Number of *On/Kun* Readings
First Grade	76	237
Second Grade	145	367
Third Grade	195	415
Fourth Grade	195	362
Fifth Grade	195	326
Six Grade	190	298

Table 7.1 Distribution of kanji characters and readings according to grade.

To give an idea of the nature of the learning task, the kanji 森 might have been mastered in its *kun* version as *mori* 'forest', with correct answers in reading 98% of the time and in writing 98% of the time. But the child might not have been mastered 森 in its *on* version as *shin*, with correct answers in reading 9.5% of the time and in writing 4% of the time (see Shimamura, 1990). There is always a discrepancy between learning the character as character, and then being able to correctly match it to its various *on/kun*-readings. For example, contrast the following figures for **mastery of kanji** as kanji, in contrast to their mastery as manifestations with multiple readings in *on/kun* representations.

Assigned Kanji	Reading Mastery Ratio (%)		Writing Mastery Ratio (%)	
	Character	*On/Kun*	Character	*On/Kun*
First Grade Kanji	93.5	58.2	88.3	54.9
Second Grade Kanji	94.9	69.3	75.7	51.2
Third Grade Kanji	93.2	75.2	67.1	52.4
Fourth Grade Kanji	93.3	82.0	64.1	55.7
Fifth Grade Kanji	90.6	80.8	57.6	50.1
Six Grade Kanji	92.0	87.0	60.4	57.4

Table 7.2 Reading and writing mastery ratios of kanji according to grade.

As can be seen, the comprehension rates level out with progression through the elementary grades, for the simple reason that the percentage of multiple readings decreases steadily, and the discrepancies are minimized. The percentage of kanji that have only one reading in the first grade is 10.5%, in the second grade 13.1%, in the third grade 32.8%, in the fourth grade 45.1%, in the fifth grade 53.8%, and in the sixth grade 61.1%. While the kanji are often more complicated in the later grades of elementary school, with the physical requirements of handwriting more taxing and writing success rates lower, the discrepancy between the kanji and its appropriate reading is much lower (see Shimamura, 1990).

Once again, this is only a subset of the entire *Jooyoo Kanji* list, and the entire set is expected to have been mastered by the end of Grade 9 of Junior High School. What this entails is mastery of the entire set of 1,945 *Jooyoo Kanji*, and their corresponding 4,087 **on/kun-readings**. The *on*-readings are slightly more numerous than the *kun*-readings, totalling 2,187 vs. 1,900, or 53.5% vs. 46.5% (see Nomura, 1981). Even this number is not entirely transparent, for the true picture is that there are some 135 'special' *on*-readings and some 29 'special' *kun*-readings among these two totals. For example, among the 135 'special' *on*-readings, one finds the less common readings of *jiki, ton, na, hon, fu* for 食, 団, 南, 反, 歩, respectively; and among the 29 'special' *kun*-readings, one finds the less common readings of *ama, nan, muna, nano, ko* for 雨, 何, 胸, 七, 木,

respectively. The statistical relationships are perhaps best seen in the following pie graph (adapted from Nomura, 1981) giving the numerical values and their percentages.

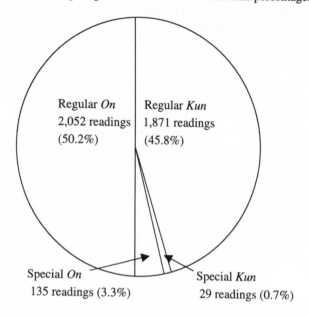

Figure 7.1 Pie graph for the percentage of regular and special *on*- and *kun*-readings.

But mastery is a relative term, for there is much to master in a system that employs a large inventory of logographic symbols which are both potentially complex and overlapping in their graphic features, falling far short of a one-to-one representational principle because of **homophonous readings** attached to different characters and kanji characters with multiple readings. In the beginning, kanji are typically simpler in form and some even have a one-to-one correspondence ratio. But inevitably, as the student passes through the grades, there will be more and more material to be mastered, and the reality of a many-to-many correspondence ratio compounds the difficulty of the learning task. For example, the kanji 分 has 3 *on*- and 4 *kun*-readings, namely, *bun, fun, bu; wakeru, wakareru, wakaru, wakatsu*, while 明 has 2 *on*- and 9 *kun*-readings, namely, *mei, myoo; akari, akarui, akarumu, akaramu, akiraka, akeru, aku, akuru, akasu*. Nomura (1981) gives a statistical inventory of the multiple possibilities, as well as a listing of the homophonic overlaps, all of which serve to remind one that learning the 1,945 *Jooyo Kanji* is not as simple as learning an itemized list of 1,945 units. Not even counting the handwriting requirements in production, the task is certainly far from simple and far from straightforward. In simplest terms, as time goes on, some children simply fail to master the kanji required for each grade (Kitao, 1984a, cited in Hirose & Hatta, 1988).

Asymmetry between Writing and Reading Abilities

Another factor to be considered in assessing 'mastery' is the clear asymmetry between children's reading and writing abilities in kanji (see Shimamura, 1990), and the fact that writing kanji is quite different from kanji reading comprehension and poses a different task to the child learner. When Yamada (1992b) tested fourth-, fifth-, and sixth-graders for their ability to read (name) and write isolated kanji, he found asymmetries in their reading and writing abilities, concluding that learning to read and learning to write kanji take place more or less independently of each other. In simplest terms, some children could read kanji they could not write, and conversely, some children could write kanji they could not read. In reading errors, the children sometimes used the *kun*-reading instead of the *on*-reading, and failure to distinguish between the two readings accounted for more than half of the reading errors in all three grades. The students would also mistake a graphically similar kanji for the one presented, or read the wrong constituent of a compound. This presages a considerable change in mastery predictions from the rosy expectations one might make on the basis of the reports of pre-schoolers with a limited number of meaningful kanji (cf. Steinberg, Isozaki & Amano, 1981; Steinberg & Yamada, 1978-1979; Steinberg, Yamada, Nakano, Hirakawa & Kanemoto, 1977). But the reasons here are obvious. The number of kanji to be mastered grows, and unpredictability and irregularity in respect to *kun*-reading vs. *on*-reading begin to appear; in addition, the increasing number of bound kanji after second-grade decrease the meaningfulness quotient. Thus, Yamada reports that the average fifth-grader can only read 61% of the kanji required by the Ministry of Education to be learned in the fourth grade. But the success rates seem to vary, according to the focus and type of study; for example, at least one study put their success rates in the 90% range for reading comprehension of individual kanji as kanji in the elementary grades tested (Shimamura, 1990). However, as already noted, their reading ability in respect to assigning the correct *on/kun*-reading always lags behind, with a 58.2% acquisition rate in the first grade moving up to a 87% rate in the sixth grade.

In writing errors, Yamada (1992b) found that his fourth-, fifth-, and sixth-graders sometimes invented kanji, gave a homophonous but incorrect kanji, gave a graphically similar character, or provided the wrong character for a two-kanji compound. In fact, the invented kanji errors and homophone errors accounted for between a third and a half of the **writing errors**, depending on which of the three grades is considered. In a study of kanji writing errors in two- and three-kanji compounds words by college students, Hatta,

Kawakami, and Hatasa (1997) also found that orthographic similarities were important, but that semantic factors contributed more to the production of kanji writing errors than phonological or morphological factors. Obviously, any notion that writing errors are simply derived from mixing up similarly shaped kanji is mistaken.

Yamada (1992b) found that single-reading kanji were easier to write than the **multiple-reading kanji**, and we note that the one constant is that kanji with single readings were much easier to both read and write than kanji with multiple readings (see also Shimamura, 1990). Older children were more likely to be successful with such kanji ambiguities, possibly because of the age factor and the fact that kanji with multiple correspondences are taught in school to older children. Curiously enough, the ratio of multiple readings for kanji drops as the child progresses through the grades; for example, only 38.9% of the kanji taught in grade six have multiple readings, but a total of 89.5% of the kanji taught in the first grade have multiple readings. But children in the higher grades also may exhibit poorer performance in kanji writing than the lower grades, likely because of the increasing complexity in kanji forms as the children advance in grade level. For example, their mastery of kanji writing for the items presented in the first grade plummets from a high 88.3% in the first grade to 60.4% in the sixth grade (Shimamura, 1990). And there are other factors at work here, namely, the fact that the absolute number of single kanji presented for mastery do not equate with the absolute number of kanji compounds to be mastered. In kanji compounds, however, it is the first kanji which suffers the most likelihood of writing error (Hatta, Kawakami & Hatasa, 1997).

Still, students do appear to make the requisite progress. Shimamura (1987) claims that compositions written by second-, fourth-, and sixth-graders consistently reflect advancement by grade level, and that sixth-graders' compositions exhibit just over 20% of the total word count represented in kanji. Shimamura (1990) further generalizes that the elementary and junior high school students she tested for the 996 *Jooyoo Kanji* showed *on*- and *kun*-readings to be relatively well-established, with an average acquisition rate in respect to reading comprehension of the items resting comfortably at 92.7%. Their kanji writing abilities, however, were considerably weaker than their reading abilities, with an average acquisition rate of the items at 66.2%. The decline in writing abilities was especially noticeable in the higher grades, but this is nothing more than the performance asymmetry in difficulty between kanji reading and kanji writing (see also Tokuda & Sato, 1988). Some suggest that while learning difficulties in the acquisition of writing skills may arise from the figural complexity of the kanji, this could be compensated for by changing a teaching tradition wherein kanji pedagogy is often arbitrary and lacking in scientific methodology (see Yamada, 1984). The time-honored method for inculcating kanji stops at tracing and copying, with enormous emphasis on the latter. There is some evidence that, at the early stages of pre-school and early grades at least, **copying** is the most effective method for learning kanji for production in handwriting (see Onose, 1988), and for later learning this same labor-intensive exercise remains the most common method of acquisition and maintenance.

It should also come as no surprise that there are those who suggest that learning to read *kanji-kana majiribun* should be pursued first, with learning to write kanji coming after (Hayashi, 1991). But all of these suggestions must pale in comparison to the boon of having a recent analysis which charts the **actual frequencies** of kanji appearances in newspaper text (Nozaki, Yokoyama, Isomoto & Yoneda, 1996). Approved lists aside, the mere fact of knowing that just 1,000 most frequently used kanji account for 95% of actual kanji usage in print is the most powerful pedagogical tool for providing practical access to written Japanese. The additional fact that the 1,600 most frequently used kanji account for an amazing 99% should obviously form the basis for the organization of learning protocols for mature students of Japanese as a Second Language, if not for native learners themselves. Given the high correlation for frequencies between newspaper texts analyzed in 1966 and 1993, one expects that reading any post-war prose on the basis of such frequency aids will benefit greatly from this kind of overview information (see Nozaki, Yokoyama, Isomoto & Yoneda, 1996).

Very simply, kanji writing is a difficult skill to acquire and maintain (see Kaiho, 1987), and not surprisingly, even college graduates make errors in their informal writing or produce cursive script in which the specific kanji cannot be deciphered (see Hatta, Kawakami & Hatasa, 1997; Hatta, Kawakami & Tamaoka, 1998). And there are also generational differences in respect to kanji reading and writing which can be attributed to kanji familiarity. They can arise from differences in schooling and educational experience, but another source is the fact that certain low-frequency kanji become familiar because of their repeated appearance in the popular media. As a result, Ukita, Sugishima, Minagawa, Inoue, and Kashu (1996) found significant differences for low frequency kanji between generations, but found little difference between generations for high frequency words which typically appeared as kanji. This was reflected in comprehension values, but one can extrapolate that it will certainly be reflected in writing abilities as well.

CROSS-CULTURAL COMPARISONS OF
READING SKILLS AND READING DISABILITIES

Non-existence of Japanese Dyslexics?

Over the past several decades, acquisition of reading skills by young children has been a perennial topic in North America, and there has been considerable debate about the suitability of reading programs in various countries. Some research has investigated the reported abilities of one cultural group as opposed to another in the matter of reading prowess, and in comparative studies of Japanese reading programs, the question of whether and "why Johnny reads differently than Noriko" (compare Overly, 1977, with Duke, 1977). There have also been corresponding claims in respect to the number and type of reading disabilities reported for the two countries. Makita (1968), for example, once noted that dyslexia is ten times lower in Japan than in Western countries, and that the syndrome is rarely encountered in Japan. He based his observations on a survey questionnaire from 247 primary school teachers reporting on 9,195 students, with the net result showing **only 0.98%** of that student population as having some degree of reading difficulty. Makita (1976) himself claimed to have never seen a single referral for reading difficulty since beginning his own children's psychiatric service in 1958. Nor, he claimed, did his colleagues see much action in this arena, on the basis of his gleanings from a series on questionnaires he sent to a limited number of child guidance clinics, educational counselling services, and other child study institutions (see Makita, 1968). The responses were all negative, except for a single case of congenital word blindness, and he concluded that there were hardly any cases that called for clinical attention (see also Sakamoto & Makita, 1973). Makita concluded that it must be the specific script type that causes reading disabilities. That is, it is the nature of the language, and the script that the language uses, that must account for the marked difference in the incidence of poor readers in Japan and in the West, and the reason why remedial reading classes and dyslexia as such are practically non-existent in Japan (Sakamoto & Makita, 1973). There is no question that, if true, such a low incidence of reading disabilities in Japan certainly stands in contrast to the incidence of reading disabilities in the United States, where estimates suggest that anywhere between 5% to 10% (Stevenson, 1984) or 3% to 15% (Sheridan, 1983) of children enrolled in primary schools show evidence of such difficulties.

There has been **criticism** of this claim that reading disabilities are virtually non-existent in Japan, and the view that the Japanese writing system is transparent because it offers readers phonetic consistency in reading kana and a direct semantic link in reading kanji has also come under scrutiny. For example, Makita's conclusions were derived from questionnaire results which reported that no children had difficulty with hiragana or katakana symbols past grade four, and that only 4% were reported to have difficulty with the kanji in their curriculum. But one of the main criticisms has been that his questionnaire only implied that the teachers should identify children who were unable to recognize individual kana or kanji symbols. They were not given explicit instructions to look for children who evidenced difficulty in **reading connected text** written in kana and/or kanji. As Yamada and Banks (1994) imply, if dyslexia in English were a simple measurement of those children who are unable to recognize and name the 26 letters of the alphabet, we might have a lower incidence in North America as well.

In English, the **vagaries of the alphabetic system** have been held to blame for acquisition problems, principally because of irregularity, redundancy, and mis-representation in respect to orthographic fit with the phonological structure it is supposed to symbolize. In turn, there have been claims about massive differences in word knowledge between readers of English and logographic languages like Chinese and Japanese. In fact, Japanese often comes in for high praise as an ideal writing system, because it is said to utilize an orthography that offers symbols for both sounds and semantics (see Gleitman & Rozin, 1977; Rozin & Gleitman, 1977; Sheridan, 1983). Not surprisingly, applications of other pictorial systems such as Blissymbolics or logographic systems such as Chinese characters have been promulgated as offering answers to English-based reading problems. For example, Rozin, Poritsky, and Sotsky (1971) taught 30 Chinese characters to eight American second-graders who exhibited reading abilities for those characters after only 4.4 hours of tutoring over a four month period. They are reporting as succeeding in mastering the Chinese characters, and the authors attribute this success to the ideographic nature of the hanzi. A close examination of the study, however, reveals that these results came from second-graders who were at an average mid-first-grade reading level at the beginning of the study, and who were continuing regular classes in which they received an average 6.4 hours in reading English. Thus, they were also receiving instruction in the English alphabet, and even showed im-provement in reading English by having improved the level of their reading skills by nearly one-fourth year.

Characterization of 'Reading Disabilities'

Stevenson (1984) questions whether the Rozin et al. children should actually be considered to have reading disabilities. The characterization of a 'reading disability' is typically a reflection of the formal definition used and the severity of the problems addressed. Downing and Leong (1982) offer the broadest, yet most comprehensive definition by noting that reading disabilities denote a broad group of children who show

varying degrees of reading difficulty for various causes, regardless of intelligence. A-
mong these is a small group of severely disabled readers who are variously characterized
as showing developmental dyslexia, reading retardation, or specific reading disabilities.
Common definitions of the elusive designation of 'reading disability', however, do typically incorporate the features of being behind in reading level by at least two years, with
average or near-average IQ, and without being emotionally or mentally disturbed. Given
the level of performance reported for these children, they seem not to qualify under these
broad guidelines.

As for their success with the Chinese characters, it is true that their knowledge of the
characters was high, with only 6 naming errors for the 137 characters used to create sentences. But comprehension lagged dramatically, with an average of fewer than 2 of the 6
questions asked being answered correctly. The results from such an exercise in paired
associate learning is impressive on the small scale, but does not begin to approach the
demands that will be made by the entire inventory of Chinese words and compounds in a
real writing system.

The gist of other research comes down on the side of the incidence of reading disabilities being much the same for alphabetic and logographic systems mastered by
English-, Japanese-, and Chinese-speaking children. For example, Stevenson, Stigler,
Lucker, and Lee (1982) attempted to determine the validity of the claim that children
learning to read Chinese and Japanese do not evidence reading disabilities. A specially-
designed reading test and a battery of ten cognitive tasks was constructed in each language (Japanese, Chinese, and English) to assess whether differences in the incidence of
reading disability is related to orthographic differences in these languages. Such an
inquiry would obviously shed light on the question of whether English orthography is the
major factor in the reading problems reported for a significant number of American
children. The results from very large samples of fifth-grade children in Japan, Taiwan,
and the United States show that reading disabilities do exist among Japanese and
Chinese children, suggesting that orthography alone is not the crucial factor which
determines the incidence of reading disabilities across cultures. The authors observe that
the reason why Japanese and Chinese professionals may have failed to acknowledge the
presence of reading disabilities among children in their own countries is largely due to
different definitions of dyslexia and reading disabilities, as well as to the manner in
which these are attributed to children. For example, in classrooms where choral reading
is favored, where slowness in reading might be attributed to lack of proper experience or
motivation, and where objective assessment instruments are not commonly available,
poor performance might not be recognized as a reading disability (see Stevenson, 1984).[3]

---

[3] Reporting disabilities can be quite subjective in other areas as well. Consider, for example, Tokuda's
(1987) correlation between visual impairment and kanji skills for 281 children in grades two to six. The

As for the lack of reading disabilities in Japan, Hirose and Hatta (1985, 1988) challenge the view that dyslexia and other reading disabilities are extremely rare in Japan, contending that frontline elementary school teachers' observations do not coincide with Makita's observations as a psychiatrist. They call attention to the fact that one of the main concerns of Japanese teachers in elementary settings is the development of remedial programs for those students who are being left behind. Makita's oft-cited data may not be valid, given his reliance on highly subjective judgments made by teachers who were simply asked to answer questions such as *"Do you have children in your class who show specific difficulties in learning to read using the ordinary method, regardless of their normal intelligence?"*. If their answer was affirmative, Makita further asked them to specify how many such children there were. In response to such loose controls, Hirose and Hatta (1988) set out to measure reading abilities in almost a thousand 11-year-old children, controlled for the variables of sex and urban vs. rural origins. They used a tighter operational definition than the Makita survey, characterizing reading disability as applicable when the reading score was more than two years behind grade level and the IQ quotient on a standardized test as equal to or greater than 85. They employed a **standardized reading test** (Kitao, 1984b), developed for assessing reading abilities in children aged 8 to 13 on five subscales which tested word discrimination in meaningful and nonsense letter sequences, sentence comprehension, sentence memory, and reasoning. Their results demonstrate that reading disabilities are as common in Japan as they are in many Western countries: 18.7% of the children tested showed a one year delay, and 10.9% showed a delay of two or more. Reading disabilities were more prevalent among male children, but urban vs. rural backgrounds did not prove to be a significant factor. If anything, reading disabilities correlated strongly with poor abilities in **sentence memory and reasoning**, instead of word discrimination ability, leading one to ask whether Rozin et al.'s emphasis on logographic symbols as a panacea is well-placed.

In this light, Yamada and Banks (1994) took the tack of examining the reading of connected text, instead of merely checking recognition of single kana or single kana words in isolation. Their results present evidence that also refutes the view that developmental dyslexia is rare in Japan. As we have already observed, fluent reading and/or full comprehension of connected text written in kana is not automatically guaranteed by the ability to recognize individual kana. Thus, in order to ascertain whether children experienced problems with processing kana in textual sequence, an oral reading test and

---

data is derived from questionnaires from instructors in schools for the blind and special classes for visually impaired children which described the nature of the children's visual impairments, as well as their physical abilities, general learning capability, and personality traits. For example, a surprising 15% of the children were classified as superior to normal children, but the exact characterization of their superior performance is not formalized.

a modified Bangor Dyslexia Test were administered to 125 fourth-graders. In the oral reading test, two texts were given: a simple text written in the normal orthographic mode (that is, a mixture of hiragana, katakana, and kanji) and a katakana text, written exclusively in katakana (an unconventional mode of presentation). Entire texts written in katakana are rare, and were thus hypothesized as likely to cause more reading difficulty for the potentially dyslexic children, and would serve to differentiate them from the non-dyslexic children. Using reading speed as the main criterion, the authors found that four boys and four girls, a total of 6% of the subjects, qualified as dyslexic. These subjects spent twice as much time as the average subjects to read the texts; they were also prone to mistakes such as mid-word pauses, transpositional errors, and intonational mistakes, indicative of problems in decoding and sequential processing. The administration of the modified Bangor Dyslexia Test also confirmed the **dyslexic status** of these eight subjects, as they performed significantly worse than normal readers on five of its seven sub-tests. These results also show parallels with children who show learning disabilities in Western reports; for example, Japanese fourth-graders who decoded kana text slowly also showed poor performance with reversed digits. In general, these Japanese dyslexic children experienced real difficulty with learning to read connected text, especially kana-only text, and appeared to labor over breaking the flow into individual kana and kanji symbols and then assembling them into meaningful words or phrases. Yamada and Banks thus caution against the uncritically accepted view that developmental dyslexia is rare in Japan, and suggest that research instead be focussed on remediating develop-mental dyslexia rather than on denying its existence.

Implications from Studies of Other Impairments

Lastly, Sasanuma's (1992; see also, 1984, 1985) overview of patterns of acquired reading impairment in Japanese neurological patients lists features which offer useful comparisons across different languages, and contribute to a universal model of reading comprehension. There are, to be sure, language-specific features unique to Japanese, but Japanese reading comprehension impairments do share some basic similarities. Most interesting, both English and Japanese exhibit instances of **double dissociation** between the comprehension and pronunciation of written words. For example, there are reported cases of post-stroke 'deep dyslexia', where the pattern of reading performance is marked by difficulty in reading aloud orthographically regular non-words as well as real words. This malfunction suggests an impairment of the ability to translate directly from orthography to phonology. In addition, such patients may also make semantically driven errors, reading <uncle> as "cousin" or <dinner> as "food". But there are also language-specific features which emerge from the unique orthographic devices in the Japanese language. In Japanese, there can be a clear-cut dissociation in performance for kanji as opposed to kana, with significantly poorer performance on kana words than kanji words, both in comprehension and reading aloud.

In the opposite direction, however, Sasanuma reports on cases of Alzheimer-type dementia for whom direct transcoding from orthographic shape to phonology, without semantic mediation, is possible in kanji reading. For example, in a single year one patient went from a nearly perfect score to chance in being able to match kanji words to corresponding pictures. Although this patient could continue to pronounce the kanji words perfectly even after three years, after one year he could not even exceed chance on 'yes-no' answers to the simplest semantic questions, such as *Is it an animal?*. It turns out that there are also cases of dissociation for kana words as well, so that the comprehension of written kana words and their pronunciation can be independently impaired.

Given that there are also reported cases for such dissociation in alphabetic scripts, the best explanation seems to be that reading in all three orthographies, alphabetic, syllabary, and logographic, involves two basic but independent processes, an orthography-to-pronunciation route and an orthography-to-meaning route (see Patterson, 1990). As a result of such **universal processing principles**, it is possible to suffer the impairments we have seen in the possible dissociation between comprehension and pronunciation of written words, be the script type kanji or kana. But we should note that there are also **language-specific** consequences of neurological impairments which are tied to the fact of Japanese having an orthography which employs both kana and kanji script types. For example, Sasanuma (1992) notes that one language-specific difference displayed by her deep dyslexia patients is a greater impairment in both the comprehension and pronunciation of kana words relative to kanji words. A second language-specific difference is to be found in the greater proportion of semantic errors in reading kanji words aloud than in reading kana words aloud. The explanation offered by Sasanuma ties in with where kanji and kana sit on the continuum of orthography-to-phonology decoding. Transcoding from orthography to phonology is less efficient, and thus slower, for kanji words than for kana words; so there is much less influence from phonology in computing meaning for kanji. For kana, the opposite will be true. Thus, if there is impairment of the orthography to phonology route, the net effect on transcoding written words will be greater on kana words for these deep dyslexics. This particular impairment will give an advantage to the indirect, semantically mediated route, thus enhancing kanji performance over kana performance somewhat, and providing for one of those script-specific features we cannot afford to simply overlook.

CONCLUSIONS

In conclusion, it is the case that differences in orthographic type alone do not provide a sufficient basis for explaining the occurrence of severe reading problems. Such problems can occur, regardless of whether the child is reading a language represented by an alphabet, logographs, or a combination of logographs and a syllabary. Some specific reading problems may be indeed be associated with the orthographic type used in each respective linguistic culture, but other factors such as definition and attribution will also critically affect reports of incidence. It probably is true that it easier to learn to read the inventory of words written in Japanese kana than it is to learn to read the inventory of words written in the English alphabet. But as soon as you add into the equation the necessity of learning to read kanji as well, the simple statement that learning to read in Japanese is easier than learning to read in English is simply a non-sequitur.

Chapter 8

EYE-MOVEMENT STUDIES

INTRODUCTORY COMMENTS

In addition to the vast body of research dealing with the acquisition of reading and writing skills, there is a smaller body of psycholinguistic literature that deals with experimental inquiry into eye movements as a measure of reading in Japanese. The measurement of eye movements as an indicator of cognitive difficulty, relating to textual density or ambiguity, as well as a global measure of the reading process, has seen some interesting results, but in general those results do not show the Japanese reader as unique in terms of fundamental reading processes. Neither the use of logographic kanji together with syllabic kana nor the traditional use of *tategaki* 'top-to-bottom' directional reading seems to alter these basic processes. For example, contrary to popular beliefs about relative ease in reading horizontal vs. vertical texts, Osaka and Oda (1991) found no difference between these two modes of reading, as measured by both eye-fixation durations and saccade lengths. The effective visual field for both vertical and horizontal readings was found to be about the same, namely, about 5 to 6 character spaces.

Work with eye-movements in reading Japanese texts does call for a reconsideration of the role of kanji vs. kana in processing text, and thus for understanding the cognitive processes in reading (see Osaka, 1991, for a convenient summary). In normal kanji-based texts, the eye skips from kanji to kanji, using them like high-profile stepping stones which stand out in relief in the field of kana. This triangulation possibility allows the reader to organize the textual sentences in a top-down processing sweep (Osaka, 1987b), a strategy which is not immediately possible with alphabetic or syllabary texts. The peripheral vision for kanji-based texts is also wider (with a range of 6 words) than for kana-only texts (with a range of only 4 words), with kanji reading allowing longer saccade patterns (see Osaka, 1992). Thus, logographic writing incorporated into the normal *kanji/kana majiribun* seems to elicit different processing strategies in reading, giving rise to shorter fixation patterns followed by longer saccades. The results show that the effective visual field for kanji-based texts, including both parafoveal and near peripheral areas, is twice as large as the visual field for kana only texts. Whether this is because kanji are accessed directly in the mental lexicon (see Osaka, 1990), and do not require phonological recoding, as per the traditional explanation, or because of the physical layout of the text, is yet to be answered satisfactorily. Before elaborating upon the findings for Japanese, we provide some basic facts about eye movements during reading.

EXPERIMENTAL METHODS IN EYE-MOVEMENT STUDIES

Depending on differences in the reader's visual acuity, the reader's eye fixation at any given time can be divided into the **foveal** vision, the **parafoveal** vision, and the **peripheral vision** (see Rayner & Sereno, 1994, for an introduction to the basic facts of eye movements). The fovea, or central focus of our vision, is designed to process details, and vision involving the area beyond the fovea dramatically loses its acuity. In terms of coverage, the fovea covers a visual angle which takes in the central two degrees of coverage, each one degree being equated to three or four letters of written word stimuli. Parafoveal vision takes in the next five degrees of coverage, angled from each side of the fixation point, and is not directly responsible for gathering detailed information. The range of parafoveal vision does, however, guide the eyes from one fixation point to another, and is responsible for the control of saccadic eye movements. The information that aids in identifying the meaning of a word is, therefore, obtained within the foveal region and the beginning of the parafoveal region. Peripheral vision covers the region beyond the area covered by parafoveal vision, but information obtained through peripheral vision is of little use in reading, and provides only general information, as for example, holistic images of text format, sentence length, and sentence endings.

Basic Eye Movements

The basic eye movements found in reading consist of a series of fixations and saccades, or movements until the next fixation point. **Fixations** are the periods in which our eyes are relatively still, and are generally measured by the duration of a fixed vision, usually lasting 150 to 350 msec. (see Rayner, 1992). The perceptual span is defined in terms of that portion of the text from which useful information is obtained during a single fixation (Rayer & Sereno, 1994). Although the exact rationale for fixation is undecided, it seems likely that fixations have three purposes: they allow transmission of the visual stimulus while the eyes are at rest; at the same time, they provide a period free from any new, interfering stimuli; and they allow cognitive downtime to comprehend the ideas just taken in, as well as their interrelationships (see McConkie, 1983). Eye fixation duration can range from 50 to 600 msec., depending on factors such as word frequency, word length, its syntactic features, and its predictability from the context that a word finds itself in. Of these, word frequency plays the most important role, with shorter fixation durations elicited by higher frequency words. After each fixation, readers will move forward a number of character spaces, as the **saccade** leads the foveal vision to the next visual target stimulus presented in the parafoveal vision area. Thus, while foveal vision is reading a fixed word or words, the parafoveal vision is looking for the next fixation point. In transferring from the current fixation point to the next fixation point, the eyes do not move smoothly, but rather move in a jerking series of movements,[1] with each saccade taking in as little as one character space or as much as fifteen character spaces, but more typically about six to eight characters.

When the eyes do move from one fixation point to another, the fixed position is not chosen at random, but the eyes consistently seek an **optimal viewing position** from which the time taken to recognize the word is minimal. If the initial fixation position differs from the optimal viewing position, the time it takes to recognize a given word increases (O'Regan, 1992). In real-time reading situations, however, the interplay between fixations and saccades is blended with **regressive movements** of the eyes, with about 10 to 15% of eye fixation being in reality regressions in which readers look back and re-read word stimuli (Rayner & Sereno, 1994). Regression is due to the processor's inability to comprehend words on-line, and so the reader has to backtrack to words that were not comprehended initially. Low-frequency words are the ones more likely to be re-fixated than high-frequency words, as are very long words (see Inhoff & Rayner, 1986; Rayner & Sereno, 1994). Such backtracking is then followed by a long saccadic sweep back to the location from which the regression started. The more difficult the text, the more regressions, and also the longer the fixations become, the shorter the saccades.

---

[1] Despite rapid saccadic movements, Nakamizo (1974) notes that readers do not experience blurred vision. Since the turn of the century, there have been two competing views to account for this stabilizing effect of **saccadic suppression**. One explanation is that the nervous system ignores blurred retinal images, while the other explanation claims that saccadic suppression is due to a built-in inhibitory process. Experimental studies in Japan generally favor the inhibitory hypothesis, because saccadic suppression starts 30-50 msec. prior to the actual saccadic movement and persists until 30-50 msec. after the movement, suggesting that saccadic suppression must take place even before the possibility of blurred retinal images (see also Osaka, 1987a).

Experimental Methods

The basic premise underlying eye-movement experiments as applied to the reading task is that the examination of fixations and saccades can function as a window through which we can make appropriate inferences about moment-to-moment language processing decisions. This premise is based on the assumption that eye movements relate to cognitive processes, and that the reading rate, as measured by way of eye-movements, and the speed of comprehension do not differ substantially. This allows, for example, an external measure by which to judge alternative accounts of the processes that accompany reading (see Rayner, 1992).

Various **techniques** have been employed as experimental methods of reading, some focussing on word-by-word presentation and others on textual presentation. Single word presentation has its limitations in terms of the processing inferences which can be made, because such methods may not reveal the true nature of the cognitive processes involved in reading continuous written text. And such tasks are somewhat unnatural, because the reading rate which emerges from such measurements is not necessarily representative of the reading processes which accompany normal reading (see Rayner & Sereno, 1994). In the 'word-by-word reading' experimental technique, subjects control the rate of word presentation themselves (for example, by pressing a button). The 'Rapid Serial Visual Presentation (RSVP) method presents subjects with words at a predetermined presentation rate in the same or slightly different spatial location. The RSVP technique lends itself to ascertaining the 'convenient viewing position' within the array of letters that constitutes a word, because the location of the array and the length of the array can both be varied (see Osaka, 1990, for an example). A third related method elicits 'completion responses', with subjects providing a typical word recognition response, such as lexical decision or naming, to a target word after they have finished reading a passage silently. A fourth method simply measures the total reading time for a segment of the text, say a phrase, clause, or sentence, so that one is measuring a grammatical block of words instead of a single word.

Other experimental methods focus on direct measurements of the span from which characters are read, allowing inferences more attuned to textual reading of written material presented sequentially. The most fruitful of these experimental methods have been the constellation of techniques that track eye movements of readers as they actually read. This paradigm has been generally viewed as more natural because **tracking eye-movements** records what is happening in the on-line processing of written text, without introducing artificial tasks to complicate both the task and the inferences therefrom. And there is the early, but comforting finding that reading rate and comprehension do not differ when subjects read in the laboratory vs. normal conditions (Tinker, 1939).

One such method is a 'moving window' method which controls the amount of text information visible around the current eye fixation; because the amount of information available to the subject in a defined region of text around the point of fixation is limited, one should in principle be able to measure the perceptual span from which relevant information is gathered. The text beyond this 'window' is altered in some way; for example, the letters may be replaced with X's. With each new fixation, another window is established; if window size matches the region from which a reader obtains information, it may be equated with the size of perceptual area from which information is adduced (McConkie & Rayner, 1975; Rayner & Sereno, 1994). That is, the window size is as large as the region from which the reader acquires information, and in this way emulates normal reading practice. The underlying assumption here, of course, is that changes in eye movements somehow match changes in the perceptual span, an assumption not always to be taken for granted (see, for example, O'Regan, 1992).

Unlike the moving window paradigm in which a display change is associated with each eye movement, a word or non-word letter string initially occupies the critical target location in the text in the 'boundary' method (Rayner, 1975, 1992). This technique allows the researcher to make inferences about the kind of information which is acquired at different distances from the target, thus allowing us to see how much and what kinds of parafoveal information are gleaned from a word before it is actually fixated upon. For example, an invisible boundary can be placed just to the left of the target location, and when the reader makes an eye movement that crosses this boundary, the initially displayed stimulus (that is, the parafoveal preview) is replaced by the target word. In this method, fixation time on the target is examined as a function of the relationship between the parafoveal preview and the target (Rayner & Sereno, 1994). The idea is that the amount of fixation time on the target itself is partially determined by the type and amount of information acquired from the items in parafoveal vision.

A last method does actually track the movement of the eyes by projecting a beam of light onto the surface of the eyeball, and tracking the movement of the eyes by constantly monitoring the angles of reflected beams. The reflections of the beam are fed into a computer monitoring device, giving an ongoing account of what the eyes are doing at any given point. In sum, so far such on-line tracking methods seem to offer the most faithful reflection of moment-by-moment processing decisions, given the fact that such methods track eye-movement while reading is taking place at a normal reading rate.

EYE-MOVEMENT STUDIES IN JAPANESE

Regular Kanji-based Texts

Several studies have examined fixation durations while reading regular kana-kanji mixed texts. Osaka (1989) presented subjects with such a text on a monochrome CRT screen, and held the ratio of that text at a 60/40 value (that is, 60 of 100 characters were kana, while 40 were kanji). A mean fixation duration of 168.26 msec. for regular texts was obtained by averaging fixations within the area of 1 degree of spatial extent which were longer than 66 msec. But a similar experimental study by Osaka (1990) reports a significantly different value of 270 msec. for mean fixation duration, pointing to a lack of absolute values for fixation durations. Such differences also call attention to the fact that mean fixation durations may be sensitive to text type and text content.

While fixation duration seems to be a relative value, there are some interesting similarities in reading English texts and Japanese texts. **Content words** are consistently fixated on, while **function words** are consistently skipped in English. However, in Japanese, content words are regularly written in kanji and function words in kana, so that the parafoveal vision skips from kanji to kanji, using them as signalling markers or high-profile stepping stones in traversing the textual path. For example, Kambe (1986) reports that fixations appear consistently on kanji (90% of the time), but not so often on hiragana (only 49% of the time). Interestingly enough, they also alight on katakana 97% of the time, underscoring the fact that most katakana words are highly information-laden and, if novel as katakana forms, quite unpredictable from their shapes. Hence, likelihood of the landing point for the eyes seems likely to correspond to kanji as well as katakana words scattered within the mixed text, suggesting that in processing Japanese texts the fixation choice points are **orthographically driven**. Parafoveal vision seeks out katakana and kanji as the next likely fixation point, perhaps not even discriminating whether the word is a content word or not. This can be an effective strategy, because as long as eye fixations do settle on katakana and kanji words, the parafoveal vision will not miss too many content words. And these words stand out in bold relief against a field of hiragana script, much in the way that numerals do in alphabetic text. In this sense, saccadic eye-movements in Japanese are more orthography-driven, to the extent that some have even suggested that, as a mixed script, the Japanese orthography is extremely efficient in processing text for reading comprehension (Taylor & Taylor, 1983), and perhaps even easier to read than a single-script text (Taylor, 1997).[2]

---

[2] When Osaka (1989, 1990) had Japanese subjects read English alphabetically-written texts as well as kana texts, he found that these texts elicited the same general type of eye movements as did kana texts, suggesting that phonologically-based writing systems (such as the kana syllabary and the English alphabet) elicit similar

The typical Japanese reader is able to skim through normal kanji-based text by relying on parafoveal detection of the kanji elements embedded within the field of kana. In a sense, English readers also employ similar text-based strategies which rely on the interaction between **word length** and **grammatical type**. For example, short words of three letters or less are likely to be skipped in English, while longer words of six letters or more are rarely skipped. Moreover, content words are fixated most of the time, while function words are only fixated on about a third of the time or much less, depending upon the specific function word (see Rayner & Sereno, 1994). It would appear that word-skipping is a natural component in the process of normal reading, but in Japanese where to alight next is conditioned by script type, katakana or kanji being likely candidates, whereas in English that decision is conditioned by the length of a word to the right of the current fixation.

McConkie and Rayner (1975) report the size of the **perceptual span** in English to be 15 character spaces in the right visual field extending from the fixation point, as well as 3 or 4 character spaces to the left of the fixation point (see also Rayner, 1983; Rayner & Sereno, 1994). In right-to-left scripts, such as Hebrew, the perceptual span appears to be the inverse, and thus asymmetric to the left of the fixation point instead (Rayner, 1983). In English, the actual word identification span, or so-called **'effective visual span'**, within which a fixed vision can obtain detailed orthographic information, is smaller than the 'perceptual span', which involves a region only 5 to 7 character spaces to the right of the fixation.

In Japanese, Ikeda and Saida (1978) have examined perceptual spans by manipulating the window span at fixation points, artificially narrowing and thus controlling the visual field size. Ikeda and Saida had Japanese subjects read text samples silently, under six different visual field size conditions: 2, 3, 5, 8, 13, and 20 degrees of visual angle, corresponding to 2.6, 3.9, 6.6, 10.5, 17.1 and 26.3 character spaces, respectively. The results reveal that an increase in visual field size elicits an increase in reading rate, but only to a point; depending upon individual differences, there was no increase in the reading rate beyond a certain visual field size, roughly between 10 and 17 letters. Thus, for example, the size of the visual field is evident in those cases where it is reduced; saccades become smaller, and there is an increase in reading time and a decrease in reading rate.

Although individual differences play a role in this work as well, Kambe (1989) reports the size of the effective visual field to be between 9 and 12 characters, with the average distance between fixations between 3 and 5 characters in kanji-based text.

---

processing strategies in reading. It is true that English texts of roughly the same difficulty made for longer fixation durations than did the Japanese texts for the Japanese subjects, and that there was a significant difference between the difficulty levels of easy vs. difficult. But one might expect that Japanese subjects reading English would exhibit longer fixations in the second language text than in the first language text.

Kambe employed the fixed window approach, and compared readers' eye movements, as they read through a special vision-restricting window which they slid along the text, with their eye movements when reading text normally and without such a window. Osaka (1992) notes that if one equates a Japanese character with a letter, then the span of reading is considerably smaller. But one might consider kanji-based text to be **more dense** than English text, because of the amount of information packed into a single kanji; if so, one might also say that more information is processed per fixation in kanji-based text, giving rise to longer saccade lengths.

Osaka and Osaka (1992) observe that the results for reading spans suggest that **working memory** for reading appears to be independent of language structure. They base their conclusions on an examination of the relationships between working memory capacity in first and second languages by measuring reading spans for Japanese and for English among Japanese students who had studied English for more than six years. Working memory involves the immediate memory processes in the simultaneous storage and processing of information, with emphasis on the efficiency of storing the partial product of comprehension for a limited period while incoming information is being processed. Working memory capacity is closely related to an individual's reading ability, and plays an important role in comprehension processes during reading. What they found was that reading span scores showed a significant correlation with reading comprehension scores, and that the high-span reader had a larger capacity to work with strategic memorization in both languages. Such findings should recall the importance of **individual differences** in language comprehension for us, with perceptual grasp of information spans just another example of this fact.

When parafoveal vision is examined from a **developmental** point of view, some interesting differences emerge between children and adults. It is generally accepted that acuity thresholds for the periphery are higher for children than for adults, and that conversely, adults are faster in visual search and reading than are children. It may be that children are not as adept at using peripheral vision in such tasks, and Osaka (1980) reports on a study which contrasts the effectiveness of **parafoveal visual field size** for adults vs. children. Three-, four-, five-, and twenty-one-year-old subjects had to identify pictures through peepholes of five different sizes, with the results showing that the effectiveness of the parafoveal vision differed among the four age groups. Response times improved as age and area increased, with adults being the most proficient at information processing involving parafoveal vision. Hatae (1982) also provides evidence that the efficiency of parafoveal vision increases as the child grows. First- and second-graders who had been characterized as good vs. poor readers were presented with hiragana targets surrounded by various kinds of **visual noise** material (hiragana, katakana, alphabetic symbols, and concrete object shapes), which they were asked to read aloud as quickly as possible. The response times, not surprisingly, varied according to grade level and to the type of noise. As the children advanced in age, moving from the first to the second grade, so also did their ability to filter parafoveal noise out from the orthographic target information. Also, good readers in general exhibited a more efficient filtering system for such visual noise (see Adachi, 1992, 1993, Sato, 1982, and Yagi, Ishida & Katayama, 1992, for other constraining factors). It would appear that this is established at a fairly early age, for the consensus seems to be that children acquire and use letter information from the same regions as college students by the fifth grade. There is no particular body of evidence that shows that the region within which letters are identified increases beyond this point, even though reading skills may increase (see McConkie, 1983).

The experimental results for **'convenient viewing position'** also show some interesting comparisons between English and Japanese texts. Convenient viewing position is the position within a word where the eye should fixate first in order for the word to be captured most quickly and efficiently. Osaka (1990) presented high frequency words in different orthographic types, differentiated by the location for each presentation, and had subjects fixate on the word presented. He found that preferred viewing positions existed for both kana and kanji formats, and these results correspond with previous findings for English, in that the convenient viewing position is located somewhat to the left of the word's center (see also Osaka, 1992). More specifically, the convenient viewing positions for katakana and hiragana formats are practically the same, namely, the fifth, fourth, third, and second letter positions for 11-, 9-, 7-, and 5-kana words, respectively (see Osaka, 1990). The probable landing place from which convenient viewing position can be established is located more toward the beginning of the word because more attention is typically devoted to the initial letter in a string than to other letters in such arrays. In the same way, some preview information is derived from previewing the first few letters in words to the right of the current fixation. The same results are reported by Kambe (1986), who found fixation to take place to the left of word center; for example, in ten-letter words, fixation took place on the fourth letter.

Saccadic distance in the available experimental studies ranges somewhere between 3 to 5 characters, although one must take into account individual differences. For example, Ikeda and Saida (1978) reports that the saccadic distance for his Japanese subjects ranged from 2.1 to 5.0 characters, with a mean value of 3.6 characters. Kambe (1986, 1989) reports the average saccadic distance between fixation points to be between 3 and 5 letters, although Osaka (1989) notes an average saccadic distance of around 5 letters.

Regression appears to be more frequent in the case of English texts than in Japanese texts. According to Rayner and Inhoff (1981), somewhere between 12% to 20% of English text reading involves regressive eye-movements. But only 2 of Kambe's (1984) 18 Japanese subjects exhibited a regressive ratio higher than 10%, while Kambe (1986) reported a regressive reading ratio of 6% among his subjects. One explanation that has been offered is that Japanese texts involve fewer regressive eye movements because they mix phonographic kana and logographic kanji. This orthographic mixing offers a visual aid to the reader by predicting whether a given word is a content word of Sino-Japanese origin (represented by kanji), a content word of a foreign origin (represented by katakana), or merely a native function word (represented by hiragana). The notion is that such pre-determined orthographic differences would make it easy to transfer the parafoveal vision from one fixation point to another, thus eliciting less need for regressive eye movements.

Kanji-based Texts vs. Kana-only Texts

In Japanese, it is possible to contrast regular kana/kanji mixed texts with exclusively hiragana or katakana texts, and this has been done to examine possible processing differences between logographically-based texts and phonographically-based texts, and how such differences might relate to orthography-specific strategies. The general finding is that kana-only texts are harder to process than normal kana/kanji texts, eliciting longer fixation durations, shorter saccadic distances, and frequent occurrences of regressive eye movements. For example, Osaka (1989) examined all three factors of fixation duration, saccade distance, and regressive eye movements, by creating three sets of written texts which differed in script type but contained exactly the same word content. An original text taken from a Japanese novel was presented to subjects in regular kana/kanji format, hiragana-only, and katakana-only formats. The results of eye movement tracking revealed mean fixation durations of 238.91 msec., 190.78 msec., and 168.26 msec. for the katakana-only formats, hiragana-only formats, and regular kana/kanji formats, respectively. Mean saccade lengths were 3.07, 4.68, and 5.01 degrees for the same three formats in the same ranked order.

Although a traditional explanation resorts to the dichotomy between the phonologically-based kana requirement of phonological recoding and the alleged logographic direct access to the mental lexicon, there is certainly an element of **script familiarity** here, compounded by textual **layout unfamiliarity**. Although Osaka (1990) found that Japanese subjects were less efficient in reading phoneme-based texts in English, this may or may not be due to alphabetic symbols being processed purely as phonological symbols. Here too, the longer fixation durations and shorter saccadic distances, at least when matched by their reading of regular mixed Japanese texts, may also be affected by the absence of word frequency and word familiarity effects, as well as script and text familiarity.

Vertical Texts vs. Horizontal Texts

Japanese text can be written in **three different directional modes**. The traditional mode follows Chinese writing practices imported more than a millennium ago, with the text written in vertical fashion, with the characters on each line running top to bottom down the page, and successive lines running from right to left across the page. Because of the influence of alphabetic writing systems, texts have also come to be written in a horizontal directional mode in recent times. This directional mode follows the same format as alphabetic texts, with script running left-to-right in individual lines (just as in this line), and the lines running top to bottom on the printed page (just as on this page). A third directional mode of writing, employing horizontal right-to-left presentation of script, is rather exceptional today, and is never put into practice for regular text presentation. It is often seen in the single-line designations found on signs, headers, and name plates for old establishments such as Buddhist temples and Shinto shrines, as well as in those establishments wishing to portray themselves as old, traditional, or estimable establishments. Thus, Japanese really employs only the two directional modes with any frequency, the traditional, vertical *tategaki* (縦書) and the imported, horizontal *yokogaki* (横書).

Until the beginning of Meiji era (1868-1911), Japanese texts were all written in *tategaki*. But increasing acquaintance with Western culture, and Western scholarship in particular, led to *yokogaki* being adopted as a directional mode in written texts. This subtle competition occasioned internal debates throughout the Meiji era as to whether *tategaki* or *yokogaki* was the more efficient mode with respect to reading and writing (see Osaka, 1991). Until the end of the Second World War, the *tategaki* mode predominated, with all government documents presented in this traditional format. The situation changed dramatically after the War, however, with the Government extolling the merits of *yokogaki* in 1946 and issuing an official recognition of its formal uses, the *Kooyoobun no Hidari-yokogaki ni tsuite* 'On the Use of Left(-to-right) Yokogaki in Official Documents'. Claims were made about *yokogaki* being easier to write, easier to read, and easier on space: supposedly, it was easier to write because the writer can see the final pieces of the characters being written, easier to read when there are references to Western languages, and more economical in its need for less paper in printing requirements (see Takebe, 1979). After this official recognition, even government decrees and official documents after 1949 began to be written in *yokogaki* (see Yasumoto, 1976), although there are still some notable exceptions, such as *koseki* 'family registry' and *kampoo* (官報) 'formal government announcements'. Since then, *yokogaki* has come to be regarded as the main directional mode in writing, while *tategaki* has taken on more the status of an old-fashioned way of writing. The degree to which *yokogaki* has spread among Japanese writers can be glimpsed in a study of preferences conducted by the

National Language Research Institute in 1964 (see Yasumoto, 1976). Among the subjects chosen for their professional pursuit of intellectual activities, such as writing or publishing, many reported using *yokogaki* all or most of the time, as can be seen in the table below. Far fewer reported using *tategaki* most or all of the time.

Preference of Yokogaki Use	Answer Rate
Exclusively	24.4%
Mostly	31.6%
Occasionally	34.9%
Hardly	4.3%
Never	1.4%
No Response	3.3%

Table 8.1 *Yokogaki* Use by professionals.

Possible **processing differences** between *tategaki* and *yokogaki* first received attention in the late 1920s (see Saito, 1980, for a review of early experimental work), when a group of ophthalmologists reported on a series of 17 experiments with nonsense symbols, nonsense orthographic stimuli, and meaningful orthographic stimuli. According to the findings reported by the *Nihon Ganka Gakkai* 'Japanese Ophthalmolgical Society' (1928), efficiency of processing the three types of visual stimuli differed between the vertical and horizontal writing modes. Meaningful orthographic stimuli were better handled by the vertical reading mode, while nonsense symbols were better handled in the horizontal mode. This finding may be attributed to the fact that the subjects were more familiar with vertical reading practices, a reasonable conclusion derived from factors not entirely unlike the script familiarity question. Nevertheless, Japanese studies have continued to search for possible processing differences between the two directional modes, and one sees the occasional volume discussing the relative merits of one directional mode as opposed to the other. For example, the special issue of *Gengo*, Volume 5, 1976, devotes itself to the topic of *Tate to Yoko no Nihongo* (縦と横の日本語) 'Vertical and Horizontal Japanese', elaborating their historical and cultural roots, efficiency and functionality, as well as data from eye movement studies.

Various claims have been made as to relative status of one directional mode vs. the other. Tanaka, Iwasaki, and Miki (1974) observe that visual resolution may fall off more rapidly in the vertical direction than in the horizontal direction, and suggest that there may be a greater ease of eye movement along the horizontal than along the vertical plane. But Watanabe (1971) claims that while horizontal reading might be thought to have some physiological advantage over vertical reading, such an advantage can only be minimal and not be reflected in relative efficiency values for the two directional modes (see Osaka & Oda, 1991). But the question of efficiency for directional modes is a **moot point** because it has never really been fully explored or even considered in most languages, except perhaps in Japanese where such options exist (see Saito, 1980). The global ubiquity of the Roman alphabet-based left-to-right framework is reflected in the fact that directionality in writing systems has never received much serious attention, though there have been occasional studies of right-to-left directionality in Hebrew (Nachson, Shefler & Samocha, 1977).

Although not using Japanese symbols, Sakamoto, Itakura, Imamura, Kinebuchi, Seki, and Hanba (1992) have experimentally examined **velocity of movement** in all four possible directions of eye movement to assess the impact of movement and directionality on the visual recognition of letters, with the express aim of designing new letters with high visual recognition capabilities. They varied the velocity of movement of a series of white squares and letters in the four directions: from left to right in a horizontal manner; from right to left in a horizontal manner; from top to bottom in a vertical manner; and from bottom to top in a vertical manner. Error rates for horizontally moving symbols were significantly smaller than for the vertically moving symbols, with non-significant differences between the two horizontal directions of left vs. right. If anything, visual recognition for letters depended more on the velocity with which they moved.

Importantly, however, eye-movement studies in general find **no significant differences** between the two types of directionality (see Osaka, 1991; Osaka & Oda, 1991). Using a moving window method which varied in size from 1 to 12 characters vertically, Osaka and Oda (1991) found that saccade length increased and fixation duration decreased as the size of the window increased. But they also found that the effective visual field size within which a fixed vision can obtain detailed orthographic information in vertical reading mode is about 5 to 6 character spaces. A field size of 5.5 character spaces was the critical value in Osaka and Oda's results, and this value is very close to the effective field size of 5.8 character spaces found by Osaka (1989) for the horizontal reading mode, as well as to the field size estimated by Kambe's (1989) analysis of the distance from fixation to fixation. (Saccadic distance is different from effective field size in notion.) The implication seems to be that *tategaki* and *yokogaki* directional modes are pretty much a matter of tradition and/or choice rather than of processing efficiency.

Scrolling Speed and Window Size

Lastly, there are efficiency considerations in respect to scrolling speed and window size for reading comprehension. Chujo, Notomi, and Ishida (1993) investigated the influence of the number of characters on the reading rate of character strings moving from left to right. They varied the number of characters on a scrolling screen, adding characters one by one until the number of characters reached 30. Subjects adjusted the movement rate themselves until they found the **optimal movement rate** for the scrolling characters. This optimal movement rate increased proportionately as the number of characters increased, but stabilized at 190 msec. per character once the characters exceeded five in number. The inference is that the field size of the moving window must be at least 5 characters in scope, so that meaningful chunking can take place; but scrolling speed is most efficient in dealing with 7 characters or more at a scrolling speed of 190 msec. per character.

In a similar vein, Kogo and Kishi (1996) examined eye movements of Japanese subjects viewing American movies with **Japanese subtitles**. The number of characters they manipulated was between 6 and 13 characters presented in one line of printed text, and between 13 and 20 characters presented in two lines of printed text. The object of the eye tracking instruments were to record eye movements at four crucial points in reading the subtitles: when the subjects' eyes jumped to the subtitled area, when they jumped to the head of the subtitle, when they read the text, and when they jumped to the head of the second line in two-line subtitles. In general, the results confirm that the larger the number of characters, the longer the reading times: two-line presentations required longer processing times than one-line presentations. Obviously, on-line eye movement research methods have more applications than simply deciding between alternative accounts of word recognition and skilled reading. They also provide useful input into applied engineering questions, such as how to design and integrate the interaction between moving pictures on the screen and their related textual presentations by way of subtitling.

CONCLUSIONS

In concluding this chapter, we should note that the work on eye movements in reading Japanese texts reveals a significant role for kanji vs. kana in the processing of written texts. However, the results of this research paradigm do not show the Japanese reader to be unique in respect to fundamental reading processes, although reading Japanese texts is more orthography-driven than reading phoneme-based texts. If anything, they suggest the underpinnings of a framework of universal strategies in reading written text for comprehension.

Chapter 9

LATERALITY

INTRODUCTION

The human brain exhibits hemispheric differences. The most obvious **hemispheric asymmetry** is observed in the fact that approximately 90% of the human population are right-handed, and such a large population bias is claimed to be atypical among species (Hellige, 1990; Levy, 1972; Sakano, 1970). Another well-established asymmetry is the left-hemisphere dominance of speech; about 95% of right-handers localize their linguistic faculty in the left hemisphere (Hellige, 1980, 1990; Kimura, 1961; Levy, 1969).[1] Besides linguistic dominance, the left hemisphere is known to be superior to the right in analytical processing and for categorizational processing (see, for example, Kosslyn, 1987). Meanwhile, the right hemisphere is superior to left for manipulospatial processing and visuospatial processing (see, for example, Bryden 1982; Kimura, 1969), including the recognition of faces (see DeSchonen & Mathivet, 1989). The right hemisphere is also claimed to be responsible for the production and perception of emotion (see, for example, Bradshaw & Nettleton, 1983).[2]

Since the pioneering era of aphasic research by Broca (1861) and Wernicke (1874), the phenomenon of lateral asymmetry for language activities has come to be well recognized. The modern study of lateral asymmetry has been further expanded by a rich variety

---

[1] According to Levy (1969: 615), "during the evolution of the hominids gestalt perception may have lateralized into the mute [right] hemisphere as a consequence of an antagonism between functions of language and perception".

[2] One sensitive, hence, perhaps not well studied, issue is gender differences in laterality. We have found three studies, Hatta and Kawakami (1994), Kashihara (1981), and Nagae (1983), which address this issue in Japanese. For instance, Kashihara investigates gender differences in laterality effects on the recall of the location of presented kana. Twenty-five adult males and 21 females were presented with a table of 16 boxes with four to eight randomly placed hiragana. A finding was that while males showed a better recall rate for kana positions, females showed a significantly better recall rate for kana characters.

of experimental and clinical inquiries, which have provided entirely new ways of looking at the nature and consequences of hemispheric asymmetry. A dramatic example of such innovative perspectives can be seen in the insights derived from **split-brain** patients first reported by Sperry and his colleagues (for example, Levy, Trevarthen & Sperry, 1972; Sperry, 1974; Sperry & Gazzaniga, 1967) in their systematic research with commissur-otomy patients. These studies, as well as clinical studies involving various types of aphasics, continue to amplify our understanding of cerebral hemispheric asymmetry.

A **variety of techniques** have been developed to probe hemispheric asymmetry for not only such neurologically impaired patients but also for normal individuals. The common strategy observed with these techniques is to present stimuli in such a way that they ostensibly reach one hemisphere more directly, so that the measurement of performance on a specific task can be treated as a function of the stimulated hemisphere (Hellige, 1990). For instance, in the auditory modality, two different stimuli are presented simultaneously, one to each ear (see for example, Hatta, Yamamoto & Hirose, 1990). With such dichotic presentation, neurological evidence indicates that the stimulus presented to one ear is projected to the contralateral cerebral hemisphere. In the case of the visual modality, visual stimuli are tachistoscopically presented to the left or right of an observer's fixation point so that the stimulus from each visual field is projected to the contralateral cerebral hemisphere. Such tachistoscopic examination has been one of the principal experimental paradigms for examining cerebral hemispheric asymmetry insofar as lexical access and word recognition strategies are concerned.

Laterality preferences are reflected in language processing functions which involve written word recognition. And since the nature of **kana/kanji processing** in Japanese is the focus of our inquiry, no such volume would be complete without some mention of this fact. Hence, this chapter briefly reviews the psycholinguistic literature in the areas of experimental psychology and clinical aphasiology, in an attempt to ascertain whether Japanese is unique in its pattern of laterality preferences involving its orthographic repre-sentations. In examining the nature of orthographic processing, we also examine whether such preferences might be influenced by the associative attributes of the script types themselves or the cognitive functions applied to aspects of their decoding. Others have e-valuated some of this literature and found it lacking. For example, Paradis, Hagiwara, and Hildebrandt (1985) find the experimental studies to that point more contradictory than consistent, and simply dismiss most of these studies as evidence for any particular model of cerebral asymmetry. While they do admit that two-kanji compounds elicit a left hemisphere advantage, they point out that the majority of studies deal with the iden-tification of single characters. And they conclude that single Chinese hanzi or Japanese kanji can produce the same laterality patterns as English words, given the right conditions of presentation. In this overview, we take a less detailed and somewhat more historical approach, because we could never do justice to the vast Japanese literature in this field and because we are more interested in introducing the scope and rationale for such Japanese research. For example, we are well aware of the widespread set of popular notions, both in Japan and elsewhere, that hemispheric involvement in respect to the Japanese orthographic system is somehow unique. Thus, we are more interested in seeing where the original sources of such laterality research have derived from, which directions it has taken, and most importantly, where such research might move on to.

DICHOTOMOUS VIEWS OF LATERALITY IN KANA/KANJI PROCESSING

The Origin of the Dichotomous View

Results from early studies by neurologists and experimental psychologists quickly gave rise to the impression that orthographic processing in **Japanese is unique** in the sense that phonemically encoded kana are processed exclusively in the left linguistic hemisphere, while visuospatially oriented kanji are processed in the right hemisphere. Historically, this processing asymmetry between kana and kanji (involving Broca's aphasics) was first noticed at the beginning of the Twentieth Century by Yamamoto (1911) and Asayama (1914). For instance, Asayama (cited in Yamadori, 1998) reported the case of a 33-year-old male who could write kanji with little difficulty but who could hardly write kana characters. However, a dichotomous view of kana and kanji processing may be traced more recently to two influential studies which were coincidentally published in the same volume of *Neuropsychologia* in 1977. One is by Sasanuma and her colleagues (Sasanuma, Itoh, Mori & Kobayashi, 977; but also see Sasanuma & Fujimura, 1971, 1972), and the other by Hatta (1977b).

Based on **tachistoscopic experiments** using hiragana and kanji words, Sasanuma et al. showed that performance ratios for kana and kanji processing are asymmetrically related. Kana processing exhibited a significant right field advantage (in that the correct answer rate of 77.4% was obtained in the right visual field in comparison to that of 66.8% in the left visual field). Meanwhile, kanji processing showed a non-significant trend toward left field superiority (in that the correct answer rate of 72.1% was obtained in the left visual field in comparison to that of 67.6% in the right visual field). Based on an examination of two significant interactions in a pair of experiments which contrasted phonological tasks with visual tasks, Sasanuma, Itoh, Kobayashi, and Mori (1980) later reiterated their assumption that the left hemisphere is more efficient in the phonological processing of kana characters, with the right hemisphere more efficient in the visual processing of kanji characters.

Based also on tachistoscopic experiments, Hatta (1977b) examined whether there were processing differences for high- and low-familiarity single kanji. His main finding was that, irrespective of familiarity, the correct response rate for the kanji stimuli presented to the left visual field was much higher than that for the kanji stimuli presented to the right visual field. And in Hatta (1978) there seemed to be further evidence for a left visual field advantage for single kanji, and a right visual field advantage for kana words. These findings are somewhat refined in an experiment (Hatta, 1977a) which added the variable of imageability, as in concrete vs. abstract. It is true that in tachistoscopically examining whether there were processing differences between single kanji associated with concrete meanings (海 *umi* 'sea', 河 *kawa* 'river') and those with abstract meanings (比 *hi* 'ratio', 忠 *chuu* 'loyalty'), Hatta found that the concrete kanji were more correctly recognized than the abstract kanji. But he also found that the ratio of correct responses was much higher for the kanji stimuli presented to the left visual field (that is, 81% for concrete kanji and 76% for abstract kanji) than those presented to the right visual field (that is, 66% for concrete kanji and 61% for abstract kanji).

Such experimental results were often matched by findings from the **clinical literature** which investigated language impairments in aphasics. For instance, tests on kanji and kana processing given to Broca's aphasics showed a clear asymmetry in processing kanji and kana (Sasanuma, 1977). Their success rate in kanji processing was roughly around the 50% mark, whereas with kana processing it was almost 0%. To account for this asymmetrical performance by the Broca's patients, Sasanuma exemplifies the classic view of cerebral lateralization: the right hemisphere, dominant for gestalt pattern-matching, would be responsible for kanji processing, and the left hemisphere, dominant for sequential, analytical processing, would be responsible for kana processing. This simple dichotomy of function for the cerebral hemispheres was extremely attractive for its elegant simplicity, and seemed to match the configurational qualities of kanji logographs. This classic view of lateralization of language insofar as it relates to script types has not been particularly supported by the published results seen in the wide range of inquiry found in the psychological and clinical literature since then.

A large number of studies have since explored the dimensions of kana and kanji processing from a variety of perspectives, and the results reported by the majority of these studies call for a **re-articulated version** of the 'dichotomous view' of kana/kanji processing. For example, the Paradis et al. (1985) and Hatta (1991) overviews of the experimental literature both note that the majority of studies show no visual field difference, although some have reported a tendency toward left visual field advantage for single kanji. Then, too, there is the clinical literature, and we now know that there are selective losses in kana vs. kanji processing in Japanese aphasic patients exhibiting alexia and/or agraphia (Iwata, 1981, 1987; Paradis et al., 1985; Sasanuma, 1974a, 1974b, 1975, 1980; Sasanuma & Fujimura, 1971, 1972; Sasanuma & Monoi, 1975). Thus, there has been great interest in seeing how the various impairments found in kana/kanji processing abilities might possibly relate to the quest for determining laterality preferences. As a consequence of their attention to experimental variables and the nature of the tasks posed to both normal and aphasic subjects, it is worth reviewing some of the more pertinent of these experimental and clinical studies because they are representative of the direction of research in the last several decades.

Kana Processing

Given that the left hemisphere is a linguistic hemisphere, the issue of laterality preferences in Japanese psycholinguistic studies can be reiterated as the extent to which the right hemisphere contributes to the processing of kana and kanji stimuli (see Yamadori, 1980). The possibility that kana words are processed by the right hemisphere seems to be somewhat remote. For instance, almost all earlier clinical studies (Sasanuma, 1974a, 1975, 1977) suggest that kana is processed largely by the left hemisphere. For instance, according to Sasanuma (1977), impairment in kana processing is found predominantly among patients whose lesions were located in such **left hemisphere speech areas** as Broca's area, Wernicke's area, and the arcuate fasciculus.

This suggestion has been mirrored in most other studies, as for instance, in more recent work by Kashihara (1986), Nagae (1992), Shimada (1981), and Law, Kanno, Fujita, Lassen, Miura, and Uemura (1991). After instructing his 15 subjects to respond either with the right or left hand depending upon the type of stimuli, Kashihara (1986) tachistoscopically presented paired stimuli which consisted of (a) symbols designating a circle or a cross and (b) corresponding kana words (まる maru 'circle' and かけ kake 'cross'). Given the clear difference in reaction times between such non-verbal and verbal stimuli, Kashihara concluded that kana words are better processed by the left than the right hemisphere. This left hemisphere superiority for kana processing is also supported by Nagae's (1992) detailed survey of previous clinical (11) and experimental (34) studies on laterality preferences. This extensive review of the literature does not list a single study or experiment which supports the claim that the right hemisphere has any crucial involvement in the processing of kana. From a different perspective, Law et al. (1991) map language processing areas of the cerebral cortex for kana stimuli by using Positron Emission Tomography (PET) scans with 13 normal Japanese male subjects. Their finding was that kana words activated the temporoparietal cortex near the 'left' supramarginal and angular gyri regions.

Thus, the left hemisphere is crucially involved in processing kana shapes, but this is all the more true when processing considerations require the left to be involved in the analytic aspect of some task. For example, this is true for **semantic classifications** of kana items, as Hatta (1977c) demonstrates with his findings for right visual field superiority with vertically written katakana words which were supposed to be classified according to superordinate category membership. Outline drawings of such items produced opposite results when their superordinate category membership was tested for.

Furthermore, to be processed by the left hemisphere, kana strings are not required to be meaningful strings. Endo, Shimizu, and Hori (1978) employed two types of stimuli: non-verbal stimuli in the form of random shapes and verbal stimuli in the form of bisyllabic Japanese **nonsense words** written in kana. Not surprisingly, recognition of the random shapes produced right hemispheric superiority, while the reaction times obtained from 18 subjects suggested a right visual field (hence left hemisphere) advantage for the kana stimuli.[3] Recognition of kana shapes, of course, is a linguistic matter which requires linguistic analysis to arrive at a decision of whether they are nonsense strings or not. Whether or not this is part of the task, subjects automatically assume a strategy of analysis, given the kana strings as stimuli, and it is only *a posteriori* that the subject would know that the string was a bogus word.

It would appear that processing of kana words which require phonemic encoding involve the left hemisphere and that the right hemisphere is dissociated from such encoding functions (see, for example, Levy, 1972). However, the assumption that the right hemisphere is dissociated with the processing of kana *words* does not necessarily mean that this hemisphere does not contribute to the processing of individual **kana *characters***. The evidence from cases of disconnection-type agraphia with alexia leads Yamadori, Nagashima, and Tamaki (1983) to claim that the neural substrate for both kana and kanji configurations is stored bilaterally, while the neural substrate for ordering these symbols into the meaningful sequence we perceive as a *word* is confined to the left hemisphere. Their suggestion for kana characters seems to be experimentally supported by Hatta, Ohnishi, Yamamoto, and Ogura (1981), who found a left visual field advantage for the simple condition of matching physical identity for word pairs constructed of two kana characters. In essence, if kana characters are processed as visuospatial configurations, even kana pattern-matching can invoke right hemisphere superiority (but see also Hatta, 1983, who found no laterality differences for physical identity matches for either katakana or hiragana).

Recall that a number of studies have pointed to the fact of **visual familiarity** and chunking as factors in processing high frequency, high familiarity kana words. But

---

[3] Sakurai, Momose, Iwata, Watanabe, Ishikawa and Kanazawa (1993) suggest that nonsense kana words are instead processed bilaterally.

Kawakami (1993) further speculates that because familiar kana words are processed as visual chunks, there may be some involvement of the right hemisphere in these instances. Kawakami examined the effect of script familiarity on lexical decision tasks by creating familiar and unfamiliar words, three to five kana in length, and writing half of the stimulus words in the kana script they are not usually written in. Subjects then had to judge whether these stimuli were real words or not. Reaction times increased in proportion to word length for unfamiliar script words (クモリ kumori 'cloudy', ヌイグルミ nuigurumi 'stuffed doll'), but this increase was not found with familiar script words (くもり kumori 'cloudy', ぬいぐるみ nuigurumi 'stuffed doll'). Kawakami concluded that visually familiar sequences of kana are treated as chunks in reading which do not require phonological processing (see also Besner & Hildebrandt, 1987, and Hirose, 1984, 1985, for similar findings) and infers that they condition more left visual field advantage than unfamiliar words because of that visual familiarity.

Nagae (1994) ties this possibility to the mental representations for concrete objects, suggesting that the right hemisphere shows some semantic processing capacity for both kana and kanji words if they denote concrete objects. Nagae used a sentence judgment task which required subjects to judge whether a laterally presented word was congruent with a sentence which had been presented just prior to the word for the sentence judgment task. He used both concrete and abstract words, and the reaction times for the concrete words were significantly faster when they were presented in the left visual field, regardless of whether they were presented in kanji or kana. In contrast, there were no significant reaction time differences for judgments of concrete vs. abstract words when they were presented to the right visual field. There is no suggestion in such studies as to exactly what the contribution is, but the inference seems to be that in some way, to some degree, the right hemisphere can contribute to the processing of kana words in some minimal, but as yet vague, way.

In sum, it would appear that the left hemisphere undertakes the linguistic analysis that kana symbols require in their usual appearance in language materials. The evidence for anything other than this conclusion seems to be weak.

Kanji Processing

Some studies have suggested that certain aspects of kanji processing may involve the right hemisphere, but the kanji stimuli which are included in such claims seem mostly to be kanji stimuli which are presented as **single characters** (see Hatta, 1991). Once kanji are presented as compounds, any right hemisphere superiority tends to disappear. In other words, the classical view that kanji processing involves the right hemisphere seems to apply primarily to the processing of single kanji. And that may be tied to the over-emphasis on visual processing instead of semantic processing and the fact that they are presented in such a manner that they function as visuospatial stimuli rather than as linguistic stimuli (Shimada & Otsuka, 1981).

Single Kanji Stimuli. In a pair of experiments, Hatta (1978) tested perceptual asymmetry in recognition for kanji words and mixed words containing both kanji and hiragana. In the first experiment, 40 single kanji (心 *kokoro* 'heart', 湯 *yu* 'hot water') and another 40 hiragana stimuli (こころ *kokoro* 'heart', ゆ *yu* 'hot water') were tachisto-scopically presented to the left or right visual fields for subjects. Unlike the processing of the hiragana stimuli, the processing of the single kanji stimuli clearly showed a left visual field advantage in respect to recognition accuracy --- 81.5% for the left visual field in contrast to 69.7% for the right visual field. A second experiment presented regular kanji compounds (安心 *anshin* 'relief', 熱湯 *nettoo* 'boiling water') and orthographically unusual kana/kanji mixed compounds (あん心 *anshin* 'relief', ねっ湯 *nettoo* 'boiling water'). In this case, the left visual field advantage that was previously observed with the single kanji stimuli disappeared with the regular kanji compounds.

Another study by Hatta also came to the same generalization about single kanji presentations. Hatta (1981a) found that in the application of the **Stroop test**, color stimuli produced greater interference in the left visual field if the stimuli were written in kanji, as for example, the kanji color terms presented as the single characters 青 *ao* 'blue', 黄 *ki* 'yellow', 緑 *midori* 'green', and 赤 *aka* 'red'. Such interference was not observed with kana stimuli in the same visual field (and, in fact, he found no visual field differences when subjects responded to kana Stroop stimuli). Hatta interpreted these findings as further indication that the right hemisphere was specialized for processing kanji, since it shows a greater **interference effect**. He also offers the possible explanation that color information, which is processed by the right hemisphere (see also Nagae, 1989), might have been the confounding factor in kanji processing under the Stroop interference condition. Although Hatta, Katoh, and Aitani (1983) later found no visual field difference in the size of the interference effect for single kanji, and a definite right visual field effect for alphabetic stimuli, they too maintain that this demonstrates that kanji have different properties from phonetic symbols and tie that to specialization for kanji in the right hemisphere.

Using tachistoscopic presentation, Foster (1990) examined whether the lateralization patterns for kanji stimuli are different from that of other types of writing systems. She tested for laterality effects in the recognition/matching and categorization of 16 familiar and 16 unfamiliar single simple kanji and nonsense figures with various **cultural groups** (Japanese, Chinese, Korean, Arabic, and Western) that differed in both writing system type and their experience with logographic scripts. Reaction times for correct responses showed that no subjects showed visual field asymmetries in the category judgment task, but that all subjects exhibited some tendency for a left visual field advantage in the matching task. Importantly, this tendency was significant with single kanji stimuli in the reaction times of the Japanese subjects.

The same appears to be true for Chinese **hanzi processing** (see Tsao, Wu & Feustel, 1981). Tseng, Hung, Cotton, and Wang (1979) report such right hemisphere superiority for single hanzi stimuli even when a verbal report was required of subjects (cf. Huang & Jones, 1980, who found no such superiority in a tachistoscopic naming task). However, when Tseng et al. employed hanzi strings that consisted of two-character or multiple-character combinations, this left visual field superiority disappeared in favor of a right visual field, and therefore, left hemisphere advantage. Tzeng et al.'s explanation revolves around the differences inherent in what each experimental task invites; that is, the holistic recognition of a single hanzi becomes an analytical process when hanzi characters are put together to form strings.

Not all are convinced, however, and the Japanese literature also offers some debate on the meaning of such results. Nagae (1989) and Shimada and Otsuka (1981) point out that those studies which demonstrate right hemisphere superiority for kanji processing tend to expose kanji stimuli only once and for extremely **short durations**. For instance, in Hatta (1977a, 1977b, 1978), single kanji stimuli were presented for 20 msec. The findings for Chinese subjects' recognition of single hanzi are similar: for example, in Tzeng et al., the mean exposure time for single hanzi was 40 msec., while the mean exposure time for two-character words was over 100 msec. And Cheng and Fu (1986) used mean exposure times that were a mere 12.43 msec. for single characters. Shimada and Otsuka also point out that these studies tend to impose visually elaborate discrimination tasks on their subjects. In Hatta's (1977a, 1977b, 1978) experiments, one kanji and one numeral were simultaneously displayed on a screen; the task for the subject was to first report which number appeared at a given focus point and then which kanji was presented either on the left or the right side of the screen. Scores for each subject were tabulated as the number of correct letter identifications in each visual field. Moreover, the critics claim that these studies did not inform their subjects as to which kinds of kanji stimuli were to be presented and how they were to be presented. Hence, some might say that the subjects were engaged in a visual discrimination task which was quite unlike the tasks they face in actual reading situations. On the other hand, as Keung and Hoosain (1989) note, it may be that two-kanji words have a higher perceptual threshold than single characters, and that longer exposure times are necessary to get an accurate reading of performance. If so, the longer exposure times might be what is benefitting the left hemisphere.

Such discussion implies that the observed right hemisphere superiority of single kanji may be due to other factors, such as kanji stimuli being interpreted as **visuospatial stimuli**. Then too, the presentation of single kanji stimuli does not invariably lead to right hemisphere superiority in processing. For example, Kawakami, and Hatta (1994) report that a lexical decision task for single kanji stimuli, such as 足 *ashi* 'foot', 寺 *tera* 'temple', and 河 *kawa* 'river' invoked ambihemispheric processing. And one of Besner, Daniels, and Slade's experiments (1982) with Japanese and Chinese subjects found left hemisphere superiority in processing both the Arabic numerals and kanji/hanzi numerals for 4 to 9. This is different than the typical claims for right hemisphere efficiency for kanji numerals and left hemisphere efficiency for Arabic numerals. Their findings lead Besner et al. to conclude that it is not the direct mapping between logographs and morphemes of a language which necessarily yields a right hemisphere superiority for single kanji, but associated stimulus characteristics which make demands on pre-processing operations which are carried out more efficiently in the right, rather than the left, hemisphere.

Compound Kanji Stimuli. If compound kanji words are used as experimental stimuli, the left visual field advantage which is observed with single kanji characters tends to disappear, with such compounds usually conditioning **left hemisphere superiority** or, somewhat less commonly, ambihemispheric processing. For instance, Shimada (1981) found that processing of compound kanji words can be ambihemispheric. He employed three-symbol kana words and two-character kanji compounds (化学 *kagaku* 'chemistry', 天気 *tenki* 'weather'), arbitrarily dividing them into 'negative' and 'positive' stimuli. The task of 26 normal subjects was to respond by key-tapping whether a given stimulus appearing on the screen belonged to either one of the groups. For kana stimuli, 22 of the 26 subjects showed a right visual field advantage, but the number of subjects showing a right visual field advantage for the kanji stimuli was equal to the number of the subjects showing a left visual field advantage. This finding leads Shimada to conclude that kanji processing involves both hemispheres.

Kawakami and Hatta (1994) conclude that processing of kanji compounds can be either ambihemispheric or be manifested as left hemisphere superiority. In one of their experiments, 40 concrete (食器 *shokki* 'tableware') and abstract (作法 *sahoo* 'manner') kanji compound stimuli were tachistoscopically presented to 16 subjects for a lexical decision task. Their main finding was that these compound kanji stimuli did not evoke an expected right hemisphere superiority. For the **abstract compound kanji** stimuli, lexical decision times for those presented to the right visual field were faster than for those presented to the left visual field, and even concrete kanji compounds did not manifest any significant tendency towards a left visual field advantage.

Mostly, however, studies have echoed Hatta's (1978) early finding that processing of kanji compounds exhibits left hemisphere superiority. As part of this early study, 40 two-character kanji compounds, all high in respect to familiarity (都会 *tokai* 'metropolitan', 馬車 *basha* 'coach'), were presented to 30 right-handed undergraduates. A kanji compound stimulus and one numeral were simultaneously displayed on-screen, and subjects had to first report which number appeared at a given focus point and then which kanji was presented either on the left or the right side of the screen. The experimental result, based on the number of correct identifications, showed left hemisphere superiority (64.23% for the right visual field vs. 57.82% for the left visual field).

With the exception of Keung and Hoosain (1989), no right hemisphere advantage has ever been found for kanji compounds in Chinese, where high visual complexity in terms of stroke number and low-frequency had such an effect in lexical decision tasks under conditions of short exposure and low luminance. The right hemisphere advantage they found does alert us to the fact that there is some support for more than perceptual factors, but the linguistic factors which might play a role are still not obvious to us. And we have no similar evidence from Japanese subjects as yet. Taken together, the studies of single kanji stimuli vs. compound kanji stimuli simply do not allow us to make the sweeping generalization that hemispheric processing is dichotomous according to script type, kanji vs. kana. Nor does it allow us to claim that processing of kanji is a domain in which right hemisphere superiority is the expected norm. If anything, kanji are generally processed as **linguistic elements**, and as a result, require the involvement of the left hemisphere.

FUNCTIONAL FACTORS IN LATERALITY PREFERENCES

The dichotomous view of kana and kanji processing by script type and hemisphere is too simplistic a view to explain the data which arise from various experimental and clinical inquiries. It is, however, equally facile to assume that single kanji stimuli condition right hemisphere involvement because they are treated as visuospatial stimuli, and, contrastively, that compound kanji stimuli always invoke left hemisphere superiority because they are treated as linguistic stimuli. There are a variety of experimental factors, related to cognitive function and task type, that can have an effect on hemispheric involvement as well. Kanji processing is sensitive to the interaction between **stimuli type** and **task type**. For example, it is often said that kanji numerals are more efficiently processed by the right hemisphere, while Arabic numerals are more efficiently processed by the left hemisphere. At the same time, it is equally common to see experimental results in which the left is better at analytical tasks such as mental calculation. As a result, one sees a left hemisphere advantage for mathematical operations because of the left's specialization for mental calculation, regardless of the kinds of numerals used as stimuli, kanji or Arabic (see Hatta & Tsuji, 1993). If the right is further specialized for other functions, say, the spatial tasks involved in mental rotation, mental transformation, or imagery operations, and the left is better at other analytical tasks such as semantic categorization and sequencing, then one can predict differential performance better keyed to the cognitive functions elicited in the experimental task than to the stimulus types used in the task. As a result, experimental studies, especially those coming from the cognitive psychology tradition, must be evaluated to examine the effect of the various experimental variables involved, especially focussing on the specific tasks posed to subjects.

Experimental Variables

When one examines those studies involving normal subjects, **physical variables** appear to show no decisive effects on laterality preferences. Such physical variables include factors like number of strokes, size, rotation angles, and duration of exposure. In contrast, **qualitative variables**, such as the concreteness, frequency, familiarity, and part-of-speech classification of the kanji stimulus item may influence hemispheric involvement. Importantly, there are also a number of studies which report that the lateralization findings are not solely influenced by such qualitative variables, but by the function and depth of processing involved in a specific experimental task as well.

Insignificant Variables. Most experimental work that has manipulated various types of physical variables associated with kanji, including the number of strokes, size and rotation angles, and duration of exposure, has not reported any decisive effects on laterality preferences (see Nagae, 1992). For instance, one might speculate that the number of strokes, or **configurational complexity**, in the orthographic presentation for kanji could be a factor which would induce a processing asymmetry in laterality preferences. However, when Büssing, Bruckmann, and Hartje (1987) tested 115 German subjects with kana, simple kanji, and complex kanji, no left visual field advantage for higher figural complexity in complex kanji was found. This was so even though the task consisted of indicating, as quickly as possible, whether two stimuli presented in sequence were the same or different. In one of a series of experimental tasks, Hatta (1992) also reports that there was no significant effect of figural complexity on laterality preferences when quantified as mean lexical decision times --- for real kanji, 568 msec. (LVF) and 571 msec. (RVF); for non-kanji, 612 msec. (LVF) and 624 msec. (RVF). But, as we have seen in earlier chapters, figural complexity may certainly speed recognition. Although at the early stage of processing, perceptual attributes such as the number of strokes may be a contributing factor, these studies in general do not suggest that figural complexity has a decisive laterality effect on the identification of kanji.

Japanese subjects are sensitive to the font types for kanji presentation in print (see Langman & Saito, 1984). However, there seems to be no experimental study which specifically focuses on the interactive effect of **font type and size** for characters on laterality preferences. If Kanda (1984, cited in Nagae, 1992) is correct in his inferences about script size, the size of kanji characters should not have any significant effect on the processing of orthographic symbols in respect to laterality preferences, though they may speed recognition.

Rotation angles may affect lateralization, and it is generally reported that inverted or rotated characters elicit a left visual field superiority. For example, Hayashi and Hatta (1978) probed laterality differences by posing several levels of cognitive processing in conjunction with a mental rotation task in which subjects matched kanji at various angles of rotation with normally presented kanji. Their findings were that not all mental rotation invokes the right hemisphere, despite its pattern-matching nature; when the mental rotation task was supplemented by the use of verbal mediators, the left hemisphere appeared to be more centrally involved in performing the task than the right hemisphere. Thus, although the mental rotation task might incur lateralization effects, the effects are likely to be mediated by the degree of rotation and the interjection of verbal mediators. This conclusion is also supported by Nishikawa and Niina (1981), who in fact failed to find visual field differences due to rotation of kanji stimuli.

Duration of exposure can be an influencing factor as well. Many tachistoscopic studies have employed exposure durations ranging from 50 msec. to 200 msec., suggesting that duration of exposure within this range does not have a significant effect on lateralization (see Nagae, 1992). However, as pointed out by Nagae (1989) and Shimada and Otsuka (1981), if the duration of exposure is extremely short, right hemisphere superiority may be manifested, especially with single kanji characters.[4] Furthermore, once the duration of exposure exceeds 200 msec., visual field effect cannot be effectively measured because information has already begun to flow across the corpus callosum (cf. Hoptman & Davidson, 1994). If one excludes those experimental studies which have failed to control for this effect, one notes that duration of exposure within the 50 msec. to 200 msec. range does not have an effect on lateralization.

Significant Variables. In contrast to the results arising from experimental manipulation of physical variables, qualitative variables, such as the part-of-speech classification, imagery/concreteness, and familiarity of the kanji stimuli can have significant effects on lateralization. For example, Elman, Takahashi, and Tohsaku (1981a) had subjects verbally report on the grammatical category each kanji word belonged to, while their reaction times to tachistoscopic presentation was taken as the response measure. The results revealed that the expected right hemisphere superiority found in studies up to that point obtained only for nouns (谷 *tani* 'valley'), but not for adjectives (細 *hosoi* 'thin') and

---

[4] The same claim is made with respect to English words by Pring (1981), whose experimental results indicate that if visually complex words are presented for short duration for a lexical decision task, a left visual field advantage can be observed.

verbs (思, *omou* 'to consider'). Adjectives and verbs were in fact processed more rapidly in the right visual field, suggesting left hemisphere superiority. One explanation offered as to why such **part-of-speech classification** shows differential lateralization effects is that nouns tend to denote high imagery objects while adjectival and verbal items fail to provoke such concrete imagery.

It has been reported in alphabetic writing systems that if concrete words are used as experimental stimuli, right visual superiority in word recognition is reduced (Hines, 1976), and it is reduced further if the stimuli are associated with high imagery values (see Marcel & Patterson, 1978; Moscovitch, 1979). With respect to **concreteness** associated with kanji stimuli, Ohnishi and Hatta (1980) found that when high concrete kanji are presented to the left visual field and low concrete kanji to the right visual field simultaneously, the high concrete kanji are processed better than the low concrete kanji. The above finding is also replicated by Elman, Takahashi, and Tohsaku (1981b), who report a right hemisphere advantage for concrete kanji nouns, and the left hemisphere significantly better in identifying abstract kanji. Recall that Nagae (1994) also tested normal subjects by having them judge whether tachistoscopically presented concrete/abstract kanji words were congruous with the meaning of a sentence presented before-hand. Subjects processed the concrete words (医者 *isha* 'doctor', 石油 *sekiyu* 'oil') significantly faster than the abstract words (事実 *jijitsu* 'fact', 古代 *kodai* 'ancient times') when these stimulus words were presented in the left visual field (although there were no significant differences when they were presented to the right visual field). Hatta (1977a) also examined whether there are differences in laterality preferences between kanji with highly concrete meanings and those with highly abstract meanings. His findings also showed that concrete kanji are more correctly recognized in the left visual field than are abstract kanji. These results lead him to argue that, since the right hemisphere facilitates pattern recognition, and since concrete kanji are high in imagery, the factor of concreteness/abstractness affects efficiency of visual information processing for orthographic symbols like kanji (see also Hatta, 1992; Hayashi, 1985). The corollary associated with this position is that the process of pattern recognition for verbal stimuli which are processed in the right hemisphere is facilitated by **imagery**.

Many studies also report the significance of familiarity and frequency on lateralization. And the influence of **familiarity** by virtue of **frequency** has already been noted for kanji recognition in earlier chapters. Certainly, familiarity has an effect on recognition, as Hatta (1977a) clearly shows. Experimental results from a visual half-field recognition test with both high- and low-familiarity items demonstrated that high familiarity kanji were recognized more accurately than low familiarity kanji in both visual fields. However, in other studies, familiarity seems to condition two different patterns of laterality preference. First, if linguistic stimuli are presented to subjects who are totally unfamiliar with the stimuli, the processing of such symbols may trigger right hemisphere superiority initially. However, the **repeated exposure** of the stimuli will eventually shift the superiority to the left hemisphere. Secondly, if linguistic stimuli are already high in frequency and very familiar to subjects, the stimuli will condition left hemisphere superiority.

Most of the studies on familiarity deal with the first pattern. For instance, in Minagawa, Yokoyama, and Kashu (1988), four different simplified **hanzi** from China that were unfamiliar to Japanese subjects were exposed to either their right or left visual field. Overall reaction times revealed that the right visual field gradually increased in superiority as the testing progressed, indicating that during the early stages of testing, unfamiliar characters were processed as meaningless symbols by the right hemisphere. However, as the stimuli became more and more familiar, they began to be processed as meaningful linguistic symbols by the left hemisphere. This familiarity effect has also been duplicated with Japanese subjects working with more unfamiliar scripts. For example, Yoshizaki and Hatta (1987) found exactly this effect in the learning of **Hebrew words** by Japanese subjects. Four experimental groups learned the pronunciation only for Hebrew words, the meaning only, both pronunciation and meaning, or nothing. Although there was no clear visual field advantage in testing prior to the learning experience, subjects who had learned pronunciation only or pronunciation plus meaning showed a right visual field advantage after learning the Hebrew words. Although Yoshizaki and Hatta suggest that the mastery of the pronunciation for the Hebrew words was what conditioned the shift in visual field advantage, it is more likely that engaging the words as linguistic objects is what accounts for the shift.

In the same fashion, increasing familiarity with novel patterns as potential linguistic symbols also seems to have an effect. This is similar to what Endo, Shimizu, and Nakamura (1981a) report for Japanese subjects who were asked to learn and remember **hangul** stimuli. Those who did learn them showed an absence of laterality difference, while those who did not learn them between Experiments 1 and 2 continued to show a left visual field superiority in Experiment 2. Endo, Shimizu, and Nakamura (1981b) found the same to be true for Japanese who knew no hangul, in contrast to Japanese-Koreans who had learned that writing system for a period of 6 months. The Japanese exhibited a left visual field superiority, while the Japanese-Koreans with some orthographic experience showed the opposite, a significant right visual field superiority. In like manner, Hatta and Konda (1992) tested Japanese subjects for sequential changes in hemispheric advantage when there was an increase in familiarity for novel stimuli, by employing unfamiliar human faces, Korean hangul, and alphabetic letters written in the ornate Palace script as stimuli. The majority of subjects showed a continuing left visual field advantage for face recognition, irrespective of increasing familiarity, confirming that the right hemisphere is specialized for human face recognition. In contrast, the visual field advantage began to disappear with an increase in familiarity with the unknown script stimuli. Although the data do not show a sudden and complete change to the opposite visual field, they do reveal a diminishing of left visual field advantage as subjects accommodated to the unfamiliar orthographic symbols.

In sum, when one considers the nature of the experimental stimuli that have been used in controlled approaches to laterality preferences, it would appear that physical variables have no significant effect on lateralization. Qualitative variables, on the other hand, can have an effect on lateralization, although this appears to arise in large part from their ability to evoke imagery.

Examination of Tasks Involved

Having cursorily examined the effects of the experimental variables used to elicit lateralization preferences in various studies, we will next turn our attention to the possible effects arising from the types of experimental tasks asked of subjects. That is, do the cognitive functions posed by the differing requirements of the various **graphemic**, **phonemic**, and **semantic tasks** employed with subjects have any effects on lateralization when it comes to kanji processing?

Graphemic Tasks. Experimental studies which employ graphemic processing tasks generally have a pair of orthographic symbols presented simultaneously to just one visual field for graphemic identification. Results of many studies with kanji stimuli are **equivocal**. First, there are some studies whose findings show right hemisphere superiority with graphemic processing. For instance, in one of his experiments, Hatta (1981b) probes laterality preferences for kanji through a simple physical matching task. Half of the 32 pairs of kanji consist of two adjacent identical kanji and the other half of two different kanji, and undergraduate subjects had to judge whether a pair of tachistoscopically presented adjacent characters was identical or not. The finding was that the subjects were able to complete the physical matching task for the paired kanji faster in the left than right visual field. As reviewed earlier, Foster (1990) also examined laterality effects in the recognition of single kanji with subjects from several cultural groups. All exhibited a tendency for left visual field superiority in a physical matching task, and this finding was particularly significant for the kanji material for Japanese subjects. Secondly, there are studies whose findings simply contrast with the above findings. For instance, Sasanuma, Itoh, Kobayashi, and Mori (1980) presented kanji in the left and right visual fields of subjects, and had them decide whether a given pair of stimuli was identical (別 *betsu* vs. 別 *betsu*) or not (別 *betsu* vs. 刷 *satsu*). Their results showed no visual field asymmetry, and this finding was later duplicated by Hatta (1981c), who failed to find a clear right hemisphere superiority for kanji employed in a graphemic matching task (see also Nagae, 1989).

Given the equivocal findings, the issue remains open. One speculation is, however, that the difference may be due to whether kanji are processed purely as visuospatial stimuli, conditioning a right hemisphere advantage, or as graphemic symbols, conditioning a left hemisphere advantage. And the work on **'kanji vs. picture'** by Minagawa and Kashu (1984) does suggest that the laterality effects can also be influenced by the strategies adopted by individual subjects. But words access the phonemic code prior to the semantic code, and kanji are not exceptions to this rule, as Flaherty (1993b) points out in her work testing pictures as opposed to kanji. And even the processing of pictures does not necessarily lead to right hemisphere superiority. For instance, Nishikawa (1982) tachisto-scopically presented kanji and picture stimuli to the left and right visual fields of 42 subjects whose task was to judge whether the shapes or concepts of these stimuli matched memory sets which had been given earlier. Analysis of the results shows a linear increase in reaction time for both left and right hemispheres, regardless of the types of stimuli, suggesting serial processing rather than parallel processing. Moreover, reaction times indicated a right visual field advantage not only for kanji/concept stimuli but also for picture stimuli. Nishikawa speculates that the picture stimuli were treated as linguistic objects by the subjects, and attributes reaction time differences between the left and right visual fields to the time associated with transfer. That is, the stimuli presented to the left visual field took longer to be processed since they had to be transferred from the right hemisphere to the left hemisphere, which is responsible for processing.

Phonemic Tasks. Phonemic tasks typically involve presentation of stimuli, in sequence or in parallel, to one of the visual fields for phonological identification. A prime example of this is the **naming task**, in which the subject must say the word, first activating and then realizing the phonological identity of the stimulus item. Much previous work in this paradigm demonstrates a right visual field advantage for kanji. For instance, in Sasanuma, Itoh, Kobayashi, and Mori (1980), subjects were asked to make decisions about phonological identity, that is, whether a given pair of stimuli had an identical pronunciation (団 *dan* vs. 段 *dan*) or not (界 *kai* vs. 晩 *ban*). Not suprisingly, the results indicated a significant right visual field superiority. As reviewed earlier, Yoshizaki and Hatta (1987) also report left hemisphere superiority in respect to phonological manipulation. Once their Japanese subjects had learned the pronunciation of Hebrew words, a right visual field advantage emerged, suggesting that **knowledge of phonological information** is an important factor in producing this advantage (see also Hatta & Konda, 1992; Minagawa, Yokoyama & Kashu, 1988). These findings are simply congruent with the interpretation that the left hemisphere is dominant in phonemic processing. In fact, the assumption that only the left hemisphere is associated with phonemic encoding functions is mirrored in the fact that our earlier inventory of Japanese research did not uncover a single study which demonstrated that phonological processing might trigger any instance of right hemisphere superiority (see Kess and Miyamoto, 1994).

Semantic Tasks. Experimental tasks which have been designated as semantic tasks in the literature usually employ some kind of **categorical identification task**. Not surprisingly, most experimental studies based on these semantic tasks report a right visual field advantage when processing kanji for their semantic affiliations. For example, Hayashi and Hatta (1982) examined the relationship between semantic processing and cerebral laterality effects by measuring response times in a categorical classification task with kanji. As stimuli, they chose 36 concrete and abstract kanji characters belonging to such semantic categories as "animal" (豚 *buta* 'pig'), "plant" (竹 *take* 'bamboo'), "emotion" (怒 *ikari* 'anger'), and "warmth" (寒 *samui* 'cold'). The subjects' task was to decide to which categories a given kanji stimulus belonged by pressing the appropriate button. The results demonstrated right visual field advantage, regardless of response hand, for both concrete and abstract kanji, suggesting superiority for the left hemisphere in the semantic processing required for kanji categorization.[5] Semantic categorization is a cognitive function which calls upon the left hemisphere primarily, and contributing factors such as concreteness and imageability, which seemed to play a role in simple recognition procedures, do not shift this advantage to the right hemisphere when deeper linguistic analysis is called for. Both concrete and abstract kanji stimuli elicited the same direction of visual field superiority in this task.

And when *pigeonholing* operations are called for, their semantic classificatory nature also produces a highly significant right visual field advantage (see Hatta, 1986a). Two of the pre-attentive mechanisms in visual processing have been said to be *filtering* and *pigeonholing*, and Hatta compared these to ascertain whether they elicited different cerebral involvement. Filtering simply matches physical features, whereas *pigeonholing* relies on **shallow semantic processing** to create pigeonhole-like categories that the input may be temporarily tossed into. When Hatta had subjects check stimulus words for a single feature difference, there was no significant accuracy difference between the left and right visual fields. But when subjects had to select a relevant stimulus word among irrelevant stimuli which did not differ in any single feature, there was a highly significant right visual field advantage.

Lastly, in a series of experiments Hatta (1981b) provides further evidence for the depth of processing interpretation, as well as for the differential effect of the tasks posed

---

[5] Using exclusively katakana words for a semantic categorization matching task, Hatta (1977c) duplicates the above finding with kana.

to subjects on laterality preferences. His series of three experiments posed tasks such as pattern matching (*Are two kanji the same or different?*), lexical decision (*Is a kanji a bona fide or a counterfeit kanji?*), and semantic comparison (*Does the kanji appear in the semantically congruent side of the visual field or not?*). The major finding is that there is a different hemispheric contribution at each level of kanji processing. In the first stage of kanji processing, that is, pattern-matching, there was a significant contribution by the right hemisphere. In the second stage of the processing, that is, lexical decision, both left and right hemispheres contributed to the processing. And at the last stage of the processing, that is, semantic comparison, there was a significant contribution by the left hemisphere. Hatta (1992) also found support for the notion that various cognitive tasks, such as lexical, naming, and semantic classification, relate to different levels of processing, as well as for the fact that deeper levels of processing elicit longer reaction times. Leong, Wong, Wong, and Hiscock (1985) found similar results for Chinese word recognition, suggesting that the **level of cognitive involvement** in processing logographs may be a cross-linguistic phenomenon which traverses kanji-using orthographic cultures.

Combinatorial Tasks. Hatta (1981c) has also examined the **interactive effects** of experimental tasks by simple comparisons of processing strategies and processing levels. Hatta reports on a first experiment which compared two matching tasks which required different processing strategies, that is, matching physical identity and matching phonological identity. A second experiment employed two matching tasks which instead differed in processing level, by matching physical identity and matching semantic category. Results from the first experiment, which employed tasks differing in processing strategies, showed no significant difference in laterality effect. However, the results from the second experiment, which employed tasks differing in processing levels, showed a significant difference in laterality effect. While the physical identity matching task did not show laterality differences, category matching did demonstrate a significant superiority for the right visual field. In addition to Hatta's (1981b, 1981c, 1992) work mentioned above, there are a few other studies which examine the interactive effects of all three types of experimental task. For example, Sekiguchi and Abe (1992) examine hemispheric differences in kanji processing by employing event-related brain potentials in order to monitor brain-wave activity. Experimental stimuli were constructed in order to test subjects in several areas: a graphemic or pattern-matching task, that is, whether the same kanji was found in a pair of compounds (休校 *kyuukoo* 'school-closure' vs. 校正 *koosei* 'editing'); a phonemic or phonological decoding task, that is, whether a given pair of kanji compounds was pronounced the same (工業 *koogyoo* 'industry' vs. 鉱業 *koogyoo* 'mining'); and a semantic decoding task, that is, whether a pair of kanji compounds belonged to a specific semantic category (先生 *sensei* 'teacher' vs. 生徒 *seito* 'student'). Brain wave activity was significant in the right hemisphere when graphemic aspects of kanji were being processed, whereas brain wave activity was significant in the left hemisphere when phonemic and semantic aspects of kanji compounds were being processed. Despite the controversial nature of event-related brain potentials as valid measurements of cognitive activity, these results in a large extent parallel other findings in suggesting that lateralization effects are directly tied to the **functional requirements** of the task before the subject.

Summary Conclusions

In sum, if one examines the experimental literature in an attempt to weigh the contribution of the experimental variables involved and the specific tasks posed, it is clear that the interaction between variable type and task type must be taken into account for a realistic explanation of cognitive processing. In particular, our examination of the effect of posed experimental tasks on laterality preferences shows that while the configurational aspects of kanji may be processed both by the right and left hemisphere, the phonemic and semantic aspects of kanji processing are predominantly handled by the left hemisphere. In other words, any cerebral shifts in respect to laterality preferences are very much affected by the functional requirements of the processing task, and since most language-related tasks are linguistically analytical, the left hemisphere is crucially involved at all levels. At the very least, these findings seriously **challenge any dichotomous view** that kanji recognition automatically invokes right hemisphere superiority, in that the joint factors of linguistic analysis and processing level generally supercede any central involvement of the right hemisphere.

CLINICAL STUDIES

Universality

In general, aphasic symptomatology for Japanese parallels that of Indo-European languages, and the essential facts are largely the same (Hamanaka, 1994; Paradis et al., 1985; Yamadori, 1985, 1998). There is a common set of **biological principles** which organize the human brain in respect to linguistic activity, and this holds true regardless of the language a person speaks. Ever since Broca's (1861) and Wernicke's (1874) insightful observations about how brain lesions in specific areas matched up to specific language disorders, we have learned much about hemispheric asymmetry. More recently, we have had equally dramatic revelations by way of those patients who have had the connection via the corpus callosum disconnected for the treatment of conditions such as severe epilepsy. In simplest terms, we can also say that the nature and range of Japanese clinical cases precludes the notion that there is a notable incidence of differential impairment of kanji after right hemisphere damage. If anything, there are clinically documented patterns of greater impairment for both kana and kanji in the left hemisphere. The correlation seems to be with the temporal region for kana and the occipito-parietal region for kanji, but the data also point to **dissociations** between performance for reading and writing for both kana and kanji after left hemisphere injuries. Clinical studies of patients with unilateral brain damage or split-brain surgery thus also provide us with convincing evidence that any simple view of kana and kanji processing cannot be maintained.

At the same time, linguistic differences in orthographic types can be reflected in the actual realization of impairments (see Sasanuma, 1984, 1985, 1988). Impairments in written word comprehension and production in Japanese aphasics and Japanese split-brain patients have revealed some behavioral differences between what seem to be relatively independent neurofunctional modules dealing with reading and writing for kana and kanji (see Paradis, 1987; Tatsumi, Itoh, Sasanuma & Fujisaki, 1985). The interaction of such abilities would be difficult, if not impossible, to isolate and detect in normal subjects' performance on experimental tasks. This may be why the experimental results arising from performance by normal subjects do not always correlate with the clinical findings (see Paradis et al., 1985), and so we have learned much from those clinical cases of impairments arising from brain lesions. In the case of Japanese written word recognition, first we have come to know that patterns of relative impairment of kana vs. kanji processing are distributed over a wide range. It is common enough to have patients with impairment of both kana and kanji; but at the two opposite ends of the continuum. It is also possible to have **selective impairment** of just kana or selective impairment of just kanji (see Sasanuma, 1985). For example, impairment of kana processing emerges typically in Broca's aphasics (Sasanuma, 1974a, 1975), while impairment of kanji processing is a characteristic of the aphasic syndrome called *gogi aphasia* (Sasanuma & Monoi, 1975; Yamadori, 1998) in which there is a severe loss of word meanings for kanji compound words (see also Sasanuma, Sakuma & Kitano, 1992). More recently, we have also come to know that **double dissociation** is found for both kana and kanji processing (see overviews in Iwata, 1988; Paradis, 1987; Paradis et al., 1985; Sasanuma, 1992). A single- or one-way dissociation is found when a patient's performance is more impaired on one cognitive task than another as a result of brain damage. In the case of both kana and kanji, we have double dissociation, with impairment in either reading or writing for kana and in either reading or writing for kanji. In essence, there are some language-specific features which have crucial implications for aphasia theory and treatment for Japanese, and these must be considered along with universalistic data to allow the construction of a comprehensive theory of aphasia (see Sasanuma, 1986).

As noted in the previous section, there is little question that the left hemisphere is largely responsible for processing the phonemic and semantic information required for the central aspects of kanji interpretation. As far as speech production is concerned, the left hemisphere is superior in the vast majority of subjects. But in respect to the recognition and production of orthographic material, this left dominance is less absolute and more a matter of degree. The basic left-right dichotomy may not be that simple, and there is some clinical evidence that reminds us of this fact.

Right Hemisphere Contribution

Clinical studies in the vast medical literature for Japanese often offer **contrasting views** as to the exact role of the right hemisphere in language processing. The literature is too large and too complex for us to attempt a synthesis here, although we hope to do this in a next book with the Japanese experts themselves. Because kanji do invoke processing which is tied to their visual configurations, one would expect that the visual association areas might be activated in a way that one does not find for kana sequences. And this is what Law, Kannao, Fujita, Lassen, Miura, and Uemura (1991) did find in PET scan measurements of regional cerebral blood flow for kanji reading; there was indeed significant bilateral activation of the visual association areas, but there was significantly greater right than left activation. Nevertheless, the question which has interested Japanese aphasiologists goes beyond visual processing, and that question is just what is the role of the right hemisphere in processing linguistic information of any kind associated with kana vs. kanji. One school argues that the right hemisphere is divorced from processing any aspect of kana and kanji whatsoever. The opposing view admits that the contribution of the right hemisphere is limited, but argues that it does make a contribution, although that contribution has yet to be specified in any detailed fashion.

For example, in reviewing previous studies of split-brain (commissurotomy) patients' abilities to manipulate visual and tactile stimuli, Sugishita (1980) offers the following conclusions regarding cerebral lateralization. First, the left hemisphere is specialized for language processing. Second, given split-brain patients' performance in copying figures such as Necker cubes and tetrahedrons, the right hemisphere is superior to the left in visuo-spatial processing. Third, the claim that the right hemisphere is involved in some types of language processing (for example, object-naming, picture-word matching, copying) must be accepted with reservation. Studies which make the claim have often employed split-brain patients who had undergone a commissurotomy several years prior to actual tests. During a 15 month post-operational period, none of Sugishita's patients exhibited any observable ability for reading kanji and kana words presented in the left visual fields, while they were capable of processing kana and kanji words presented in the right visual field. As a result, Sugishita observes that the results with split-brain patients confirm that the left hemisphere processes both kana and kanji, while the right hemisphere's contribution to kana and kanji processing abilities are extremely limited, and are only observed a few years after commissurotomy. In sum, Sugishita questions the view which claims that both left and right hemispheres are involved in language processing, and sees these functions as resident in the intact left hemisphere (see also Iwata, 1988; Sugishita, Iwata, Toyokura, Yoshioka & Yamada, 1978; Sugishita & Yoshioka. 1987).

Furthermore, Sugishita and his colleagues also question the textbook assumption that a specific aphasic type or lesion site is always associated with a particular impairment pattern in kana or kanji reading. The clinical observations, when carefully examined and matched, often fail to coincide with such generalizations. For example, Sugishita, Otomo, Kabe, and Yunoki (1992) point out that the methodology and analytical procedures in many previous studies have simply been inadequate to support such generalizations. The test materials that were used were unspecified or inappropriate, the number of test items was too small, conclusions were presented without providing individual performance to support those conclusions, and in some cases, single cases were used to associate patterns of reading impairment with lesion sites (but see also Caramazza & Badecker, 1989). Sugishita et al. carried out their own comprehensive examination in an attempt to counteract these shortcomings, and found no consistent linkage between aphasia type and patterns of impairment in single kana and kanji reading in a subject pool that included 7 pure alexics, 23 Broca's aphasics, 13 Wernicke's aphasics, and 7 patients with alexia and agraphia. In fact, the impairment patterns were not even uniform across patients within the same aphasic syndrome grouping, and a majority of cases in each group were unselectively impaired for kana and kanji reading.

Others are less prone to actively deny that the right hemisphere may have some part in processing kana and kanji. For example, Iwata (1977) has shown that, in a kanji and picture matching task which required semantic processing, split-brain patients did indeed exhibit 100% performance with their left hemisphere. But they also exhibited a 56% success rate with the right hemisphere, suggesting that the right hemisphere does play some part in processing certain semantic features for kanji. Otsuka and Shimada (1988) similarly report that 36 unilaterally brain-damaged patients showed left hemisphere dominance for both kana and kanji processing, but that the right hemisphere did exhibit some semantic processing capabilities, despite its inability to make graphemic-phonemic linkages. Furthermore, Yamadori, Nagashima, and Tamaki (1983) report a case of a-graphia with alexia, caused by lesions at the posterior half of the corpus callosum and the left medial occipital lobe. The result was a dissociated agraphia of the disconnection type for kana and kanji. The ability of the left hand to realize kanji characters was imprecise, but the right hand showed normal capacity for kanji writing. For kana characters, the right hand retained normal writing ability, while the left hand could write correct kana characters but was unable to connect these into a meaningful word (but see also Tanaka, Yamodori & Murata, 1987).

Yamadori (1980) elsewhere discusses two case studies of right-handed Broca's patients whose symptoms seem to support the above hypothesis. After noting that there is little question that the left hemisphere processes both kana and kanji more efficiently and more accurately than the right hemisphere, Yamadori goes on to suggest that the neural substrate necessary for writing both kana and kanji is stored bilaterally, while the neural substrate for ordering these graphemes into a meaningful sequence is confined to the left hemisphere. While his two patients could write single characters with their left hands, they could not sequence these characters into words and phrases with their left hands while this continued to be possible with their right hands. Obviously, **organized serial output** of more than one character is under the control of the left hemisphere because it requires phonetic knowledge and control of lexical access procedures. Examples of such abilities can be seen in the following selection taken from Yamadori's (1980) report on productions by one of his patients. The left side of the figure shows the copying by his left hand and the right side by his right hand. (The right side of the figure contains the proverb, 泣きつらにはち *Nakitsura ni hachi* 'A bee sting onto a crying face', meaning 'Bad things tend to pile up'. The left side of the figure is written only as far as 泣き *naki* 'crying ...', the rest being scratched out.)

Figure 9. 1 Copying by Yamadori's patient.
(Reprinted with permission from Yamadori, 1980))

These findings are congruent with the observation that the right hemisphere critically lacks the ability to sequence phoneme-dependent linguistic units. If so, we cannot say that the right hemisphere is crucially involved in processing orthographic symbols, except for their configurational and kinetic production aspects. What is not clear is just which orthographic aspects of kana and kanji processing are contributed to by the right hemisphere, and the manner and extent of this involvement. So far as we know at this point, the phonemic and semantic processing capabilities of the right hemisphere appear to be severely limited when compared to the left hemisphere, and so far no one has clearly demonstrated the extent of its involvement in kana and kanji processing at any level beyond the configurational and kinetic aspects of graphemic production and processing.

CONCLUSIONS

It is clear that we cannot maintain the view that the cognitive considerations in processing Japanese orthography are unique, with kana processed by the left hemisphere and kanji processed by the right hemisphere. And we should not be surprised to learn that clinical studies report impairments for both kana and kanji after left hemisphere injury, suggesting that the cognitive underpinnings for both as writing system tokens are resident in the left hemisphere. After all, we implicitly knew this when we first noted that the Japanese orthographic system does not use kana and kanji in mutually exclusive ways. Rather, both script types are **mixed into one orthography** when presented in normal text, and even when individual words are considered, we found considerable overlap between them in terms of script type and script familiarity. Where there are differences reported, the issue has more to do with the types of processing tasks involved and the cognitive requirements they impose.

And of course, we have not even begun to touch the evidence for **individual differences** (see Sugishita, Otomo, Kabe & Yunoki, 1992) and the possibility of partial lateralization of functions to the other hemisphere. For example, Abe, Yokoyama, and Yanagihara (1995) report a right-handed man with selective agraphia for kana after damage to the non-dominant right hemisphere. Kanji comprehension, reading, and writing were unaffected, and he did not suffer from other aphasic symptoms. Abe et al. suggest that some aspects of the language functions for some right-handers might be partially lateralized to the right hemisphere, and by implication, we might expect the same to be true for left-handers. Very simply, the evidence does not always allow a perfectly transparent view of left vs. right functions in respect to each and every aspect of language in each and every individual.

What really awaits elucidation at this point, however, is a better understanding of the **interactive relationship** between the two hemispheres. Although the evidence is as yet insufficient to be precise, it is likely that both left and right hemispheres collaborate in processing certain aspects of the graphemic, phonemic, and semantic information necessary for decoding words written in kana and kanji. There are some encouraging signs in this direction, and some recent research has attempted to find the extent of interhemispheric cooperation. For example, recent experimental findings reveal that simultaneous bilateral presentation is superior to unilateral presentation in the processing of both Arabic and kanji numerals (Hatta & Tsuji, 1993). Clinical neuropsychological studies have also probed whether kana and kanji processing employ different **inter-hemispheric connections** (Kawamura, 1990; Kawamura & Hirayama, 1991; Kawamura, Hirayama & Yamamoto, 1989). But so far, we are severely limited in knowing how the left and right hemispheres integrate various informational modules, even those limited to lexical access and word recognition procedures in language processing, and this will obviously be the challenge for future studies in psycholinguistics, neuropsychology, and clinical aphasiology.

Chapter 10

CONCLUSIONS

UNIVERSALITY

Japanese research into the processing dimensions of a mixed orthography sheds light on the basic questions of word recognition and lexical access research in psycholinguistics. Our purpose in this book has been to introduce this rich psycholinguistic paradigm, and to show which considerations affect the path by which **lexical access** becomes **word recognition** in processing written Japanese when presented in exclusively syllabary or Chinese kanji characters. But in running text, Japanese mixes the two principles of logographic and phonological script in its overall orthography, and so we have considered the processing strategies involved with mixed scripts as well. We have surveyed a number of different areas to see if the experimental results point to the possibility of different processes correlating exclusively with different orthographic representations. In doing so, three distinct orthographic systems with three different ratios of representation have consistently claimed our attention. We have focussed on the Japanese kana, in which a symbol almost always represents the same pronunciation, and the Japanese kanji, in which the same character may represent pronunciations which are varied and un-predictable. But we have often alluded to the English alphabet, in which the relation-ship between letter and phoneme form is irregular. The comparisons are inevitable, especially given our backgrounds and the readership of this manuscript. Our review of a wide range of studies suggests that the same basic principles of lexical access operate across the **three types of orthographic activity**. That is, orthographic configurations can be used to jump directly to phonological form, to meaning, or to both, depending upon the processing task at hand and their advantageous or necessary interaction. While the role and importance of these factors may differ somewhat for each orthography in respect to the processing strategy favored and the processing time required for a given cognitive task, it would appear that humans reading scripts bring the same cognitive arsenal to the idiosyncratic requirements of the world's writing systems. Others have reached the same conclusions, but from different vantage points (see, for example, DeFrancis, 1989;

Paradis, Hagiwara & Hildebrandt, 1985; Patterson, 1990), and our exhaustive search of the Japanese literature has not convinced us to conclude otherwise.

Universal Constraints in Processing Models

Still, it is worth reviewing what we have learned about kana/kanji access to the Japanese mental lexicon, for the picture for kana/kanji processing is not a simple one. Certainly kana and kanji processing is not dichotomous, so that a simple, thorough-going explanation that places logographic scripts on one side and kana scripts on the other is too facile. The totality of evidence supports neither an orthography-independent processing route for kanji nor an orthography-dependent processing route for kana. A better way of looking at the problem might be to suggest that kanji processing can, depending upon the context and the circumstance, make use of either of two processing routes in accessing the specific properties of a lexical item presented in kanji script. As we have seen, even purportedly non-phonological scripts such as Chinese hanzi and Japanese kanji do in fact have phonological elements mixed into their orthographies. In fact, this notion of **parallel processing** is not limited to logographic systems, but it also applies to access strategies in alphabetic or syllabic systems which are phonologically based. After all, phonologically based writing systems offer a continuum of regularity, ranging from extremely regular scripts, such as Tagalog, Finnish, Spanish, and Italian, right on through to English and French on the irregular side of the continuum. The fact is that the alphabetic principle of one-to-one correspondence is rarely realized as the orthographic reality in a given language. Sometimes the unit relationships overlap in the correspondence between alphabetic letters and individual speech sounds, as is the case with /f/ represented by *f, ph, -gh*. And sometimes the units are tied to a particular class of words, as is the case with the initial /sk-/ in words like *school, scholastic, scholarship, scholar* vs. the initial palatal sibilant in *schist, schloss, schluss*. Words outside the specific word class go either way, according to regional dialect or personal idiolect, as is the case with *schedule, schism*.

Nevertheless, we would never posit that kanji processing is essentially the same as kana or alphabetic processing, particularly in the earliest stages of processing. It seems obvious from our review of the literature that pattern recognition processes are often different for stimuli of the logographic type, with logographic stimuli typically displaying a greater dependence on the various graphic features to be found within the visual stimulus. There is a vast array of experimental literature using a variety of experimental tasks which suggests a central contributory role of graphemic information in kanji processing in Japanese (see Kess & Miyamoto, 1996; Miyamoto & Kess, 1995). But, by the same token, we cannot support the equally simplistic view that kanji processing has but a single route, which goes from orthography to semantics, entirely bypassing the contribution of phonological information. The most plausible cognitive model to explain all this mixing and matching of information within and across levels will likely reside in an **interactive explanation** which mixes the basic tenets of the orthography-independent and the orthography-dependent processing explanations. If there are a variety of favored strategies for reading in different types of orthographies, it is also likely that the same language may use different strategies if it has more than one script type (see Bridgeman, 1987). But it can also mean that the same language can mix these various strategies in dealing with the same script type. And this is what we have seen with Japanese mixing phonological recoding and visual access for both the kana and the kanji scripts, depending upon the task, familiarity with the written stimulus, and so forth. That is, depending upon the contextual setting for a given kanji, and its specific features of familiarity, frequency, and complexity, one of the two processing routes may be realized as the most efficient path to word recognition. Both processing routes ultimately access semantic information, but one route is a sound-mediated route and the other route is a grapheme-mediated route. For many processing tasks that involve natural language, kanji symbols do resemble alphabetic symbols in that they too will invoke phonological properties as the decoder marches through the mental lexicon. Tasks that are not simple pattern-matching maneuvers are likely to take the decoder from grapheme through phonology to semantics, so that phonological properties may also be accessed in those analytical tasks that are not pattern-matching or category-matching in nature.

But there is also a cognitive routing that can travel a grapheme-mediated route. This is the only way that we can account for how the reader will access information about, as well as make decisions on, those tasks involving kanji logographs that do not require phonological mediation. One expects, then, that kanji will employ a direct route especially in cases where kanji exhibit high frequency and high familiarity. There are, of course, examples in alphabetic systems like English where the cognitive route travelled is also a direct route. For example, the English lack of a perfectly transparent sound-letter correspondence is overlooked in cases of morphophonemic identity such as the plural <-s>, the past tense <-ed>, the alternation /haws > hawz-/ in *houses*, and so forth. This is certainly the case in repeated instances of familiar, but highly idiosyncratic spellings; these quickly become immune to phonological analysis and their spellings are soon ignored. Words like *Ubyssey* (the U.B.C. student newspaper at the University of British Columbia) in Canadian English, the name for Queen *Liliuokalani* (missing its /-uo-/ in favor of /-o-/ in Hawaiian English, place names and personal names like *Thames*, *Gloucester*, and *the admirable Crichton* in British English, as well as common words like *thyme, often, catsup* in American English, are forms of this type. For speakers of these dialects of English, the words present an immediate visual referent; for those who are not, the words are parsed for possible hints to their phonological identity. In general, the direct visual route may be the primary means of lexical access for familiar words, and this is especially true for skilled readers when they encounter such words.

When we considered the findings for kana in Japanese, we found some interesting parallels there as well. Even though the kana syllabaries in Japanese are based on the phonological information they represent, there were some interesting differences for high- vs. low-frequency items. For one thing, **katakana** shapes for high frequency words are more likely to be processed directly by using their visual shapes, whereas lower frequency words have to undergo the process of phonological recoding. This advantage might not be as available to longer hiragana shapes, because such content words are often written in kanji as the first option, thus negating the possibility of a frequent visual shape. But the shorter hiragana words, such as function words, are likely to use visual shape as a factor in word recognition, although in mixed, running text these are simply skipped over, as eye-movement studies demonstrate.

We also found parallels in experimental results that credited **frequency** with whether words are recognized on a visual basis or through phonological mediation in both Chinese and English. High frequency words were recognized visually, without phonological decoding, in both Chinese and English, while infrequent or newly-coined words invoked phonological decoding (Seidenberg, 1985; Seidenberg, Waters, Barnes & Tanenhaus, 1984). In Chinese, phonetic compounds were read more quickly than non-phonetic compounds when the characters were of a low frequency. The inference which ensued from this set of findings was that phonological recoding may be more closely tied to the processing of lower frequency words in languages, implying that the extent to which written words encode phonology may be irrelevant to the recognition of high frequency words. If this is true, then differences between orthographies will reside more in how the lower frequency items are represented phonologically, and the way in which phonology plays out its reduced role in reading (see Seidenberg, 1985). It is certainly true that every language has a highly skewed distribution of its lexical items; some words are more common than others, and a very small number accounts for a high percentage of spoken or written language. The prototypical example of this must be the function words, which are by their nature high in frequency and rarely invoke phonological recoding rules. But it also appears to be true for many content words, which may not require phonological recoding because of their frequency. We already know that frequency is an important factor in other aspects of kanji processing, and it would not be surprising if lexical access procedures for kanji are highly sensitive to relative frequency of a lexical item.

One conclusion that arises from the literature is that the **early dichotomies** do not necessarily offer the best explanations, even if they are the simplest. Kana are not always superior to kanji in accessing the phonological code, and kanji do not always invoke rapid and automatic access to the semantic code. The processing situation is never as simple or as elegant as that. Although the dual route notion, with its suggestion of two alternative routes to lexical representation, catalyzed much of the earlier research (see Foss, 1988) in alphabetic languages, it has severe shortcomings[1] as an explanatory model of real-time processing for a complex object like a written language with multiple scripts. Dual route models are too much like **flow chart models**, with this or that choice to be made, but offering no insight into the time course of processing events (Seidenberg, 1985). They do offer a choice of alternative pathways, but fail to chart the interaction between them, or even parallel processing with competition taking place between the pathways. It should not be an all-or-none hypothesis that we entertain, for a number of critical factors enter into the question of choosing the most efficient strategy for achieving the task at hand. That choice will depend upon the type of stimulus and the individual contributions of factors, such as the complexity, overlap, and distinctiveness of kanji configurations, the frequency of both individual kanji and kanji compounds, as well as the reader's own ability and his/her degree of familiarity with the word itself. All of these factors have parallels in reading other orthographies, and we suggest that the support for the absolute uniqueness of logographic hanzi/kanji systems is considerably weaker than has been posited by some. Rather than the grapheme-mediated primary route being unique to Chinese and Japanese, it is a matter of degree, reflecting how often this route is activated as the primary route in an orthography. Thus, in Japanese, rather than kana and kanji access being inherently different from one another in all instances, we begin to see that at times they share some similarities. Direct access is possible for kana, and phonetic information may be invoked, when it is available, for certain instances of kanji processing.

Looking again at the question of word recognition across orthographies, such considerations encourage discussion of the parallels between the Japanese scripts and the English orthography, where the same possibilities of direct access or phonological decoding arise according to circumstance. After all, even in alphabetic languages like English, the assemblage of letters or cluster combinations to phonological representations is not a particularly efficient strategy. Just because there are grapheme-to-phoneme conversion rules in alphabetic languages does not mean that the processing algorithms are always used, or that they must exclude other processing strategies. Both the phonological and the orthographic pathways can interact as the processor seeks to identify and activate the mental representation of the words. In fact, a **realistic interactive explanation** should postulate that all information is being accessed, namely, phonological, orthographic (or graphemic), kinetic (or motoric), and semantic information; lexical access procedures

---

[1] For one thing, phonological information need not even be activated. We know that the congenitally deaf can learn to read and we know that they can learn to perform well on IQ tests, despite the fact that these largely test verbal abilities (see Furth, 1966).

utilize what they can and what they need from these sources until successful word recognition takes place. There may be differences in the degree to which one or the other informational source is applied, but this is to be expected within the realm of cross-linguistic specifics. For example, the Japanese situation places heavier emphasis on the role of kinetic information derived from the motoric images stored along with other features of the lexical entry. This kind of information is perhaps more important in orthographic systems in which effort is expended in kinetic memorization of logographic shapes in both the acquisition of and maintenance of writing skills. But errors such as 'slips of the pen' suggest that such information may not be entirely absent even in alphabetic and syllabic scripts.

Having said this, we should here note that languages and their orthographies differ, and there should be room in a useful explanatory model of lexical access and word recognition to show where Japanese, or any other language, can differ in its favored choices among processing strategies and its utilization of them. We have been aware that the current philosophy of science inexorably draws our attention to the question of **universal constraints** on how the mental lexicon is searched, and thus we have adduced the Japanese findings to illuminate the nature of such universal constraints. As a result, we have noted that there are processing strategies which respond to correspondence regularity, frequency, familiarity, as well as the fact that the analytical task type may drive the choice of the most efficient route for turning lexical access into word recognition. But as we search the mental lexicon for the correct interpretation of a lexical item appearing in its written shape, we use the information available to varying degrees in languages like Japanese, English, or Chinese. The degree to which we employ these routes may differ across languages, although the fact of their availability does not vary across these languages. So, at this point, we should pay some attention to **language specifics**, and now assess what Japanese has told us about Japanese.

LANGUAGE SPECIFICITY

The first, and perhaps most fundamental, fact about lexical access and word recognition in Japanese is that it employs three different script types to represent three different sets of lexical items. But it does so asymmetrically and with some degree of overlap. All **three sets of lexical items** are really part of contemporary written Japanese, although they are often viewed as being at various stages of acculturation into the 'regular' vocabulary inventory. A vocabulary item can be a native Japanese word which finds its historical or contemporary origins in native elements; or it can be a Sino-Japanese word, originally borrowed from Chinese or more recently created within Japanese from historically imported Chinese roots; or it can be a borrowing from languages other than Chinese. It is not the case that Japanese uses one script type for each and only each type, but it variously represents those vocabulary subsets with its three orthographic types. There is by no means a perfect one-to-one correspondence between type of vocabulary item and script type. It is true that Sino-Japanese content words are usually written in kanji, that native Japanese function words are written in hiragana, and that borrowings from other languages are always written in katakana. But it also true that any native Japanese content word or Sino-Japanese content word can be written in hiragana, just as any word can be written in katakana for purposes of emphasis, italicization, style, and so forth. The very fact that there is not a perfect separation among the three script types gives rise to varying degrees of script familiarity as a factor in both processing and production. Certainly, the **partial overlap** among script types is a consideration which must be factored into a processing framework that already tabulates word frequency and word familiarity.

Kanji

When one considers kanji in isolation, the fact of **frequency** is an inescapable reality in kanji recognition. Educational experience only accounts for a certain percentage of the experience needed to deal with the vast range of potential kanji. Although 3,000 kanji will cover 99% of what Japanese readers will encounter (see Nozaki, Yokoyama, Isomoto & Yoneda, 1996), they still require an additional 3,000 kanji over and above that to completely predict kanji usage in the typical newspaper. But frequencies for individual kanji are not the same as frequencies for kanji words, and the number of compounds that a given kanji can enter into provides yet another table of frequencies. When one considers the research on priming from single kanji to compound kanji, or from kanji elements in compound kanji to other compound kanji, the inference seems to be that single kanji and compound kanji can and often do live separate lexical lives. And the same principles of change in frequency which apply to changes in the relative rankings of single kanji will apply to the relative rankings of kanji compounds. From an educational point of view, there can be little doubt that the recently published frequency tables for single kanji (Yokoyama, Sasahara, Nozaki & Long, 1998), the frequency and familiarity tables for Japanese words (Amano, Kondo & Kakehi, 1995, 1999), and the proposed frequency tables for compounds, will go a long way toward supplementing the pedagogical focus on the limited list of *Jooyoo Kanji*. An accurate picture of lexical access strategies for Japanese kanji will only be achieved with a knowledge of their relative frequencies in portraying words, both synchronically and diachronically.

Single Kanji. For kanji words which consist of a single complex kanji, the results suggest that processing of both phonetic information and **configurational information** is initiated. The character as a whole is scanned for whatever relevant information is available, and both contribute to achieving the point of word recognition for such single kanji. This is the only way to explain the Wydell, Patterson, and Humphreys (1993) and the Sakuma, Sasanuma, Tatsumi, and Masaki (1998) results for homophony effects and graphic similarity effects both emerging from the same characters. The divergent findings for homophone confounds in these experiments contrast with the English results (Van Orden, 1987; Van Orden, Johnston & Hale, 1988) and certainly suggest differences in the early stages of word recognition for Japanese kanji words and English alphabetic words. While phonological activation is early and effective for English words, the same may not be as true for kanji words. Phonological activation may take place in kanji formats, but not early enough or completely enough to carry the full burden of activation of semantic information. It would appear that orthography is here the critical factor, even though phonology is activated during access procedures, perhaps encouraged by the fact that phonological and graphic information in kanji recognition are statistically tied in Japanese. The results seem to point to orthography as the primary source of activation, but do not deny the possibility that the phonology of kanji words is also activated. Such findings are also consistent with a parallel access view of the total package of informational features in lexical access, one in which both phonology and orthography come into play. The Japanese situation simply reminds us that the time course of reading processes is not necessarily the same across orthographies, and that the idiosyncratic design features of these symbolic systems condition the effectiveness of the cognitive strategies underlying reading in each.

However, these are findings germane to the issue of word recognition. When one considers the memory findings, the experimental literature seems to suggest that verbal may take precedence over visual information, depending upon the frequency of the logographic unit. For Chinese subjects, hanzi which were frequent and had pronunciations which were well-known were maintained better in their verbal form in short-term memory. In contrast, hanzi which were infrequent and had poorly known readings were stored in their orthographic form instead. The unfamiliar characters were also subject to more interference by intervening visual tasks, while the familiar characters with well-known pronunciations were subject to more interference by intervening verbal tasks. For memory at least, storing and accessing phonological information seems to be tied to the frequency of the specific character and the likelihood that it is known, as well as the task to which the subject must turn his/her attention to (see Hue & Erickson, 1988).

As to radicals in **complex kanji**, we have gone far beyond the simplistic notion that semantic radicals give clues to meaning, or that phonetic radicals give clues to phonology in any far-reaching and reliable way. Though the elements are present in a select number of complex kanji, we have learned that they provide other evidence which may complement or even supercede such traditional expectations. We began by asking about the role of the **'semantic' radicals** in kanji processing, hoping that their function would illuminate a universal theory of word recognition. If Japanese readers were at some unconscious level to process the semantic information purported to be carried by the radicals embedded in complex kanji, this would certainly have informed the debate regarding analytic decomposition of morphologically complex words in other languages. This would have been even more interesting if the information about embedded radicals had only a tenuous, opaque relationship to the meaning of the total kanji. Unfortunately, the evidence for this is weak, and priming across single kanji, from radical to radical, is not as robustly convincing as one would expect it to be, if this were indeed the important processing clue it is held out to be. This should not be surprising, because the so-called semantic radicals more often than not offer vague 'semantic' information about proto-typical semantic categories in the mental lexicon. But they do convey other categorical information, which may be more informative and more reliable than expectations about the semantic information. Family relationships are a better way of thinking of these categorial groupings, rather than groupings centered around a semantic focal point in the familiar prototypical frame of reference (cf. Rosch, 1973, 1975, 1978; Rosch & Mervis, 1978). Instead, we know that the location and frequency of the traditional radicals in complex kanji differ in respect to their contribution to word recognition. Saito et al. (1995a, 1995b, 1995c, 1997) deconstructed and then tested those JIS kanji which had both left-hand and right-hand components, and found that the right-hand radical is more informative than the left-hand radical in reducing the number of possible candidates in the search for the correct kanji. The average reader appears to rely more on configu-rational considerations than on historically-derived etymological considerations, and it is their frequency, not absolute numbers, that are important. Equally important are their collocational possibilities with other components in creating complex kanji. Saito, Masuda, and Kawakami's (1998) data suggest that radicals embedded in a complex kanji activate such information both at the radical level and at the whole-kanji level, with such **activation spreading** across that part of the mental lexicon which stores related representations for other kanji mediated by the same radical. This all-at-onceness effect in whole-word activation of its various components further points to an interactive model as the best explanatory model for word recognition in Japanese. The whole word is processed, as well as its components, and there is interactive feedback within the levels and between the levels.

Other studies are suggestive of the fact that highly complex kanji are taken in at a processing glance, their very complexity providing identificational clues as to their identity. Inversely, the same must be true for very simple kanji, so that the two configu-rational types, extremely simple and extremely complex, occupy opposite ends of the distributional curve. Their relative simplicity or complexity in itself offers a holistic processing clue. The same may be true for highly symmetrical kanji, although we only have experimental evidence of subjective judgments which see them as less complex, despite the number of strokes which they contain. And yet other kanji may be identified in part or whole by some specific part of the kanji, one which makes a given kanji unique in the context.

Compounds. Kanji compound words constitute another large and important grouping in the total inventory of kanji words. Not only are they worthy of attention because of their absolute numbers within the vocabulary inventory, but also because they contain within themselves the morphological principles by which new words are built on *on-kun* morphological patterns. This aspect of Japanese orthography provides one of the most interesting dimensions of the Japanese mental lexicon. It also accounts for the historically robust interest in written word recognition. The processing of morphological elements derived from *on* or *kun* origins, as they enter into collocational partnerships to create compound words, is a central dimension in Japanese word processing. It also fosters an implicit, but far-reaching cross-modal etymological awareness in the Japanese mental lexicon that goes further than, say, English language awareness of Greco-Roman roots in compound coinages. And this is what many Japanese scholars must be alluding to in their claims that the written medium is inextricably tied to the spoken medium. The spoken language does often reflect orthographic considerations of shape, style, range of readings, and iconicity that outreaches the interplay of such factors in the speech-to-writing continuum in most other languages. In Japanese, the **writing-to-speech** direction of influence is, simply stated, a powerful processing factor that must be understood not only for a theory of lexical access, but also for its value in understanding the popular beliefs about language and the Japanese language. It is in the construction of compound words that such considerations come to the fore, and where the range of *on-* and *kun-* readings pose unique demands on the reader.

The relationship of a single kanji as a word to its appearance as an element inside a kanji combination as a compound word is not a simple one. It is true that various experimental results indicate that the **first kanji** in the compound, and its relative frequency values, are important. After all, this is where lexical access procedures begin, checking the left-hand member of the compound for initial matches in the mental lexicon, and passing through to the right hand member in the compound for confirmation of the whole compound word. Very simply, the first kanji narrows down the number of choices as to the right-hand kanji, and defines the range of possible collocations in the **cohort** of potential kanji compounds (see, for example, Hirose, 1992a; Tamaoka & Takahashi, 1999).

The principles underlying such a collocational range are not entirely unlike the narrowing down described by Saito et al. (1995a, 1995b, 1995c, 1997) in their findings for the left- and right-hand components in single complex kanji. This is also what Yamada and Kayamoto's (1998) evaluations of 'high-valency' members of kanji compounds is tapping into; such high-valency kanji are richer in **associative values** because they activate more related kanji in the mental lexicon. This could be because of meaning or their orthographic shape, but it could also arise simply by virtue of frequency of co-occurrence with other kanji in such compounds. Such kanji also have greater probability of forming new compounds, because the template is already there, bolstered by their existing frequency patterns in word-building exercises. In addition to the frequency of the compound itself, the findings in general suggest that the first kanji of a compound is the best predictor of the ease of word recognition, as well as the predictability of whether a pairing is even an existing word entry with a real address in the mental lexicon.

But other research also points to the word as word, namely, compound as compound, that is processed as a whole and that acts as the ultimate arbiter for the pho-nological realization of the kanji reading. Thus, frequency tables for compounds are essential not only for assessing lexical decision tasks, but also for naming tasks in which the pho-nological realization of a given *on-* or *kun*-reading is variable and dependent upon context. Much research seems to point to two-kanji compounds being stored as and being accessed as **whole word units**, with the identification process sensitive to the holistic word level, rather than decomposition for access at the individual kanji level. Such a position is not incompatible with the findings regarding the importance of the frequency of the initial kanji in the compound, for the final realization of the compound as a whole word is where the lexical address will be ultimately realized. This does not imply that initiation of lexical access procedures is not triggered upon viewing the first kanji in the compound. Given the weighting of the orthographic features we have seen in other studies for both single and compound kanji, the first kanji of the pair will provide the first pointers to the area in which the kanji is stored. The two positions are not all incompatible; one expects the first kanji to be critical for the beginning stages of the identification process, but the ultimate goal is identification of the compound as a whole word.

The evidence from cases of neurological impairment also points to the possibility of two processing strategies for kanji compounds, one which addresses the whole word as word and another which takes into account the sub-word values of the constituent kanji in kanji compounds. Either one of these strategies can remain or be impaired, depending upon the specifics of the neurological damage. If we make the analogy with what happens in normal readers, perhaps the most efficient strategy is that kanji compounds are stored and accessed as whole units, except when they are infrequent, unknown, or unfamiliar. In such instances, kanji compounds are analyzed by breaking them into their component parts, and in these cases, the search procedures focus on finding the most likely fit in terms of both pronunciation and meaning.

Kana

As for the kana syllabaries, they seem to have taken a back seat to the logographic kanji in respect to the amount of psycholinguistic research which focusses on word recognition. Kanji do have a special place in the popular and professional consciousness, and it is not surprising that the kanji script has attracted considerable interest in both past and current research. One promising counter-trend has been the recent attention paid to the question of **script familiarity** and its effects on lexical access. The issue has at times been posed as the possibility of competing lexicons in the language, one arranged along the lines of hiragana native words vs. katakana borrowed words. But the early work by Hirose (1984, 1985) and the formidable paradigm of research pursued by Kashu, Ukita, and their colleagues over the last decade (see, for example, Ukita, Sugishima, Minagawa, Inoue & Kashu, 1996) has been a fruitful re-direction of effort, providing answers that do much to show the mixed nature of Japanese orthographic practices. There are overlapping vocabulary sets, but not neatly defined as kanji vs. kana, or even kanji vs. hiragana vs. katakana. The results so far published do much to even out the burden of energy placed on kanji alone, and show how lexical items can be variously represented in all three scripts, in the style of multiply overlapping Venn diagrams. We already know that word familiarity, in addition to word frequency, is closely related to ease of recognition. But word familiarity in Japanese has another dimension, that of script familiarity with the common orthographic shape(s) for a given word. These findings have implications for word recognition, but they also have serious implications for literacy studies and educational practice. For example, we have learned that variation is common even for high frequency words for which kanji is the typical representation (see Inoue, 1995; Inoue, Sugishima, Ukita, Minagawa & Kashu, 1994; Kashu, 1995). Almost a fifth of the highest frequency 750 words in magazine corpora exhibited variation in script type, as did a sixth of the words in newspaper headlines. Perhaps even more importantly, the **subjective expectations** about script type for those 750 words exceeded the 50% mark when college students gave opinions as to their possible orthographic manifestations. The fluidity in orthographic practice is thus matched by an even greater fluidity in script expectations, and seems to implicitly reinforce such practices in actual production. The point for us is that script familiarity is useful for a theory of word recognition in Japanese in two ways. In some cases, the theory must reckon with script familiarity in the exclusive assignment of script for certain words. In other cases, it must deal with statistical approximations of script type assignments for other words, for script type assignments in these cases are not defined in binary terms. For example, the subjective frequencies of the three script types assessed for those 750 words generated a total of ten classificatory types (Ukita et al., 1996). Thus, while this situation offers fluidity for some items, it also reinforces script type for other items. On the one hand, there is a positive correlation between high frequency content words in print and script type expectations, so that such words are deemed most appropriate in kanji representations. A high exposure rate for a common word is usually matched by a high expectation that the word will appear in a kanji format. On the other hand, unusual words, low frequency words, and words with low familiarity ratings will show variation in written forms, especially across generations (Ukita et al., 1996).

As to the kana syllabaries, it is not the case that they are simply representational variants of the same syllabic structures from a processing point of view. From a transcriptional point of view, it is true that hiragana and katakana share the same syllabic reference point, and that both can transcribe the same word according to the same principles. And there is some evidence of cross-modal priming, with a word written in the one syllabary priming the same word written in the other syllabary. The strength of this priming is not, however, as complete as the same word in the same script (Hatta & Ogawa, 1983). Such **cross-script priming** may be partially due to the fact of the same semantic content being accessed, as well as to the issue of script variation discussed above, namely, that for many words, more than one script type appearance is possible. However, from an information processing point of view, the two kana systems are not equivalent for native readers of Japanese in at least three important ways. First of all, they show differential frequencies with individual words, and this issue of script familiarity has measurable consequences in processing and even production terms. Secondly, the findings from eye-movement studies call attention to the fact that katakana words receive the longest eye fixations, invoke shorter saccades, and invite regressive movements more than even kanji and certainly far more than hiragana. These are interesting processing differences which are tied to more than just the fact of borrowings being transliterated into Japanese. Some of the critical difference appears to be tied to the fact of content words being represented in katakana, and like kanji, these angular katakana renditions stand out in a field of cursive hiragana. But a third point has to do with the fact that katakana themselves may be more difficult to process because of their minimalist angular shapes, the fact that they often overlap in whole or part, and the fact that they give rise to perceptual confusion in a way that the more distinctive, cursive hiragana do not. This is apparently true for Optical Character Readers as well as human readers, as evidenced by success rates when noise is interpolated (see Yokoyama, 1995; Yokoyama & Yoneda, 1995).

In terms of future research, **katakana words** are surely an area that merit more attention. Katakana words can no longer be considered a small subset of the vocabulary, limited to a few eccentric loanwords scattered throughout the text. Increasingly, katakana borrowings appear in greater and greater numbers, keeping pace with the number of importations into Japanese. Given their status in eye movement results, and their increasing prominence on the vocabulary landscape, they deserve to be the object of the research focus they are now receiving in recent attempts to plot frequency curves for katakana words in newspaper corpora (see Nozaki & Yokoyama, 1996; Yokoyama & Nozaki, 1996b). They are central to future word recognition studies within Japanese itself, but they also merit examination for inclusion in 'Japanese as a Second Language materials', where too much is expected of foreigners learning so-called 'familiar' katakana borrowings and not enough is provided them in terms of learning aids that are truly useful. One way of making them more familiar, of course, is to introduce the romaji renditions of such borrowed words, calling attention to the ways in which they have been integrated into Japanese vocabulary from either their spoken English or written English renditions. The surprising thing about Japanese orthographic research is that more has not been done to study the role of romaji intrusions upon Japanese print schemes. From a pedagogical point of view, more effort should be directed at finding how these increasingly common alphabetic symbols might aid foreign learners of Japanese vocabulary.

Kanji-Mixed Texts. Because Japanese is typically written in the 'kanji-mixed sentence' style, with all three scripts appearing in the same sentence, psycholinguistic research on Japanese reading practices should illuminate the way in which fundamental principles of orthographic processing at the word level interact 'top-down' processes derived from decisions about phrasal and sentence levels. But not much comes to us from possible research about contextual, **higher level decisions** affecting lower-level ones, except for the tendency to ignore 'typos' on 'mis-spelled' kanji in such larger contexts. If it does not always matter whether some small component of the total kanji configuration is wrong when that kanji is placed in a larger context (see Shimomura & Yokosawa, 1995), then the holistic processing uptake of a kanji form must supercede the decompositional analysis which takes place at lower levels for words presented in isolation. The whole-word shapes, or distinctive stroke patterns, be they recognized radicals or not, may deliver more information than the possible decompositional process. Decomposition may then be fall-back strategy, like phonological recoding, to be employed when familiarity and context do not provide enough information for global word recognition. This is an area which needs to be further investigated than it has been.

Certainly the way in which longer texts and top-down processes have been enlightened is through the eye-movement studies largely associated with Osaka and his colleagues (Osaka, 1990, 1991, 1992; Osaka & Oda, 1991; Osaka & Osaka, 1992). We already know that reading times are faster for kana/kanji mixed normal texts, and so is processing for comprehension. This coincides with the findings for eye movement studies, which seem to mesh with studies in English reading skills and levels of cognitive difficulty, as defined by textual density or ambiguity. Here too in Japanese, texts which are normal kanji-mixed texts are easier and faster to read than kana-only texts. Just as English content words are signalled by length, kanji word elements seem to signal the likelihood of a densely packed, semantically-laden content word in Japanese texts. But so also do katakana words, and for similar reasons. The eye glides through the landscape of curvy hiragana, seeking angular promotories of kanji or katakana on which to alight, fixate upon, and run saccades to and from. There is no question that kanji are important in such an organizational scheme, but not so much because they are directly accessed in the mental lexicon; rather they offer quick and reliable clues as to what is worth accessing in the mental lexicon.

Acquisition

The acquisition of orthography skills provides clues as to how **individual differences** will be enacted in word recognition skills, as well as paving the way for the differences to be found between 'good' vs. 'bad' readers in the educational system. The likelihood of individual differences among normal readers must be embedded within a strategic model of reading, for specific individuals will favor specific strategies.

Then, too, the orthographic material to be mastered by the child presents its own learning demands. Learning the list of approved kanji is not so simple as learning an itemized list of thus-and-so-many kanji. Their mastery, first of all, involves a pattern-matching system that employs a large inventory of logographic symbols which are often complex in their configurational shape, often overlapping in their various graphic features. In respect to symbol assignments, the system falls far short of a one-to-one representational principle; homophonous readings for graphically different characters abound, and the same kanji character can often have **multiple readings**. As children move up through the grades, the reality of the ambiguous correspondence ratio which characterizes the system comes to the fore. Moreover, there is a clear **asymmetry** between reading and writing abilities in kanji, and this is just as true for adults as it is for children. Writing kanji is a different task from reading kanji, and this is one area where the truism about comprehension outstripping production is certainly the case. The advent of the word processor has certainly come at an opportune time to redress this imbalance for many, but it would appear that it has become part of the problem rather than the answer to it. At the same time that mechanical devices now offer an external memory with easy look-up procedures, they also remove the need for direct access to kinetic memory and the active production of kanji. Handwriting skills may become more and more of an art form, just as good penmanship is hardly a school subject in Western countries the way it once was. And we may begin to see two distinct kanji sets in processing terms, one a large set of kanji items which is easily read and recognized and the other a somewhat reduced set which is readily produced from memory in written production. There is no question that this push-pull relationship has already blunted the direction of kanji simplification policies. The **dichotomy** between the number of kanji potentially used and the number of kanji actually used has been blurred in many instances, and the increased capability of electronic storage offers the enticement of a wider, rather than a narrower, range of kanji use in both popular literature and the media.

As to the grand question of whether Japanese is more or less efficient as an orthographic system, this is a question hardly worth asking. Those reading theorists who have sought solutions to reading difficulties in various orthographic types seem to have forgotten that every orthography has its shortcomings, just as it has its specific advantages. And every orthographic system poses a task of some enormity to the child, every one of whom has already mastered a first language with the naturalness that innate programming predicts. Unfortunately, the acquisition of orthographic skills for reading and for writing does not involve programmatic, innately enforced abilities, and the child must put out effort to master what is required to adapt existing language abilities to this secondary symbol system. As a result, it should not be surprising that children the world over, regardless of writing system typology, experience reading disabilities of one kind or another, and Japanese is no exception to this rule.

CONCLUSION

In concluding, then, we should end by noting that our original intention was survey the rich field of Japanese psycholinguistic research on the mental lexicon. We have found this work to be enormously enlightening about Japanese topics, and by extension, of universal issues in lexical access, word recognition, and reading skills. We stood in awe of the vast range of intellectual talent which has gone into consolidating this key area in Japanese scholarship, and we can only hope that we have done it justice.

APPENDIX

INTRODUCTORY COMMENTS

Japanese titles of books, chapters, contributions, and journal articles in the bibliography were transliterated, instead of being presented in the original Japanese, in order to conserve space. In an attempt to sharpen the focus of a book or journal article, the translations in the bibliography are occasionally different from the printed English version in accompanying abstracts. Names of authors were left just as we found them, so there is some variety in the actual presentation of certain proper names. Titles which were published in English were of course left just as they appeared. Titles which were published in Japanese were transliterated by using a modified Hepburn Romaji transcription system. The only point that we might call attention to in our use of the Hepburn Romaji system is that long vowels in the bibliography are not represented, but appear as single vowels without the distinguishing diacritic /^/ that Hepburn recommends. For the reader of Japanese, the referent will be immediately clear; for the non-reader of Japanese, the difference may not be important. In the text of the book itself, however, we have adopted the practice of citing actual words with length shown by doubling the vowels since there are many occasions where this phonological information is crucial to the discussion. However, for proper names and journal or book titles we have simply transliterated with a single vowel, unless the author has specifically employed a particular spelling in the English rendition.

JAPANESE JOURNALS

Japanese journal names are translated in the following appendix, with their respective translations and source of publication, if relevant. Rather than repeat the full citation and its translation after every entry, we have included this information once only in the ordered list below. A complete list of relevant Japanese journals is listed in our earlier work (Kess and Miyamoto, 1994).

Ann. Bull. RILP = Annual Bulletin, Research Institute of Logopedics and Phoniatrics. Tokyo: Tokyo University.

Daini Gengo to Shite no Nihongo no Gaksuhu Kenkyu (第二言語としての学習研究) = *Acquisition of Japanese as a Second Language.*

Dokusho Kagaku (読書科学) = *The Science of Reading.* Tokyo: Nihon Dokusho Gakkai [The Japan Reading Association].

Gengo (言語) = *Language.* Tokyo: Taishukan Shoten.

Gengo Kenkyu (言語研究) = *The Journal of the Linguistic Society of Japan.* Tokyo: Nihon Gengo Gakkai [Linguistic Society of Japan].

Gengo Seikatsu (言語生活) = *Language Life.*

Hattatsu Shinrigaku Kenkyu (発達心理学研究) = *The Japanese Journal of Developmental Psychology.* Tokyo: Nihon Hattatsu Shinri Gakkai [Japan Society of Developmental Psychology].

Japanese Psychological Research. Tokyo: The Japanese Psychological Association.

Jido Shinrigaku no Shinpo (児童心理の進歩) = *Advances in Child Psychology.* Tokyo: Nihon Jido Kenkyusho [The Center for the Development of Child Psychology], distributed by Kaneko Shobo, Tokyo.

Keiryo Kokugogaku (計量国語学) = *Mathematical Linguistics* Tokyo: Keiryo Kokugo Gakkai [The Japanese Society of Mathematical Linguistics].

Kiso Shinrigaku Kenkyu (基礎心理学研究) = *The Japanese Journal of Psychonomic Science.* Tokyo: Nihon Kiso Shinri Gakkai [The Japanese Psychonomic Society].

Kokuritsu Kokugo Kenkyusho Hokoku (国立国語研究所報告) = *Bulletin of the National Language Research Institute.*

Kyoiku Shinrigaku Kenkyu (教育心理学研究) = *The Japanese Journal of Educational Psychology.* Tokyo: Nihon Kyoiku Shinri Gakkai [The Japanese Association of Educational Psychology].

Kyoiku Shinrigaku Nenpo (教育心理学年報) = *The Annual Report of Educational Psychology in Japan.* Tokyo: Nihon Kyoiku Shinri Gakkai [The Japanese Association of Educational Psychology], distributed by Kokudosha, Tokyo.

Nihongo Kyoiku (日本語教育) = *Journal of Japanese Language Teaching.* Tokyo: Nihongo Kyoiku Kai [The Society for Teaching Japanese as a Foreign Language].

Nihongogaku (日本語学) = *Japanese Linguistics.* Tokyo: Meiji Shoin.

Nihon Kyoiku Kogaku Zasshi (日本教育科学雑誌) = *The Japanese Journal of the Educational Technology.*

Nihon Kyoiku Kogaku Kaishi (日本教育工学会誌) = *Proceedings of the Japanese Educational Technology Association Meetings.* Tokyo: Nihon Kyoiku Kogaku Gakkai [Japanese Society for Educational Technology].

No to Shinkei (脳と神経) = *Brain and Nerve.* Tokyo: Igaku Shoin.

Oyo Butsuri (応用物理) = *Applied Physics*. Tokyo: Oyo Butsuri Gakkai [Japanese Applied Physics Society].

Rinsho Shinkeigaku (臨床神経学) = *Clinical Neurology*. Tokyo: Nihon Shinkei Gakkai [The Japanese Society of Clinical Neurology].

Shinkei Igaku (神経医学) = *Neurological Medicine*. Tokyo: Igaku Shoin.

Shinkei Kenkyu no Shinpo (神経研究の進歩) = *Advances in the Neurological Sciences*. Tokyo: Igaku Shoin.

Shinkei Naika (神経内科) = *Internal Medicine in Neurology*.

Shinkei Shinrigaku (神経心理学) = *Japanese Journal of Neuropsychology*. Ishikawa: Nihon Shinkei Shinri Gakkai [Neuropsychology Association of Japan].

Shinrigaku Hyoron (心理学評論) = *Japanese Psychological Reviews*. Kyoto: Kyoto Daigaku Shinrigaku Hyoron Kankokai [The Kyoto University Publishing Association for Psychological Reviews].

Shinrigaku Kenkyu (心理学研究) = *The Japanese Journal of Psychology*. Tokyo: Nihon Shinri Gakkai [The Japanese Psychological Association].

Shizen (自然) = *Nature*. Tokyo: Chukoronsha.

Shitsugosho Kenkyu (失語症研究) = *Higher Brain Function Research*. Shizuoka: Nihon Shitsugosho Kenkyukai [The Japanese Society of Aphasia].

Tetsugaku Kenkyu (哲学研究) = *The Journal of Philosophical Studies*. Kyoto: Kyoto Tetsugakukai [Kyoto Philosophical Society].

Tokushu Kyoikugaku Kenkyu (特殊教育学研究) = *Japanese Journal of Special Education*. Tsukuba: Nihon Tokushu Kyoiku Gakkai (Japanese Society of Special Education).

JAPANESE RESEARCH PUBLICATIONS

Japanese university and research institute publications that we cited are presented below, with their respective translations and source of publication, if relevant. Once again, rather than repeat the translation after every entry, we have included the translation once in the ordered list below. A complete list of relevant Japanese research publications is also listed in our earlier work (Kess and Miyamoto, 1994).

Hiroshima Daigaku Kyoiku Gakubu Kiyo (広島大学教育学部紀要) = *The Bulletin of the Faculty of Education, Hiroshima University*. Hiroshima: Hiroshima University.

Hiroshima Daigaku Nihongo Kyoiku Gakka Kiyo (広島大学日本語教育学課紀要) = *The Bulletin of the Department of Japanese Language Education, Hiroshima University.* Hiroshima: Hiroshima University.

Kobe Yamate Joshi Tanki Daigaku Kiyo (神戸山手女子短期大学紀要) = *The Bulletin of Kobe Yamate Women's College.*

Kwansei Gakuin Daigaku Jinbun Ronkyu (関西学院大学人文論究) = *The Bulletin of the Humanities, Kwansei Gakuin University.* Kobe: Kwansei Gakuin University.

Kyoto Daigaku Kyoiku Gakubu Kiyo (京都大学教育学部紀要) = *The Bulletin of the Faculty of Education, Kyoto University.* Kyoto: Kyoto Unisversity.

Kyoto Kyoiku Daigaku Kiyo (京都教育大学紀要) = *The Bulletin of the Faculty of Letters, Kyoto University of Education.* Kyoto: Kyoto University of Education.

Matsuyama Daigaku Gengo Bunka Kenkyu (松山大学言語文化研究) = *Matsuyama University Research Reports in Language and Culture.* Matsuyama: Matsuyama University.

Matsuyama Daigaku Sogo Kenkyusho Soho (松山大学総合研究所総報) = *Matsuyama University General Research Center Report.* Matsuyama: Matsuyama University.

Nagoya Daigaku Kyoyobu Kiyo (名古屋大学教養部紀要) = *The Bulletin of the College of General Education, Nagoya University.* Nagoya: Nagoya University

Tohoku Psychologia Folia. Sendai: Tohoku University.

REFERENCES

Abe, J. 1994. *Ningen no Gengo Joho Shori: Gengo Rikai no Ninchi Kagaku [Linguistic Information Processing by Humans: The Cognitive Science of Language Comprehension]*. Cognitive Science and Information Processing, 12. Tokyo: Saiensusha.

Abe, K., R. Yokoyama & T. Yanagihara. 1995. "A Crossed Kana Agraphia". *Behavioural Neurology* 8.121-124.

Adachi, J. 1992. "Shikaku Taisho no Keitai ni Yotte Yudo Sareru Hietsu Gankyu Undo [Saccadic Eye Movement Guided by the Visual Form]". *Shinrigaku Kenkyu* 63.118-122.

Adachi, J. 1993. "Shuhenshi Shigeki Sentaku ni Yoru Sakkeda ni okeru Shikaku Joho Shori [The Visual Information Processing in Generating Saccades through the Selection of the Peripheral Stimulus]". *Shinrigaku Kenkyu* 63.363-370.

Agency for Cultural Affairs. 1987. *Kogata Kokugo Jiten ni Sairoku Sarete Iru Gairaigo [Loan Words Recorded in Japanese Dictionaries]*. Tokyo: Bunkacho.

Akamatsu, T. 1997. *Japanese Phonetics: Theory and Practice. LINCOM Studies in Asian Linguistics 03*. Munchen-Newcastle: LINCOM EUROPA.

Akita, K., T. Muto, M. Fujioka & K. Yasumi. 1995. "Yoji wa Ika ni Hon o Yomu ka?: Kana Moji no Shutoku to Yomikata no Kanrensei no Judanteki Kento [The Development of Children's Reading of Story Books: A Longitudinal Study of Relations between the Acquisition of Kana-letters and Book Reading]". *Hattatsu Shinrigaku Kenkyu* 6.58-58.

Amano, K. 1970. "Go no Oninkozo no Bunsekikoi no Keisei to Kanamoji no Yomi no Gakushu [Formation of the Act of Analyzing the Phonemic Structure of Words and Its Relation to Learning Japanese Syllabic Characters (Kanamoji)]". *Kyoiku Shinrigaku Kenkyu* 18.76-89.

Amano, S., T. Kondo & K. Kakehi. 1995. "Modality Dependency of Familiarity Ratings of Japanese Words". *Perception and Psychophysics* 57.598-603.

Amano, S., T. Kondo & K. Kakehi. 1999. *NTT Psycholinguistic Database*. Tokyo: NTT Communication Science Laboratories.

Araki, T. 1985. "Kanji Kensaku no tame no Kanji Kodo Kaizen [Development of Kanji Codes for Kanji Retrieval]". *Keiryo Kokugogaku* 15.100-117.

Asahi Shimbun. 1994. CD-ROM, 1993 Editions of the *Asahi Shimbun*. Tokyo: Kinokuniya & Nichigai Associates.

Asayama, T. 1914. "Uber die Aphasie bei Japanern". *Deutsche Archive für Klinische Medizin* 113.523-529.

Azuma, H. & H. Imada. 1994. "Origins and Development of Psychology in Japan: The Interaction between Western Science and the Japanese Cultural Heritage". *International Journal of Psychology* 29.707-715.

Besner, D. 1990. "Orthographies and Their Phonologies: A Hypothesis". *Bulletin of the Psychonomic Society* 28.395-396.

Besner, D. & M. Coltheart. 1979. "Ideographic and Alphabetic Processing in Skilled Reading of English". *Neuropsychologia* 17.467-472.

Besner, D., D. S. Daniels & C. Slade. 1982. "Ideogram Reading and Right Hemisphere Language". *British Journal of Psychology* 73.21-28.

Besner, D. & N. Hildebrandt. 1987. "Orthographic and Phonological Codes in the Oral Reading of Japanese Kana". *Journal of Experimental Psychology* 13.335-343.

Biederman, I. & Y-C. Tsao. 1979. "On Processing Chinese Ideographs and English Words: Some Implications from Stroop-Test Results". *Cognitive Psychology* 11.125-132.

Boltz, W. G. 1994. *The Origin and Early Development of the Chinese Writing System.* New Haven: American Oriental Society.

Bradley, L. & P. E. Bryant. 1983. "Categorizing Sounds and Learning to Read--A Causal Connection". *Nature* 301.419-421.

Bridgeman, B. 1987. "Is the Dual-Route Theory Possible in Phonetically Regular Languages?". *Behavioral and Brain Sciences* 10.331-332.

Bradshaw, J. L. & N. C. Nettleton. 1983. *Human Cerebral Asymmetry.* Englewood Cliffs, NJ: Prentice-Hall.

Broca, P. P. 1861. Remarques sur le Siège de la Faculté du Langage Articulé: Suivies d'une Observation d'Aphémie (Perte de la Parole). *Bulletin de la Société Anatomie de Paris* 36.330-357.

Brown, R. & D. McNeill. 1966. "The 'Tip of the Tongue' Phenomenon". *Journal of Verbal Learning and Verbal Behavior* 5.325-337.

Brown, H., N. K. Sharma & K. Kirsner. 1984. "The Role of Script and Phonology in Lexical Representation". *Quarterly Journal of Experimental Psychology* 36A.491-505.

Bryden, M. P. 1982. *Laterality: Functional Asymmetry in the Intact Brain.* New York: Academic Press.

Büssing, A., R. Bruckmann & W. Hartje. 1987. "Influence of Figural Complexity on the Identification of Kanji and Kana Characters". *Cortex* 23.325-330.

Caramazza, A. & W. Badecker, 1989. "Patient Classification in Neuropsychological Research". *Brain and Cognition* 10.256-295.

Carroll, J. B., P. Davies & B. Richman. 1972. *Word Frequency Book.* New York: American Heritage Dictionary.

Chen, H-C. 1996. "Chinese Reading and Comprehension: A Cognitive Psychology Perspective". *The Handbook of Chinese Psychology* ed. by M. H. Bond, 43-62. Hong Kong: Oxford University Press.

Chen, Y. P., D. A. Allport & J. C. Marshall. 1996. "What Are the Functional Orthographic Units in Chinese Word Recognition: The Stroke or the Stroke Pattern?". *Quarterly Journal of Experimental Psychology* 49A.1024-1043.

Chen, H-C., G. B. Flores d'Arcais & S-L. Cheung. 1995. "Orthographic and Phonological Activation in Recognizing Chinese Chracters". *Psychological Research* 58.144-153.

Cheng, C. M. & G. L. Fu. 1986. "The Recognition of Chinese Characters and Words under Divided Field Representation". *Linguistics, Psychology, and the Chinese Language* ed. by H. S. R. Kao & R. Hoosain. Hong Kong: University of Hong Kong Centre of Asian Studies.

Chen, H-C. & K-C. Tsoi. 1990. "Symbol-Word Interference in Chinese and English". *Acta Psychologica* 75.123-138.

Chen, M. J. & J. C-K. Yuen. 1991. "Effects of Pinyin and Script Type on Verbal Processing: Comparisons of the China, Taiwan, and Hong Kong Experience". *International Journal of Behavioral Development* 14.429-448.

Chikamatsu, N. 1996. "The Effects of LI Orthography on L2 Word Recognition: A Study of English and Chinese Learners of Japanese". *Studies in Second Language Acquisition* 18.403-432.

Chikamatsu, N., S. Yokoyama, H. Nozaki, E. Long, H. Sasahara & S. Fukuda. 1998. "Development of a Japanese Kanji Character Frequency List". Paper given at the 12th International Unicode Conference. Tokyo, Japan. April, 1998.

Chikamatsu, N, S. Yokoyama, H. Nozaki, E. Long, H. Sasahara & S. Fukuda. (n.d.). "A Japanese Logographic Character Frequency List for Cognitive Science Research".

Chua, F. K. 1995. "Reading a Chinese Logograph: Meaning from Spelling and Sound". *Asian Journal of Psychology* 1.47-53.

Chujo, K., K. Notomi & T. Ishida. 1993. "Yoko Sutororu Hyoji no Yomi no Sokudo ni Oyobosu Mojisu no Koka [The Effects of the Number of Characters on the Reading Rate of Character Strings Moving Horizontally on a CRT]". *Shinrigaku Kenkyu* 64.360-368.

Collier-Sanuki, Y. 1996. "Review of N. Gottlieb: *Kanji Politics: Language Policy and Japanese Script*". *The Japan Foundation Newsletter* 14.17-19.

Coulmas, F. 1989. *The Writing Systems of the World*. Oxford: Blackwell Publishers.

Dairoku, H. 1995. "Mora ni Taisuru Ishiki wa Kana Moji no Yomishutoku no Hitsuyo Joken ka? [Is Awareness of Morae a Necessary Condition for Kana Reading?]". *Shinrigaku Kenkyu* 66.253-260.

DeFrancis, J. 1989. *Visible Speech: The Diverse Oneness of Writing Systems*. Honolulu: University of Hawaii Press.

DeSchonen, S. & E. Mathivet. 1989. "First Come, First Served: A Scenario about the Development of Hemispheric Specialization in Face Recognition during Infancy". *European Bulletin of Cognitive Psychology* 9.3-44.

Duke, B. C. 1977. "Why Noriko Can Read". *The Educational Forum* 41.229-236.

Ebbinghaus, H. 1885. *Uber das Gedachtnis [On Memory]*. Leipzig: Duncker & Humblot.

Eko, R. & S. Nakamizo. 1989. "Kanji, Kana, Zukei no Fugoka Katei [Coded Representations of Kanji, Kana, and Figures]". *Shinrigaku Kenkyu* 60.265-268.

Elman, L. J., K. Takahashi & Y. Tohsaku. 1981a. "Asymmetries for the Categorization of Kanji Nouns, Adjectives, and Verbs Presented to the Left and Right Visual Fields". *Brain and Language* 13.290-300.

Elman, L. J., K. Takahashi & Y. Tohsaku. 1981b. "Lateral Asymmetries for the Identification of Concrete and Abstract Kanji". *Neuropsychologia* 19.407-412.

Endo, C. 1983. *Kotoba no Shinrigaku [The Psychology of Language]*. Kyoto: Nakanishiya Shuppan.

Endo, M., A. Shimizu & T. Hori. 1978. "Functional Asymmetry of Visual Fields for Japanese Words in *Kana* (Syllable-Based) Writing and Random Shape-Recognition in Japanese Subjects". *Neuropsychologia* 16.291-297.

Endo, M., A. Shimizu & I. Nakamura. 1981a. "Laterality Differences in Recognition of Japanese and Hangul Words by Monolinguals and Bilinguals". *Cortex* 17.391-400.

Endo, M., A. Shimizu & I. Nakamura. 1981b. "The Influence of Hangul Learning upon Laterality Differences in Hangul Word Recognition by Native Japanese Subjects". *Brain and Language* 14.114-119.

Endo, Y. 1988. "The Role of a Motoric Aspect of Representation: Spontaneous Writing-Like Behavior in Japanese". *Practical Aspects of Memory: Current Research and Issues*, Vol. 2, *Clinical and Educational Implications* ed. by M. M. Gruneberg, P. E. Morris & R. N. Sykes, 459-463. New York: John Wiley.

Endo-Misawa, M. 1990. "Yoji no Yoonsetsu no Yomi Kaki no Shutoku Katei [How Young Children Learn to Read and Spell Small-Sized Kana]". *Kyoiku Shinrigaku Kenkyu* 38.213-222.

Erickson, D., I. G. Mattingly & M. T. Turvey. 1977. "Phonetic Activity in Reading: An Experiment with Kanji". *Language and Speech* 20.384-399.

Fang, S-P., O. J. L. Tzeng & L. Alva. 1981. "Intralanguage vs. Interlanguage Stroop Effects in Two Types of Writing Systems". *Memory and Cognition* 9.609-617.

Feldman, L. B. & M. T. Turvey. 1980. "Words Written in Kana Are Named Faster Than the Same Words Written in Kanji". *Language and Speech* 23.141-147.

Flaherty, M. 1993a. "Perception of Japanese Kanji: Differences between Japanese Children and Second Language Learners". *Psychological Studies* 38.15-20.

Flaherty, M. 1993b. "Are Japanese Kanji Processed Like Pictures?". *Psychologia* 36.144-150.

Flaherty, M. 1994. "Word-Picture Interference Effects in Chinese, Japanese Kanji and Kana, and English". *Psychologia* 37.169-179.

Flores d'Arcais, G. B. & H. Saito. 1990. "Semantic Activation and Lexical Decomposition in the Recognition of Complex Kanji Characters". *Cognition in Individual and Social Contexts* ed. by A. F. Bennett & K. M. McConkey, 101-109. Amsterdam: North-Holland.

Flores d'Arcais, G. B. & H. Saito. 1993. "Lexical Decomposition of Complex Kanji Characters in Japanese Readers". *Psychological Research* 55.52-63.

Flores d'Arcais, G. B., H. Saito, and M. Kawakami. 1995. "Phonological and Semantic Activation in Reading Kanji Characters". *Journal of Experimental Psychology: Learning, Memory, and Cognition* 21.34-42.

Flores d'Arcais, G. B., H. Saito, M. Kawakami & H. Masuda. 1994. "Figural and Phonological Effects in Radical Migration with Kanji Characters". *Advances in the Study of Chinese Language Processing, Vol. 1*, ed. by H-W. Chang, J-T. Huang, C-W. Hue & O. J. L. Tzeng, 241-254. Taipei: National Taiwan University.

Foss, D. J. 1988. "Experimental Psycholinguistics". *Annual Review of Psychology* 39.301-348.

Foster, M. 1990. "A Cross-Cultural Study on Hemispheric Asymmetries in Tachistoscopic Recognition of Kanji Characters". *Tohoku Psychologica Folia* 49.1-14.

Fox, B. & D. K. Routh. 1975. "Analyzing Spoken Language into Words, Syllables, and Phonemes: A Developmental Study". *Journal of Psycholinguistic Research* 4.331-342.

Fujihara, K. 1989. "Kanamoji to Suji no Shori Katei no Chigai [Differences in Processing Kana and Numerals]". *Shinrigaku Kenkyu* 60.76-82.

Fujita, T. 1992. "Tango Kansei wa Deta Kudokei Tesuto to Ieru ka? [Is Word Fragment Completion a Data-driven Test?]". *Shinrigaku Kenkyu* 63.326-332.

Fukuzawa, S. 1987. *Jido no Kotoba [Children's Language]. Kodomo no Gengo Shinri [Psychology of Children's Language]* ed. by S. Fukuzawa. *Gendai Shinrigaku Bukkusu [Contemporary Psychology Books]*, 79. Tokyo: Dainihon Tosho.

Fukuzawa, S., ed. 1996. *Kotoba no Shinri to Kyoiku [Education and the Psychology of Language]*. Tokyo: Kyoiku Shuppan.

Furth, H. 1966. *Thinking without Language*. New York: The Free Press.

Gelb, I. J. 1963. *The Study of Writing*. Revised Edition. Chicago: University of Chicago Press.

Gile, D. 1986. "Kango Recognition in Japanese Speech Perception". *Lingua* 70.171-189.

Gipson, P. 1984. *A Study of the Long-term Priming of Auditory Word Recognition.* Unpublished Doctoral dissertation, Cambridge University.

Gleitman, L. R. & P. Rozin. 1977. "The Structure and Acquisition of Reading I: Relations between Orthographies and the Structure of Language". *Towards a Psychology of Reading* ed. by A. S. Reber & D. L. Scarborough, 1-53. Hillsdale, NJ: Lawrence Erlbaum Associates.

Gottlieb, N. 1995. *Kanji Politics: Language Policy and Japanese Script.* London and New York: Kegan Paul International.

Green, D., P. Meara & S. Court. 1989. "Are Numbers Logographs?". *Journal of Research in Reading* 12.1.49-58.

Haga, J. 1979. *Nigengo Heiyo no Shinri: Gengoshinrigakuteki Kenkyu [Psychology of Bilingualism: Psycholinguistic Research].* Tokyo: Asakura Shoten.

Haga, J. 1988. *Gengoshinrigaku Nyumon [Introduction to Psycholinguistics].* Tokyo: Yuhikaku.

Haga, J. & M. Koyasu, eds. 1990. *Metafa no Shinrigaku [The Psychology of Metaphor].* Tokyo: Seishin Shobo.

Haga, Y. 1979. *Nihonjin no Hyogen Shinri [Psychology of Japanese Expression].* Tokyo: Chuko Sosho.

Hakoda, Y. & M. Sasaki. 1990. "Shudanyo Suturupu, Gyaku Suturupu Tesuto: Oyo Yoshiki, Junjo, Renshu no Koka [The Stroop and Reverse-Stroop Test: The Effects of Reaction Mode, Order, and Practice]". *Kyoiku Shinrigaku Kenkyu* 38.389-394.

Hamada, J. 1986. "Junko oyobi Gyakko Fukusho, Saisei Joken ni okeru Randamu Sujiretsu ni Taisuru Shikaku Kioku to Chokaku Kioku no Sogo Sayo [Visual and Auditory Memory for Random Digit Series Under Forward and Backward Rehearsal/Recall Conditions]". *Kiso Shinrigaku Kenkyu* 5.55-61.

Hamanaka, T. 1994. "One Hundred Years of Neuropychology in Japan: Retrospect and Prospect". *Neuropsychology Review* 4.289-298.

Harada, E. 1987. "Tango o Koeru Chokusetsu Puraimingu Koka: Tangotsui ni okeru Koka no Kento [Direct Priming Effect Beyond Words: A Case of Word Pairs]". *Shinrigaku Kenkyu* 58.302-308.

Haryu, E. 1989. "Yoji ni okeru Kanji to Hiragana no Dokuji Gakushu: Sono Shidohoho ni Tsuite no Kento [What Facilitates Learning to Read Characters by Children?]". *Kyoiku Shinrigaku Kenkyu* 37.264-269.

Hasuike, R., O. J. L. Tzeng & D. L. Hung. 1986. "Script Effects and Cerebral Lateralization: The Case of Chinese Characters". *Language Processing in Bilinguals: Psycholinguistic and Neuropsychological Perspectives* ed. by J. Vaid, 275-288. Hillsdale, NJ: Lawrence Erlbaum Associates.

Hatae, T. 1982. "The Different Effects of Parafoveal Information Processing of Kana Reading in Poor and Good Readers of Elementary School First and Second Grades". *Psychologia* 25.155-163.

Hatano, G., K. Kuhara & M. Akiyama. 1981. "Kanji Help Readers of Japanese Infer the Meaning of Unfamiliar Words". *The Quarterly Newsletter of the Laboratory of Comparative Human Cognition* 3.30-33.

Hatano, K. 1936. *Gengoshinrigaku [Psycholinguistics]*. Series entitled *Iwanami Kooza Kokugo Kyoiku; Kokugo Kyoiku no Gakuteki Kikoo [Iwanami Lectures in National Language Education; Scholastic Organization of National Language Education]*. Tokyo: Iwanami Shoten.

Hatano, K. 1958. *Kotoba to Bunsho no Shinrigaku [The Psychology of Words and Sentences]*. Tokyo: Shinchosha.

Hatta, T. 1977a. "Lateral Recognition of Abstract and Concrete Kanji in Japanese". *Perceptual and Motor Skills* 45.731-734.

Hatta, T. 1977b. "Recognition of Japanese Kanji in the Left and Right Visual Fields". *Neuropsychologia* 15.685-688.

Hatta, T. 1977c. "Hanchuka Ido Handan Kadai ni okeru Daino Hankyu Kinosa ni Tsuite [Hemispheric Differences in a Categorization Matching Task]". *Shinrigaku Kenkyu* 48.141-147.

Hatta, T. 1978. "Recognition of Japanese Kanji and Hiragana in the Left and Right Visual Fields". *Japanese Psychological Research* 20.51-59.

Hatta, T. 1981a. "Differential Processing of Kanji and Kana Stimuli in Japanese People: Some Implications from Stroop-Test Results". *Neuropsychologia* 19.87-93.

Hatta, T. 1981b. "Different Stages of Kanji Processing and Their Relations to Functional Hemisphere Asymmetries". *Japanese Psychological Research* 23.27-36.

Hatta, T. 1981c. "Kanji Zairyo Ninchi no Daino Hankyu Kinosa ni okeru Shori Horyakusa to Shori Suijun no Eikyo [Task Differences in Tachistoscopic Kanji Recognition and Their Relations to Hemisphere Asymmetries]". *Shinrigaku Kenkyu* 52.139-144.

Hatta, T. 1983. "Level of Processing Effects on Hemispheric Asymmetries with Kana (Japanese Phonetic Symbols) Words". *International Journal of Psychology* 18.285-296.

Hatta, T. 1985. "Reading Processes in Japanese: Do the Japanese Have Script-Specific Mechanism?". *Language Sciences* 7.355-363.

Hatta, T. 1986a. "Differential Hemispheric Engagement in Covert Preattentive Processes: Filtering and Pigeonholing Mechanisms". *Psychologia* 29.42-49.

Hatta, T. 1986b. "Review of Michel Paradis, Hiroko Hagiwara, and Nancy Hildebrandt: *Neurolinguistic Aspects of the Japanese Writing System*". *Journal of Neurolinguistics* 2.383-387.

Hatta, T. 1991. "Kanji Ninchi no Raterariti [Laterality in Kanji Recognition]". *Yonjunen no Ayumi* [*Progress in Forty Years*] ed. by M. Ikuzawa, 527-550. Osaka: Osaka City University.

Hatta, T. 1992. "The Effects of Kanji Attributes on Visual Field Differences: Examination with Lexical Decision, Naming and Semantic Classification Tasks". *Neuropsychologia* 30.361-371.

Hatta, T., T. I. Hatae & K. Kirsner. 1984. "Orthographic Dominance and Interference Effects in Letter Recognition Among Japanese-English and English-Japanese Bilinguals". *Psychologia* 27.1-9.

Hatta, T. & T. Hirose 1984. "Gairaigo, Higairaigo no Ninchi Shori ni Kansuru Kenkyu: Nihonjin Daigakusei to Gaikokujin Daigakusei no Yomi Jikan no Kekka Kara [Reading of Japanese and Foreign Loan Words by Japanese and Australian Students]". *Dokusho Kagaku* 28.121-129.

Hatta, T., Y. Honjoh & H. Mito. 1983. "Event-Related Potentials and Reaction Times as Measures of Hemispheric Differences for Physical and Semantic Kanji Matching". *Cortex* 19.517-528.

Hatta, T., H. Katoh & N. Aitani. 1983. "Does Single Kanji Process Dominantly in the Right Hemispheres? Some Implications from Stroop-Test Results". *International Journal of Neuroscience* 18.67-72.

Hatta, T., H. Katoh & K. Kirsner. 1984. "Lexical Representation of Foreign Loan Words in Japanese Learners Among Native Readers of English". *Psychologia* 27.237-243.

Hatta, T. & A. Kawakami. 1994. "Cohort Effects in the Lateral Preference of Japanese People". *Journal of General Psychology* 121.377-380.

Hatta, T. & A. Kawakami. 1996. "Lexical and Naming Processes of Non-prototypical Kanji: Evidence of the Component Parts Activation". *Asia Pacific Journal of Speech, Language and Hearing* 1.55-64.

Hatta, T., A. Kawakami, & Y. Hatasa. 1997. "Kanji Writing Errors in Japanese College Students and American Japanese Students". *Cognitive Processing of Chinese and Related Asian Languages* ed. by H-C. Chen, 401-416. Hong Kong: The Chinese University Press.

Hatta, T., A. Kawakami & K. Tamaoka. 1998. "Writing Errors in Japanese Kanji: A Study with Japanese Students and Foreign Learners of Japanese". *Reading and Writing* 10.457-470.

Hatta, T. & T. Konda. 1992. "Changes in Visual Field Advantage in Processing Face and Unknown Letter with Increasing Stimulus Familiarization". *Psychologia* 35.21-32.

Hatta, T. & T. Ogawa. 1983. "Hiragana and Katakana in Japanese Orthography and Lexical Representation". *Language Sciences* 5.185-196.

Hatta, T., H. Ohnishi, M. Yamamoto & H. Ogura. 1981. "Cerebral Laterality Effects on Levels of Kana Word Processing". *Psychologia* 24.202-206.

Hatta, T. & S. Tsuji. 1993. "Interhemispheric Integration of Number Stimuli: Comparison of Arabic with Kanji Numerals". *Cortex* 29.359-364.

Hatta, T., M. Yamamoto & T. Hirose. 1990. "Ryoji Bunricho Kensa ni Yoru Gengoon Ninchi no Sayuji Kino no Hattatsu [Development of the Right Ear Advantage in Dichotic Listening Test: Comparison of the Findings by Cross-sectional and Longitudinal Studies]". *Shinrigaku Kenkyu* 61.308-313.

Hayashi, O. 1991. "Kanji no Kaiho to Moji Kyoiku [Kanji Liberation and Character Education]". *Gengo* 20.44-49.

Hayashi, R. 1985. "Hemispheric Asymmetry as a Function of Word Imageability in Recognition Memory Task". *Japanese Psychological Research* 27.63-71.

Hayashi, R. 1988. "Stroop Kansho Kadai de no Hyokisa ni okeru Bogaigo no Imi Zokusei no Yakuwari ni Tsuite [The Role of Semantic Attributes and Script Type Effects in Stroop Color-Word Interference]". *Shinrigaku Kenkyu* 59.1-8.

Hayashi, R. & T. Hatta. 1978. "Hemispheric Differences in Mental Rotation Task with Kanji Stimuli". *Psychologia* 21.210-215.

Hayashi, R. & T. Hatta. 1982. "Visual Field Differences in a Deeper Semantic Processing Task With Kanji Stimuli". *Japanese Psychological Research* 24.111-117.

Hayashi, R. & T. Hayashi. 1991. "Concurrent Vocal Interference Effect on Reading Comprehension of Kana Alone and Kanji-Kana Mixed Form Sentence". *Psychologia* 34.118-125.

Hellige, J. B. 1980 "Cerebral Hemisphere Asymmetry: Methods, Issues, and Implications". *Educational Communication and Technology* 28.83-98.

Hellige, J. B. 1990. "Hemispheric Asymmetry". *Annual Review of Psychology* 41.55-80.

Hieshima, I. 1994. *Kotoba no Shinri: Hajimete Gengoshinrigaku o Manabu Hito no Tame ni [The Psychology of Language: Psycholinguistics for Those Beginning Its Study]*. Tokyo: Kitaki Shuppan.

Higuchi, H., K. Saito, M. Tominaga, Y. Shimada, J. Yamaguchi, N. Motomura, T. Kashiwagi & A. Yamadori. 1996. "A Single Case of Multiple Sclerosis with a Peculiar Kanji Alexia". *Proceedings of the Twentieth Meeting of the Japanese Neuropsychological Association*, p. 142.

Hines, D. 1976. "Recognition of Verbs, Abstract Nouns, and Concrete Nouns from the Left and Right Visual Half-fields". *Neuropsychologia* 14.211-216.

Hirose, H. 1992a. "Jukugo no Ninchi Katei ni Kansuru Kenkyu: Puraimingu-ho ni Yoru Kento [Using the Priming Paradigm to Investigate Word Recognition for Kanji Compound Words]". *Shinrigaku Kenkyu* 63.303-309.

Hirose, H. 1992b. "Kanji no Yomi Katei ni okeru Keitai Joho no Koka: Onin Macchingu Kadai ni okeru Kento [The Effects of Graphemic Information on Kanji Reading:

An Experiment Using the Phonemic Matching Task]". *Kiso Shinrigaku Kenkyu* 2.109-113.

Hirose, T. 1984. "Kanji oyobi Kana Tango no Imiteki Shori ni Oyobosu Hyoki Hindo no Koka [The Effect of Script Frequency on Semantic Processing of Kanji and Kana Words]". *Shinrigaku Kenkyu* 55.173-176.

Hirose, T. 1985. "Tango no Ninchi ni Oyobosu Hyoki no Shinkinsei no Koka [The Effects of Orthographic Familiarity on Word Recognition]". *Shinrigaku Kenkyu* 56.44-47.

Hirose, T. & T. Hatta. 1985. "Reading Disabilities in Japan: Evidence against the Myth of Rarity". *International Journal of Neuroscience* 26.249-252.

Hirose, T. & T. Hatta. 1988. "Reading Disabilities in Modern Japanese Children". *Journal of Research in Reading* 11.152-160.

Hishitani, S. 1980. "Kioku ni Oyobosu Hikensha to Zairyo no Tokusei no Koka: Fugoka Horyaku no Kojinsa ni Tsuite no Kento [Subject and Stimulus Effect on Memory: Individual Differences in Coding Strategies]". *Kyoiku Shinrigaku Kenkyu* 28.251-255.

Hoptman, M. J. & R. J. Davidson. 1994. "How and Why Do the Two Cerebral Hemispheres Interact?". *Psychological Bulletin* 116.195-219.

Hoshino, A. 1979. "Current Major Trends in Psychology in Japan". *Psychologia* 22.1-20.

Hoshino, A. & T. Umemoto. 1987. "Japanese Psychology: Historical Review and Recent Trends". *Psychology Moving East* ed. by G. H. Blowers & A. M. Turtle, 183-196. Boulder, Colorado: Westview Press.

Hoshino, Y. 1991. "Inhibitory Effects of Irrelevant Information on Reaction Time in Classifying Target Items". *Japanese Psychological Research* 33.53-63.

Hotta, O. 1984. "Moji Onsetsu no Shiyo Hindo ni Yoru Hiragana no Moji Shutoku Yoin ni Kansuru Kenkyu [Kana Acquisition Based on the Frequency of Letters and Syllables". *Kyoiku Shinrigaku Kenkyu* 32.68-72.

Hue, C-W. & J. R. Erickson. 1988. "Short-term Memory for Chinese Characters and Radicals". *Memory and Cognition.* 16.196-205.

Humphreys, G. W. & L. J. Evett. 1985. "Are There Independent Lexical and Nonlexical Routes in Word Processing? An Evaluation of the Dual-Route Theory of Reading". *Behavioral and Brain Sciences* 8.869-740.

Hung, D. L. & O. J. L. Tzeng. 1981. "Orthographic Variations and Visual Information Processing". *Psychological Bulletin* 90.377-414.

Huang, Y. L. & B. Jones. 1980. "Naming and Discrimination of Chinese Ideograms Presented in the Right and Left Visual Fields". *Neuropsychologia* 18.703-706.

Ikeda, M. & S. Saida. 1978. "Span of Recognition in Reading". *Vision Research* 18.83-88.

Ikeda, S. 1988. "The Japanese Word Processor". *Journal of Reading* 31.498-504.

Ikeda, S., N. Matsumi & T. Mori. 1994. "Eigo-Nihongokan de Shojiru Gengonai, Gengokan Suturupu Koka no Kento: Daigakusei to Chugakusei no Hikaku [Stroop and Reverse Stroop Interference in English and Japanese: A Comparison of High School and University Students]". *Hattatsu Shinrigaku Kenkyu* 5.31-40.

Imai, Y. 1983. "Kana no Dokuji Gakushu ni Oyobosu Kaigaka to Gengoka no Koka [The Effect of Pictorial and Verbal Familiarization on Learning to Read Kana Scripts]". *Kyoiku Shinrigaku Kenkyu* 31.203-210.

Imai, Y. 1987. "Yoji no Moji no Yomi [Script Reading by Children]". *Kodomo no Gengo Shinri, 2: Yoji no Kotoba [Child Psycholinguistics, Vol. 2: Child Language]* ed. by S. Fukuzawa, 57-93. Tokyo: Dainihon Tosho.

Imai, Y. & M. Sakai. 1991. "Yoji ni okeru Nihongo Tokushu Onsetsu no Yomi no Gakushu [Teaching Young Children to Read Japanese Special Syllables]". *Dokusho Kagaku* 35.94-103.

Inhoff, A. W. & K. Rayner. 1986. "Parafoveal Word Processing during Eye Fixations in Reading: Effects of Word Frequency". *Perception and Psychophysics* 40.431-439.

Inoue, M. & T. Tsujino. 1992. "Kokugo Kankei Shimbun Kiji Detabesu ni Tsuite (Chukan Hokoku) [Database of Japanese Language Nespaper Articles: Interim Report]". *Kokuritsu Kokugo Kenkyusho Hokoku* 104.165-193.

Inoue, M. 1980. "Kanji no Keitaiteki Shori, Oninteki Shori, oyobi Imi Shori no Kanrensei ni Tsuite: Keitai Macchingu Kadai o Mochiite [Graphemic, Phonemic, and Semantic Processing of Kanji, as Assessed by a Graphemic Matching Task]". *Shinrigaku Kenkyu* 51.136-144.

Inoue, M. 1995. "Gohyoki no Yure kara Tayosei e: Shukanteki Hyoki Hindo to Shinbun no Yure [Word Representations and Diversity: Subjective Representational Rates and Newspaper Variations]". *Kobe Yamate Joshi Tanki Daigaku Kiyo* 38.15-23.

Inoue, M, H. Saito & Y. Nomura. 1979. "Kanji no Tokusei ni Kansuru Shinrigakuteki Kenkyu: Keitai, Onin Shori to Imi no Chushutsu [Psychological Research on Kanji Characteristics: The Effects of Graphemic and Phonemic Processing on Information Extraction from Kanji]". *Shinrigaku Hyoron* 22.143-159.

Inoue, M., I. Sugishima, J. Ukita, M. Minagawa & K. Kashu. 1994. "Nihongo no Hyoki Keitai ni Kansuru Kenkyu (2): Shukanteki Hyoki Hindo to Go no Shutsugen Hindo [Research on Japanese Orthographic Representations (2): Subjective Representational Rates and Frequency Rates]". *Nihon Shinri Gakkai Dai-58kai Taikai, Happyo Rombunshu [Proceedings of the 58th Meeting of the Japan Psychological Association]*, p. 867.

Inoue, M., J. Ukita, M. Minagawa, I. Sugishima & K. Kashu. 1995. "Nihongo no Hyoki Keitai ni Kansuru Kenkyu (5): Hyoki no Tayosei--Bunsho Hikki Jikken ni Yoru Bunseki [Research on Japanese Orthographic Representations (5): Orthographic Variations--An Analysis of Transcription Experiments]". *Nihon Shinri Gakkai*

Dai-59kai Taikai, Happyo Rombunshu [*Proceedings of the 59th Meeting of the Japan Psychological Association*], p. 850.

Inui, T. 1983. "Moji Ninchi no Suri Moderu [Mathematical Models of Letter Identification]". *Shinrigaku Hyoron* 26.289-311.

Iritani, T. 1964. *Gengoshinrigaku: Komyunikeshon no Shinriteki Kiso* [*Psycholinguistics: The Psychological Basis of Communication*]. Tokyo: Seishin Shobo.

Iritani, T. 1965. *Kotoba no Shinrigaku* [*The Psychology of Language*]. Tokyo: Chuo Koronsha.

Iritani, T. 1971. *Kotoba to Ningen Kankei* [*Language and Human Relationships*]. Tokyo: Kodansha.

Iritani, T. 1975. *Gengoshinrigaku: Komyunikeshon no Shinriteki Kiso* [*Psycholinguistics: The Psychological Basis of Communication*]. Expanded edition. Tokyo: Seishin Shobo.

Iritani, T. 1983. *Gengoshinrigaku no Susume* [*Invitation to Psycholinguistics*]. Tokyo: Taishukan Shoten.

Ishii, H. 1991. "Kana oyobi Oto no Shutsugen Hindo no Shochosa [Surveys of the Frequency of Sounds and Kana]". *Keiryo Kokugogaku* 18.84-97.

Ishio, A. 1990. "Senga Tango Kadai ni okeru Chokaku, Shikaku Suturupu Kansho [Auditory-Visual Stroop Interference in Picture-Word Processing]". *Shinrigaku Kenkyu* 61.329-335.

Ishino, H. 1992. "Gairaigo no Zogoryoku [Word Formation of Loan Words]". *Nihongogaku* 11.45-52.

Ishiwatari, T. 1991. "Koseki to Moji [Family Registry and Characters]". *Gengo* 20.36-37.

Ishizawa, H. & T. Furugori. 1990. "Bunsho no Yomi to Sono Katei no Keisan Moderu [A Computational Model of the Reading Comprehension Task]". *Keiryo Kokugogaku* 17.227-240.

Ito, K. 1979. "Keisei Moji to Kanji Shido [Character Formation and Kanji Teaching]". *Gengo Seikatsu* 326.68-79.

Ito, K. 1990. *Kodomo no Kotoba: Shutoku to Sozo* [*Child Language: Learning and Creativity*]. Tokyo: Keiso Shobo.

Ito, Y. 1995. "Shikakuteki Kioku to Gengo [Visual Memory and Language]". *Nihongogaku* 14.47-55.

Itsukushima, Y. 1981. "Gojuon no Junjo Handan ni Arawareru Shinteki Kisei no Kento [Mental Mechanisms Underlying Order Judgments in the Japanese Syllabary]". *Shinrigaku Kenkyu* 51.310-317.

Iwabuchi, E. 1968. *Kotoba no Tanjo: Ubu Koe kara Gosai made* [*The Birth of Language: From Birth Cry to the Age of Five*]. Tokyo: Nihon Hoso Shuppan Kyokai.

Iwata, M. 1977. "Junsui Shitsugoshokogun no Shinkeishinrigakuteki Sokumen [Neuropsychological Aspects of Pure Alexia Syndrome]". *Shinkei Kenkyu no Shinpo* 21.930-940.

Iwata, M. 1981. "Yomikaki no Shinkei Kiko [Neurological Structure of Reading and Writing]". *Shizen*, April of 1981 issue, 38-45.

Iwata, M. 1987. *No to Komyunikeshon [Communication and the Brain]*. Tokyo: Asakura Shoten.

Iwata, M. 1988. Neuropsychological Substrate of Reading and Writing in Japanese Writing System. *Higher Nervous Functions: International Symposium during the Asian Oceanian Congress of Neurology, Bali: 20-24, September, 1987*, ed. by W. M. Hermann, 51-62. Braunschweig, Germany: Vieweg.

Japanese Applied Psychology Association. 1954. *Bunka Shinri [Cultural Psychology]*. *Shinrigaku Koza [Lectures in Psychology]* ed. by the Japanese Applied Psychology Association, 12. Tokyo: Nakayama Shoten.

Japanese Ophthalmolgical Society. 1928. "Kokuji ni Kansuru Gankagakuteki Kenkyu [Ophthalmolgical Studies on Japanese Characters]". *Nihon Ganka Gakkaishi* 32.

Jimbo, K. 1934. *Gengoshinrigaku [Psycholinguistics]*. *Kokugo Kagaku Koza [Lectures in the Science of National Language]* Tokyo: Meiji Shoin.

Kabashima, T. 1977. "Kanji kara Romaji made [From Kanji to Romaji]". *Nihongo no Rekishi [The History of the Japanese Language]* ed. by A. Sakakura, 114-152. Tokyo: Taishukan.

Kabashima, T. 1984. "Kompyuta to Kanji no Unmei [Computers and the Destiny of Kanji]". *Gengo Seikatsu* 13.43-48.

Kabashima, T. 1991. "JIS Kanji no Igi to Hyoka [The Significance and Evaluation of JIS Kanji]". *Gengo* 20.24-28.

Kaiho, H. 1968. "Katakana Moji no Miyasusa no Kitei Yoin: Jukaiki Bunseki ni Yoru Kento [Factors Determining the Legibility of Katakana Letters: A Multiple Regression Analysis]". *Shinrigaku Kenkyu* 39.13-20.

Kaiho, H. 1979. "Kanji Joho Shori Kisei o Megutte [Information Processing for Kanji]". *Keiryo Kokugogaku* 11.331-340.

Kaiho, H. 1987. "Ningen ni okeru Kanji Joho Shori [Kanji Information Processing in Humans]". *Keiryo Kokugogaku to Nihongo Shori [Mathematical Linguistics and Japanese Language Processing]*, 49-61. Tokyo: Akiyama Shoten.

Kaiho, H. & Y. Inukai. 1982. "Kyoiku Kanji no Gaikei Tokucho no Shinriteki Bunseki [An Analysis of Gestalt Characteristics of 881 Japanese/Chinese Kanji]". *Kyoiku Shinrigaku Kenkyu* 53.312-315.

Kaiho, H. & Y. Nomura. 1983. *Kanji Joho Shori no Shinrigaku [The Psychology of Kanji Processing]*. Tokyo: Kyoiku Shuppan.

Kaiho, H. & M. Sasaki. 1984. "Sentenmo no Kanji Sonzai Kankaku to Kanji Tensaku Katei [Sensitivity to the Correspondence between Words and Kanji and the Retrieval Process of Kanji in the Blind]". *Tokushu Kyoikugaku Kenkyu* 21.7-16.

Kaiho, H. & F. Toda. 1981. "Moji Ninshiki Kenkyu ni okeru Walsh Henkan no Riyo o Megutte [On Walsh Transformation as a Research Tool for Letter Recognition]". *Shinrigaku Hyoron* 24.490-500.

Kajiwara, K. 1982. "Shinbun no Kanji Ganyuritsu no Hensen: Meiji, Taisho, Showa o Tsujite [Shifts in Occurrence Rate for Newspaper Kanji: Through the Meiji, Taisho, and Showa Eras]". *Kokuritsu Kokugo Kenkyusho Hokoku* 71.209-236.

Kambe, N. 1984. "Kanji Kana Majiribun no Yomi ni okeru Kanji no Yakuwari [The Role of Kanji in Reading Kanji-Kana Mixed Texts]". *Nihon Shinri Gakkai Dai-48kai Taikai, Happyo Rombunshu* [*Proceedings of the 48th Meeting of the Japan Psychological Association*], p. 434.

Kambe, N. 1986. "Yomi no Gankyu Undo to Yomi Katei [The Eye Movement of Reading and Reading Processes]". *Kokuritsu Kokugo Kenkyusho Hokoku* 7.29-66.

Kambe, N. 1989. "Yomi no Gankyu Undo ni okeru Hitotsu no Teiryuchu no Joho Juyo Hani [The Span of the Effective Visual Field during a Fixation in Reading Eye Movement]". *Kokuritsu Kokugo Kenkyusho Hokoku* 10.59-80.

Kamiya, S. 1985. "Komoku no Keitaiteki Joho ga Sainin Kioku ni Oyobosu Koka [Orthography Effects on Recognition]". *Shinrigaku Kenkyu* 56.15-21.

Kamiya, S., H. Tajika & K. Takahashi. 1994. "Effects of Subliminal Perception of Words in Explicit and Implicit Memory". *Psychologia* 37.72-80.

Kanda, Y. 1984. "Kanji Shori no Raterariti ni Kansuru Kenkyu [Study on Lateralization of Kanji Processing]". *Hiroshima Daigaku Kyoiku Gakubu Kiyo* 10.131-138.

Kashihara, E. 1981. "Ninchi aruiwa Kioku no Yoshiki to Seisa [Laterality and Gender Differences in Recognition and Memory]". *Kyoiku Shinrigaku Kenkyu* 29.46-50.

Kashihara, E. 1986. "Moji to Zukei no Doji Niju Benbetsu Hanno Jikan ni okeru Shiya Koka [Visual Field Effects on Simultaneous Discrimination for Letters and Figures]". *Kyoiku Shinrigaku Kenkyu* 34.79-83.

Kashu, K., ed. 1994. "Nihongo no Hyoki Keitai no Suijunka to Sono Ninchi Shinrigakuteki Datosei no Kenkyu [Standardization of Japanese Orthographic Representation and Its Applicability to Cognitive Psychology Research]". *Heisei 4/5-Nendo Kagaku Kenkyuhi Hojokin Kenkyu Hokoku Seika Hokokusho* [*Report on Scientific Research Expenses for Heisei 4/5*].

Kashu, K., ed. 1995. "Nihongo no Hyoki Keitai no Suijunka to Sono Ninchi: Shinrigakuteki Datosei no Kenkyu [Standardization of Japanese Orthographic Representation and Cognitive Science Research]". *Kagaku Kenkyuhi Hojokin Hokokusho* [*Research Report for Scientific Grant Award Expenses*].

Kashu, K., M. Inoue & I. Ishihara. 1980. "Kanji no Shikakuteki Fukuzatsusei ni Kansuru Shoyoin [Factors Determining the Visual Complexity of Kanji]". *Kwansei Gakuin Daigaku Jinmon Ronkyu* 30.23-34.

Kashu, K., I. Ishihara, M. Inoue, H. Saito & Y. Maeda. 1979. "Kanji no Shikakuteki Fukuzatsusei [Visual Complexity of Kanji]". *Kwansei Gakuin Daigaku Jinmon Ronkyu* 29.103-121.

Katayama, W. & A. Yagi. 1992. "The Effect of Word Processing Time on Eye Movements in Visual Search". *Psychologia* 35.173-179.

Kawaguchi, J. 1985. "Kanji Chikaku ni okeru Imiteki Puraimingu Koka [Semantic Priming Effects on Kanji Processing]". *Shinrigaku Kenkyu* 56.296-299.

Kawaguchi, J. 1987. "Senko Shigeki Shori no Imiteki Suijun to Puraimingu Koka [Conscious Levels of Processing a Preceding Stimulus and Priming Effect]". *Shinrigaku Kenkyu* 57.350-356.

Kawai, Y. 1966. "Kanji no Butsuriteki Fukuzatsusei to Yomi no Gakushu [The Effect of Physical Complexity on Learning Kanji]". *Kyoiku Shinrigaku Kenkyu* 14.129-138.

Kawakami, A. & T. Hatta. 1994. "Visual Field Differences in Kanji Recognition: Are Single and Compound Kanji Processed Differently?". *Psychologia* 37.180-187.

Kawakami, M. 1993. "Kanago no Goi Kettei Kadai ni okeru Hyoki no Shinkinsei to Shori Tani [Script Familiarity in Lexical Decision Tasks with Kana Words]". *Shinrigaku Kenkyu* 64.235-239.

Kawamura, M. 1990. "Junsui Shitsugo, Junsui Shissho, Shitsugo Shissho no Byotai [Localization and Symptomatology of Pure Alexia, Pure Agraphia, and Alexia with Agraphia]". *Shinkei Shinrigaku* 6.16-24.

Kawamura, M. & K. Hirayama. 1991. "Moji no Shikakuteki Ninchi [Visual Recognition of Characters]". *Shinkei Kenkyu no Shinpo* 35.479-488.

Kawamura, M., K. Hirayama & H. Yamamoto. 1989. "Different Interhemispheric Transfer of Kanji and Kana Writing Evidenced by a Case with Left Unilateral Agraphia without Apraxia". *Brain* 112.1011-1018.

Kayamoto, Y. 1995. "Doitsu Kanji ni okeru Chugokugoon to Nihongo no Onyomi no Ruijido ni Kansuru Chosa [Similarities and Differences in Readings for Chinese Characters and Japanese On-Readings]". *Hiroshima Daigaku Nihongo Kyoiku Gakka Kiyo* 5.67-75.

Kayamoto, Y., J. Yamada & H. Takashima. 1998. "The Consistency of Multiple-Pronunciation Effects in Reading: The Case of Japanese Logographs". *Journal of Psycholinguistic Research* 27.619-637.

Kess, J. F. 1983. "The Wundtian Origins of Early Bloomfieldian Psycholinguistics". Introduction to *An Introduction to the Study of Language.* (= *Classics in Psycholinguistics*, 3.) by L. Bloomfield, xvii-xxxviii. Amsterdam: John Benjamins. Publishers.

Kess, J. F. 1992. *Psycholinguistics: Psychology, Linguistics, and the Study of Natural Language*. Amsterdam: John Benjamins Publishers.

Kess, J. F. & R. A. Hoppe. 1981. *Ambiguity in Psycholinguistics*. Amsterdam: John Benjamins Publishers.

Kess, J. F. & T. Miyamoto. 1994. *Japanese Psycholinguistics: A Classified and Annotated Research Bibliography*. Amsterdam: John Benjamins Publishers.

Kess, J. F. & T. Miyamoto. 1996. "Psycholinguistic Evidence for Laterality Preferences and Information Processing in Japanese". *Language Research* 32.351-371.

Kess, J. F. & T. Miyamoto. 1997. "Psycholinguistic Aspects of Hanji Processing in Chinese". *Mon-Khmer Studies* 27.349-359.

Kess, J. F. & Y. Nishimitsu. 1990. *Linguistic Ambiguity in Natural Language: Japanese and English*. Tokyo: Kuroshio Shuppan.

Keung, H. S. & R. Hoosain. 1989. "Right Hemisphere Advantage in Lexical Decision with Two-Character Chinese Words". *Brain and Language* 37.606-615.

Ki, J. S. 1986. "Remarks on Modern Sino-Korean". *Language Research* 22.469-502.

Kikushima, K. 1964. *Kotoba no Shakai Shinri [Social Psychology of Language]*. Tokyo: Meiji Tosho.

Kim, D. 1990. "Nigengo Heiyoji no Gengo Kansho ni Kansuru Kenkyu: Chosen Gakko no Seito, Gakusei no Baai [Linguistic Interference in Bilingual Children: Students in a Korean School]". *Kyoiku Shinrigaku Kenkyu* 38.205-212.

Kimura, D. 1961. "Cerebral Dominance and the Perception of Verbal Stimuli". *Canadian Journal of Psychology* 15.166-171.

Kimura, D. 1969. "Spatial Localization in Left and Right Visual Fields". *Canadian Journal of Psychology* 23.445-458.

Kimura, Y. 1984. "Concurrent Vocal Interference: Its Effects on Kana and Kanji". *Quarterly Journal of Experimental Psychology* 36A.117-127.

Kimura, Y. & P. Bryant. 1983. "Reading and Writing in English and Japanese: A Cross-cultural Study of Young Children". *British Journal of Developmental Psychology* 1.143-154.

Kindaichi, H. 1988. *Nihongo [Japanese]*. Tokyo: Iwanami Shoten.

Kindaichi, H., O. Hayashi & T. Shibata, eds. 1988. *Nihongo Hyakka Daijiten [Encyclopaedia of the Japanese Language]*. Tokyo: Taishukan.

Kindaichi, K. 1991. *Shineikai Kokugo Jiten [New Japanese Word Dictionary]*. Tokyo: Sanseido.

Kinoshita, S. & H. Saito. 1992. "Effects of Concurrent Articulation on Reading Japanese Kanji and Kana Words". *The Quarterly Journal of Experimental Psychology* 44A.455-474.

Kitao, H. 1960. "Hiraganabun to Kanji Majiribun no Yomiyasusa no Hikaku Kenkyu [Comparative Study on Readability of Hiragana-only and Kanji-Mixed Texts]". *Kyoiku Shinrigaku Kenkyu* 7.195-199.

Kitao, N. 1984a. "What is a Learning Disability?". *Ochikobore Ochikoboshi [Learning Disability]* ed. by N. Kitao & E. Kajita. Tokyo: Yuhikaku.

Kitao, N. 1984b. *Reading Ability Test TK-1*. Tokyo: Yuhikaku.

Kitao, N., T. Hatta, M. Ishida, Y. Babazono & Y. Kondo. 1977. "Kyoiku Kanji 881-ji no Gutaisei, Shokeisei oyobi Jukuchisei [Concreteness, Hieroglyphicity and Familiarity of 881 Kanji]". *Shinrigaku Kenkyu* 48.105-111.

Kobayashi, H. & M. Sasaki. 1997. *Kodomotachi no Gengo Shutoku [Language Acquisition by Children]*. Tokyo: Taishukan.

Koga, K. & R. Groner. 1989. "16 Intercultural Experiments as a Research Tool in the Study of Cognitive Skill Acquistion: Japanese Character Recognition and Eye Movements in Non-Japanese Subjects". *Knowledge Acquisition from Text and Pictures* ed. by H. Mandl & J. R. Levin, 279-291. Amsterdam: North Holland.

Kogo, C. & M. Kishi. 1996. "Jimaku Eiga no Shicho ni okeru Gankyu Undo no Bunseki [Analysis of Eye Movements during Viewing of Subtitled Movies]". *Nihon Kyoiku Kogaku Zasshi* 20.161-166.

Kohn, S. E., A. Wingfield, L. Menn, H. Goodglass, J. B. Gleason & M. Hyde. 1987. "Lexical Retrieval: The Tip-of-the-tongue Phenomenon". *Applied Psycholinguistics* 8.245-266.

Koizumi, T. 1991. "Nihon ni okeru Moji Seisaku no Rekishi [The History of Character Policy in Japan]". *Gengo* 20.38-43.

Komatsu, S. & M. Naito. 1992. "Repetition Priming With Japanese Kana Scripts in Word-Fragment Completion". *Memory & Cognition* 20.160-170.

Komendzinska, A. 1995. "Do Second-Language Learners of Japanese Make Use of the Same Mental Lexicon for Kana Words as Native Speakers?". *Psychologia* 38.146-154.

Kosslyn, S. M. 1987. "Seeing and Imagining in the Cerebral Hemispheres: A Computational Approach". *Psychological Review* 94.148-175.

Kubozono, H. 1989. "The Mora and Syllable Structure in Japanese: Evidence From Speech Errors". *Language and Speech* 32.249-278.

Kucera, H. & W. N. Francis. 1967. *Computational Analysis of Present-day American English*. Providence: Brown University Press.

Kuhara-Kojima, K., G. Hatano, H. Saito & T. Haebara. 1996. "Vocalization Latencies of Skilled and Less Skilled Comprehenders for Words Written in Hiragana and Kanji". *Reading Research Quarterly* 31.158-171.

Kuroda, Y. 1969. "Characteristics of Social Science Journals in Japan". *The American Behavioral Scientist* 12.46-50.

Kurosu, M. 1984. "Kompyuta ni Totte Kanji to wa: Kanji no Kogaku [Kanji Processing by Computer: Kanji Engineering]". *Kanji o Kagaku Suru [Making Kanji Scientific]* ed. by H. Kaiho, 67-120. Tokyo: Yuhikaku.

Lam, A. S. L., C. A. Perfetti & L. Bell. 1991. "Automatic Phonetic Transfer in Bidialectal Reading". *Applied Psycholinguistics* 12.299-311.

Langman, P. & H. Saito. 1984. "Cross-Linguistic Categorization of Kanji Characters". *Japanese Psychological Research* 26.93-102.

Law, I., I. Kannao, H. Fujita, N. A. Lassen, S. Miura & K. Uemura. 1991. "Left Supramarginal/Angular Gyri Activation During Reading of Syllabograms in the Japanese Language". *Journal of Neurolinguistics* 6.243-251.

Leck, K. J., B. S. Weekes & M. J. Chen. 1995. "Visual and Phonological Pathways to the Lexicon: Evidence from Chinese Readers". *Memory & Cognition* 23.468-476.

Leong, C. K. 1986. "What Does Accessing a Morphemic Script Tell Us About Reading and Reading Disorders in an Alphabetic Script?". *Annals of Dyslexia* 36.82-102.

Leong, C. K. 1991. "From Phonemic Awareness to Phonological Processing to Language Access in Children Developing Reading Proficiency". *Phonological Awareness in Reading: The Evolution of Current Perspectives* ed. by D. J. Sawyer & B. J. Fox, 217-254. New York: Spring-Verlag.

Leong, C. K., P-W. Cheng & R. Mulcahy. 1987. "Automatic Processing of Morphemic Orthography by Mature Readers". *Language and Speech* 30.181-196.

Leong, C. K. & R. M. Joshi. 1997. "Relating Phonologic and Orthographic Processing to Learning to Read and Spell". *Cross-Language Studies of Learning to Read and Spell: Phonologic and Orthographic Processing* ed. by C. K. Leong & R. M. Joshi, 1-29. Dordrecht: Kluwer Academic Publishers.

Leong, C. K. & K. Tamaoka. 1995. "Use of Phonological Information in Processing Kanji and Katakana by Skilled and Less Skilled Japanese Readers". *Reading and Writing: An Interdisciplinary Journal* 7.377-393.

Leong, C. K. & K. Tamaoka, eds. 1998. *Cognitive Processing of the Chinese and Japanese Languages*. Boston: Kluwer Academic Publishers.

Leong, C. K., S. Wong, A. Wong & M. Hiscock. 1985. "Differential Cerebral Involvement in Perceiving Chinese Characters: Levels of Processing Approach". *Brain and Language* 26.131-145.

Levy, J. 1969. "Possible Basis for the Evolution of Lateral Specification of the Human Brain". *Nature* 224.614-615.

Levy, J. 1972. "Lateral Specialization of the Human Brain: Behavioral Manifestations and Possible Evolutionary Basis". *The Biology of Behaviour* ed. by A. Kiger, 159-180. Corballis: Oregon University Press.

Levy, J., C. Trevarthen & R. W. Sperry. 1972. "Perception of Bilateral Chimeric Figures Following Hemispheric Deconnexion". *Brain* 95.61-78.

Liberman, I. Y., D. Shankweiler, F. W. Fischer & B. Carter. 1974. "Explicit Syllable and Phoneme Segmentation in the Young Child". *Journal of Experimental Child Psychology* 18.201-212.

Liberman, I. Y., D. Shankweiler, A. M. Liberman, C. Fowler & F. W. Fischer. 1977. "Phonetic Segmentation and Recoding in the Beginning Reader". *Toward a Psychology of Reading* ed. by A. S. Reber & D. L. Scarborough, 207-225. Hillsdale, NJ: Lawrence Erlbaum Associates.

Lima, S. D. 1987. "Morphological Analysis in Sentence Reading". *Journal of Memory and Language* 26.84-99.

Liu, I-M. 1983. "Cueing Function of Fragments of Chinese Characters in Reading". *Acta Psychologica Taiwanica* 25.85-90.

Liu, I-M., C-J. Chuang & S-C. Wang. 1975. *Frequency Count of 40,000 Chinese Words.* Taipei: Lucky Books.

Liu, I-M., Y. Zhu & J-T. Wu. 1992. "The Long-term Modality Effect: In Search of Differences in Processing Logographs and Alphabetic Words". *Cognition* 43.31-66

Lunde, K. 1993. *Understanding Japanese Information.* Sebastopol: O'Reilly & Associates, Inc.

Makioka, S. 1994. "Tango no Shikakuteki Ninchi Katei ni okeru Moji Ichi Joho no Hyogen [Representation of Letter Position in Visual Recognition Process]". *Shinrigaku Kenkyu* 65.224-232.

Makita, K. 1968. "The Rarity of Reading Disability in Japanese Children". *American Journal of Orthopsychiatry* 38.599-614.

Makita, K. 1976. "Reading Disability and the Writing System". *New Horizons in Reading* ed. by J. E. Merritt, 250-254. Newark, DE: International Reading Association Press.

Mann, V. A. 1984. "Temporary Memory For Linguistic and Nonlinguistic Material in Relation to the Acquisition of Japanese Kana and Kanji". *Ann. Bull. RILP* 18.135-151.

Mann, V. A. 1986. "Phonological Awareness: The Role of Reading Experience". *Haskins Laboratories: Status Report on Speech Research* SR-85.1-22.

Marcel, T. & K. Patterson. 1978. "Word Recognition and Production: Reciprocity in Clinical and Normal Studies". *Attention and Performance VII* ed. by J. Requin, 209-226. Hillsdale, N. J.: Lawrence Erlbaum Associates.

Martin, S. E. 1972. "Non-alphabetic Writing Systems: Some Observations". *Language by Ear and by Eye* ed. by J. F. Kavanaugh & I. G. Mattingly, 81-102. Cambridge, MA: MIT Press.

Matsubara, T. & Y. Kobayashi. 1966. "Kana Moji no Miyasusa ni Kansuru Kenkyu [A Study of the Legiblity of Kana-Letters]". *Shinrigaku Kenkyu* 37.359-363.

Matsuda, M., H. Shotenmoku, K. Nakamura, Y. Nakatani & N. Suzuki. 1996. "A Case Study of Alexia with Left Temporal Lobe Lesion". *Proceedings of the Twentieth Meeting of the Japanese Neuropsychological Association*, p. 138.

McConkie, G. W. 1983. "Eye Movements and Perception during Reading". *Eye Movements in Reading: Perceptual and Language Processes* ed. by K. Rayner, 65-96. New York: Academic Press.

McConkie G. W. & K. Rayner. 1975. "The Span of the Effective Stimulus during an Eye Fixation in Reading". *Perception and Psychophysics* 17.578-586.

Minagawa, N. & K. Kashu. 1984. "Daino Hankyu no Hataraki ni okeru Kojinsa: Kikino Tesuto no Shinraisei ni Tsuite no Kento [Individual Differences in Hemispheric Function: The Reliability of a Hemisphericity Test]". *Kwansei Gakuin Daigaku Jinmon Ronkyu* 34.95-112.

Minagawa, N., T. Yokoyama & K. Kashu. 1988. "The Effect of Repetitive Presentation and Inducement of Simplified Form of Kanji on Visual Field Differences". *Psychologia* 31.217-225.

Misumi, J. & M. F. Peterson. 1990. "Psychology in Japan". *Annual Review of Psychology* 41.213-241.

Mizuno, R. 1997. "Kanji Hyokigo no Onin Shori Jidoka Kasetsu no Kensho [A Test of a Hypothesis of Automatic Phonological Processing of Kanji Words]". *Shinrigaku Kenkyu* 68.1-8.

Miura, T. 1978. "The Word Superiority Effect in a Case of *Hiragana* Letter Strings". *Perception and Psychophysics* 24.505-508.

Miyagi, O., ed. 1953. *Kotoba no Shinri [The Psychology of Language]*. Tokyo: Kawade Shobo.

Miyagi, O., ed. 1954. *Kotoba no Shinri [The Psychology of Language]*. New Edition. Tokyo: Kawade Shobo.

Miyamoto, T. & J. F. Kess. 1995. "The Japanese Brain: Information Processing in the Right vs. Left Hemispheres". *Proceedings of the Japan Studies Association of Canada*, Victoria, September 30, 1995.

Miyamoto, T. & J. F. Kess. 1997. "Japanese Psycholinguistics: Its Historical Development, Contemporary Focus, and Future Challenges". *Japan at Century's End: Changes, Challenges, and Choices* ed. by H. Millward & J. Morrison, 203-214. Halifax: Fernwood Publishing.

Mojikyo Research Society. 1999. *Pasokon Yuyu Kanji Jutsu [An Guide to Easy Use of Kanji Fonts]*. Tokyo: Kinokuniya.

Morais, J., L. Cary, J. Alegria, & P. Bertelson. 1979. "Does Awareness of Speech as a Sequence of Phones Arise Spontaneously?". *Cognition* 7.323-331.

Mori, C. & J. Yamada. 1988. "Copying Span as an Index of Written Language Ability". *Perceptual and Motor Skills* 66.375-382.

Mori, K. 1992. *Minichua Jinko Gengo Kenkyu: Gengo Shutoku no Jikken Shinrigaku [Research in Miniature Artificial Language: Experimental Psychology Approach to Language Acquisition]*. Tokyo: Kazama Shobo.

Mori, Y. 1998. "Effects of First Language and Phonological Accessibility on Kanji Recognition". *The Modern Language Journal* 82.69-82.

Morikawa, Y. 1981. "Stroop Phenomena in the Japanese Language". *Perceptual and Motor Skills* 53.66-77.

Morikawa, Y. 1986. "Stroop Phenomena in the Japanese Language (II): Effects of Character-Usage Frequency and Number of Strokes". *Linguistics, Psychology, and Chinese Language* ed. by H. S. R. Kao & R. Hoosain, 73-80. Hong Kong: Centre of Asian Studies, University of Hong Kong.

Moro, Y., ed. 1997. *Taiwa to Chi: Danwa no Ninchi Kagaku Nyumon [Conversation and Knowledge: Introduction to a Cognitive Science of Discourse]*. Tokyo: Shinyosha.

Morohashi, T. 1989. *Daikanwa Jiten [Japanese Kanji Character Dictionary]*, Vol. 1-12. Tokyo: Taishukan.

Morton, J. & S. Sasanuma. 1984. "Lexical Access in Japanese". *Orthographies and Reading: Perspectives From Cognitive Psychology, Neuropsychology, and Linguistics* ed. by L. Henderson, 25-42. Hillsdale, NJ: Lawrence Erlbaum Associates.

Morton, J., S. Sasanuma, K. Patterson & N. Sakuma. 1992. "The Organization of the Lexicon in Japanese: Single and Compound Kanji". *British Journal of Psychology* 83.517-531.

Moscovitch, M. 1979. "Information Processing and the Cerebral Hemispheres". *Handbook of Behavioral Neurology: Vol. 2 Neuropsychology* ed. by M. S. Gazzaniga, 379-446. New York: Plenum Press.

Muraishi, S. & S. Hayashi. 1958. *Kodomo no Shiko to Kotoba [Child Language and Thought]*. Tokyo: Meiji Tosho Shuppan.

Murakami, Y. 1980. "Nodo made Dekakaru Gensho ni okeru Kana to Kanji Tango no Kioku Tani ni Tsuite [Memory for Kana and Kanji Words in the Tip-of-the-Tongue Phenomenon]". *Shinrigaku Kenkyu* 51.41-44.

Murata, K. 1968. *Yoji no Gengo Hattatsu [Children's Language Development]*. Tokyo: Baifukan.

Murata, K. 1972. *Yochienki no Gengo Hattatsu [Language Development during the Kindergarten Period]*. Tokyo: Baifukan.

Murata, K. 1977. *Gengo Hattatsu no Shinrigaku [Psychology of Language Development]*. Tokyo: Baifukan.

Murata, K. 1981. *Gengo Hattatsu Kenkyu: Sono Rekishi to Gendai no Doko [Research in Language Development: History and Current Directions]*. Tokyo: Baifukan.

Murata, K. 1983. *Kodomo no Kotoba to Kyoiku [Child Language and Education]*. Tokyo: Kaneko Shobo.

Muto, T., ed. 1991. *Kotoba ga Tanjo Suru Toki: Gengo-Jodo-Kankei* [*When Language is Born: Language-Emotions-Relationships*]. Series entitled *Shinrigaku no Furontia* [*Frontiers in Psychology*]. Tokyo: Shinyosha.

Nachson, I., G. E. Shefler & D. Samocha. 1977. "Directional Scanning as a Function of Stimulus Characteristics, Reading Habits, and Directional Set". *Journal of Cross-Cultural Psychology* 8.83-99.

Nagae, S. 1983. "Kodomo no Gengo to Kukan Joho no Kioku to Seisa [Child Language and Sex Differences in Memory for Spatial Information]". *Kyoiku Shinrigaku Kenkyu* 31.171-176.

Nagae, S. 1989. Migi Hankyu no Shikaku Joho Shori [Visual Information Processing of the Right Hemisphere]". *Shinrigaku Hyoron* 32.387-406.

Nagae, S. 1992. "Shiya Bunkatsu Kenkyu kara Mita Kanji Joho Shori [Kanji Information Processing from the Viewpoint of Research on Half-Visual Fields]". *Shinrigaku Hyoron* 35.269-292.

Nagae, S. 1994. "Migi Hankyu ni okeru Kanji to Kana no Imi Shori Kino [Semantic Processing Functions of *Kanji* and *Kana* Words in the Right Hemisphere]". *Shinrigaku Kenkyu* 65.144-149.

Naito, M. & S. Komatsu. 1988. "Puraimingu Koka ni Kanyo Suru Kioku Zokusei no Kento [On Memory Attributes Which Mediate Priming Effects in Perceptual Identification]". *Shinrigaku Kenkyu* 58.352-358.

Naka, M. 1984. "Imi Nettowaku ni okeru Kasseika Sareta Joho no Sogo Sayo [Interaction of Activations in a Semantic Network]". *Shinrigaku Kenkyu* 55.1-7.

Naka, M. & H. Naoi. 1995. "The Effect of Repeated Writing on Memory". *Memory and Cognition* 23.201-212.

Nakahara, N. 1991. "Itaiji no Gainen to Jittai [The Concept and Status of Deformed Kanji]". *Gengo* 20.62-83.

Nakamizo, S. 1974. "Saccadic Suppression o Meguru Shomondai [Issues in Saccadic Suppression]". *Shinrigaku Hyoron* 17.319-339.

Nakau, M. 1994. *Ninchi Imiron no Genri* [*Principles of a Cognitive Theory of Meaning*]. Tokyo: Taishukan.

National Language Research Institute of Japan. 1962. *Gendai Zasshi Kyujusshu no Yogo Yoji* [*The Vocabulary and Their Written Forms in Ninety Contemporary Magazines*]. Daiichi Bunsatu. Tokyo: Shuei Shuppan.

National Language Research Institute of Japan. 1976. *Gendai Shimbun no Kanji* [*Kanji Characters in Modern Newspapers*]. *Report 56 of the National Language Research Institute*. Tokyo: Shuei Shuppan.

National Language Research Institute of Japan. 1983. *Gendai Hyoki no Yure* [*Variations in Contemporary Orthography*]. *Report 75 of the National Language Research Institute*.

National Language Research Institute of Japan. 1997. *Gendai Zasshi Kyujusshu no Yogo Yoji* [*The Vocabulary and Their Written Forms in Ninety Contemporary Magazines*]. Floppy Disk Format. Tokyo: Sanseido.

Neisser, U. 1967. *Cognitive Psychology*. New York: Appleton.

Nihei, Y. 1986a. "Dissociation of Motor Memory From Phonetic Memory: Its Effects on Slips of the Pen". *Graphonomics: Contemporary Research in Handwriting* ed. by H. S. R. Kao, G. P. Van Galen & R. Hoosain, 243-252. Amsterdam: North-Holland.

Nihei, Y. 1986b. "Experimentally Induced Slips of the Pen". *Linguistics, Psychology, and the Chinese Language* ed. by H. S. R. Kao & R. Hoosain, 309-315. Hong Kong: Centre of Asian Studies, University of Hong Kong.

Nihei, Y. 1988. "Effects of Pre-activation of Motor Memory for Kanji and Kana on Slips of the Pen: An Experimental Verification of the Recency Hypothesis for Slips". *Tohoku Psychologica Folia* 47.1-7.

Nihei, Y. 1991. "Bonyo Undo Puroguramu o Meguru Undo Kioku Kenkyu no Tenkai: Shoji no Mondai o Chushin ni [A Generalized Movement Program for Kinetic Memory: Focussing on the Problem of Handwriting]". *Shinrigaku Hyoron* 34.358-382.

Nishikawa, Y. 1982. "E Joho to Moji Joho no Shori Yoshiki to Daino Hankyu Kinosa [Modes of Information Processing for Picture and Letter Stimuli and Functional Hemispheric Differences]". *Kiso Shinrigaku Kenkyu* 1.14-21.

Nishikawa, Y. & S. Niina. 1981. "Joho Shori Yoshiki kara Mita Daino Ryohankyu no Kinoteki Sai [Modes of Information Processing Underlying Hemispheric Functional Differences]". *Shinrigaku Kenkyu* 51.335-342.

Nomura, M. 1980. "Shukanshi no Kanji Ganyuritsu [Kanji Content in Weekly Publications]". *Keiryo Kokugogaku* 12.215-222.

Nomura, M. 1981. "Joyo Kanji no OnKun [On-Kun Statistics for the Joyo Kanji]". *Keiryo Kokugogaku* 13.27-33.

Nomura, M. 1984. "Kanji no Tokusei o Hakaru: Kanji no Keiryo Kokugogaku [Measuring the Characteristics of Kanji: Mathematical Linguistics and Kanji]". *Kanji o Kagaku Suru* [*Making Kanji Scientific*] ed. by H. Kaiho, 1-34. Tokyo: Yuhikaku.

Nomura, M. 1991. "Johoka Jidai no Kanji to Seishoho [Orthography and Kanji in the Information Age]". *Gengo* 20.30-35.

Nomura, Y. 1978. "The Information Processing of Chinese Characters (Kanji): Chinese Reading, Japanese Reading, and the Attachment of Meaning". *Shinrigaku Kenkyu* 49.190-197.

Nomura, Y. 1979. "Kanji no Joho Shori: Ondoku-Kundoku no Tansaku Katei [Information Processing of Kanji: Retrieval Processes in Chinese *On*-Readings and Japanese *Kun*-Readings]". *Shinrigaku Kenkyu* 50.101-105.

Nomura, Y. 1981a. "Kanji Kana Hyokigo no Joho Shori: Yomi ni Oyobosu Deta Suishinkei Shori to Gainen Suishinkei Shori no Koka [Information Processing of Kanji and Kana Script: Data-Driven vs. Concept-Driven Processing on Reading]". *Shinrigaku Kenkyu* 51.327-334.

Nomura, Y. 1981b. "Data-Driven and Conceptually-Driven Processing in the Reading of Kanji and Kana Script". *Psychologia* 24.65-74.

Nozaki, H. & S. Yokoyama. 1996. "Shinbun to Zasshi ni okeru Kanji Shiyo Hindo no Bunseki [The Analysis of Kanji Frequency in Newspapers and Magazines]". *Proceedings of the 24th Meeting of the Behaviometric Society of Japan*, 266-267.

Nozaki, H., S. Yokoyama & N. Chikamatsu. 1997. "Shinbun to Zasshi ni okeru Kanji Shiyo Hindo no Bunseki [The Analysis of Kanji Frequency in Newspapers and Magazines]". *Nihon Kyoiku Kogaku Zasshi* 21.21-24.

Nozaki, H., S. Yokoyama, N. Chikamatsu & Y. Isomoto. 1997. "Shinbun to Zasshi ni okeru Kanji Shiyo Hindo no Bunseki [The Analysis of Kanji Frequency in Newspapers and Magazines]". *Nihon Kyoiku Kogaku Kaishi* 1.1-4.

Nozaki, H., S. Yokoyama, Y. Isomoto & J. Yoneda. 1996. "Moji Shiyo ni Kansuru Keiryoteki Kenkyu: Nihongo Kyoiku Shien no Kanten kara [A Study of Character Frequency: From the Point of View of Japanese Language Education]". *Nihon Kyoiku Kogaku Zasshi* 20.141-149.

Oden, G. C. & J. G. Rueckl. 1986. "Is the Difference between *gill* and *girl* More than a Letter?". *Bulletin of the Psychonomic Society* 24.7-10.

Ohnishi, H. & T. Hatta. 1980. "Lateral Differences in Tachistoscopic Recognition of Kanji-Pairs with Mixed Image Values". *Psychologia* 23.233-239.

Ohta, N. 1991. "Chokusetsu Puraimingu [Direct Priming]". *Shinrigaku Kenkyu* 62.119-135.

Oka, N., T. Mori & S. Kakigi. 1979. Yoji no Kanji to Kana Moji no Yomi no Gakushu [Learning to Read Kanji and Kana by Young Children]". *Shinrigaku Kenkyu* 50.49-52.

Okada, A. 1969. *Gengo Kyoiku no Shinri [Psychology of Language Education]*. Tokyo: Shinkokaku Shoten.

Okada, R. 1985. "Comments on a Model of Japanese Kana Processing". *Psychologia* 28.182-185.

Okamoto, N. 1982. *Kodomo to Kotoba [Children and Language]*. Tokyo: Iwanami Shoten.

Okubo, T. 1968. *Kokugo-Bungaku Kyoiku to Kotoba no Shinri [National Language-Literature Education and the Psychology of Language]*. Tokyo: Daimeido.

Omori, S. 1955. *Kotoba ga Jiyu ni Hanasetara: Kitsuon no Shinri to Chiryoho [For Language to be Freely Spoken: The Psychology of Stuttering and Methods of Treatment]*. Tokyo: Kaneko Shobo.

Onose, M. 1987. "Yoji Jido ni okeru Nazori oyobi Shisha no Renshu ga Shoji Gino no Shutoku ni Oyobosu Koka [The Effect of Tracing and Copying Practice on Handwriting Skills for Pre-School and First Grade Children]". *Kyoiku Shinrigaku Kenkyu* 35.9-16.

Onose, M. 1988. "Nazori oyobi Shisha Renshu no Kumiawase ga Yoji Jido no Shoji Gino ni Oyobosu Koka [The Effect of the Combination of Tracing and Copying Practice on Handwriting Skills for Pre-School and First Grade Children]". *Kyoiku Shinrigaku Kenkyu* 365.129-134.

O'Regan, J. K. 1992. "Optimal Viewing Position in Words and the Strategy-Tactics Theory of Eye Movements in Reading". *Eye Movements and Visual Cognition: Scene Perception and Reading* ed. by K. Rayner, 323-354. New York: Springer-Verlag.

Osaka, N. 1980. "Effect of Peripheral Visual Field Size upon Visual Search in Children and Adults". *Perception* 9.451-455.

Osaka, N. 1987a. "Variation of Saccadic Suppression with Target Eccentricity". *Ophthalmic and Physiological Optics* 7.499-501.

Osaka, N. 1987b. "Effect of Peripheral Visual Field Size upon Eye Movements during Japanese Text Processing". *Eye Movements From Physiology to Cognition: Selected/Edited Proceedings of the Third European Conference on Eye Movements, Dourdan, France, September 1985*, ed. by J. K. O'Regan & A. Levy-Schoen, 421-429. Amsterdam: North-Holland.

Osaka, N. 1989. "Eye Fixation and Saccade during Kana and Kanji Text Reading: Comparison of English and Japanese Text Processing". *Bulletin of the Psychonomic Society* 27.548-550.

Osaka, N. 1990. "Spread of Visual Attention during Fixation while Reading Japanese Text". *From Eye to Mind: Information Acquisition in Perception, Search, and Reading* ed. by R. Groner, G. d'Ydewalle & R. Parham, 167-178. Amsterdam: North-Holland.

Osaka, N. 1991. "Yomi no Seishin Butsurigaku: Yuko Shiya no Yakuwari o Chushin ni [The Psychophysics of Reading Japanese Text: The Role of Effective Visual Field]". *Tetsugaku Kenkyu* 558.588-612.

Osaka, N. 1992. "Size of Saccade and Fixation Duration of Eye Movements during Reading: Psychophysics of Japanese Text Processing". *Journal of the Optical Society of America* 9.5-13.

Osaka, N. & K. Oda. 1991. "Effective Visual Field Size Necessary for Vertical Reading during Japanese Text Processing". *Bulletin of the Psychonomic Society* 29.345-347.

Osaka, M. & N. Osaka. 1992. "Language-Independent Working Memory as Measured by Japanese and English Reading Span Tests". *Bulletin of the Psychonomic Society* 30.287-289.

Osgood, C. E. & R. Hoosain. 1974. "Salience of the Word as a Unit in the Perception of Language". *Perception and Psychophysics* 15.168-192.

Ota, N. & H. Tajika, eds. 1991. *Ninchi Shinrigaku: Riron to Deta [Cognitive Psychology: Theory and Data]*. Tokyo: Seishin Shobo.

Otake, T., G. Hatano, A. Cutler & J. Mehler. 1993. "Mora or Syllable? Speech Segmentation in Japanese". *Journal of Memory and Language* 32.258-278.

Otsu, Y. 1989. "Shinrigengogaku [Psycholinguistics]". *Eigogaku no Kanren Bunya [Related Disciplines in English Linguistics]* ed. by M. Shibatani, Y. Otsu & A. Tsuda, 183-386. Tokyo: Taishukan.

Otsuka, A. & M. Shimada. 1988. "Kana and Kanji Processing in Patients with Unilateral Brain Damage". *Studia Phonologica* 22.28-38.

Overly, N. V. 1977. "Why Johnny Reads Differently than Noriko". *The Educational Forum* 41.236-245.

Ozawa, A. & Y. Nomura. 1981. "Yoji no Kanji to Kana no Yomi ni Oyobosu Benbetsu oyobi Kaidoku Katei no Koka [Discrimination and Decoding Processes in Reading Kanji and Kana Script by Young Children]". *Kyoiku Shinrigaku Kenkyu* 29.199-206.

Paradis, M. 1987 "The Neurofunctional Modularity of Cognitive Skills: Evidence from Japanese Alexia and Polyglot Aphasia". *Motor and Sensory Processes of Language* ed. by E. Keller & M. Gopnik, 277-289. Hillsdale, NJ: Lawrence Erlbaum.

Paradis, M., H. Hagiwara & N. Hildebrandt. 1985. *Neurolinguistic Aspects of the Japanese Writing System*. Orlando: Academic Press.

Park, S. & T. Y. Arbuckle. 1977. "Ideograms vs. Alphabets: Effects of Scripts on Memory in 'Biscriptual' Korean Subjects". *Journal of Experimental Psychology* 3.631-642.

Patterson, K. E. 1990. "Basic Processes of Reading: Do They Differ in Japanese and English?". *Shinkei Shinrigaku* 6.4-14.

Perfetti, C. A. 1985. *Reading Ability*. New York: Oxford University Press.

Perfetti, C. A. & S. Zhang. 1995. "Very Early Phonological Activation in Chinese Reading". *Journal of Experimental Psychology: Learning, Memory, and Cognition* 21.24-33.

Perfetti, C. A., S. Zhang & I. Berent. 1992. "Reading in English and Chinese: Evidence for a 'Universal' Phonological Principle". *Orthography, Phonology, Morphology, and Meaning* ed. by R. Frost & L. Katz, 227-248. Amsterdam: North Holland.

Potter, M. C. & B. A. Faulconer. 1975. "Time to Understand Pictures and Words". *Nature* 253.437-438.

Prem, M. 1991. "Nihongo Kyoiku no Neck: Gairaigo [Loanwords: The Bottleneck in Teaching Japanese to Foreigners]". *Nihongo Kyoiku* 74.28-33.

Pring, T. R. 1981. "The Effect of Stimulus Size and Exposure Duration on Visual Field Asymmetries". *Cortex* 17.227-240.

Rayner, K. 1975. "Perceptual Span and Peripheral Cues in Reading". *Cognitive Psychology* 7.65-81.

Rayner, K. 1983. "The Perceptual Span and Eye Movement Control during Reading". *Eye Movements in Reading: Perceptual and Language Processes* ed. by K. Rayner, 97-120. New York: Academic Press.

Rayner, K. 1992. *Eye Movements and Visual Cognition: Scene Perception and Reading.* New York: Springer-Verlag.

Rayner, K. & W. Inhoff. 1981. "Control of Eye Movements during Reading". *Model of Oculomotor Behavior and Control* ed. by B. L. Zuber, 209-231. Florida: CRC Press.

Rayner, K. & S. C. Sereno. 1994. "Eye Movements in Reading". *Handbook of Psycholinguistics* ed. by M. A. Gernsbacher, 57-81. San Diego: Academic Press.

Read, C., Y-F. Zhang, H-Y. Nie & B-Q. Ding. 1986. "The Ability to Manipulate Speech Sounds Depends upon Knowing Alphabetic Writing". *Cognition* 24.31-44.

Rosch, E. 1973. "On the Internal Structure of Perceptual and Semantic Categories". *Cognitive Development and the Acquisition of Language* ed. by T. E. Moore, 111-144. New York: Academic Press.

Rosch, E. 1975. "Cognitive Representations of Semantic Categories". *Journal of Experimental Psychology* 104.192-233.

Rosch, E. 1978. "Principles of Categorization". *Cognition and Categorization* ed. by E. Rosch & B. Lloyd, 27-48. Hillsdale, NJ: Lawrence Erlbaum Associates.

Rosch, E. & C. B. Mervis. 1975. "Family Resemblances: Studies in the Internal Structure of Categories". *Cognitive Psychology* 7.573-605.

Rozin, P. & L. R. Gleitman. 1977. "The Structure and Acquisition of Reading II: The Reading Process and the Acquisition of the Alphabetic Principle". *Towards a Psychology of Reading* ed. by A. S. Reber & D. L. Scarborough, 55-141. Hillsdale, NJ: Lawrence Erlbaum Associates.

Rozin, P., S. Poritsky & R. Sotsky. 1971. "American Children with Reading Problems Can Easily Learn to Read English Represented by Chinese Characters". *Science* 171.1264-1267.

Rubenstein, H., S. S. Lewis & M. A. Rubenstein. 1971. "Evidence for Phonemic Reading in Visual Word Recognition". *Journal of Verbal Learning and Verbal Behavior* 10.645-657.

Saint-Jacques, B. 1987. "The Roman Alphabet in the Japanese Writing System". *Visible Language* 21.88-105.

Saito, H. 1987. "Hikari Disuku o Shiyo Shita Tairyo Nihongo Deta no Chikuseki [On Large-scale Japanese Language Storage on Optical Disks]". *Kokuritsu Kokugo Kenkyusho Hokoku* 90.95-123.

Saito, H. 1988. "Kanji Joho Detabesu [Kanji Information Data-Base]". *Kokuritsu Kokugo Kenkyusho Hokoku* 94.27-47.

Saito, H. 1994. "Ichi Mojitai ni Ichi Fugo o Taio Saseru Kanji Fugoka no Hoho [A Method of Encoding a Standard Form to One Code for Structural 4-byte Kanji Code Used in Information Interchange]". *Keiryo Kokugogaku* 19.223-233.

Saito, H. 1998. "Tagengo o Toitsu Suru Joho Kokanyo 4 Baito Kodo no Kenkyu [Research on the 4-Byte Information Retrieval Code as a Unificational Device for Various Languages]". *Report at the Annual Seika Happyokai, National Language Research Institute, March 7, 1998.*

Saito, H. 1980. "Nihongo ni okeru Tategaki to Yokogaki [Horizontal and Vertical Reading in Japanese]". *Shinrigaku Hyoron* 23.89-105.

Saito, H. 1981a. "Toward Comparative Studies of Reading Kanji and Kana". *The Quarterly Newsletter of the Laboratory of Comparative Human Cognition* 3.33-36.

Saito, H. 1981b. "Kanji to Kana no Yomi ni okeru Keitaiteki Fugoka oyobi Oninteki Fugoka no Kento [Use of Graphemic and Phonemic Encoding in Reading Kanji and Kana]". *Shinrigaku Kenkyu* 52.266-273.

Saito, H. 1980c. "Nihongo ni okeru Tategaki to Yokogaki [Horizontal vs. Vertical Reading in Japanese]". *Shinrigaku Hyoron* 23.89-105.

Saito, H. 1982. "Kanji no Yomi ni Kansuru Joho Shori Katei [Information Processing in Kanji Reading]". *Jido Shinrigaku no Shinpo* 21.328-351.

Saito, H. 1986. "Cost of Information and Integration Based on Inference". *Linguistics, Psychology, and the Chinese Language* ed. by H. S. Kao & R. Hoosain, 55-71. Hong Kong: Centre of Asian Studies, University of Hong Kong.

Saito, H., M. Inoue & Y. Nomura. 1979. "Information Processing of Kanji (Chinese Characters) and Kana (Japanese Characters): The Close Relationship Among Graphemic, Phonemic, and Semantic Aspects". *Psychologia* 22.195-206.

Saito, H. & M. Kawakami. 1992. "Renso Kioku ni okeru Kensaku Katei: Giji Jukugo no Jukugo Rashisa no Hyoka ni okeru Shinteki Jisho no Kanyo [Retrieval Processes in Associative Memory: Pseudo-Compound Words and the Mental Lexicon]". *Nagoya Daigaku Kyoyobu Kiyo* 36.67-99.

Saito, H., M. Kawakami & H. Masuda. 1995a. "Kanji Koosei ni okeru Buhin no Shutsugen Hindohyo [Frequencies for Semantic and Phonetic Radical Components in Complex Kanji Radicals]". *Bulletin of the Nagoya University Graduate School of Informatics and Science* 1.113-134.

Saito, H., M. Kawakami & H. Masuda. 1995b. "Kanji Koosei ni okeru Buhin (Bushsu): Onin Taiyohyo [Table of Phonetic Correspondences for Radical Components in Complex Kanji]". *Bulletin of the Nagoya University Graduate School of Informatics and Science* 2.89-115.

Saito, H., M. Kawakami & H. Masuda. 1995c. "Phonological Effect in Radical Migration with Kanji Characters". *Proceedings of the 12th Annual Meeting of the Japanese Cognitive Science Society* 186-187.

Saito, H., M. Kawakami & H. Masuda. 1998. "Form and Sound Similarity Effects in Kanji Recognition". *Reading and Writing* 10.323-357.

Saito, H., M. Kawakami, H. Masuda & G. B. Flores d'Arcais. 1995. "Conjunctionability Effects on Radical Migration with Kanji Characters". Paper presented at the *Seventh International Conference on the Cognitive Processing of Chinese and other Asian Languages*. Hong Kong.

Saito, H., M. Kawakami, H. Masuda & G. B. Flores d'Arcais. 1997. "Contributions of Radical Components to Kanji Character Recognition and Recall". *Cognitive Processing of Chinese and Related Asian Languages* ed. by H-C. Chen, 109-140. Hong Kong: The Chinese University Press.

Saito, H. & P. Langman. 1984. "Intra-Linguistic Categorization of Obsolete Kanji". *Japanese Psychological Research* 26.134-142.

Saito, H. & T. Tsuzuki. 1989. "Retrieval Processes in Associative Memory: Norms of Retrieval Variability for Forty-Eight Homophones in Japanese Kanji". *Nagoya Daigaku Kyoyobu Kiyo* 33.70-106.

Sakamoto, I. 1952. *Kotoba no Shinri [The Psychology of Language]*. Tokyo: Kanekoshobo.

Sakamoto, I. 1955. *Yomi to Sakubun no Shinri [The Psychology of Reading and Composition]*. Tokyo: Maki Shoten.

Sakamoto, I., K. Okamoto, S. Muraishi, & S. Yasumasa. 1956. *Gengoshinrigaku [Psycholinguistics]*. Tokyo: Gakugei Tosho.

Sakamoto, K., N. Itakura, K. Imamura, N. Kinebuchi, K. Seki & S. Hanba. 1992. "On the Visual Recognition of Moving Letters". *Annual of Physiological Anthropology* 11.611-624.

Sakamoto, T. & K. Makita. 1973. "Japan". *Comparative Reading* ed. by John Downing, 440-465. New York: Macmillan.

Sakano, N. 1970. "Kinoteki Sayu Hitaishosei to Sono Hattatsuteki Igi [Functional Asymmetry and Its Significance to Human Development] ". *Shinrigaku Hyoron* 13.38-53.

Sakano, N. & K. Amano. 1976. *Gengoshinrigaku [Psycholinguistics]*. *Gendai Shinrigaku Sosho [Current Psychology Series]*, Volume 3. Tokyo: Shindokusyosha.

Sakano, N. & K. Amano. 1993. *Gengoshinrigaku [Psycholinguistics]*. Tokyo: Shindokusyosha.

Sakuma, N., M. Itoh & S. Sasanuma. 1989. "Puraimingu Paradaimu ni Yoru Kanji Tango no Ninchi Yunitto no Kento [Recognition Units of Kanji Words: Priming Effects on Kanji Recognition". *Shinrigaku Kenkyu* 60.1-8

Sakuma, N., S. Sasanuma, I. F. Tatsumi & S. Masaki. 1998. "Orthography and Phonology in Reading Japanese Kanji Words: Evidence from the Semantic Decision Task with Homophones". *Memory and Cognition* 26.75-87.

Sakurai, Y., T. Momose, M. Iwata, T. Watanabe, T. Ishikawa & I. Kanazawa. 1993. "Semantic Processing in Kana Word Reading: Activation Studies with Positron Emission Tomography". *Neuro Report* 4.327-330.

Sanseido Publishing. 1977. *Kotoba to Shinri [Language and Psychology]*. Series entitled *Nihongo to Bunka-Shakai [Japanese and Culture-Society]*, 1. Tokyo: Sanseido.

Sasahara, H., S. Yokoyama, H. Nozaki & J. Yoneda. 1998. "Asahi Shinbun CD-ROM to Shimen ni okeru Yurei Moji to Jisho Hikeisaiji [Phantom Characters and the Value of Electronic Newspaper Corpora]". *Keiryo Kokugogaku* 21.145-161.

Sasaki, M. 1984a. "Mojin ni Totte Kanji to wa: Kanji no Fukushigaku [Kanji for the Blind]". *Kanji o Kagaku Suru [Making Kanji Scientific]* ed. by H. Kaiho, 225-263. Tokyo: Yuhikaku.

Sasaki, M. 1984b. "Kusho Kodo no Hattatsu [The Development of Kanji Finger-Spelling]". *Kyoiku Shinrigaku Kenkyu* 32.34-43.

Sasaki, M. 1987a. "Why Do Japanese Write Characters in Space?". *International Journal of Behavioral Development* 10.135-149.

Sasaki, M. & A. Watanabe. 1983. "Kusho Kodo no Shutsugen to Kino: Hyosho no Undo Kankakuteki na Seibun ni Tsuite [The Appearance and Functions of Kanji Finger-Spelling Behavior]". *Kyoiku Shinrigaku Kenkyu* 31.273-282.

Sasaki, M. & A. Watanabe. 1984. "Kusho Kodo no Bunkateki Kigen [The Cultural Origins of Kanji Finger-Spelling]". *Kyoiku Shinrigaku Kenkyu* 32.182-190.

Sasanuma, S. 1974a. "Impairment of Written Language in Japanese Aphasics: Kana and Kanji Processing". *Journal of Chinese Linguistics* 2.141-158.

Sasanuma, S. 1974b. "Kana vs.Kanji Processing in Alexia with Transient Agraphia: A Case Report". *Cortex* 10.89-97.

Sasanuma, S. 1975. "Kana and Kanji Processing in Japanese Aphasics". *Brain and Language* 2.369-383.

Sasanuma, S. 1977. "Shitsugosho ni okeru Kana to Kanji no Shogai [Impairments of Kana and Kanji Processing in Japanese Aphasics]". *Gengo* 6.66-74.

Sasanuma, S. 1980. "Acquired Dyslexia in Japanese: Clinical Features and Underlying Mechanisms". *Deep Dyslexia* ed. by M. Coltheart, K. Patterson & J. C. Marshall, 48-90. London: Routledge & Kegan Paul.

Sasanuma, S. 1984. "Can Surface Dyslexia Occur in Japanese?". *Orthographies and Reading: Perspectives from Cognitive Psychology, Neuropsychology, and Linguistics* ed. by L. Henderson, 43-56. Hillsdale, NJ: Lawrence Erlbaum Associates.

Sasanuma, S. 1985. "Surface Dyslexia and Dysgraphia: How Are They Manifested in Japanese?". *Surface Dyslexia* ed. by K. E. Patterson, J. C. Marshall & M. Coltheart, 225-249. Hillsdale, NJ: Lawrence Erlbaum Associates.

Sasanuma, S. 1986. "Universal and Language-Specific Symptomatology and Treatment of Aphasia". *Folia Phoniatrica* 38.121-175.

Sasanuma, S. 1988. "Cognitive Neuropsychology Approach to the Study of Aphasia: A Case of Reading Impairment". *Aphasiology* 2.395-400.

Sasanuma, S. 1992. "Neuropsychology of Reading: Universal and Language-Specific Features of Reading Impairment". *International Perspectives on Psychological Science. Vol. 1: Leading Themes* ed. by P. Bertelson, P. Eelen & G. d'Ydewalle, 105-125. Hillsdale, NJ: Lawrence Erlbaum Associates.

Sasanuma, S. & O. Fujimura. 1971. "Selective Impairment of Phonetic and Non-phonetic Transcription of Words in Japanese Aphasic Patients: Kana vs. Kanji in Visual Recognition and Writing". *Cortex* 7.1-18.

Sasanuma, S. & O. Fujimura. 1972. "An Analysis of Writing Errors in Japanese Aphasic Patients". *Cortex* 8.265-282.

Sasanuma, S., M. Itoh, Y. Kobayashi & K. Mori. 1980. "The Nature of the Task-stimulus Interaction in the Tachistoscopic Recognition of Kana and Kanji Words". *Brain and Language* 9.298-306.

Sasanuma, S., M. Itoh, K. Mori & Y. Kobayashi. 1977. "Tachistoscopic Recognition of Kana and Kanji Words". *Neuropsychologia* 15.547-553.

Sasanuma, S. & H. Monoi. 1975. "The Syndrome of *Gogi* (Word-meaning) Aphasia: Selective Impairment of Kanji Processing". *Neurology* 25.627-632.

Sasanuma, S., N. Sakuma & K. Kitano. 1992. "Reading Kanji Without Semantics: Evidence from a Longitudinal Study of Dementia". *Cognitive Neuropsychology* 9.465-486.

Sasanuma, S., N. Sakuma & I. Tatsumi. 1988. "Lexical Access of Kana Words and Words in Kana". *Ann. Bull. RILP* 22.117-123.

Satake, H. 1991. "Wapuro to Hojo Kanji [Word Processing and Supplementary Kanji]". *Gengo* 20.50-51.

Sato, E. 1992. "Moji--Hyoki [Characters--Representations]". *Kokugogaku* 169.82-93.

Sato, K. 1973. *Japanese Ideomatic Letter Kanji: Design of Japanese Letters*. Volume 5. Tokyo: Maruzen.

Sato, K. 1982. "Guhatsu Kioku Kadai ni okeru Jido no Chui Haibun to Sentakuteki Kioku ni Kansuru Kenkyu [Children's Attention Allocation and Selective Memory in Incidental Memory Tasks]". *Kyoiku Shirigaku Kenkyu* 30.201-210.

Sawaki, M. & N. Hagita. 1996. "Recognition of Degraded Machine-printed Characters Using a Complementary Similarity Measure and Error-correction Learning". *IEICE Transactions on Information and Systems*, Vol. E79-D.491-497.

Sawaki, M. & N. Hagita. 1998. "Text-line Extraction and Character Recognition of Document Headlines with Graphical Designs Using Complementary Similarity Measure. *IEEE Transactions on Pattern Analysis and Machine Intelligence*, 20.1103-1109.

Sawaki, M., N. Hagita & K. Ishii. 1997. "Robust Character Recognition of Gray-scaled Images with Graphical Designs and Noise". *Proceedings of the International Conference on Document Analysis and Recognition*, 491-494. Los Alamitos, CA: IEEE Computer Society.

Scott A. J. & L. C. Ehri. 1990. "Sight Word Reading in Prereaders: Use of Logographic vs. Alphabetic Access Routes". *Journal of Reading Behavior* 22.149-166.

Seeley, C. 1984a. "Introduction". *Aspects of the Japanese Writing System*, Special Issue of *Visible Language* ed. by C. Seeley. *Visible Language* 18.213-218.

Seeley, C. 1984b. "The Japanese Script since 1900". *Aspects of the Japanese Writing System*, Special Issue of *Visible Language*, ed. by C. Seeley. *Visible Language* 18.267-302.

Seidenberg, M. S. 1985. "The Time Course of Phonological Code Activation in Two Writing Systems". *Cognition* 19.1-30.

Seidenberg, M. S. 1989. "Visual Word Recognition and Performance: A Computational Model and Its Implications". *Lexical Representation and Process* ed. by W. Marslen-Wilson, 25-74. Cambridge, MA: MIT Press.

Seidenberg, M. S., G. S. Waters, M. Barnes & M. K. Tanenhaus. 1984. "When Does Irregular Spelling or Pronunciation Influence Word Recognition?". *Journal of Verbal Learning and Verbal Behavior* 23.383-404.

Sekiguchi, H. & I. Abe. 1992. "Kanji Ninchi Shori ni okeru Daino Hankyu Kinosa ni Tsuite [Functional Hemisphere Differences in Kanji Recognition]". *Kyoiku Shinrigaku Kenkyu* 40.315-322.

Sheridan, E. M. 1983. "Reading Disabilities: Can We Blame the Written Language?". *Journal of Learning Disabilities* 16.81-86.

Shim, J-K. 1987. "Formation of Korean Alphabet". *Language Research* 23.527-538.

Shimada, M. 1981. "Kana and Kanji Processing in Japanese With Special Reference to Functional Hemisphere Specialization". *Tohoku Psychologica Folia* 40.24-34.

Shimada, M. & A. Otsuka. 1981. "Kanji Shori ni okeru Daino Hankyu Kinosa [Functional Hemisphere Differences in Kanji Processing]". *Shinrigaku Hyoron* 24.472-489.

Shimamura, A. P. 1987. "Word Comprehension and Naming: An Analysis of English and Japanese Orthographies". *American Journal of Psychology* 100.15-40.

Shimamura, N. 1987. "Jido no Kanji Shiyo: Kadai Sakubun no Kanji Ganyuritsu Kara [Use of Chinese Characters by Japanese Children in Guided Compositions]". *Kokuritsu Kokugo Kenkyusho Hokoku* 8.77-94.

Shimamura, N. 1990. "Kanji no Shutokuritsu: Haito Kanji ni Yoru Chigai [Acquisition Rates of Kanji by School Children: Differences in Kanji by Grade Level]". *Keiryo Kokugogaku* 17.273-279.

Shimamura, N. 1997 "Senzen no Kodomo no Kanji [Kanji Ability of Pre-war Children]". *Dokusho Kagaku* 41.124-128.

Shimamura, N. & H. Mikami. 1994. "Yoji no Hiragana no Shutoku: Kokuritsu Kokugo Kenkyusho no 1967 Nen no Chosa to no Hikaku o Toshite [Acquisition of Hiragana Letters by Pre-school Children: A Comparision with the 1967 Survey by the National Language Research Institute]". *Kyoiku Shinrigaku Kenkyu* 42.70-76.

Shimomura, M. 1998. "The Relationship between Kanji Words and Kanji Characters in the Mental Lexicon". Paper given at the *First International Conference on the Mental Lexicon*, Edmonton, Alberta. September, 1998.

Shimomura, M. & K. Yokosawa. 1991. "Processing of Kanji and Kana Characters Within Japanese Words". *Perception and Psychophysics* 50.19-27.

Shimomura, M. & K. Yokosawa. 1995. "The Processing of Constituent Characters in Kanji Words in Proofreading Japanese Sentences". *Psychological Research* 58.51-60.

Sperry, R. W. 1974. "Lateral Specialization in the Surgically Separated Hemispheres". *Neurosciences* ed. by F. O. Schmitt & F. G. Worden. Cambridge, MA: MIT Press.

Sperry, R. W. & M. S. Gazzaniga. 1967. "Language Following Surgical Disconnection of the Hemispheres". *Brain Mechanisms Underlying Speech and Language* ed. by F. L. Darley, 108-121. New York: Grune and Stratton.

Steinberg, D. D. & J. Yamada. 1978-1979. "Are Whole Word Kanji Easier to Learn Than Syllable Kana?". *Reading Research Quarterly* 14.88-99.

Steinberg, D. D., J. Yamada, Y. Nakano, S. Hirakawa & S. Kanemoto. 1977. "Meaning and the Learning of Kanji and Kana". *Hiroshima Forum for Psychology* 4.15-24.

Steinberg, D. D., M. Isozaki & S. Amano. 1981. "Yoji no Kana to Kanji no Yomi Gakushu [Learning to Read Kana and Kanji by Young Children]". *Shinrigaku Kenkyu* 52.309-312.

Steinberg, D. D., K. Yoshida & R. Yagi. 1985. "Issaiji oyobi Nisaiji ni Taisuru Katei de no Yomi no Shido [Teaching Reading to One- and Two-year-olds at Home]". *Dokusho Kagaku* 29.1-17.

Stevenson, H. W. 1984. "Orthography and Reading Disabilities". *Journal of Learning Disabilities* 17.296-301.

Stevenson, H. W., J. W. Stigler, G. W. Lucker & S-Y. Lee. 1982. "Reading Disabilities: The Case of Chinese, Japanese, and English". *Child Development* 53.1164-1181.

Stroop, V. R. 1935. "Studies of Interference in Serial Verbal Reactions". *Journal of Experimental Psychology* 18.643-662.

Sugimura, T. 1974. "Yoji ni okeru Tango no Yomi no Gakushu [Learning to Read Words by Young Children]". *Kyoiku Shinrigaku Kenkyu* 22.34-38.

Sugishima, I. & K. Kashu. 1992. "Nihongo ni okeru Hyoki Keitai ga Tango no Naihoteki Imi ni Oyobosu Eikyo [The Effect of Orthographic Representation on Lexical Connotation]". *Kwansei Gakuin Daigaku Jinbun Ronkyu* 41.15-30.

Sugishima, I., J. Ukita, M. Minagawa & K. Kashu. 1994. "Nihongo no Hyoki Hindo ga Go no Ondoku Senji to Sainin Kioku ni Oyobosu Eikyo [The Effect of Script-Frequency on Reading and Recalling of Japanese Words]". *Kwansei Gakuin Daigaku Jinbun Ronkyu* 43.71-82.

Sugishita, M. 1980. "Noryo Sonsho ni Yoru *Disconnexion* Syndrome ni okeru Kanji Kana Mondai [Kanji and Kana Processing in Japanese Patients with Partial Split-brain] ". *Shinkei Naika* 13.317-325.

Sugishita, M., M. Iwata, Y. Toyokura, M. Yoshioka & R. Yamada. 1978. "Reading of Ideograms and Phonograms in Japanese Patients after Partial Commissurotomy". *Neuropsychologia* 16.417-426.

Sugishita, M., K. Otomo, S. Kabe & K. Yunoki. 1992. "A Critical Appraisal of Neuropsychological Correlates of Japanese Ideogram (Kanji) and Phonogram (Kana) Reading". *Brain* 115.1563-1585

Sugishita, M. & M. Yoshioka. 1987. "Visual Processes in a Hemialexic Patient with Posterior Callosal Section". *Neuropsychologia* 25.329-339.

Suzuki, T. 1969. "Hyoki to Shite no Kanji [Kanji as Representations]". *Gengo Seikatsu* 214.17-25.

Suzuki, T. 1975. "On the Twofold Phonetic Realization of Basic Concepts: In Defence of Chinese Characters in Japanese". *Language in Japanese Society: Current Issues in Sociolinguistics* ed. by F. C. C. Peng, 175-192. Tokyo: University of Tokyo Press.

Suzuki, T. 1977. "Writing Is Not Language, or Is It?". *Journal of Pragmatics* 1.407-420.

Tabata, Z. 1936. *Shakaigaku yori Mitaru Gengo [Language as Viewed from Sociology]*. Series entitled *Iwanami Koza Kokugo Kyoiku; Kokugo Kyoiku no Gakuteki Kiko [Iwanami Lectures in National Language Education; Scholastic Organization of National Language Education]*. Tokyo: Iwanami Shoten.

Tada, H. 1975. "Syllable Effects on Reaction and Recognition Times in Reading Letters in Japan". *Tohoku Psychologica Folia* 34.17-26.

Taft, Marcus. 1991. *Reading and the Mental Lexicon*. Hillsdale, NJ: Lawrence Erlbaum Associates.

Tajika, H. A. Taniguchi, S. Kamiya & E. Neumann. 1991. "Individual Differences in Speed of Semantic Memory Retrieval and Stroop Interference". *Psychologia* 34.28-35.

Tajika, H., S. Kamiya & K. Takahashi. 1993. "Effects of Perceptual Processing of Information in Explicit and Implicit Retention Tests". *Psychologia* 36.21-26.

Tajika, H., J. Kawaguchi, T. Ikegami & H. Yama. 1992. *Joho Shori no Shinrigaku: Ninchi Shinrigaku Nyumon* [*The Psychology of Information Processing: An Introduction to Cognitive Psychology*]. Tokyo: Saiensusha.

Takahashi, A. & D. Green. 1983. "Numerical Judgments with Kanji and Kana". *Neuropsychologia* 21.259-263.

Takahashi, T. & K. Tamaoka. 1992. "Script Familiarity Effects on the Efficiency of Processing Numerals by Japanese University Students with High and Low English Proficiency". *Matsuyama Daigaku Gengo Bunka Kenkyu* 11.33-48.

Takata T. 1991. "Kanji no Unmei [The Fate of Kanji]". *Gengo* 20.52-58.

Takebe, Y. 1979. *Nihongo no Hyoki* [The Representation of Japanese]. Tokyo: Kadokawa Shoten.

Tamaoka, K. 1991. "Psycholinguistic Nature of the Japanese Orthography". *Studies in Language and Literature* 11.49-82. Matsuyama: Matsuyama University.

Tamaoka, K. 1994. "Kana to Kanji ni Yoru Goi Shori no Mekanizumu [Kana and Kanji Word Processing Mechanisms]". *Matsuyama Daigaku Sogo Kenkyusho Soho*, Number 15. Matsuyama: Matsuyama University. Pp. 101.

Tamaoka, K. (n.d.). "Romaji wa Yuzai ka? Romaji o Baikai to Shita Eigokei Nihongo Gakushusha no Bogo kara no Onin Kansho no Zofuku ni Kansuru Kensho [Is Romaji Guilty? An Examination of Phonological Interference in English-speaking Learners of Japanese through the Romaji Script]".

Tamaoka, K. & M. Hatsuzuka. 1995. "Kanji Niji Jukugo no Shori ni okeru Kanji Shiyo Hindo no Eikyo [The Effect of Kanji Frequency on Processing Japanese Two-Morpheme Compound Words]". *Dokusho Kagaku* 39.121-137.

Tamaoka, K. & M. Hatsuzuka. 1997. "Hiragana to Katakana no Shori ni okeru Kankaku Benbetsu oyobi Kankaku Shikibetsu Kino [Sense-discriminative and Sense-determinative Functions in the Processing of Japanese Hiragana and Katakana]". *Dokusho Kagaku* 41.15-28

Tamaoka, K. & M. Hatsuzuka. 1998. "The Effect of Morphological Semantics on the Processing of Japanese Two-Kanji Compound Words]". *Reading and Writing* 10.293-322.

Tamaoka, K. & M. Hatsuzuka. (n.d.). "Goi Shori ni okeru Kanji Jukugo Koseisu to Kanji Shiyo Hindo no Tsunahiki Gensho [A 'Tug-of-War' between Kanji Word-Construction Size and Kanji Printed Frequency in the Processing of Japanese Words]".

Tamaoka, K., M. Hatsuzuka, J. F. Kess & D. R. Bogdan. 1998. "Hiragana tai Katakana: Goi oyobi Gijigo no Shori ni okeru Hyoki no Shinkinsei Koka [Hiragana vs. Katakana: The Script Familiarity Effect on the Processing of Japanese Words and Pseudo-words]". *Dokusho Kagaku* 42.1-13.

Tamaoka, K., C. K. Leong & T. Hatta. 1991. "Processing Numerals in Arabic, Kanji, Hiragana and Katakana by Skilled and Less Skilled Japanese Readers in Grades 4-6". *Psychologia* 34.200-206.

Tamaoka, K., C. K. Leong & T. Hatta. 1992. "Effects of Vocal Interference on Identifying Kanji, Hiragana and Katakana Words by Skilled and Less Skilled Japanese Readers in Grades 4-6". *Psychologia* 35.33-41.

Tamaoka, K. & B. Menzel. 1994. "Nihongo Kyoiku ni okeru Romaji Shiyo Shihan no Ronriteki Konkyo ni Kansuru Gengo Shinrigakuteki Kosatsu [To Use or Not to Use Romaji: A Psycholinguistic Evaluation of the Arguments Against the Use of Romaji for Teaching Japanese with Learners of Alphabetic Mother Tongues]". *Dokusho Kagaku* 38.104-116.

Tamaoka, K. & M. Taft. 1994. "Haku ga Onin Shori no Saisho Tani to Nariuru no ka?: Giji Gairaigo no Goi Shogo Handan kara no Kosatsu [Is the Smallest Unit in Phonological Processing Equivalent to the Smallest Unit in Orthographic Processing?: Lexical Judgments of Katakana Non-words]". *Shinrigaku Kenkyu* 65.377-382.

Tamaoka, K. & N. Takahashi. 1999. "Kanji Niji Jukugo no Shoji Kodo ni okeru Goi Shiyo Hindo oyobi Shojiteki Fukuzatsusei no Eikyo [The Effects of Word Frequency and Orthographic Complexity on the Writing Process of Japanese Two-morpheme Compound Words]". *Shinrigaku Kenkyu* 70.45-50.

Tamaoka, K., Y. Yanase & K. Kirsner. (n.d.). "Joyo Kanji 1945-ji no Shotokusei ni Kansuru Detabesu [The Data Base for Characteristics of the 1945 Japanese Joyo Kanji]".

Tan, L. H., R. Hoosain & D-L. Peng. 1995. "Role of Early Presemantic Phonological Code in Chinese Character Identification". *Journal of Experimental Psychology: Learning, Memory, and Cognition* 21.43-54.

Tan, L. H. & C. A. Perfetti. 1997. "Visual Chinese Character Recognition: Does Phonological Information Access to Meaning?". *Journal of Memory and Language* 37.41-57.

Tanaka, A. 1991. "Gendai Hyoki ni Hitsuyo na Kanjisu [The Necessary Number of Kanji in Contemporary Orthography]". *Gengo* 20.59-61.

Tanaka, H. & K. Konishi. 1990. "Katakana Hyoki Tango no Shori Katei: Hyoki Hindo no Eikyo [Semantic Processing of Katakana Words: Effects of Script Frequency]". *Shinkei Shinrigaku* 6.231-239.

Tanaka, T. 1977. "Moji Ninchi ni Kansuru Hattatsu III [Development of Orthographical Recognition III]". *Shinrigaku Kenkyu* 48.49-53.

Tanaka, Y., A. Yamadori & S. Murata. 1987. "Selective Kana Agraphia: A Case Report". *Cortex* 23.679-684.

Tanaka, T., J. Iwasaki & C. Miki. 1974. "Moji Ninchi ni Kansuru Hattatsu [Development of Orthographical Recognition]". *Shinrigaku Kenkyu* 45.37-45.

Tanaka, Y. 1966. "Status of Japanese Experimental Psychology". *Annual Review of Psychology* 17.233-272.

Tanaka, Y. & G. W. England. 1972. "Psychology in Japan". *Annual Review of Psychology* 23.695-732.

Tasaki, K. 1992. "Moji no Nodoteki Shoku Ninchi ni Oyobosu Shigeki no Okisa no Koka [The Effect of Letter Size on Haptic Letter Recognition]". *Shinrigaku Kenkyu* 63.201-204.

Tatsumi, I. F., M. Itoh, S. Sasanuma & H. Fujisaki. 1985. "Span of Short-term Memory for Auditorily and Visually Presented Word Sequences". *Ann. Bull. RILP* 19.283-299.

Taylor, I. 1988. "Psychology of Literacy: East and West". *The Alphabet and the Brain: The Lateralization of Writing* ed. by D. de Kerckhove & C. J. Lumsden, 202-233. Berlin: Springer-Verlag.

Taylor, I. 1997. "Psycholinguistic Reasons for Keeping Chinese Characters". *Cognitive Processing of Chinese and Related Asian Languages* ed. by H-C. Chen, 299-319. Hong Kong: The Chinese University Press.

Taylor, I. & M. M. Taylor. 1983. *The Psychology of Reading.* New York: Academic Press.

Taylor, I. & M. M. Taylor. 1995. *Writing and Literacy in Chinese, Korean, and Chinese.* Amsterdam: John Benjamins Publishers.

Thorndike, E. L. & I. Lorge. 1944. *The Teacher's Word Book of 30,000 Words.* New York: Teachers' College Press, Columbia University.

Tinker, M. A. 1939. "Reliability and Validity of Eye-movement Measures of Reading". *Journal of Experimental Psychology* 19.732-746.

Tokuda, K. 1987. "Jakushiji no Kanji Yomi Kaki Seiseki o Kitei Suru Gakushusha no Yoin no Kento [Kanji Reading and Writing Abilities in Visually Impaired Children]". *Kyoiku Shinrigaku Kenkyu* 35.155-162.

Tokuda, K. & Y. Sato. 1988. "Kanji no Kaki no Nanisei Hyotei ni okeru Kanji Zokusei no Koka [The Effect of Kanji Properties on Judgments of Writing Difficulty]". *Keiryo Kokugogaku* 16.175-181.

Toma, C. & T. Toshima. 1989. "Developmental Change in Cognitive Organization Underlying Stroop Tasks of Japanese Orthographies". *International Journal of Psychology* 24.547-559.

Tomita, T. 1991. "Nihongo Kyoiku to Gairaigo oyobi Sono Hyoki [Loanwords in Teaching Japanese and its Orthography]". *Nihongogaku* 10.37-44.

Tsao, Y., M. Wu & T. Feustel. 1981. "Stroop Interference: Hemispheric Difference in Chinese Speakers". *Brain and Language* 13.372-378.

Twine, N. 1983. "Toward Simplicity: Script Reform Movements in the Meiji Period". *Monumenta Nipponica* 38.115-132.

Tzeng, O. J. L. & D. L. Hung. 1980. "Reading in a Non-alphabetic Writing System: Some Experimental Studies". *Orthography, Reading, and Dyslexia* ed. by J. F. Kavanaugh & R. L. Venezky, 223-248. Baltimore: University Park Press.

Tzeng, O. J. L., D. L. Huang, B. Cotton & W. S-Y. Wang. 1979. "Visual Lateralization Effect in Reading Chinese Characters". *Nature* 282.499-501.

Tzeng, O. J. L., D. L. Hung & W. S-Y. Wang. 1977. "Speech Decoding in Reading Chinese Characters: An Information Processing View". *Journal of Experimental Psychology: Human Learning and Memory* 6.621-630.

Tzeng, O. J. L. & W. S-Y. Wang. 1983. "The First Two R's". *American Scientist* 71.238-243.

Ukita, J. & K. Kashu, eds. 1996. *Gengo to Kioku [Language and Memory]*. *Gendai Shinrigaku Sirizu [Modern Psychology Series]*, 5. Tokyo: Baifukan.

Ukita, J., M. Minagawa, I. Sugishima & K. Kashu. 1991. "Nichijo Buppinmei no Hyoki Keitai ni Kansuru Kenkyu: Kaku Hyoki no Shukanteki Shutsugen Hindo to Tekisetsusei ni Tsuite no Hyotei [On the Orthographic Representation of Everyday Objects: Evaluation of the Frequency of Orthographic Types and Subjective Judgments of Appropriateness]". *Kwansei Gakuin Daigaku Jinbun Ronkyu* 40.11-26.

Ukita, J., I. Sugishima, M. Minagawa, M. Inoue & K. Kashu. 1996. *Nihongo no Hyoki Keitai ni Kansuru Shinrigakuteki Kenkyu [Psychological Research on Orthographic Forms in Japanese]*. *Psychological Monograph No. 25*. Tokyo: Japanese Psychological Association.

Ukita, J., I. Sugishima, M. Minagawa & K. Kashu. 1993. "Nihongo no Hyoki Keitai ni Kansuru Kenkyu (1): Doitsugo ni okeru Kanji, Hiragana, Katakana Kaku Hyoki no Shukanteki Shutsugen Hindo ni Tsuite no Hyotei [Research on Japanese Orthographic Representations (1): Evaluation of the Subjective Frequency Rates of Kanji, Hiragana, Katakana Representations of the Same Word]". *Nihon Shinri Gakkai Dai-57kai Taikai, Happyo Rombunshu [Proceedings of the 57th Meeting of the Japan Psychological Association]*, p. 434.

Umemura, C. 1981. "Kana to Kanji no Moji Kino no Sai ni Tsuite: Kioku Kadai ni Yoru Kento [Functional Properties of Kana and Kanji in Memory Tasks]". *Kyoiku Shinrigaku Kenkyu* 29.123-131.

Unger, J. M. 1984. "Japanese Orthography in the Computer Age". *Visible Language* 18.238-253.

Unger, J. M. 1987. *The Fifth Generation Fallacy: Why Japan is Betting Its Future on Artificial Intelligence*. Oxford: Oxford University Press.

Vance, T. 1980. "The Psychological Status of a Constraint on Japanese Consonant Alternation". *Linguistics* 18.245-267.

Venezky, R. L. 1967. "English Orthography: Its Graphical Structure and Relation to Sound". *Reading Research Quarterly* 2.75-105.

Venezky, R. L. 1970. *The Structure of English Orthography*. The Hague: Mouton.

Van Orden, G. C. 1987. "A ROWS is a ROSE: Spelling, Sound and Reading". *Memory and Cognition* 15.181-198.

Van Orden., G. C., J. C. Johnston & B. L. Hale. 1988. "Word Identification in Reading Proceeds from Spelling to Sound to Meaning". *Journal of Experimental Psychology: Learning, Memory, and Cognition* 14.371-385.

Wang, J. 1988. "Kanji no Onin Shori to Imiteki Shori wa Doji ni Kanryo Suru ka [Does Phonological and Semantic Processing of Kanji Finish at the Same Time?]". *Shinrigaku Kenkyu* 59.252-255.

Wang, J. & T. Kikuchi. 1989. "Shunkan Teiji Joken ni okeru Kanji Tango no Onin Shori oyobi Imi Shori ni Tsuite [Phonological and Semantic Processing of Kanji under Brief Exposure Duration Conditions]". *Tsukuba Psychological Research* 11.11-16.

Wang, J. & T. Kikuchi. 1989. "Puraimu no Dotei ga Dekinai Joken ni okeru Kanji no Hampuku Koka oyobi Imiteki, Oninteki Puraimingu Koka [Repetition, Semantic Priming, and Phonological Priming from Masked Kanji Characters]". *Tsukuba Psychological Research* 13.33-40.

Wang, W. S-Y. 1971. "Review of Liu: *Chinese Characters and Their Impact on Other Languages of East Asia*". *Modern Language Journal* 15.187-188.

Wang, W. S-Y. 1981. "Language Structure and Optimal Orthography". *Perception of Print: Reading Reserch in Experimental Psychology* ed. by O. J. L Tzeng & H. Singer, 223-236. Hillsdale, NJ: Lawrence Erlbaum Associates.

Watanabe, A. 1971. "Chushiten to Gankyu Undo [Eye Fixation and Eye Movement]". *Oyo Butsuri* 40.330-334.

Watanabe, A. 1977. "Interferences of Visual Noises with the Peripheral Matching of Letters". *Tohoku Psychologica Folia* 46.101-110.

Watanabe, Y. 1991. "Latency in the Transcription, Transliteration, and Pronunciation of Japanese Ideographs and Syllabic Letters". *Tohoku Psychologica Folia* 50.25-34.

Watanabe, Y. 1993. "Whole Word Advantage in Reading Japanese Syllabic Letters and Ideographs". *Tohoku Psychologia Folia* 52.36-44.

Wernicke, C. 1874. *Der Aphasische Symptomenkomplex*. Breslau: Cohn and Weigert.

Wydell, T. N., B. Butterworth & K. E. Patterson. 1995. "The Inconsistency of Consistency Effects in Reading: The Case of Japanese Kanji". *Journal of Experimental Psychology: Learning, Memory, and Cognition* 21.1155-1168

Wydell, T. N., K. E. Patterson & G. W. Humphreys. 1993. "Phonologically Mediated Access to Meaning for Kanji: Is a *Rows* still a *Rose* in Japanese Kanji?". *Journal of Experimental Psychology: Learning, Memory, and Cognition* 19.491-514.

Yagi, A., K. Ishida & J. Katayama. 1992. "Contour Effects on Potentials Associated with Eye Fixations". *Psychologia* 35.50-54.

Yamada, H. 1983. "Certain Problems Associated with the Design of Input Keyboards for Japanese Writing". *Cognitive Aspects of Skilled Typewriting* ed. by W. E. Cooper, 305-407. New York: Springer-Verlag.

Yamada, J. 1984. "Kodomo ni Totte Kanji to wa: Kanji no Kyoikugaku [Kanji for Children: Kanji Education]". *Kanji o Kagaku Suru [Making Kanji Scientific]* ed. by H. Kaiho, 121-154. Tokyo: Yuhikaku.

Yamada, J. 1992a. "Why Are Kana Words Named Faster Than Kanji Words?". *Brain and Language* 43.682-693.

Yamada, J. 1992b. "Asymmetries of Reading and Writing Kanji by Japanese Children". *Journal of Psycholinguistic Research* 21.563-580.

Yamada, J. 1994. "Latencies for Naming Bound Morphemes and Words in Kanji". *Language and Speech* 37.251-258.

Yamada, J. & A. Banks. 1994. "Evidence for and Characteristics of Dyslexia among Japanese Children". *Annals of Dyslexia* 44.105-119.

Yamada, J., H. Imai & Y. Ikebe. 1990. "The Use of the Orthographic Lexicon in Reading Kana Words". *Journal of General Psychology* 117.311-323.

Yamada, J. & Y. Kayamoto. 1998. "Valency, Secondary Frequency, and Lexical Access: A Japanese Study". *Applied Psycholinguistics* 19.87-97.

Yamada, J., N. Matsuura & Y. Yanase. 1988. "Does Knowledge of Romaji Facilitate English Reading?". *The Journal of General Psychology* 115.229-239.

Yamada, J., M. Sasaki & N. Motooka. 1988. "Copying, Reading, and Writing of Kana and Simple Forms by Japanese Preschoolers". *Perceptual and Motor Skills* 66.387-394.

Yamadori, A. 1975. "Ideogram Reading in Alexia". *Brain* 98.231-238.

Yamadori, A. 1980. "Kanji Kana Mondai to Daino Hankyu no Sayusa [Cerebral Laterality and Kanji-Kana Processing]". *Shinkei Kenkyu no Shinpo* 24.556-564.

Yamadori, A. 1985. *An Introduction to Neuropsychology.* Tokyo: Igaku Shoin.

Yamadori, A. 1986. "Category Specific Alexia and a Neuropsychological Model of Alexia". *Linguistics, Psychology, and the Chinese Language* ed. by H. S. R. Kao & R. Hoosain, 255-264. Hong Kong: Centre for Asian Studies, University of Hong Kong.

Yamadori, A. 1998. "Aphasia in Ideograph Readers: The Case of Japanese". *Aphasia in Atypical Populations* ed. by P. Coppens, Y. Lebrun & A. Basso, 143-174. Mahweh, NJ: Lawrence Erlbaum Associates.

Yamadori, A., T. Nagashima & N. Tamaki. 1983. "Ideogram Writing in a Disconnection Syndrome". *Brain and Language* 19.346-356.

Yasumoto, B. 1976. "Tate to Yoko no Kino to Koritsu [Function and Efficiency of Vertical and Horizontal Texts]". *Gengo* 5.14-28.

Yamamoto, S. 1911. "Motor Aphasia: A Case Report". *Reports of the Third Conference of the Medical Society of Japan*, 1233-1234.

Yasunaga, M. 1981. "Joyo Kanjihyo ga Umareru Made [Until the Joyo Kanji Was Born]". *Gengo Seikatsu* 355.24-31.

Yatabe, T. 1956. *Jido no Gengo [Children's Language]*. Tokyo: Tokyo Sogensha.

Yatabe, T. 1983. *Jido no Gengo [Children's Language]*. *Yatabe Tatsuro Chosakushu [Collected Works of Yatabe Tatsuro]*, 8. Tokyo: Baifukan.

Yi, K-O. 1987. "Tango Ninchi ni okeru Jiritsusei to Bunmyaku Izonsei [Autonomy and Context Dependency in Word Recognition]". *Shinrigaku Hyoron* 30.387-401.

Yokoyama, S. 1991a. "Ondoku Shori Sareta Shigeki Komoku no Saisei ni Oyobosu Hyoki no Jukuchisei no Koka [The Effect of Orthographic Familiarity on Recall of Stimulus Items Read Aloud]". *Shinrigaku Kenkyu* 62.195-199.

Yokoyama, S. 1991b. *Gengo Shigeki no Kioku ni okeru Shikakuteki Joho no Kino [The Function of Visual Information in Memory for Linguistic Stimuli]*. Ph.D. dissertation, Tsukuba University, Tsukuba, Ibaraki-ken, Japan.

Yokoyama, S. 1995. "Nihongo Hyoki to Ninchi [Cognition and Orthgraphic Representations of Japanese]". *Nihongogaku* 14.65-72.

Yokoyama, S. 1997. *Hyoki to Kioku [Orthography and Memory]*. *Psychological Monograph No. 26*. Tokyo: Japanese Psychological Association.

Yokoyama, S. & M. Imai. 1989. "Kanji to Kana no Hyoki Keitai no Sai ga Tango no Guhatsu Kioku ni Oyobosu Koka [The Effect of Orthographic Difference between Kanji and Kana Words on Incidental Memory]". *Shinrigaku Kenkyu* 60.61-63.

Yokoyama, S., M. Imai & S. Furukawa. 1991. "Ondoku Shori Sareta Shigeki Komoku no Saisei ni Oyobosu Hyoki Keitai to Imejika no Koka [The Effect of Orthography and Imagery on Recall of Stimulus Items Which Were Read Aloud]". *Shinrigaku Kenkyu* 61.409-412.

Yokoyama, S. & H. Nozaki. 1996a. "Compilation of Kanji Frequency List for Psychology [Shinrigaku no tame no Kanji Hindo Kijunhyo no Sakusei]". *Proceedings of the 60th Meeting of the Japanese Psychological Association*, p. 599. Tokyo: Japanese Psychological Association.

Yokoyama, S. & H. Nozaki. 1996b. "Asahi Shimbun CD-ROM ni yoru Kanji Hindo Kijunhyo no Sakusei to Suryo Bunseki [The Statistical Analysis of Kanji Frequency in the Asahi Shinbun]". *Simpojumu Jinmon Kagaku ni okeru Suryoteki Bunseki [The Symposium on Quantitative Analysis in the Human Sciences, March 11, 1996]*. Statistics and Mathematics Research Institute, Ministry of Education. Pp. 1-4.

Yokoyama, S. & H. Sasahara. 1998a. "Kyujitai ga Konomareru Kanji no Dotei: Joshi Daigakusei o Taisho ni Shita Chosa [Older Kanji Forms Are Preferred in Kanji Choices: A Survey of Women University Students]". *Report at the Annual Seika Happyokai, National Language Research Institute, March 7, 1998*.

Yokoyama, S. & H. Sasahara. 1998b. "Itaiji Sentaku ni Eikyo Suru Yoin [The Pragmatics of Choosing Kanji Variants]". *Keiryo Kokugogaku* 21.291-310.

Yokoyama, S., H. Sasahara, H. Nozaki & E. Long. 1998. *Shimbun Denshi Media no Kanji: Asahi Shimbun CD-ROM ni yoru Kanji Hindohyo* [*Kanji in the Electronic Newspaper Media: Kanji Frequency Tables from the Asahi Newspaper CD-ROM*]. *Kokuritsu Kokugo Kenkyujo Purojekuto Sensho 1* [*National Language Research Institute Project, Special Publication 1*]. Tokyo: Sanseido.

Yokoyama, S., H. Sasahara, H. Nozaki & J. Yoneda. 1997. "Asahi Shimbun ni okeru Jisho Hikeisai Kanji no Shutsugen Jokyo [On the Appearance of Unlisted Kanji in the Asahi Newspaper]". *Report at the Annual Seika Happyokai, Third Language Processing Conference*, Faculty of Engineering, Kyoto University.

Yokoyama, S. & J. Yoneda. 1995. "Noizu ni Uzumoreta Kanji to Kana no Ninchi [Recognition of Kanji and Kana with Additive Noise]". *Kokuritsu Kokugo Kenkyusho Hokoku* 110.99-119.

Yoshimura, M. 1995. *Ninchi Imiron no Hoho: Keiken to Doki no Gengogaku* [*Methods of a Cognitive Theory of Meaning: The Linguistics of Experience and Motivation*]. Kobe: Jimbun Shoin.

Yoshizaki, K. & T. Hatta. 1987. "Shift of Visual Field Advantage by Learning Experience of Foreign Words". *Neuropsychologia* 25.589-592.

AUTHOR INDEX

SUBJECT INDEX